HNC Early Education & Childcare

Frances Scott

Elaine Anderson

Liz Johnstone

Mary MacMillan

Margaret Paterson

Sarah Sayers

www.heinemann.co.uk

✓ Free online support
✓ Useful weblinks
✓ 24 hour online ordering

01865 888118

Heinemann is an imprint of Pearson Education Limited, a company incorporated in England and Wales, having its registered office at Edinburgh Gate, Harlow, Essex, CM20 2JE. Registered company number: 872828

www.heinemann.co.uk

Heinemann is a registered trademark of Pearson Education Limited

Text © Pearson Education Limited 2008

First published 2008

12
10 9 8 7 6 5

British Library Cataloguing in Publication Data is available from the British Library on request.

ISBN 978 0 435 401 01 6

Designed by Hicks Design
Typeset by Tek Art
Original illustrations © Pearson Education Limited
Illustrated by Harriet Staines and Tek Art
Picture research by Kath Kollberg
Printed in China by Pearson Asia (SWTC/05)

Acknowledgements

The front cover shows a detail from *Going Down a Rainbow*, a painting by Jade Williamson (aged 9 years) of Balhousie Primary School, Scotland, a winner of the Children in Scotland art competition in 2005. Reproduced with kind permission from Jade Williamson and Children in Scotland.

Children in Scotland (www.childreninscotland.org. uk) is the national agency for voluntary, statutory and professional organisations and individuals working with children and their families in Scotland.

Elizabeth Johnstone would like to thank the early education and childcare practitioners in Edinburgh and surrounding areas including her PDA students who were willing to discuss how they were implementing the Curriculum for Excellence. She would also like to thank the HNC students and early years children she has been fortunate enough to observe.

Sarah Sayers would like to thank her grandchildren – William, Sam, Matthew, Evie, Alice and Edward – for providing her with endless sources of examples to illustrate the theory that underpins practice in early education and childcare.

The author and publisher would like to thank the following individuals and organisations for permission to reproduce photographs:

© Pearson Education Ltd / Tudor Photography – 20; © Pearson Education Ltd / Jules Selmes – 22; © Pearson Education Ltd / Jules Selmes – 22; © Pearson Education Ltd / Jules Selmes – 22; © iStockPhoto.com / Jeremy Edwards – 36; © Pearson Education Ltd / Lord & Leverett – 37; © Pearson Education Ltd / Peter Morris – 69; © Alamy / Picture Partners – 72; © Alamy / Bubbles PhotoLibrary – 76; © Digital Vision – 78; © Alamy / Image Source Black – 79; © iStockPhoto.com / Elena Koren Baum – 88; © Alamy / Kazki – 94; Author photo – 95; Author photo – 96; © Learning & Teaching Scotland – 100; © Learning & Teaching Scotland – 100; © Learning & Teaching Scotland – 100; © Pearson Education Ltd / Gareth Boden – 102; © Corbis –105; © Pearson Education Ltd / Tudor Photography – 114; © Pearson Education Ltd / Jules Selmes – 121; © Bubbles – 136; © Alamy / Scott Camazine – 140; © Getty / Veer Renee DeMartin – 140; © Alamy / Ariadne van Zandbergen – 140; © iStockPhoto.com / Adam Borkowski – 143; © Pearson Education Ltd / Tudor Photography – 152; © Pearson Education Ltd / Jules Selmes – 154; © iStockPhoto.com / Ivana Starcevic – 171; © Corbis / Ron Nickel / Design Pics – 171; © Action Plus – 216; © Pearson Education Ltd / Gareth Boden – 227; © Bubbles – 236; © Fotolia / Rob Marmion – 250; © Fotolia / Pavel Losevsky – 253; © iStockPhoto.com / Sean Locke – 255; © iStockPhoto.com / John Prescott – 274; © iStockPhoto.com / Htuller – 274; © Getty / Bruce Ayres – 277; © iStockPhoto.com / Jaimie Duplass – 290; © Corbis – 291; © Pearson Education Ltd / Tudor Photography – 294; © iStockPhoto.com / Martin Purmensky – 322; © Pearson Education Ltd / Ian Wedgewood – 322; © Getty / Altrendo Images – 331.

Crown Copyright Material is reproduced with permission of the Controller of HMSO and the Queen's Printer for Scotland.

Crown Copyright material on pages 3, 39-40, 41, 42, 54, 56, 59, 64, 100, 101, 106, 107, 109, 115, 120, 123, 133, 134, 135, 136, 137, 177, 185, 186, 189, 196, 207, 260, 272, 274, 285, 288 and 289 is reproduced under the terms of the Click-Use Licence.

Material on pages 51, 101, 103, 105, 115, 122, 123, 128, 130, 132 and 136 is reproduced with permission from Learning and Teaching Scotland.

Material on pages 30 and 296 is reproduced with the kind permission of the Scottish Social Services Council ©June 2008.

The diagram illustrating how the Children's Hearing System works on page 61 is reproduced with kind permission of the Scottish Children's Reporter Administration.

Material on page 135 is reproduced by kind permission of Fields in Trust, formerly the National Playing Fields Association.

Material on page 142 is reproduced with kind permission of Colwyn Trevarthen and the Research Centre for Child Development, Graduate School of Education, Hokkaido University.

Every effort has been made to contact copyright holders of material reproduced in this book. Any omissions will be rectified in subsequent printings if notice is given to the publishers.

The websites used in this book were correct and up-to-date at the time of publication. It is essential for tutors to preview each website before using it in class so as to ensure that the URL is still accurate, relevant and appropriate. We suggest that tutors bookmark useful websites and consider enabling students to access them through the school/college intranet.

Contents

---

[1]Pages vi–viii provide a full outline of the HNC units covered by this book.

About the authors

Frances Scott

Frances Scott is a senior learning and development advisor with a regulatory body in Scotland where she has a lead role in supporting the early years and childcare workforce.

Prior to this she worked for twelve years as a senior lecturer and curriculum head with responsibility for the HNC in Early Education and Childcare in one of Scotland's largest colleges.

Frances is a qualified teacher with two specialist awards in early education and childcare and an MSc in Childhood Studies from Edinburgh University.

Elaine Anderson

Elaine Anderson is a lecturer in Early Education and Childcare at Angus College in Arbroath, a post which she has held for nine years. Elaine gained her BEd degree in 1976 from the University of Edinburgh and since then has worked in childcare and adult services in a variety of roles. Her experience includes infant teaching, teaching basic skills in literacy and numeracy for Community Education.

While living in England, Elaine was employed by Mencap working with adults and children in a residential setting. Prior to her present post she was a Child and Family Centre worker at a busy social work department.

Mary MacMillan

Mary MacMillan has worked in further education for the last twelve years. She manages the HNC Early Education and Childcare at Stevenson College, Edinburgh, one of Scotland's largest colleges. Before working in further education, Mary worked as a teacher in a variety of educational contexts, including primary, nursery and learning support.

In addition to teaching various units within the HNC framework, Mary has worked with the Scottish Qualifications Authority (SQA) in the development of both the HNC and the PDA Early Education and Childcare. She is currently a member of the Qualification Development Team for a new HND in Childhood Practice.

Sarah Sayers

Sarah Sayers achieved a MEd (Honours) degree from Dundee University. She is currently the Senior External Verifier in Childcare for the Scottish Qualifications Authority. She worked for ten years supporting children and their families in their homes and monitoring children's development in child health clinics, nursery, primary and secondary schools. Sarah has taught health, social and childcare courses from Intermediate 1 to Advanced Higher, psychology and sociology for twelve years in further education colleges and university.

Sarah was the Principal Assessor for the Early Years Care and Education Higher for the SQA for five years, setting and marking examination papers.

Margaret Paterson

Margaret Paterson is a Curriculum Leader in Care in a college of further education in Glasgow. This involves her in training a wide variety of students preparing for careers in Early Education and Childcare. She is currently Senior Examiner for the Early Education and Childcare Higher exam in Scotland.

Before working in further education, Margaret worked with young children and their families in a variety of educational and social care settings. During this time she developed a particular interest in supporting children who had experienced domestic abuse while working as a Family Resource Worker within Scottish Women's Aid. In her spare time Margaret serves as a voluntary Children's Panel Member.

Liz Johnstone

Liz Johnstone is an experienced teacher qualified in primary and drama education. She has worked with primary and early years children in mainstream and special schools in Scotland and England. Liz has also been a play leader in a community playgroup in the voluntary sector.

Liz is a lecturer at Stevenson College in Edinburgh where she teaches Early Education and Childcare to Higher National Certificate and PDA students.

Introduction

The Scottish Government has a vision that children in Scotland will become confident individuals, effective contributors, successful learners and responsible citizens. To achieve this vision, children must be safe, nurtured, healthy, active, achieving, respected, responsible and included.

This means that practitioners who work with children have to be able to respond to their needs and to engage with and support children by providing them with carefully considered, well-paced and well-constructed opportunities, activities and experiences. They need to be aware of how children can be supported intellectually and emotionally, and how they can be provided with safe, healthy and physically challenging opportunities from the earliest stages of their lives. Working with children also means having a key role to fulfil working with parents and children's carers.

The role of an early education and childcare practitioner is therefore a varied and often highly demanding one. In recent years, registration and regulation has helped to make sure children are provided with play, care and learning opportunities that are safe and which meet a national standard. It has also meant children and families can expect a service which offers them protection and which values diversity and equality. High-quality training for these roles is essential to maintain and improve the quality of services that children and families require.

About the HNC in Early Education and Childcare

You have chosen to do the HNC in Early Education and Childcare and this book is designed to support some of the key learning required for this award. The HNC is a Scottish Qualifications Authority (SQA) award and is one of two main qualifications required by practitioners to work with children in a day care of children setting in Scotland.

It requires the successful completion of twelve Higher National (HN) credits. Each HN credit provides eight credit points on the Scottish Credit and Qualifications Framework (SCQF) at Level 7. This means that on successful completion of this award you will have 96 credit points at SCQF Level 7.

The core of the HNC is made up of five mandatory units plus two specialist options, from which at least one must be chosen, plus an additional five credits to be taken from the optional section of 13 units. If you are doing the HNC at one of Scotland's colleges it is likely the college staff will advise you of the optional units they offer.

The HNC covers the age range birth–12 years and you can select an early years route, a playwork route or both. You are required to complete all of the mandatory core units but can select from the core either the unit 'Curriculum and assessment in an early education and childcare setting' or 'Facilitating play facilities'. You may select both these units but if you do so you can only choose four rather than five optional units. Your college or training provider tutor will guide you through this when you start the course.

About this book

This book is designed to support you through some of the key units in the HNC. It is primarily designed for those working in an early years setting, but there are many examples throughout of how you might support older children in an out-of-school care setting.

Individual chapters relate to a specific unit or a range of units, and this is shown later in the introduction. Each chapter describes the learning and content from the HNC that it covers. This learning supports but does not match identically the outcomes of the units covered. The book is designed to show the interrelationship between HNC units.

Each chapter provides you with case studies that are working examples from practice. These case studies integrate theory and practice, allow you to debate and discuss issues with colleagues and tutors and to consider how you might deal with or respond to each scenario. You will also find case studies provide you with opportunities to consider issues relating to the age range covered by this award, including work with babies and older children, and those with additional support needs.

There are explanations of key words and phrases in every chapter. These will help you to understand some of the specialist language that might be used in this sector, and which you may be unfamiliar with.

Each chapter has a selection of learning features such as: *Activity*; *Consider this*; and *Further research*. These features are intended to support you by providing activities, thought-provoking questions and points for group discussion. The *Further research* feature will signpost you to look beyond the information contained in this book by suggesting useful websites, articles, texts and reports. Some features may direct you to consider additional research and activities to allow critical analysis of practice. The features have been included to support your learning and because the HNC

involves extensive reading, writing, research, personal reflection and evaluation. Each chapter finishes with a *Check your progress* feature, providing questions designed to allow you to test your knowledge and understanding of the chapter you have just read.

A key feature of all HNC awards in Scotland is the final graded unit, which requires a range of skills and careful writing and analysis to be used. The graded unit determines the overall grade you receive and whether you pass or fail the award. It is a very important part of the course. Successful completion of the graded unit means you will have managed to integrate the practice and the knowledge required in the mandatory section, and Chapter 10 provides you with support for completion of this unit.

The chart on pages vi–viii shows the HNC units covered by this book.

This book has been written by people who are currently teaching HNC students or who have had extensive experience of doing so. I hope you will find it helpful and hope you enjoy your career in the early education and childcare sector.

Frances Scott

HNC units covered by this book

	Key units covered	Other units covered
Chapter 1 Working in an early education and childcare setting	*Mandatory Unit* **DF4Y 34:** Working in an early education and childcare setting	*Mandatory Units:* • DF5E 34: Group award graded unit 1 *Group A Specialist Optional Units:* • DF51 34: Curriculum and assessment in an early education and childcare setting • DF53 34: Facilitating playwork opportunities *Group B Optional Units:* • DF55 34: Children and young people with additional support needs • DF57 34: Strategies and initiatives to support children's health and well-being • DF59 34: Working with children 0–3 years • DF5A 34: Working with children 3–5 years • DF5C 34: Working with children 5–8 years • DF5D 34: Working with children 8–12 years • DG5D 35: Team working in care settings

	Key units covered	Other units covered
Chapter 2 Children and young people's rights: provision, protection and participation	*Mandatory Unit* **DF50 34:** Children and young people's rights: provision, protection and participation	All other HNC Early Education and Childcare units
Chapter 3 Theoretical approaches to development and learning	*Mandatory Unit* **DF52 34:** Theoretical approaches to development and learning	*Group A Specialist Optional Units:* • DF53 34: Facilitating playwork opportunities *Group B Optional Units:* • DF55 34: Children and young people with additional support needs • DF59 34: Working with children 0–3 years • DF5A 34: Working with children 3–5 years • DF5C 34: Working with children 5–8 years • DF5D 34: Working with children 8–12 years
Chapter 4 Curriculum, play and transitions	*Group A Specialist Optional Unit* **DF51 34:** Curriculum and assessment in an early education and childcare setting	*Mandatory Units:* • DF4Y 34: Working in an early education and childcare setting *Group A Specialist Optional Units:* • DF53 34: Facilitating playwork opportunities *Group B Optional Units:* • DF55 34: Children and young people with additional support needs • DF58 34: Promoting language, literacy and numeracy in early education and childcare • DF59 34: Working with children 0–3 years • DF5A 34: Working with children 3–5 years • DF5C 34: Working with children 5–8 years • DF5D 34: Working with children 8–12 years
Chapter 5 Promoting language, literacy and numeracy	*Group B Optional Unit* **DF58 34:** Promoting language, literacy and numeracy in early education and childcare	*Mandatory Units:* • DF4Y 34: Working in an early education and childcare setting *Group B Optional Units:* • DF59 34: Working with children 0–3 years • DF5A 34: Working with children 3–5 years • DF5C 34: Working with children 5–8 years
Chapter 6 Children and young people with additional support needs	*Group B Optional Unit* **DF55 34:** Children and young people with additional support needs	*Mandatory Units:* • DF50 34: Children and young people's rights: provision, protection and participation • DF52 34: Theoretical approaches to development and learning *Group A Specialist Optional Units:* • DF53 34: Facilitating playwork opportunities *Group B Optional Units:* • DF56 34: Contemporary issues for children and families • DF59 34: Working with children 0–3 years

	Key units covered	Other units covered
		- DF5A 34: Working with children 3–5 years - DF5C 34: Working with children 5–8 years - DF5D 34: Working with children 8–12 years - DG5D 35: Team working in care settings
Chapter 7 Team working and communication	*Group B Optional Units:* - **DG5D 35:** Team working in care settings - **DE3R 34:** Personal development planning - **DE1K 33:** Workplace communication in English	*Mandatory Units:* - DF4Y 34: Working in an early education and childcare setting *Group B Optional Units:* - DF55 34: Children and young people with additional support needs - DF59 34: Working with children 0–3 years - DF5A 34: Working with children 3–5 years - DF5C 34: Working with children 5–8 years - DF5D 34: Working with children 8–12 years
Chapter 8 Understanding and supporting children's behaviour	*Group B Optional Unit* **DF54 34:** Understanding and supporting children's behaviour	*Mandatory Units:* - DF4Y 34: Working in an early education and childcare setting - DF50 34: Children and young people's rights: provision, protection and participation - DF52 34: Theoretical approaches to development and learning *Group B Optional Units:* - DF55 34: Children and young people with additional support needs - DF59 34: Working with children 0–3 years - DF5A 34: Working with children 3–5 years
Chapter 9 The impact of government policy on the lives of children in Scotland	*Group B Optional Units:* - **DF57 34:** Strategies and initiatives to support children's health and well-being - **DF56 34:** Contemporary issues for children and families	*Mandatory Units:* - DF4Y 34: Working in an early education and childcare setting - DF50 34: Children and young people's rights: provision, protection and participation *Group A Specialist Optional Units:* - DF51 34: Curriculum and assessment in an early education and childcare setting *Group B Optional Units:* - DF54 34: Understanding and supporting children's behaviour - DF55 34: Children and young people with additional support needs
Chapter 10 The graded unit: a survival guide	*Mandatory Units:* - **F290 34:** Graded Unit 1 - **DF5E 34:** Group award graded unit 1	*Mandatory Units:* - DF4Y 34: Working in an early education and childcare setting - DF50 34: Children and young people's rights: provision, protection and participation - DF52 34: Theoretical approaches to development and learning

Chapter 1

Working in an early education and childcare setting

Introduction

Working with children is interesting and varied. It is a job that requires careful planning and preparation, personal skills and capabilities. These include skills of communication, problem-solving and the ability to work with others. You will also find you need to have the skills to organise and plan activities for children and to prepare and manage the play environment for them.

In this chapter you will learn about some of the practicalities of working in the early education and childcare sector. This will help you to develop the professional skills you need to organise day-to-day experiences for children in the setting you work in. You will learn about the importance of reporting and recording what young children do and how this is used in planning appropriate experiences to support their learning and development. The process of reporting and recording will also be vital when you work with other key professionals such as teachers, educational psychologists, social workers and health professionals.

In Chapter 4 you will learn how to develop play-based activities for children, and with information from this chapter you will begin to develop a clearer understanding of some of the key features of children's learning and development and how you can contribute to supporting this. This will include understanding what you can provide, how it can be provided, why you should do this and the type of important relationships that will be involved in the process.

When you work with children and with other team members, it is essential to be able to stand back and evaluate what has gone on. This means thinking about the successes of the day and what might have been done differently. This chapter will help you understand some of the subtleties of doing this and will support your understanding of why it is important to be evaluative when offering a professional service to children.

As an early education and childcare practitioner in Scotland, you are part of a regulated workforce. This chapter will guide you through some of the key points about the Scottish Social Services Council's (SSSC) Codes of Practice (2003) and how they impact on the day-to-day work you do.

In this chapter you will learn:

- How appropriate skills are used to create a nurturing and stimulating learning and play environment

- How to plan, organise and implement development and learning opportunities in an early education and childcare setting

- How reporting and recording supports the work of the early education and childcare practitioner

- How other professionals support the early education and childcare practitioner

- How to evaluate your own contribution in creating a nurturing and professional service for children

- Ways in which codes of practice inform the work of the early education and childcare practitioner

How appropriate skills are used to create a nurturing and stimulating learning and play environment

Early education and childcare practitioners quickly discover that working with children isn't an easy option. It's a job that requires knowledge and understanding, with professional values, skills and abilities, and personal commitment. When you put these together you achieve professional action. It is through professional action that the early education and childcare practitioner provides an effective service for children and their families.

Early education and childcare is an important profession and you should never underestimate the skills required to do the job.

Key term

Professional action is the way you apply the knowledge and skills you have learned and the observations you have made to the day-to-day actions in your chosen profession. It combines the way in which you behave at work with your professional values and the knowledge and skills you have developed.

Activity

Working in small groups with others from your class, consider the skills you have that you think will make you a good practitioner. Discuss these as a group and choose one person to list all the skills that everyone in your group has.

How do you think these skills can be used?

Make a group poster of these skills then compare the poster with others in the class. Are there similarities common to each group?

Not all children are the same

Children are unique individuals and you should be aware of how to work with a range of children with varying needs. This includes understanding that children will have different dispositions with different ways of playing and learning, and understanding what additional support a child may need from time to time. You will already be aware that some children may be quite outgoing while others are more introverted; some children prefer to be alone while others seek the company of peers. Some children will be very tenacious and spend a lot of time trying to solve a problem while others will give up easily. As an early education and childcare practitioner you should respect and value children as unique, whole individuals who have a right to participate and be consulted about what they want to do and how they like things done. You will learn more about this in Chapter 2. Part of the skills of an early education and childcare practitioner involves supporting children's play and learning as well as helping children who move quickly from activity to activity to concentrate for longer periods. This may mean sitting with a child and gently encouraging or posing questions that help the child to rethink or reconsider what he or she is doing. These strategies sometimes help children to concentrate for longer.

You may also find some children favour only one type of play or stay for very long periods at one activity. As you become more experienced, you will learn to use your professional judgement to decide whether this is unusual or undesirable for the child. You will learn techniques that help you gauge accurately the preferences of each child. This, in turn, will help you to plan activities that are appropriate for each child's age and stage of development.

In Chapter 4 you will read about the type of experiences children should have in a setting, but it is useful to mention here that children should have opportunities for play that is freely chosen and will help them to explore, observe, listen and talk, respond, think, experiment and be active, among other skills.

As an early education and childcare practitioner you will have high expectations for all children and you will be committed to making sure they are provided with opportunities to achieve their full potential.

At some point in their lives, most children will have additional support needs. These may be long-term needs such as a disability, or may be for the short term such as going into hospital for a procedure. As an early education and childcare practitioner, you will develop skills to deal with specific and additional support needs in the course of your day-to-day work. This could involve the need to develop specialist skills in communicating with children by alternative methods. It could also involve researching a specialist area or bringing in a specialist practitioner, such as a hospital play specialist to talk to and try to reassure a child.

The Scottish Government's *Skills for Scotland: A Lifelong Skills Strategy* (Edinburgh, 2007) has identified some of the key skills needed by employers in all sectors as being 'soft skills'. It describes these skills as less definable but nevertheless essential. They are listed below.

- Effective time management
- Planning and organising
- Effective oral and written communication skills
- The ability to solve problems
- The ability to undertake tasks or make submissions at short notice
- The ability to work with others to achieve common goals
- The ability to think critically and creatively
- The ability to learn and continue learning
- The ability to take responsibility for professional development
- Having the skills to manage, or be managed by, others

(*Skills for Scotland: A Lifelong Skills Strategy*)

All of the skills highlighted by the Scottish Government are relevant to you as a practitioner and with regard to the way you approach your placement experience. Many of these skills will be looked at in detail in Chapter 7, which looks at team working. Later in this chapter, there is an opportunity to consider the skills you think you currently have and to see how you use them when you go to placement. This list of skills will also be a useful reference point for you. Other skills are discussed below.

The skill of listening and responding

When you are in placement and in your day-to-day work, you will begin to develop the skill of active listening. This will be explained further in Chapters 2 and 7, but essentially it means you should listen without interrupting and make sure you are giving the person who is talking your full attention. Children and adults are very aware when someone is only partly listening or when that person's body language suggests a lack of interest. This might mean you are staring into the distance when a child or adult is speaking, or you have a tendency to butt in to a conversation before it is finished, or you don't stop what you are doing to give the child or adult your full attention.

One way of showing you are actively listening is by repeating the child or adult's comment or question when they have finished talking. For example, if a child tells you she is 'gonna be a bridesmaid at my auntie's wedding', you might helpfully respond: 'Oh, you're going to be a bridesmaid, Lucy. Tell me all about it. What is it that a bridesmaid has to do?'

In the same way, if a child tells you he 'cannae get thae boxes to stick together', you might want to say: 'I see what you mean, Ryan. They're just not sticking together, are they? How can we solve that?' This type of response shows a child you are interested and have been listening.

Consider this

How do you feel when someone you are talking to yawns or is distracted by something that's going on elsewhere?

How would you feel if you had an important piece of information that you were dying to tell someone, but when you told them they simply said 'That's good' and walked away?

Listening is an important aspect of childcare

Approachability, adaptability and flexibility

Among the key skills needed by the early education and childcare practitioner is the ability to be approachable, adaptable and flexible. Children and parents will often come to you with news they want to share or for advice or reassurance. As with listening skills, being approachable means sending out the correct messages or cues. The cues you give are an indicator to the recipient of what they might expect. These cues can be verbal or non-verbal and will be explained in greater detail in Chapter 7. However, non-verbal communication will cue children in without any spoken language. So, if you are talking to a child without making eye contact or while scowling, this is likely to cue indifference or annoyance. Any cues you give should suggest openness, so don't stand with your arms folded or tap your foot in frustration or impatience. You can use positive cues such as smiling, making good eye contact, lightly touching a child's arm when you are giving praise and getting down to the child's level when he or she is speaking to you. Remember, children also use cues, so you have to be alert to what these might be indicating verbally or non-verbally.

Some nurseries and out-of-school centres operate a 'key workers' system. This means you will have a small group of children for whom you have particular responsibility. So, the child knows you are the adult he or she needs to go to each morning. This is important in a busy centre as children can often be intimidated by large numbers or the noise of a strange environment.

In some settings, practitioners are encouraged to put children at ease by shaking hands and saying 'hello' to each child when they arrive in the morning and 'goodbye' when they leave. This can be good practice because it means you are actively welcoming the child every day, saying his or her name, and it is a polite acknowledgement that you are pleased each child is there. It is also a way of showing approachability and friendliness. Please check out whether there are any cultural sensitivities associated with handshaking and don't assume it will be acceptable to everyone. Other strategies include starting the day with circle time and a song that acknowledges each child in turn: 'Molly Ross, Molly Ross, how are you?' Molly would reply: 'Here I am, here I am, how do you do?' However you do the daily introductions and goodbyes, it is really important the child is made to feel welcome.

Introductions are important in giving the child adult contact and a chance to share with you something that may have happened since you last met or something special the child is looking forward to.

Approachability matters to children and parents and to other team members. If you seem unapproachable, the child and his or her family are less likely to feel able to discuss or raise important issues with you. This means you will miss out on building a professional relationship in which you can form an accurate picture of the child and of the significant things that are happening in his or her life.

Making a child feel welcome

Further research

Often centres will have posters displaying different ways of saying welcome and good day. It is always important to welcome children in a way they can understand. Try to find out how your placement supports children and their families whose first or preferred language is not English. Comparing and contrasting your experience with those of others in your group might be a useful discussion point.

Adaptability and flexibility

Some people come into childcare with quite fixed and rigid views about what they think children should know and how they think children should behave. The best practitioners are those who are flexible and adaptable to change because when you are working with children the pattern is constantly changing. It is a truism that no two children are alike. Even if something works well for one child it may not for the next. So you need to be prepared to change your approach and to be flexible. It can be annoying if you have planned to do something and it has to be altered in some way, particularly if you are in a centre on placement for just a few weeks, but this happens. Occasionally, because of staff absence or when other situations occur in the centre, you have to change the original intentions and you have to be prepared to go with those changes. This is also true when you have prepared something because the child was really interested in it the day before but you find he or she just isn't interested in it the next day. Again, you have to be prepared to change your plans to accommodate a new interest.

Flexibility means you will have a fairly relaxed or open approach to change. You may be asked to step in for another colleague at short notice or to take responsibility for a part of the centre you hadn't anticipated being in. The more flexible and adaptable you are, the greater the asset you will be and the more likely you will be to learn quickly.

The Scottish Government identified the ability to step in and adapt at short notice as a skill many employers seek. For example, you could occasionally be asked to stay later than you had anticipated or to come in early to help set up the centre. Nurseries are collaborative spaces and it's important that all the practitioners in the centre are sufficiently flexible to help each other out and are mutually cooperative.

Working with others

Most of the time you will be working as one of a team of people. However, you might also be working as a sole provider such as a childminder or in a parent-led playgroup that is reliant on parents and volunteers. Often you will be involved with key people in the child's local or cultural community. Key to working with others is to understand and value the contribution each person has to make. Your behaviours are important to others you work with, so you should learn to be dependable and make sure you follow through on any commitments you make. It is vital to the team and to children and families that the centre opens on time every day. Some workplaces operate a shift system which means they are open for an extended day; this can mean 7 am to 7 pm. It is unlikely you will work a 12-hour day, but you may start work when a colleague finishes. It is important you are on time so that you can relieve other members of staff, and you need to be prompt to make sure you don't disrupt the work of the centre.

As well as working with colleagues, you will work with parents and carers of the children. You may also work with key people in the child's cultural community. All are integral to the child's

---

Case study *Pulling together*

You work with two other colleagues in a 20-place centre. The children are putting on a small event at harvest time for their families. This involves working with the children to set up displays of their work in the days preceding the event, making, printing and copying programmes and ordering refreshments. On the day before the event the manager discovers the programmes have mistakes in them. Also, the janitor has gone home sick so no seating has been set up for the following day, and the delivery you have been expecting with the refreshments hasn't arrived. You usually go home at 3.45 pm but you have been asked to stay to help sort out this difficulty.

1 Do you think this is a reasonable request?

2 If you are unable to stay, are there ways you might still be able to help?

Sandeep has just come back to the nursery having spent six months with his mother in Pakistan. He cries for most of the morning and is reluctant to settle to any activity. He keeps looking out of the window and asks when his mum will come back for him. He is following you round the nursery all the time and doesn't like to lose sight of you.

The area in which you work has a thriving Pakistani community who support the school really well.

1 Describe some ways you might help to settle Sandeep.

2 How can you best use your skills to ensure Sandeep's needs are met effectively?

life and it is important for you to link with them, to be welcoming and to communicate well.

What skills?

Sometimes, it might seem the early education and childcare practitioner needs to be superman or superwoman. In reality, you do need to have a range of skills to work with children. You have already heard about some of the skills you require and others that have been identified by the Scottish Government.

Some of the key skills which will be discussed in more detail throughout the book include: empathy; the ability to listen and respond well to children and adults; the ability to read and understand instructions; the ability to show a caring and committed attitude towards children; a willingness to take on a range of roles in the course of your working day; a professional approach to your work; an ability to understand the role of other colleagues and to respond positively to coworkers and other professional

Activity

You might like to complete the chart below and keep it at the start of a folio or log book you are asked to keep for placement activities.

It's a useful device to keep checking back to remind yourself of the skills you actually

have, as well as to remind yourself how you are developing these on a day-to-day basis. You will see how you are becoming more proficient. It's always good to remember what you can do but also to think of ways to improve.

Skills I have	How I demonstrate these skills

Skills I am developing	How I demonstrate these in placement

colleagues for the benefit of the children; practical skills; professional skills and abilities; kindness and a caring approach.

One of the professional skills you will develop through going to placement and by reading and research is the ability to understand children and to put into context their developmental stages with an understanding of their behaviours. Chapter 3 describes some of this in more detail.

When you are working with children, you need to respond to them appropriately. Sometimes, you may think a child shouldn't be behaving in a particular way but are not sure what to do about it. You should be aware of your own limitations and know how and when to ask for help or support. This means you will learn by observing others, become aware of any particular existing strategies that may be in place and start to develop your own strategies for dealing with difficult situations. Asking for support and being aware of personal and professional limitations shows a mature response and provides you with a positive learning experience. It is not an admission of defeat to explain you are not sure what to do. Remember, the only 'stupid' question is the question you don't ask.

Different types of provision in early education and childcare

HNC Early Education and Childcare is a vocational course. This means you will have placement experiences as part of the course and will need to use and develop skills in those placements. During your HNC year you are likely to have more than one placement and each may provide a different experience and new opportunities. Some colleges send candidates on three placements during their course. These are likely to be for a range of centres, including those shown in the table opposite. This tells you a little about each type of placement, the way it is funded and managed, and the age ranges of children you could be working with in each. In Chapter 9 you will learn how Scottish and central government policy provides some financial support for parents. The way it appears in the table is 'government funded'. If you are clear about the different types of provision you can be sent to, this may help you to consider in advance the type of skills you are likely to need.

Provision	Age ranges	Who inspects	How it is funded	Duration of service
Childminder	From 12 weeks to 12 years (or older)	Scottish Commission for Regulation of Care (Care Commission)	Individual families pay. Can be claimed back through tax credit or through government-funded places.	Varies from one hour to all-day care; varying times of the week and varying times of the year.
Nursery school or class (local authority)	3–5 years	Care Commission and HM Inspectorate of Education (HMIE) (if providing pre-school education)	Government funded, usually up to 15 hours a week but in some cases can be full-time.	Usually 5 days x 2.5 hours, term times only.
Child and family centres including voluntary providers	Birth to 5 years	Care Commission and HMIE (if providing pre-school education)	Usually by referral and to support families with particular needs. Government funded.	Varying times but can be for up to 2–3 hours daily or longer. Can be for a set period depending on circumstances of referral.
Private nursery	12 weeks to 5 years. May also run after-school care for 5–10-year-olds.	Care Commission and HMIE (if providing pre-school education)	Mixed economy. Some government-funded places are up to 15 hours a week but with additional hours privately funded by families.	Varies from hourly to all-day sessions. Can be up to 10 hours a day.
Playgroups (voluntary sector)	Often 2.5 to 5 years	Care Commission and HMIE (if providing pre-school education)	Some government-funded places up to 15 hours a week but with hours privately funded by families.	Usually for 2–3 hours daily, term times only, but can vary to full-year provision.
Out-of-school care	Usually children aged 4–10 years but can be for children up to 12 years	Care Commission	Usually privately funded but families can claim tax credits to help with funding.	Usually for 2–3 hours daily, but can be extended in school holidays to full-day provision.
Crèches	Can be children from 12 weeks to 10 years, but often children 2–8 years	Care Commission	Usually privately funded by parents. Can be free to parents depending on who is running the service.	Usually for a limited time from one hour to a maximum of 3 to 4 hours. Can be open all year or can be for specific occasions.
Schools including special schools and classes	Children from 4.5 to 16 years plus. You would normally be in a P1 but could work with older children with ASN.	HMIE	Government funded, unless in the independent sector where funded wholly by parents. Special schools independently run receive grants from a variety of sources and normally offer free places for children.	Usually 9 am–3.30 pm, term times only.

How to plan, organise and implement development and learning opportunities in an early education and childcare setting

Planning is used by professionals to consider, prepare and organise a suitable environment and materials for children's play, development and learning. When you are planning you need to consider what the purpose of it is. Sometimes it may be related to different stages of children's development. In other circumstances it is to extend and elaborate play experiences or to provide a suitable environment for learning to take place. Where nursery schools and classes are using Curriculum for Excellence, planning may be considered against the four capacities you will read about in Chapter 4.

Planning is an important feature of what you need to do for this unit. You will be asked to plan activities while you are in placement, but will be supported in this by key people. In placement you will be working with a mentor or a placement supervisor, who should be consulted every day, so you need to agree times at the start of your placement for discussing your plans. At college you are likely to have a placement tutor or workplace assessor, who will support your understanding of what you need to do to provide evidence for the unit.

Planning is the key to any successful activity. It takes place in collaboration with others in the early education and childcare team, with parents and with children, and is one of the most important professional skills you will acquire.

Good planning helps to ensure you provide children with the right opportunities at the right time to achieve positive outcomes. Plans can be long term and short term. The short-term plan can be broken down into individual plans.

Long-term planning

The purpose of a long-term plan is to be more strategic about what you intend doing and how you will embed interests that you know are likely to occur, such as seasonal or cultural ones. Long-term plans outline the programme for the centre. This means you are prepared for interests that will most likely occur throughout the year or that you can predict are very likely to occur, and you will know who is doing what and when. In a nursery school or class this can be achieved over a school session. It provides an opportunity for staff to be proactive in organising to ensure resources are in place and allows them to source materials if they have to be secured from elsewhere. It also allows forward planning, such as any required site visits and other key activities.

Short-term planning

Short-term plans allow you to focus on more specific objectives which enables you to build on children's current interests or identified needs. The observations the staff make are fed into the short-term plans and staff discussion is an important part of constructing a plan. Often the long-term plan, e.g. 'Where our food comes from', will generate visits and additional activities. These need to be considered against key development or curricular areas. An example would be how a particular centre ensured opportunities for listening, talking and recording within the broad theme of a visit to a local farm. This centre would also pick up on particular interests the children showed while there and would develop activities or play opportunities based on these. Short-term planning will vary from centre to centre but generally the long-term plan is distilled into smaller, specific key themes or actions. The short-term plans closely follow observed needs, including play needs.

Individual plans

Within the short-term plans will be the daily or weekly plans for children. They provide a clear focus of the child's needs and how those needs can be met in relation to planned provision and activities. These are likely to be discussed either daily or weekly depending on the type of service provider you are working in. These daily discussions will be specific to what staff observed daily to be the child's needs or interests.

Some centres outline their weekly plans by taking broad headings, such as 'Taking part in sustained conversations about a topic of interest': with the assessment focus *listening and responding to questions*. A plan is written up to show this, including: starting points for activities; what it is anticipated the children will gain from these experiences; any particular children who key staff are being asked to observe that week; and, finally, what resources are needed and who will provide these.

Any planning is subject to change but generally it helps to build up a picture of the child, what the starting point is for the child, what is needed to support that child's development or learning and how the centre will go about providing for this. This gives the practitioner a clearer idea of general and specific objectives for children's play and learning, and how to evaluate successes or identify ways needed to help the child consolidate learning, play or skills. Planning meetings give staff an opportunity to discuss and contribute to the overall planning in the centre. You will be invited to take part in meetings but may feel you want to watch and listen when you first go to placement. Later on you will feel you can contribute more confidently to discussions, as they are an important way of finding out who has responsibility for what part of the day-to-day activities in the centre.

Why planning is important

The planning process helps to set goals for children and aims for staff. It is directed at what children need and defines how the practitioners supporting them are going to provide for this effectively. Planning also means the environment is kept fresh and children are given new choices in their play. Some children

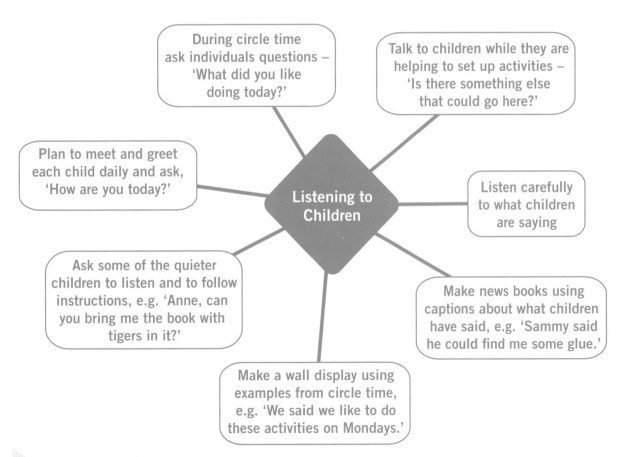

During circle time ask individuals questions – 'What did you like doing today?'

Talk to children while they are helping to set up activities – 'Is there something else that could go here?'

Plan to meet and greet each child daily and ask, 'How are you today?'

Listening to Children

Listen carefully to what children are saying

Ask some of the quieter children to listen and to follow instructions, e.g. 'Anne, can you bring me the book with tigers in it?'

Make news books using captions about what children have said, e.g. 'Sammy said he could find me some glue.'

Make a wall display using examples from circle time, e.g. 'We said we like to do these activities on Mondays.'

Developing a plan for listening to children

are in full day care for five days a week. These children need variety and choice. Planning will support children's independence, and a well-organised environment will make it easy for the children to find and to put away activities of their choosing. This doesn't mean rigidity, lack of choice or the loss of spontaneity for children. The well-designed and carefully structured environment will be planned in a way that means those working with children are clear and confident about developmental, play or learning needs, and what and how they are providing for these needs. Effective planning means that contingencies can be dealt with easily, so staff know where and how they can source materials quickly and according to the required need of the child. Good planning allows opportunities for change to occur and provides a backdrop of support for children's all-round development.

Ways to plan

There are different types of planning processes. Some of these may seem quite informal while others may be more formal. Below and opposite are two examples of planning sheets that are used in centres.

Sunnyside Nursery: Planning Sheet

Child's name: Sui Ling

Date of Birth: 02 05 2004

Sui Ling's own comments:

I saw lots of bugs when I was helping my nan dig her garden. I like looking at the bugs but they move quite fast you know

Key worker's comments:

Tuesday 08 September 2007

Putting out magnifiers for Sui Ling and Amy to use.

Suggesting we might dig in the garden and look under some leaves that have accumulated outside the door.

Resources required: spades, bug boxes, books.

Provide some slate-coloured and brown paints in painting area and some pictures of centipedes and beetles on table as inspiration to paint some insects.

Laurel Kindergarten Planning Sheet

Name: Tommy

D.O.B. 11.12.2006

Planning for week beginning: 01.10. 2007.

Tommy is starting to move on his feet while holding on to furniture for support. – Enjoys knocking down blocks and bricks; he laughs and tries to build them up so he can knock them down again. Starting to vocalise.

This week we will: provide Tommy with safe areas to move around with a key worker on hand to support him.

Make sure he has a range of activities to stimulate his interest including large blocks, soft blocks and Brio which he can build up and knock down.

Make sure we have time for alliteration rhymes and for songs. Use look-and-tell books with single images on each page.

Activity

When you first visit your placement, find out how staff plan for children's needs. Do they plan every day or every week, or do they use thematic or seasonal planning?

Does each child have a personal learning plan?

Establish who is involved in the planning process, how this is recorded and how the staff keep planning records up to date.

Finally, find out what the centre expects you as a student to plan.

One example of planning you will hear more about in placement is the personal learning plan. The personal learning plan, or PLP, is a way of providing appropriate learning that is targeted at an individual child's needs. In some local authorities in Scotland, every child has an individualised learning plan, including children in the nursery. This could be similar to the one shown above for Tommy. Throughout Scotland, personal learning plans are key to providing effective development opportunities and learning for children with additional support needs. You are less likely to find this type of planning in out-of-school care. However, this doesn't mean that you don't need to plan for children in out-of-school settings. Planning can be informal but it is important as it ensures practitioners know their role and the expectations of them.

Planning the child's environment

A Curriculum for Excellence (Scottish Executive, 2004) is one of the key documents used in nurseries in Scotland to support children's play and learning. You will read more about this in Chapter 4 and it is important to remember it when discussing planning. Scottish ministers believe it underlines how children will acquire what are described in the document as four capacities, namely to become successful learners, confident individuals, responsible citizens and effective contributors. So, when planning for children's development and learning, pre-fives practitioners need to keep this in mind. It will be an important feature of many of the settings in which you work and it is important you learn more about this curriculum document while you are doing the HNC course.

A Curriculum for Excellence: Building the Curriculum 2 – Active Learning in the Early Years (Scottish Executive, 2007) speaks about the need for active learning. This means learning that engages children and in which they are actively involved. This can be described as planned purposeful and spontaneous play that engages and challenges children to think and respond by becoming actively engaged in real life or imaginary experiences.

Further research

The Scottish Government's Curriculum for Excellence programme is described in more detail in Chapter 4 of this book. There is also a range of web-based materials about *A Curriculum for Excellence: Building the Curriculum 2 – Active Learning in the Early Years*, which looks at it in relation to early years. The website www.curriculumforexcellencescotland.gov.uk is a good place to start your research.

Try to locate some of these sources and consider how you might use the information you find to support your placement experience.

Keep some of this material filed away. You may want to use it later in the course when you are writing your graded unit.

Planning in placement

When you are in placement, one of the key purposes is to learn to create engaging environments for children. This means you will learn to plan and create spaces where children can thrive, develop, explore, experiment and learn. A well-organised environment will be calm, creative and organised. It will give children lots of scope for exploratory and imaginative play among other types of play; it will ensure children have space in which they can be creative and can have fresh air and exercise; it will be a space in which children can be nurtured and feel safe. This doesn't mean an environment that is too quiet, over tidy or rigidly controlled; a calm atmosphere can be created that still gives children freedom and scope for movement and play.

Some nurseries organise rooms according to children's ages. A key requirement of planning for different age groupings is an awareness of child development (see spider diagram opposite). When you work with children under 12 months, your first considerations will be about developmental and exploratory play

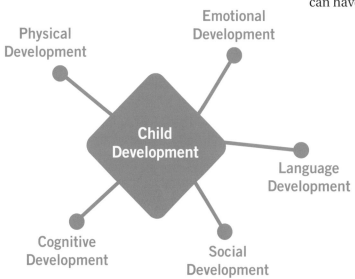

The different types of development opportunities that children require

opportunities for the child. These will be based on aspects of child development that include: physical development; emotional development; social development; language development; cognitive development. You will use the child's developmental stage and needs to plan what you need to provide for him or her.

When you are working with older children, developmental needs and, sometimes, curricular needs and progression will play a part. When you are planning a play-rich environment for children, you have to be able to create an environment that is suitable for a variety of play experiences.

The environment is the space in which children play and the space that surrounds them. It may be restricted by physical constraints or it may be a large outdoor area. One nursery in Edinburgh uses roof space for outdoor play, while another uses a church hall that has to be set up and put away every day. Often playgroups are limited by the space they have and are usually expert at maximising space for children's play.

One of the first things you could usefully do on placement is to draw a floor plan of the nursery, indicating where key play and discovery areas are situated. This provides a way of considering play areas and gives an opportunity to think about how children use the space. Sometimes it is called 'looking at the geography of space'. You may want to look at how the children use space by drawing lines to indicate how they move across the floor area and how they navigate the space. Eventually, this might seem to be just random patterns that you have created, but if you use a different colour for each child you will soon see areas of heavy usage and areas that are visited less frequently. It allows you to consider why that might be and whether the space is being used effectively.

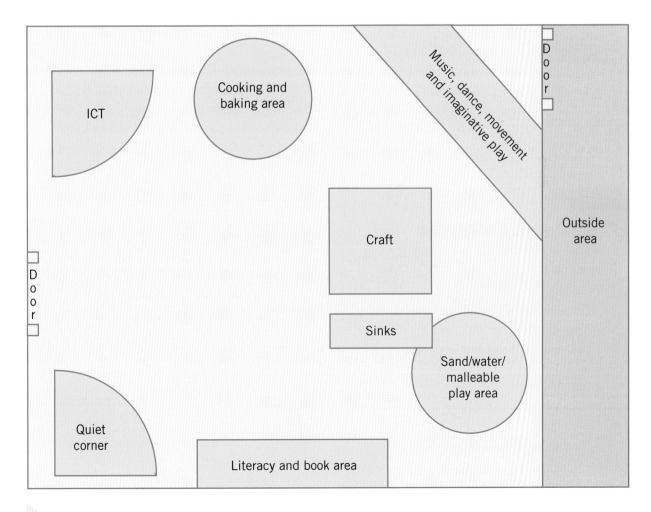

Example floor plan of a nursery

Sometimes areas don't work together. This can be because noisy and quiet areas are inappropriately put together or because there simply isn't enough space for children to spread out. Wherever possible, nurseries and out-of-school care should aim to maximise the space they have. They can include outdoor space for activities you might naturally think of as indoor. So, sand and water can be put outside as can painting, discovery activities and activities that use large motor movement.

If there is space available it can be useful to plan a quiet room or a white room, where there is calming music playing, some lava lamps or bubble tubes, and lots of soft furnishings and different textured cushions. It's helpful to include listening tapes or CDs and to have lots of books available, so that children can relax in this space. You need to think about the core purpose when planning this type of space. While adult supervision is essential, keep it low key and keep noise to a minimum. This creates a calm space to take a distressed child or a child who may be new and nervous about his or her environment. Planning and creating a quiet area, and its effectiveness in calming children, may be an interesting topic for future research in your graded unit.

Activity

Consider the diagram on page 15 of a floor plan of a nursery. Can you suggest improvements on the arrangement of the activities in this floor plan?

Draw your own nursery floor plan showing what activities are offered in each area and how children naturally move from area to area. Try to work out your own floor plan that will keep a quiet space separate from the other activities.

One of the key concepts the Scottish Government wants to embed across children's learning, their day-to-day lives and the communities in which they live is citizenship. Citizenship will be explained in later chapters but it is important to remember here how it can support planning for learning, play and development. It includes cooperation with others and peer learning, which is often a more effective way to learn and consolidate facts. The case study below is an example of how children can actively support the planning process and can support each other's learning. It also shows how practitioners can effectively intervene to support and develop learning.

Key term

Peer learning means learning from those who are your friends or contemporaries. In nurseries, schools and out-of-school care, this would mean children looking at and learning from each other. As adults we use peer learning in our day-to-day lives. This may mean that, as learners, one of your friends is able to explain a new concept or show you a format they have used for a report. In our personal lives peer learning can be about day-to-day occurrences. An example of this would be if you bought a new mobile phone and weren't clear how it worked. One of your friends might sit with you and show you the different functions. People often find this a more relaxed way of learning and children do it together all the time.

Case study *Working together*

Jimmy and Daisy are working together on the computer. Daisy tells Jimmy her dad has a new digital camera and she says they have got lots of new pictures at home to look at. Jimmy remembers they have a digital camera in the centre and goes off to find it for Daisy. Daisy says 'Here, I'll show you how it works', takes some photographs of Jimmy at the computer and shows him how to see the pictures on the screen of the camera. Mrs Kohl watches and observes what they are doing and asks Jimmy and Daisy if they would like to know how to see the pictures on the computer screen and how to print them off.

This is an example of spontaneous, active learning for the two children.

1 In what way do you think the staff in the centre had planned for the children's learning here?

2 Do you think Mrs Kohl's intervention here was appropriate?

3 What types of materials do you think Mrs Kohl would need to have near at hand to easily support these children?

Play opportunity offered (describe briefly)
Reason for choice (this should relate to a need you have observed or one that you have been told about)
What is the active learning experience (Refer to *A Curriculum for Excellence*, if appropriate)
My role in this will be and this is how it relates to other team members
Anticipated benefits to the child
Resources required and how this was planned and organised
Evaluation of my role

Evidence gathering and the planning process

When you go to your placement you may be asked to provide some written evidence of how you have planned for children's play, learning or development. Most courses ask candidates to prepare a folio of what they have achieved in their placement, and these usually need to be signed by your placement supervisor to show they were authentically done by you.

You will gradually build up confidence and the folio will show how your judgement has developed over the year. By the end of the year you will be writing well-constructed plans and will know how to observe and record evidence effectively and professionally.

In your placement you may be asked to provide a specific learning or play experience, and to record how you planned it. You will identify the reason for choosing a particular activity or experience, what your role is in the process and how your role fits with others in the team. You may also be asked to consider some of the resources you need to deliver or to develop the activity, and what the anticipated benefits are for the child who is doing it. Remember, you need to carefully observe the activity before you can actually say what the child has gained from any experience.

Above is an example of the type of planning record used by some colleges for candidates' folios.

It is likely your tutors will give you specific activities or tasks to do each time you are out in placement. These will vary according to the stage of learning you have reached in your course. They may involve developing play for particular age ranges such as babies; they may involve working with older children. Eventually, it will involve you being asked to provide specific activities or play that relates to the full range of experiences you would expect children to have. These will include providing play that supports children's literacy, numeracy and language development, as well as exploratory and investigative play that will allow children to create problems and work out solutions.

You will be asked to plan and contribute to children's outdoor play and to play that provides calculated and acceptable risk and physical challenge. This is particularly important to make sure children are fit, healthy, active and achieving. These are key priorities of the Scottish Government. When you are planning this type of activity or an activity that takes you outside the centre, you will need to carry out a risk assessment and be clear about how you are going to ensure children's safety. The Royal Society for the Prevention of Accidents (RoSPA) provides advice on how to minimise the risk of accidents and it might be useful to download this from their website (www.rospa.com).

Each placement will vary but it is likely that you will be asked to provide a minimum of one and a maximum of two planned experiences for children's play, development or learning each week you are in placement. These should be taken from a wide range that will be described in Chapter 4, but which could include creative and aesthetic experiences for children such as dressing up, dance, music, creative crafts, and construction, along with any other play or activities that allow children to be imaginative and inventive.

When children are inventive and use their imagination, they learn how to construct new possibilities or new experiences. You need to know how to support this by carefully considering if the activities that are there for children are becoming tired and need to be refreshed. If you are attentive and actively involved in planning, you will notice whether, for example, the sand and water have the same equipment in them week in and week out, and if the children are reluctant to go to the activities because there is no further challenge for them. You could bring this as an observation to the daily planning meeting. This may lead you to suggest a new activity, which can be planned, implemented and evaluated as a placement activity. If successful you may be asked to consider other areas of the nursery or your observations may be used to inform further change.

Planning, observation and evaluation together form a cycle, sometimes called the planning cycle. This circular process helps inform all you do in the centre. If used well, you will be considering and reconsidering what you need to offer and refining what you think is appropriate, according to what you have observed.

Sometimes you will be working with families and will need to explain why you have planned particular experiences for their child and how you think they will benefit the child. You may be working alongside parents and need to be clear about the rationale behind all you are doing. You will provide a role model and your effective planning and organisation will support a better understanding in parents who, for a number of reasons, may be unable to play effectively with their children. Once qualified, you are expected to be able to speak with authority to parents and to other professionals whose backgrounds will not be play-based. This will mean keeping up to date with web materials, articles, books and other research that is written about how to plan and organise children's play. This type of personal planning is valuable for the research activities you will be doing for this and other units, and for your graded unit.

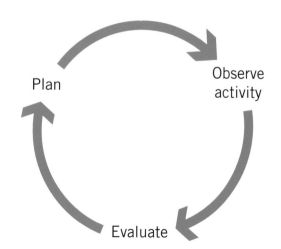

The planning cycle

Keep up to date with research about how to plan and organise children's play

Children and the planning process

Children of all ages can be actively involved in determining their own play and learning, and it is important when you are planning that you take account of this. As you progress through the HNC, you will have the opportunity to offer a range of experiences. Sometimes, you will note that children get stuck at an area or at a single activity. This can happen for a variety of reasons, including the child feeling secure at a particular area and apprehensive about joining other children, or it can be because the child isn't particularly confident about trying something new. Children can easily be discouraged and it may be that the child has found something too difficult to manage in the past. If you are planning with the child, you can engage him or her in conversation about what he or she currently likes to do and might potentially do. You can also find out about whoever a child plays with now and anyone he or she might like to play with in the future. The planning sheets on pages 12 and 13 show how a child's comments were used to create a learning experience. When you plan with the child you can use his or her ideas to help resolve issues.

Parents and the planning process

Parents and carers are integral to children's lives so involving parents in the process of planning is important. Some children are looked after by others and these key people are equally aware of the child's needs and can also be included in planning. Centres will have their own processes to involve parents and carers, and will have procedures in place to ensure parents' comments are taken account of in the planning process. This might mean an informal discussion with a parent about their child or inviting a parent in to the nursery or centre to work with staff. Either approach allows parents and staff to make decisions that support the child and that make sure a parent or carer feel they have been part of the process.

Organising a play or learning experience

Earlier in this chapter, you considered how planning can be carried out on a daily, weekly, monthly or termly basis, and is described as long-term and short-term planning. In long-term planning there are likely to be key seasonal or cultural trends. For example, the centre can anticipate they will be celebrating seasonal changes such as spring and autumn or annual cultural or religious festivals such as Diwali or Christmas. This helps in organising, preparing and storing props, books, storysacks, drapes, and other key items or equipment required. The well-organised centre keeps these clearly labelled, and part of the organisation and storage is ensuring materials are kept in good condition, are clean and are complete before storing them for use in the future. As an HNC student you will be asked to help put up displays and to change areas of the centre to reflect a particular theme that has emerged.

When you are planning activities for your folio, you should try to be well prepared. Ask in placement whether you can use materials from there and if you can spend some time looking at these. It might mean you need to stay late or come in early to investigate. You may also need to source your own materials. Develop contacts and sources for ends of paper, materials and other odds and ends. Improvise by making really interesting visual aids such as puppets – but always be aware of health and safety issues. You can also develop your own database of where you have sourced materials in the past and add this to your contacts list. Parents often have useful contacts and can be very supportive of the centre; they are also a useful point of contact for the local community.

When you plan activities for your folio, you need to keep the following in mind:

- Do you know the aim of the experience?
- What are the ages of the children?
- How many children are you working with?
- What materials will you need?
- Is the area you will be working in safe and free from hazards?
- Do you need to store materials before you start your activity?
- How are you going to encourage children to take part in the experience?

- Is everything you need clean and displayed in a way that makes children want to take part?

If you are organising materials for activities like painting, crafts or cooking, make sure you've got the right quantities ready for when the children want to use them. Finally, think about how you will clear away and tidy up. You can encourage the children to help with this.

If you are baking or cooking, try out recipes first, using the same equipment you will be using on the day, to make sure it works! If you are encouraging children to follow printed instructions, make sure you've pitched them at the correct level of understanding for the child and check the instructions make sense. This is something you might like to try out on your friends first of all. If you are using symbols or pictures on recipe cards, it's better if you print them off and laminate them and it's often more professional to use web-based images.

Remember to involve the children in the organisation, preparation and clearing away of activities. It is a really effective way of engaging interest and extending choice where you think children have become self-limiting. Children usually love being involved and this type of experience provides excellent opportunities for them to practise problem-solving and working together.

Involve children in helping with preparation and clearing away

Personal organisation

Your workplace folio or folder will provide evidence of what you have accomplished and of how you've planned and completed workplace activities. Different course providers may have varying ways they want to generate evidence for this unit. Normally, you will have a workplace supervisor who will be asked to sign and authenticate any work you have done on your placement. It will save you a great deal of anxiety if you try to keep as well organised as possible. Try to:

- write up any work you've done on the day you do it
- save your work in a placement folder in your documents
- back up all your work on a memory stick so you have a copy
- photocopy any handwritten work and keep it in a separate folder so you have a copy
- keep your folder with you at all times, such as when you get off the bus.

Some HNC candidates like to keep personal resources in an ideas book or folder. Many early education and childcare practitioners find they still add to books they started as students. You can make a paper-based folder or an electronic folder with different types of activities such as: songs and rhymes; poems; stories; art and craft; discovery activities; seasonal and cultural activities; miscellaneous items. As you go from placement to placement, you can add ideas you see there and you can include ideas from professional journals. It's a useful resource when you need to think of an activity fast.

How reporting and recording supports the work of the early education and childcare practitioner

Reporting and recording

It's very tempting to think you will remember everything you have done and what everyone has said on a daily basis. This is true of what children say to you. If it is particularly funny or engaging you may think you are bound to remember. In reality, few of us have the capacity to do this. This is one of the reasons why reporting and recording are important in early education and childcare settings and are skills you will develop when you are in placement.

Reporting and recording is the process by which we write down and feedback information we have. This important process can be carried out either formally or informally. In Chapter 2 you will read about the need for the accurate recording and reporting of child protection issues. In Chapter 4 you will see that observation of what children do is a key component of recording.

Observation involves watching and listening to what children are doing or saying. It is a professional skill and should be done as unobtrusively as possible. By watching what children are doing and recording it in a way that is meaningful, observations provide us with some evidence for the statements or claims we make about the children. Observations will be central to completing workplace folios and are integral to the planning process. Focused observation allows you to see what a child is doing in a given situation and to take appropriate actions. An example of this is given in the case study below. This is a typical example of how observation can be used to support a child and to work with the parent or carer.

What is reporting and recording?

Reporting and recording are ways of helping staff keep track of how children are developing and learning. They allow practitioners to speak with understanding to parents and other professionals about individual children. Records provide a way of showing progression and sometimes regression in children, and centres use them to inform staff when children are making a transition from one centre to another. You will read more about transitions in Chapters 3 and 6.

Key term

Making a transition occurs when a child moves from one stage to another. Transitions include moving from baby room to toddler room, nursery to primary school, and primary school to secondary school.

Case study *Observing Katie*

Katie has just started in Primary 1. She had been really happy to go to school for the first week when the children were finishing at 12 o'clock. In the second week they are staying until after lunch. On Thursday, Katie's mum has told the centre that Katie has been quite tearful about coming to school this week and the teacher and practitioner have said they will try to find out if there is anything upsetting Katie. At lunchtime the practitioner observes that Katie is last to finish her lunch and all her friends have gone out to play. Katie is observed to be agitated, pushing her food around and starting to get upset. The practitioner observes this the following day as well and concludes Katie is happy in the dining room until her friends finish and leave her. When the practitioner speaks to Katie about this, Katie says it's too noisy and she doesn't like it there.

The practitioner and teacher explain what they have observed to Mum and they all discuss ways of resolving the situation. Katie's mum tells them Katie has always been a slow eater.

1 Consider how you have used observation, or seen others in your placement use observations, to reassure or inform.

2 Can you think of ways to improve your recording of observations? List any ideas you may have. See if you can put these ideas into practice during the next few weeks.

There are some key features of keeping records, as follows:

- Records provide accurate information about individual children and the progress they have made. This is sometimes called the child's profile. Parents and carers are provided with a written record of the child's progress at set intervals each year.

- They are a means of planning the next steps in the centre. Plans will be built around need that has been recorded in profiles or otherwise observed.

- Records ensure staff are clear about particular actions they may need to take at a given time because a particular need has arisen.

- They are a means of being selective and of making professional judgement. It is not possible to record everything that goes on in a centre. Professional judgement has to be used by early education and childcare practitioners to decide what to record and how to record it.

- They encourage collaboration among staff and with other key professionals.

How to report and record

There are various ways to report and record and you will see examples in your placements. Some centres, with permission from parents, use photographs and multimedia to record what children are doing in the centre and ways they are collaborating with others. This can be a really useful way of showing parents and other professionals how children respond in given

Photographs can be used to record collaboration

situations. The illustration above shows how a photograph can be used to record collaboration in a setting. An example of a multimedia record is shown below. Kevin's dad had been telling the nursery he was concerned that Kevin didn't speak about other children he played with and he was worried that Kevin had no friends. The practitioner was able to show Kevin's dad a range of images which had been put together as 'Kevin's Book'. Below are some of the things in Kevin's Book.

This helped to reassure Kevin's dad that Kevin played well with other children.

Some centres use video images in the same way. It should be stressed that this can only be done with explicit permission from the parent

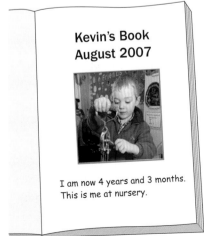

Kevin's Book
August 2007

I am now 4 years and 3 months. This is me at nursery.

I was playing with the musical instruments with Ben today.

Johnny and I love playing outside with the spades and sand.

We managed to build a sandcastle today.

or authorised adult dealing with the child, who should be informed at the outset of the purpose of the recording. All images need to be kept in secure files. They should not, in any circumstances, leave the centre unless they are required for a legitimate, professional reason following a request by another agency which has been made known to the child and parent, and for which their permission has been granted. There are ethics and guidelines governing this, which you need to be absolutely clear about.

Further research

Investigate the policies that are in place in centres and within local authorities concerning the use of images of children for professional observation purposes. The British Psychological Society has a code of ethics that describe how they view this (see www.bps.org.uk).

Following your investigation, create a list of key points from the code of ethics that you think are relevant to your work as an early education and childcare practitioner.

Other methods of recording

Some centres still favour paper-based methods of recording information. This includes day-to-day snapshot recording done on Post-its. At the end of the session these are transferred into the child's individual record or on to the planning sheet as a way of planning the following day's activities, and to take account of individual children's interests.

Some centres adopt a 'Plan do and review' approach, and the children are encouraged to record their own interests or what they have done that morning on a large sheet of paper or on a whiteboard. This recording can be done on their behalf by an adult or they can draw their own picture. For example, in Stoneypark Nursery the children go to their key worker at the end of the morning to review what they have enjoyed that day. Kylie tells her key worker that she really liked shining the torch through some coloured glass. The key worker writes this down. Timmy says he liked playing with the cars best and he draws a picture of a car to illustrate this point. At the end

of the morning the key worker takes her record to the planning meeting to discuss with others.

Parents will often come into the centre with important information for staff. In some centres they are encouraged not only to provide this information verbally but to write it into the child's home book. A home book is a book that the child brings from nursery to home and then back again, and is a way of encouraging two-way dialogue. Mary's gran wrote this in her home book: 'Mum went into hospital yesterday. The new baby should be here today and Mary and I are going to see her after nursery.' This is helpful for the staff and alerts them to think about bringing out the baby dolls, the prams and the bath, so the home corner has a 'baby' theme.

Recording should be done over time and evidence from observations should be used in context. It is wrong for staff to try to use a single observation as evidence of fact. However, if you gather information over time you will see patterns of behaviour emerge and how progress has been made. You may find you need further evidence or that you feel the child is lacking opportunity in a particular area of play or needs some challenge to help their developmental progression. Keeping accurate records enables you to do this effectively.

Reporting

Reporting back provides you with an opportunity to reflect on what has been achieved with the child involved. It is a really important part of what you do and encourages children as active participants in their learning. You will use reporting skills in feedback sessions to parents, colleagues and to other professionals. An important skill to learn is to be succinct in what you say, accurate – so make sure you can always back up what you say – and positive. Reporting is always much more effective if it is based on what a child has achieved rather than a deficit model that focuses only on lack of achievement. It is very disheartening to hear about what we can't do rather than what we can do. So, if a child has struggled with completing a jigsaw but has finally managed it, it is much more encouraging to say: 'with encouragement, Dolly managed to complete the jigsaw today'.

How other professionals support the early education and childcare practitioner

One of the key skills spoken about earlier in this chapter was the need to be able to work with others and to see what you are doing as part of a bigger picture. While you are an HNC candidate, you may notice there are a range of other professionals who work with you in centres or are called into the centre to support the child.

For Scotland's Children: Better Integrated Children's Services (Scottish Executive, 2001) identified the need for all those who are working with children to be more integrative in how they go about this. It is an important document because it outlines expectations for children and their families. It concludes there are gaps in sharing information across agencies and across professional groupings that mean children in need don't always get the level of service or the level of support they need. Often children and families who need the support of other professionals find those professionals don't always coordinate what they are doing. The result is that children and parents often have to provide the same information to a range of people who may or may not take a coordinated approach to supporting them. It is also possible to make mistakes or to fail to follow something through because the support hasn't been well coordinated.

Sometimes, working with others is called inter-professional working. This means working with people from different professional groups.

Intra-professional working, on the other hand, means working across professional groups – that is, with people from the same profession as yourself.

At other times you may hear about inter-agency working. This means different agencies are dealing with a child and family at the same time. So, the education service, the health service and the social work department may all be working with the same family. If you are working across agencies you will find you are carrying out inter-professional working. For example, you may go to a Child and Family Centre on your placement, where you are likely to be working with a range of other professional groups including social workers, community health workers and (occasionally) psychologists, speech and language therapists or physiotherapists. If you are sent to a special school on placement there is likely to be a diverse range of inter-disciplinary staff there, including teachers, speech and language therapists, occupational therapists, physiotherapists, educational psychologists and social workers from the local child and family teams.

Which workers contribute to the early education and childcare team?

Social workers

Social workers are degree-qualified, specialist practitioners whose role is to support and guide individuals and families with complex needs and problems, to find solutions to those problems and enable them to live successfully within their local communities. Social workers often work with families with complex problems or short-term need and support them to find a way through particular difficulties they may encounter. This may mean working with other agencies such as health and education services. Social workers try to empower individuals to take personal responsibility and will work with service users to construct packages of care. They need to make sure the most effective measures are put in place to protect children from possible risk from abuse (*Key Capabilities in Child Care and Protection*, Scottish Executive et al., 2006).

Public health nurses

Public health nurses (health visitors) are qualified nurses who work within communities to support the health and well-being of individuals. To this end they support a better understanding in communities, and with individuals and families, of health and well-being. They also provide what has been called 'anticipatory care'. This means supporting people to lead healthier lives that will help to reduce the need for hospital admissions and acute care. Working with families is an important part of this drive, as is working within nurseries and other childcare centres in communities. These nurses will work with individual families at key points in the child's life, including with newborns. They are intended to support children's and families' general and mental health and well-being, and should work closely with others in doing this.

Educational psychologists

Educational psychologists are degree-qualified individuals with an additional specialist award in educational psychology. They support and advise on educational programmes for children who are experiencing difficulties with their learning so that they can enhance that learning. They are asked to provide evidence if the child is being assessed for a place in a special education programme or school. They work closely with others in the team to build up a clear and accurate picture of the child and will use techniques such as observation and assessment to make recommendations about the best way of helping the child achieve and develop potential.

Speech and language therapists

Speech and language therapists are qualified specialist practitioners who work with the child and family to identify any speech, language or communication difficulties a child may have. They work as part of a multi-disciplinary team to make sure any programmes they devise for children are understood by the people who are supporting the child and are followed appropriately. The programmes might include making sure the correct environmental conditions are in place to help the child. They may support children who have difficulty forming particular words and sounds because of a physical difficulty they have had or because of general developmental delay.

Teachers

A teacher's main role is to transmit learning and to support children in reaching their full potential. Teachers are degree-qualified and those working in a nursery or pre-school may have an additional specialist qualification. They work closely with other partners to ensure the planning and organisation of learning opportunities is appropriately provided, to evaluate what they have provided and to ensure this is reported appropriately to parents and to others. They are accountable for the quality and standards of what they teach and have a responsibility to work with parents and others in the best interests of the child.

Visiting specialists

Visiting specialists are sometimes introduced by centres that need practitioners with particular specialisms to add value to what the centre is offering. These individuals usually have personal skills that are required by the centre and may include one-off visitors or individuals who come on a more regular basis. One example is centres that offer specialist foreign language teaching. Often, a teacher or member of a local community will come into the centre to teach children that language. This is also true of music and dance specialists. Some centres that are attached to primary schools will work with an Active Schools Coordinator. This person may work closely with the staff and children in the centre and with a health visitor to provide suggested healthy eating and exercise programmes for children and families.

Working with other professionals and specialists

When you are working with others, one of the key requirements is to develop a positive working relationship based on mutual trust and respect. We each have our own professional skills and develop judgements based on these. It is important to remember that different practitioners have their own skills, too. This means you should listen to what others are saying, make sure they have all the facts about the children or groups they will be working with, and work to develop relationships that have a common goal for the child or children involved. You should make sure you have time to discuss strategies and aims with other professionals. This might mean providing evidence such as observations or records so that other professionals can support the children appropriately. It may mean following up the work of other professionals by adopting a particular programme, or it may be that you simply work with them for the benefit of the child.

Activity

Consider the type of additional professional support that might be involved in the following circumstances.

Family 1

The Gray family have recently moved to Scotland. John, age 4 years, is the youngest in a family of six children and has been identified as having communications difficulties.

Family 2

Susan and Ben both misuse drugs. Ben has recently been in prison. Both are extremely caring parents who are trying to get their lives back on track. Lindy, their 12-month-old daughter, is attending the Child and Family Centre.

How to evaluate your own contribution in creating a nurturing and professional service for children

When you are in placement you will be asked to plan and organise activities and experiences for the children you are working with. This is important, but what is more important is how well you are able to evaluate what you have done. A key requirement of an early education and childcare practitioner is to be able to say what you did, why you did it and how well it worked, so that you are able to consider carefully what the next steps should be. The final step is the process of evaluating.

Evaluating as a skill is something that runs through all parts of the HNC. Evaluation allows practitioners to make a judgement based on evidence of whether something has worked and allows us to constantly improve what we do and what we offer children. A really important component of your graded unit is the evaluation. One thing to remember is that no matter how well you have planned and organised activities, they don't always go to plan. This doesn't matter. What does matter is the ability to stand back from an experience and consider why it didn't go to plan and how you might alter it the next time so that you do achieve your goal. You may also need to accept that, while the activity wasn't appropriate, children still got something beneficial from the experience. Good evaluation is a key research skill. It is concerned with extrapolating information from a range of sources and making judgements based on evidence.

How to gather evidence

Evidence can be derived from a range of sources. One of the main sources in an early education and childcare setting is observation. So, a straightforward way to consider if an activity is popular is to stand back and watch how many different children go to it in a given time. Another way of looking at an activity is considering if it is fulfilling its aim. For example, you may have set up a painting activity because you hoped children would be inspired by something you had spoken about that day. An example of this is the practitioner reading 'The Tiger Who Came to Tea' to a small group of children. The children become excited about the story and start talking about tigers, what they look like, how furry their paws are and whether or not they are very fierce. When John, the practitioner, plans for the following day, he decides to limit the colour of paint available to orange and black. He also puts up a picture of a tiger as a prompt and decides to tell the story of the 'Tiger Skin Rug'. John sits back and observes as one by one the children produce pictures of 'their scary tigers'. John also observes some really interesting discussions about visits to the zoo to see the new tiger cub. In this situation it would be fair to say the children had a continuing interest in tigers and John would need to consider how to take this interest forward.

As an early education and childcare practitioner, you will be able to gather evidence from other sources. Some HNC candidates need to produce taped observations of children's conversations, so they can consider their stage of language acquisition. Sometimes you will be asked to transcribe this. This means writing down accurately what the children are saying from the tape.

Case study

Scenario 1: *Observing Jake*

Jake has been attending the out-of-school club for three weeks now. A practitioner has been observing Jake carefully to make sure he is settling in well. Every day when Jake arrives he goes straight to the café area and helps himself to some fruit. His friends tend to go off to play with the Playstation. Jake joins them after about 10 minutes.

Which option would you choose and why?

1. You tell Jake's parents he seems hungry when he comes into the club and ask if Jake is used to having a snack straight after school.

2. You tell Jake's parents he seems to have an eating disorder and they need to get it checked out immediately.

Scenario 2: *Working with Louise*

You have been asked by the physiotherapist to work with Louise. She has suggested you try throwing and catching a beanbag to encourage Louise's large motor movements. On day one, Louise doesn't manage to catch or throw with any accuracy. On day two, Louise catches the bag once and doesn't throw. By day three, Louise catches the bag three times and manages to throw it once. On day four, Louise throws and catches the bag three times out of six.

Which option would you choose and why?

1. You tell the physiotherapist that Louise is fine at throwing and catching now and she enjoyed it.

2. You show the physiotherapist the chart you have made and explain you have observed that Louise has made some incremental progress on a day-by-day basis. You suggest you continue with this work to see if this progress is consolidated.

Being objective

If you are evaluating your own contribution, you need to be able to stand back and be objective. Objectivity is usually concerned with the examination of facts. Subjectivity usually describes opinions that are based on personal beliefs and values. So, a subjective view would be that all 2-year-olds have temper tantrums. An objective view would be that those 2-year-olds you observed in the nursery often became frustrated, some cried due to frustration and some cried, kicked their legs and screamed when they were frustrated. As an HNC candidate you are encouraged to be objective and to evaluate

your contribution based on evidence. This is called self-evaluation.

Centres are also asked to carry out self-evaluation for their Care Commission and Her Majesty's Inspectorate of Education (HMIE) inspections. This involves asking key questions about how good the experiences being offered are and if there are ways of improving these for the benefit of the children and their families. There is no virtue in self-delusion – that is, pretending something is going well when it isn't. This type of behaviour means you don't make improvements and the service suffers as a result. There is also nothing wrong in admitting something didn't go as well as it might have done. Providing you can see why and can identify ways of changing this in future, this approach is very positive.

Sometimes, others evaluate your contribution to the centre or what you are offering to the children. Mentors or workplace supervisors will do this in an objective way and will provide feedback based on fact: for example, 'I saw you working with Amy earlier. You spoke very kindly to her when she was upset,' or, 'I'm a little disappointed you haven't brought in those books you said you would bring in today.' You will usually receive a report at the end of the placement that will identify the key skills you brought to that placement, the successes of it and the key areas for improvement or further development. Accept this type of evaluation as a positive experience.

Evaluating your folio

When you are completing evidence for your workplace folio it is likely to be divided into key sections. The section on evaluation provides you with an opportunity to think about what you contributed and how well you planned, organised and carried out the experience. It also provides an opportunity to evaluate what you think the children have gained from it. Usually your discussion with your placement mentor will help to support your understanding of this, as will discussion with the children. Try to find ways of asking children how they enjoyed an activity or whether they thought you provided them with the right materials or equipment. This is part of the overall evaluation. Your mentor is likely to ask you what you think the children learned or gained from an experience, or how you think it contributed to a child's development or play. This is sometimes called *reflective practice*, because it refers to how you think about or reflect on what you have done. Being reflective isn't just about what you think, it is also about what you can prove through observations.

To help you reflect, you need to be well prepared, which includes knowing as much about a child as possible. It is much easier to reflect when you have some background to help you. So, if you know a child doesn't concentrate for long periods but has stayed at your activity for longer than usual, you can point this out in your evaluation. When you are writing an evaluation, try to remain positive, pointing out what the child was able to do well and identifying key points for development rather than deficits.

Receiving verbal feedback

The feedback you receive from other adults is important in building up your confidence and skills. Make a point of asking for feedback, although good placements will do this anyway. If you receive feedback which you think is wrong or undeserved, ask politely if you might discuss it. Ask if there are examples of when you worked in this way so that you can learn from them and try to rectify a problem. Make sure you share feedback with your college supervisor so that it can be discussed openly at three-way meetings.

Parents and others will often give impromptu feedback. This is useful and can be encouraging. An important aspect of feedback is to be clear about what is being said and how you can move forward as a result of it. This is sometimes described as personal or professional development.

Using evaluation in other HNC units

Part of undertaking the HNC is to develop the necessary professional skills and competences to allow you to make professional judgements and so take professional action. This means that sometimes you will be asked to comment on books, articles and journals based on the facts you have read. You may disagree with what has been said, and another key skill is to be able to

evaluate what you have read, sum up what you think is being said and offer evidence-based or enquiry-driven solutions. These solutions require careful thought and consideration of other points of view that have been arrived at through research or observation. Because your graded unit is based on your workplace experience, it is really important to develop the skills of analysing what you are reading and what you are being told, and to ask the following questions:

- How do I know this to be the case?
- How can I find out more about this and is there sufficient evidence to back this up?

You will read more about the skills of analysis in Chapter 10, which looks at the graded unit in more detail.

Ways in which codes of practice inform the work of the early education and childcare practitioner

Early education and childcare is part of a regulated profession, and Chapter 9 looks at the policy drivers behind this. It is regulated through the Regulation of Care (Scotland) Act (2001). Those working in the service, unless they are teachers registered with the General Teaching Council for Scotland or are registered by another professional body such as the Nursing and Midwifery Council, are required to register with the Scottish Social Services Council (SSSC). Early education and childcare services are inspected by the Care Commission and sometimes jointly inspected by the Care Commission and HMIE. Employers and those working in the sector are expected to adhere to the SSSC's Codes of Practice for Social Service Workers and Employers.

The SSSC Codes of Practice

These describe the standards of conduct and practice within which social services practitioners should work. They are intended for both employers and employees and should be seen as complementary to each other. This means that both workers and employers have responsibilities to behave in an appropriate way.

The SSSC Codes of Practice list statements that describe the standards of professional conduct and practice required of practitioners. The statements are intended to reflect existing good practice and a shared understanding of the standards practitioners need to aim for when working with children and other service users. They are a key step in the introduction of a system of regulation and the SSSC (and other councils in the UK) need to take account of them when considering issues of workers' or employers' misconduct. The standards are important when making a decision about whether a registered practitioner should remain on the register.

The SSSC Codes of Practice highlight employers' responsibilies to service users and workers, and employees' responsibilities to the people they work with and to their employer.

Key term

Service users in the social services sector in Scotland are those people who use any service that falls within the scope of the Regulation of Care (Scotland) Act (2001). This includes those who are providing a day care of children service which covers early education and childcare. In this case, service users will be children, their parents and carers.

Codes for employers

The SSSC Codes of Practice include five key requirements for employers of social service workers. These are:

- making sure people are suitable to enter the workforce
- having written policies in place to enable social service workers to meet the SSSC's Codes of Practice
- providing training and development opportunities to enable practitioners to strengthen and develop their skills and knowledge

- putting in place and implementing written policies and procedures to deal with dangerous, discriminatory and exploitative behaviour and practice
- promoting the SSSC Codes of Practice to workers, service users and carers, and cooperating with the SSSC's proceedings.

For social service workers, the five key requirements of the SSSC Codes of Practice are:

- protect the rights and promote the interests of service users and carers
- strive to establish and maintain the trust and confidence of service users and carers
- promote the independence of service users while protecting them as far as possible from danger or harm
- respect the rights of service users while seeking to ensure their behaviour doesn't cause harm to self or others
- uphold public trust and confidence in the social services. This includes: not abusing trust, exploiting service users or abusing or harming colleagues; considering whether your behaviour out of work as well as in work might call into question your suitability to work in the sector.

(Adapted from *Codes of Practice for Social Service Workers and Employers*, Scottish Social Services Council, 2005.)

You should have been given a copy of the SSSC Codes of Practice when you started your course. However, it can be downloaded from the SSSC website (www.sssc.uk.com) or you can request a copy through the website.

In practical day-to-day terms, the SSSC Codes of Practice should provide you with a strong sense of values as you progress your career in the social services sector. They should also help you to see what your responsibilities are as a social service worker. The codes serve as a useful reminder of what employers need to put in place for their workers and how they can act positively, decisively and effectively in protecting children from practitioners whose practice does not meet an appropriate standard.

What you have learned in this chapter

This chapter has provided you with information about the key skills you will need when working with children. It has shown you some of the ways you will need to plan and organise day-to-day activities and experiences for children when you are out in placement. It has also emphasised the importance of team working and of effective communication with children and their parents and carers.

You will find that other features of Unit DF4Y 34: Working in an early education and childcare setting are covered in other chapters in this book; these are detailed in the chart below.

During the HNC there is an expectation you will keep a record of all activities you have done in placement, and you will be expected to work with different age groups of children. Your placement experiences will help support the work you do for the graded unit. This is explained fully in Chapter 10, but as well as keeping records for this you will be expected to develop skills of analysis and reflection. Some colleges suggest you keep a placement diary, where you can note significant outcomes from each day's placement experience, what you have learned about a child or group of children that day, and how your contribution has supported change or improvement in the centre. By analysing your contribution you will start to build up the skills you require for the graded unit. You will also be able to reflect on what has gone well and how you might improve your contribution for the benefit of the children in the setting. It is also useful to consider the impact you have had on a particular setting or a situation in the setting. Sometimes this can be positive, but sometimes the presence of another adult can have a negative impact. You need to be able to stand back and consider this and listen to feedback from others, including children. Feedback will be essential in helping you decide what activities and experiences you want to develop in your placement and, ultimately, what topic or theme you want to pursue for your graded unit.

Working in an early education and childcare setting (Unit DF4Y 34)				
Outcome 1 How learning or play takes place in an early education and childcare setting	Chapter 1	Chapter 3	Chapter 4	Chapter 10
Outcome 2 How to plan, organise and implement development and learning opportunities	Chapter 1	Chapter 2	Chapter 4	Chapter 10
Outcome 3 Identify and demonstrate how appropriate skills are used to create a nurturing and stimulating learning and/or play environment	Chapter 1	Chapter 4	Chapter 6	Chapter 10
Outcome 4 Evaluate your own contribution in creating a nurturing and professional service for children	Chapter 1	Chapter 4	Chapter 7	Chapter 10

Complete the following questions, to see what you have learned from this chapter.

1. Why is planning important for the early education and childcare practitioner?

2. In what way can planning help you organise day-to-day activities for children?

3. Explain why team working is important in an early education and childcare setting.

4. Describe your role as an early education and childcare practitioner in setting up and putting away activities for children.

5. Explain why the SSSC Codes of Practice for Social Service Workers are important to your day-to-day work.

6. How would you describe some of the key skills required to work with children?

7. In what way does observation support a child making a transition from nursery to Primary 1?

8. How can an early education and childcare practitioner make sure parents and children are involved in reporting?

9. Explain why objectivity is important when working with children.

10. Explain why it is important to be able to evaluate your own performance in the centre.

References

Crown Office (2001) *The Regulation of Care (Scotland) Act (2001)*, Edinburgh

Scottish Executive (2004) *A Curriculum for Excellence*, Edinburgh

Scottish Executive (2007) *A Curriculum for Excellence: Building the Curriculum 2 – Active Learning in the Early Years*, Edinburgh

Scottish Executive (2001) *For Scotland's Children: Better Integrated Children's Services*, Edinburgh

Scottish Executive et al. (2006) *Key Capabilities in Child Care and Protection*, Edinburgh

Scottish Government (2007) *Skills for Scotland: A Lifelong Skills Strategy*, Edinburgh

Scottish Social Services Council (2005) *Codes of Practice for Social Service Workers and Employers*, Dundee

Chapter 2

Children and young people's rights: provision, protection and participation

Introduction

As an early education and childcare practitioner you have chosen to work with children. People who make this choice often have views about how children should be treated and protected.

Some people's views about how children should behave may be based on how they feel they were treated as children or cultural expectations. As a practitioner, you should challenge views that are poorly informed or dangerous to children's welfare, and you may need to become an advocate for children and their rights. You will need to understand what is meant by active participation by children and facilitate this in a range of ways that are appropriate for children's age and stage of development. To do this well, you will need to reflect on your own values and beliefs. This chapter will provide you with some of the reading that allows you to do this.

In this chapter you will look briefly at what is meant by childhood and how perceptions of childhood have changed. Sometimes adults hold too much power over children,

so that children don't have a voice. You will consider some of the power relationships that children may experience and ways that children can be empowered. Some of the charters and policies described in this chapter are concerned with children across the world. This means that all children, irrespective of where they live, should have the same rights and entitlements. You will read about the legislation passed by the Scottish Government to support children's universal rights.

One of the most important considerations for practitioners is to make sure children are protected from harm or abuse. While legislation concerning child protection may change from time to time, the child's right to be protected and to be listened to will not. By researching the issues of children's rights, participation and protection, you will be able to remain as up to date as possible in your professional role. This will allow you to act appropriately and proportionately in your day-to-day work with children.

In this chapter you will learn about:

- Charters and legislation that support children's rights
- Values and principles underpinning a rights-based approach
- How adults can support a process of children's participation
- The importance of listening to children
- Child protection, policies and issues
- Protecting children and young people
- Putting it into practice: policies and procedures

Charters and legislation that support children's rights

Understanding childhood

Childhood as a concept seems to be self-evident: it is the stage in which you are a child. However, different people hold varying views about what childhood should be, when it starts and when it ends. People who work with teenagers or adolescents will tell you that this age group don't like to be referred to as children. Adolescence is a stage of development that you will consider in Chapter 3. It is still considered to be part of childhood studies because it isn't yet adulthood.

In *Theorising Childhood* (2001), James, Jenks, and Prout describe some of the conventional wisdom about childhood, and explain that children are often looked at from a range of perspectives. They consider how the views of researchers and philosophers regarding the state of childhood have changed over time, and offer four examples of this. The first concept they describe is the view that children are evil – that is, a belief that children are born evil and it is the adult's role to save them from further corruption and train them to be adults. This view was adopted by the Puritans of the sixteenth century and more recently by some fundamentalist groups in the United States. Such groups believe that punishment is for the child's own good and is character forming.

A second view of childhood is that of the innocent child who is naturally good and who needs to be protected from evil. This was the view of the philosopher Rousseau (1712–78), who believed that children are innately good but that the world in which children live makes them corrupt.

A third belief is that children are like empty vessels waiting to be filled with knowledge and moulded into the adults' view of what children should be like – in effect, that childhood is a preparation for adult life. This position regards children as incompetent and waiting to be made competent by adults.

The fourth view of childhood, supported by some psychologists, takes a developmental approach. It views children as immature, naturally developing beings who go through a maturational and developmental process to 'become' self-sufficient and capable individuals.

Some of these views have been challenged by new, sociological approaches to childhood. These are quite complex to understand but essentially sociologists view childhood as a stage in its own right that is not a sub-set of adulthood or emerging adulthood. You may want to read more about childhood theories: examples of texts are given in the reference section to this chapter (pages 64–65). Recently there has been a lot of debate about how children, and so childhood, is viewed, with many contradictory views.

Sometimes children are portrayed as demonic and out of control. Anti-Social Behaviour Orders (ASBOs) are issued to children as young as 12 years, ordering them to disperse. Sometimes shops near to schools have notices stating 'Only two children at a time', giving the impression that young people are likely to cause trouble if they go into shops in larger numbers. NHS

Key terms

Sociological approaches to childhood are the ways in which childhood is thought of in terms of how children are positioned in society and how they affect society.

Anti-Social Behaviour Orders (ASBOs) are intended to prevent anti-social behaviour or behaviour that is disruptive or offensive in communities. They are issued under the Anti-Social Behaviour (Scotland) Act (2004). This Act was broadened to allow orders to be granted against children aged 12–15 years as well as older people. An order can be issued to an individual or a group of people.

Scotland reported that, in 2005, almost 1,100 children under 15 years were admitted to A&E departments suffering the effects of alcohol consumption.

A current concern is the growth of the 'cotton wool' child. This means children who are protected by parents and are not allowed to travel home from school independently, to leave home unaccompanied or to go out to play alone. Some high-profile abduction cases have made parents increasingly wary about giving their children freedom to play outdoors, in case they are hurt or corrupted in some way. However, critics consider this approach to be harmful to children's ability to calculate and take acceptable risks, to gain understanding of how to deal with risky situations and to develop resilience.

Further research

Look in your local papers for some articles about children. Consider the different ways children are portrayed in them.

Do you think there are any contradictory messages given about children in the articles? Discuss your views with colleagues in class.

Every child's childhood is set in a particular context so it is difficult to compare them. Some children in Scotland may live in inner city or rural poverty, but is it possible to equate this to the poverty of street children in Brazil? Can child soldiers in Africa be compared with gang culture in an inner city? In some parts of the world there is an expectation by families that a child as young as 9 or 10 years will work and contribute to the family income; how does this differ from cultural norms in Scotland?

You will see that it is very difficult to assess how these variables impact on childhood and to make a judgement about whether some children have 'better' or 'worse' childhoods when you are not comparing like for like.

Consider this

In what way do you think experiences of childhood vary from area to area in Scotland?

How do you think childhood is affected for children who:

1 act as carers to parents or other siblings

2 are required to work to help families make a living

3 are forced to leave home because they live in abusive situations, and end up sleeping rough?

Children's rights

Irrespective of the type of childhood they have, children are now regarded as having rights. Children's rights have been described as being about self-determination (*Sparing The Rod: Schools, Discipline and Children's Rights*, M. Parker-Jenkins, 1999) and about moving away from an adult-centric society to a society where children are valued as children and not as mini-adults or adults in waiting.

Rights describe what is morally and socially acceptable in a society and what a person should be able to expect. There is an inference of protection in a right: namely, a right should offer someone protection from particular actions.

An example of a right in the UK would be the right to freedom of speech. This means you have the right to speak out on issues that concern you without fear of being persecuted for saying these things. This contrasts with an entitlement. An entitlement means you should get something. An example is all children have the right to education but they have an entitlement to education in Scotland from the age of 5 years until they are 16 years. Education must therefore be provided by local councils for all children aged 5 to 16.

Some researchers, including C. Smith ('Children's rights: have carers abandoned values?', 1997) and M. Woodhead ('Psychology and cultural construction in children's needs', 1990), claim that where there is a needs-based approach to making decisions about children, it leaves too much power in the hands of adults, who are then able to take decisions that affect children's lives. A recent development across the world and advocated in the UK has been the growing belief among campaigners that children have rights that are separate from the rights adults have on behalf of their child.

Children's rights have been in the spotlight for a long time. However, since 1989, when the United Nations (UN) signed a charter for children's rights (see below), there has been an increased awareness of what this actually means. Much of the children's legislation across the UK since 1989 has been rights-based in approach.

The United Nations Convention on the Rights of the Child (UNCRC)

The United Nations is an organisation that supports peace and is committed to improving the lives of citizens of the world by working across nations to achieve it. It represents all nations and provides them with an important voice.

In 1989, the United Nations approved an international human rights treaty known as the Convention on the Rights of the Child. This charter was signed by every nation in the world with the exception of the United States

of America and Somalia. The USA is the richest nation in the world and Somalia is one of the poorest. The USA doesn't think it is necessary to have the UNCRC as they consider their own Constitution to cover many of the articles of the UNCRC. Others disagree with this view and argue that it's vital that all nations sign up to the UNCRC, because it means every government has to report back on the progress it is making to implement the charter in their own country. The UNCRC is not part of UK law, but the UK central government and the devolved governments in the UK have all agreed to abide by it.

> **Consider this**
>
> What might the implications be for children in a country that isn't committed to the UNCRC?

In Scotland, following the Commissioner for Children and Young People (Scotland) Act (2003), a Children's Commissioner was appointed to advocate on behalf of children, to make sure children's voices are heard and to ensure fairness in all matters affecting children. The Commissioner can call the Scottish Government or other agencies to account for their actions if they consider that they have not been working to achieve this, either through legislation passed or other actions taken.

> **Key terms**
>
> **Constitution** is a set of laws or principles that describe the way the country should be run.
>
> An **advocate** is someone who speaks or writes in support of another person or position.

Scotland's Commissioner for Children and Young People (SCCYP) is Kathleen Marshall (correct at the time of printing). The Children's Commissioner website (www.sccyp.org.uk) is a child-friendly site that encourages children to participate and ask questions. The role of the Children's Commissioner includes:

United Nations headquarters in New York

- promoting and safeguarding rights with regard to the United Nations Convention on the Rights of the Child
- involving children and young people in research
- carrying out investigations into issues that are important to children and young people.

Among other work, the Policy and Research element of SCCYP investigates the policies and practices of organisations and government bodies to ensure they are consulting with children and young people on issues that affect them and in a way that is accessible to them.

Other organisations such as Children in Scotland (www.childreninscotland.org.uk) undertake research and raise awareness of issues that affect children's day-to-day lives. Children in Scotland works with over 400 voluntary, statutory and professional organisations, as well as individuals, to support children and their families in Scotland.

It provides useful resources for early education and childcare practitioners, including information on policy and consultations that affect children. It also has resources to help children and practitioners understand the experience of growing up in Scotland today.

> ### Further research
>
> Visit the SCCYP website and the Children in Scotland website. Identify how each organisation offers support to children and their families. Consider how each website is written. If you were a child, how do you think you might feel about the accessibility of each site?

Articles of the UNCRC

The UNCRC has 54 Articles, or key statements, about what children can expect from the charter. Articles 43–54 describe the ways adults and their governments can help to make sure the charter is working. Articles 1–42 are directed at what children can expect. Here is an example of two of the Articles:

Article 1: For the purposes of the present Convention, a child means every human being below the age of eighteen years unless under the law applicable to the child, majority is attained earlier.

Article 3: In all actions concerning children, whether undertaken by public or private social welfare institutions, courts of law, administrative authorities or legislative bodies, the best interests of the child shall be a primary consideration.

You can see that the way these Articles are phrased doesn't make them particularly easy to read. There are child-friendly versions available, such as those on the United Nation's Children's Fund (UNICEF) website (www.unicef.org.uk/ youthissues) and the SCCYP website (www.sccyp. org.uk), where the Articles are explained in a more straightforward way.

All of the Articles of the charter are important to your work with children and you should be aware of how they impact on your practice. Two that are worth highlighting for this unit are Articles 3 and 12. Article 3 talks about putting the best interests of the child at the centre of everything you do, while Article 12 is about the need to consider children's views and opinions in all matters that affect them. Both of these Articles have informed some of the legislation that is currently being used in Scotland, including the Children (Scotland) Act (1995), the Regulation of Care (Scotland) Act (2001),

Articles 3 and 7 of the UNCRC emphasise the importance of listening to children

and the Education (Additional Support for Learning) (Scotland) Act (2004).

Issues that Articles 3 and 12 affect include:

- children being allowed to give or withhold consent to treat illness

- being protected when asked to give evidence

- putting the child's best interests and opinions at the centre of child protection hearings

- making sure children are allowed to give their views on how they are being treated and to give feedback in schools and in other contexts.

There are many other UNCRC Articles that you may want to consider in class.

> **Consider this**
>
> What are some of the implications in a day-to-day context for Articles 3 and 12 of the UNCRC? You may want to think about how you currently use children's views to inform practice or make changes in your centre.
>
> How does your placement ensure children are listened to in any major decisions that may affect them?
>
> Is there a policy that states how practitioners will go about listening to children?

Understanding a rights-based approach

The UNCRC and the drive for better awareness of children's rights has informed other key policies now being delivered in Scotland. One of the main improvements brought about by the UNCRC is the level to which children are actively involved, instead of being passive in processes that have a direct impact on them and on their lives. Among the intentions behind the charter was the intention to embed a rights-based culture where children have a voice, are listened to and are protected from exploitation and abuse. This has been central to the way that organisations deal with children and with children's issues since the mid-1990s, and has helped move organisations and some governments away from

a 'paternalistic' style of decision making to a rights-based, child-centred approach.

In a paternalistic style, adults make decisions for children because of a belief that this is best for the child, or because a child needs protecting in the way a father would traditionally have protected his child from harm.

A rights-based approach works on the premise that children can be supported to make decisions and don't always need to be told what is best. A rights-based approach also recognises that children need protection and that they are vulnerable to adults that might prey on them or abuse them. It places responsibilities on adults to be aware which children might need to be kept safe from harm and how children would like to be treated. This is dealt with in more detail later in this chapter (see pages 53–64).

Most people who advocate children's rights also believe that with rights come responsibilities. This means that while children have the right to expect to be treated in a particular way, they also have the responsibility to behave in ways that respect other children's and adults' rights as well.

> **Further research**
>
> Look at the UNCRC and try to identify which Articles might promote the following rights for children:
>
> - the right to play
> - the right to be protected
> - the right to be free from discrimination
> - the right to follow a chosen religion.
>
> Describe ways that an adherence to these rights should provide safeguards for children.

Legislation that support a rights-based approach to children

Acts of Parliament are the formal decisions made by parliament. In the UK there is a devolved government in Scotland that is able to make its own laws on key policy areas. One of those areas is children, including: children's health; social work and social care; education and criminal justice.

The Children (Scotland) Act (1995) – which you will read more about later in this chapter and in Chapter 9 – was seen by the Conservative government of the time as a way for it to meet its obligations under the UNCRC (*The Children (Scotland) Act 1995: Developing Policy and Law for Scotland's Children*, E. Tisdall, 1997). In particular, the Act was strongly influenced by UNCRC Articles 3 and 12. For example, the Act states: 'The welfare of the child should be the paramount consideration in making decisions about the child' (sections 11, 16, 17, 95) and 'Due regard should be given to the child's views' (sections 6, 11, 16, 17, 35).

The basic principles of the Children (Scotland) Act (1995) are:

- the child's welfare is paramount
- attention must be given to a child's views subject to the child's age and maturity
- state intervention should be limited unless in the child's best interests
- attention must be given to the child's religious persuasion, racial origin and cultural and linguistic background. *(The Children (Scotland) Act 1995: Developing Policy and Law for Scotland's Children).*

Advocates of children's rights have some concerns about the way parts of the Act are qualified and in their view have been manipulated. They consider it uses 'let outs' in its interpretation of the intention of the UNCRC by using phrases such as: 'taking into account the age and the maturity of the child'. Critics think this still allows adults to make decisions without consulting children by allowing agencies to take the view that children are not mature enough to be able to have an opinion. These children's rights advocates believe that even very young children can have valid opinions that should be listened to. They consider there are ways that young children can show they have understood and are agreeing to action. However, in Scotland's law, often 'age and maturity' or competency is taken to mean older than 12 years.

One of the main benefits of the Children (Scotland) Act (1995) was the requirement for agencies to work more closely together (you will read more about this in Chapter 9) and to review the methods that professionals had previously used to listen and talk to children.

> **Consider this**
>
> What is your view?
>
> Is it possible to be clear about when a child shows 'sufficient maturity'?
>
> Can you think of examples of children under 12 years being able to make informed decisions?

Legislation that supports children's rights will change from time to time. Some of the current legislation you need to look at for this unit is also detailed in Chapter 9. Although all the legislation you will be looking at seeks to protect children, the legislation that directly affects child protection is looked at later in this chapter. Information about the Education (Additional Support for Learning) (Scotland) Act (2004) is in Chapter 6.

Other rights-supporting legislation that is applied in Scotland includes the European Convention on Human Rights (1998). This is important because although it is concerned with all individuals it affects children and their families and is sometimes used to appeal against decisions that may have been made in Scottish courts. It includes Articles that are designed to protect the individual's rights to do or to be free from certain things, including:

- the right to life
- freedom from torture and inhumane or degrading treatment or punishment
- freedom from forced or compulsory labour
- the right to liberty and security
- the right to a fair and public trial within a reasonable time
- the right to respect for private and family life, home and correspondence
- freedom of thought, conscience and religion

- freedom of expression
- freedom of assembly and association
- the right to marry and to found a family
- the right to peaceful enjoyment of possessions
- the right to education
- the right to free elections.

(*Source: The European Convention on Human Rights, the Scotland Act and the Human Rights Act*, The Scottish Office, 1999)

Some of the rights listed are absolute, which means there are no exceptions or exceptional circumstances allowed, while others, such as Article 2: the right to education, are qualified. This means that there are situations where the Article can be changed slightly if there is a strong legal reason for doing so. One reason given for 'qualifying' the right to education is to avoid unreasonable public expenditure. In some rural and remote areas this may mean children don't have a local school. Parents could try to challenge that decision under European human rights legislation, but sometimes this type of challenge has been unsuccessful because of 'unreasonable public expenditure'.

Consider this

One of the Articles of European human rights legislation is the freedom to assemble (Article 11), and Article 15 of the UNCRC talks about the right to 'freedom of association and of peaceful assembly'.

Recent legislation in Scotland that allows Anti-Social Behaviour Orders (ASBOs) to be issued has been used by local authorities and the police to disperse groups of young people. Is there a possible contradiction between what these charters are saying and the reality in some Scottish towns? Explain your answer.

Asylum and Immigration Act (1996)

Immigration and asylum legislation changes frequently and it is important to keep up to date with such changes via government websites.

Key terms

Reserved power is a power retained by the UK government, meaning that the Scottish Government cannot amend or alter the legislation.

Devolved power is a power held by the Scottish Government. This means that the Scottish Government decides and amends the legislation.

Immigration and nationality is a reserved power and so it is the UK government in Westminster that deals with issues relating to it; the Scottish Government does not have any powers to amend or alter the Act.

Under the Asylum and Immigration Act (1996) the UK government recognises asylum seekers and can give them refugee status. The Home Office can grant asylum to people who have a 'well founded belief they will be persecuted' if they return to their own country (*Source:* The Asylum and Immigration Act (1996)). Article 22 of the UNCRC protects the rights of children who are refugees whether or not they are accompanied by adults to: 'receive appropriate protection and humanitarian assistance in the enjoyment of applicable rights'.

However, in the UK, a distinction is made between refugees and asylum seekers. Asylum seekers with children are not entitled to benefits or government entitlements other than those allowed by the National Asylum Support Service. This includes any support other children and families would get because of the requirements of the Children (Scotland) Act (1995).

If children are unaccompanied asylum seekers – that means, if the children are under 18 years old and have arrived in the UK without their family or another adult – they *are* entitled to help under the Children (Scotland) Act (1995) and the local authority has an obligation to support them.

Some children's rights activists believe that the Asylum and Immigration Act (1996) supports adults marginally better than it does children. There have been examples in

Scotland of children being detained in secure accommodation while their parents are waiting to be deported. There have also been examples of children and families taken from their homes in 'dawn raids' to be deported.

Consider this

Do you think the removal of asylum seekers and their children is an infringement of children's rights under Article 22 of the UNCRC? You might want to undertake a search of local or national newspapers or the Internet to look for stories of ways children have been removed under this Act.

Regulation of Care (Scotland) Act (2001)

The Regulation of Care (Scotland) Act (2001) helps to support children's rights by making a requirement on Scottish ministers to 'prepare and publish National Care Standards'. These standards, where they apply to children, are based on ensuring children's welfare and well-being is placed at the centre of all care services that are provided for them.

The range of children's care services include:

- adoption services
- care homes for children and young people
- childcare agencies
- childminding services
- day care of children services
- fostering services
- school care accommodation services.

The National Care Standards define what Scottish ministers expect children will receive from care services targeted at them. The responsibility to inspect care services is given to the Scottish Commission for the Regulation of Care (Care Commission), which has a duty to report back to Scottish ministers on the quality of care in services for children. This helps to ensure children's basic rights are upheld. Each set of standards for children confirms the principles behind the standards as 'reflecting the rights of children and young people as set down in the UNCRC'.

The Care Standards describe the need to provide children with: dignity; privacy; choice; safety; opportunities for realising potential; equality and diversity. Each set of standards is written from the child's point of view. An example of a standard in the *National Care Standards: Care Homes for Children and Young People* (Scottish Executive, revised 2005) is:

> **Standard 1:** You are welcomed to the care home and know what to expect during your stay.

Children who are in care homes need to be given access to the standards and to have them explained to them where necessary. This is a way of ensuring they are aware of their basic rights.

An example of the care standards you would use in a nursery or out-of-school care club, from *National Care Standards: Early Education and Childcare up to the Age of 16* (Scottish Executive, revised 2005), is:

> **Standard 5:** Each child or young person can experience and choose from a balanced range of activities.

This is directed at practitioners who might be explaining to very young children what they are entitled to expect.

Care Commission and Scottish Social Services Council

The Regulation of Care (Scotland) Act (2001) established the Care Commission as the regulator of services and the Scottish Social Services Council as the regulator of the people delivering services.

Further research

Go on to the Care Commission website (www.carecommission.com) and follow the link to the Scottish Government website for a copy of the National Care Standards.

The National Care Standards are part of the process that Care Commission Officers and others use when inspecting the services that are being offered to children. The standards provide them with a way of ensuring children's rights are not being violated.

The SSSC Codes of Practice for Social Service Workers and Employers (see pages 29–30) describe the values and principles that all social services workers should uphold when working in the sector. In addition, all registrants agree to abide by the SSSC Codes of Practice when they register. Registering the workforce allows those who are providing services to show they are of good character and have values that support children and their rights.

Activity

In *National Care Standards: Care Homes for Children and Young People*, children are addressed directly. For example, Standard 6 says: 'You feel safe and secure in all aspects of your stay in the care home'.

In *National Care Standard: Early Education and Childcare up to the Age of 16* the standards talk about 'each child'. For example, Standard 6 says: 'Each child or young person receives support from staff who respond to his or her individual needs'.

1   What do you consider the rationale to be in one set of standards addressing the child directly and the other referring to 'each child'?

2   Do you think it is acceptable for this difference to be made?

3   As an early education and childcare practitioner, how would you go about ensuring young children knew about what they can expect to happen under the National Care Standards?

Equality Act (2006)

The Equality Act (2006) came into effect on 30 April 2007 and applies to all education establishments including nurseries. The Act makes it unlawful to discriminate on the grounds of religious convictions or beliefs in accordance with Article 9 of the UNCRC. It also extends to children or young people who do not have faith or religious beliefs and makes it unlawful to discriminate against them for *not* believing. It affects schools because:

*   it makes it unlawful for any school to refuse to admit a child because he or she does or does not adhere to a particular religion
*   schools must treat all children equally irrespective of their religious beliefs, lack of belief or the beliefs of their parents.

Schools are asked by the Scottish Government to look at their policies to make sure they meet the requirements of the Act.

Data Protection Act (1998)

The Data Protection Act (1998) affects all individuals in the UK. It became law in 2000 and, among other requirements, is designed to make sure that any data that is held by a person or agency about individuals is:

*   used only with the express permission of that person
*   used only for the purpose for which permission was given and is not transferred to others
*   stored securely.

The Data Protection Act (1998) is important for the early education and childcare practitioner because it potentially affects the way you do research with children. Article 16 of the UNCRC speaks of the child's right to privacy, and more will be written in this chapter about children giving informed consent. Key points to remember as a student researching with children are to make sure:

*   that the child or family cannot be identified
*   that any data you collect has been collected in a clear and honest way
*   that data has been obtained with the participant's permission
*   that data is used only for the purpose for which you said you would use it
*   that data is not held longer than is necessary
*   that all data will be destroyed when you have finished using it
*   that data is held securely.

Case study *Valerie's research project*

Valerie is an HNC student who is hoping to do her graded unit research project on how the centre team supports children who are refugees and whose first language is not English.

The centre have been very helpful and have provided Valerie with open access to all their records. However, they have not explained to her that the records can't be removed from the centre. Valerie writes down some useful information about the families and children and decides to take two of the files home with her that night. Unfortunately, she leaves the files on the bus.

Describe the possible repercussions of Valerie's actions in terms of the Data Protection Act (1998). In what ways have her actions compromised:

- the rights of the children concerned
- the rights of the families involved?

Values and principles underpinning a rights-based approach

One of the philosophies behind the UNCRC and other rights-led policies is that children are equal to adults and have the same inherent value as adults. It is accepted that to enjoy those rights fully children often need additional support, and it is the responsibility of those who are protecting children to make sure this support is adequately given.

Rights can be seen as motivational: namely, rights make people or governments do things. The values that underpin those rights can motivate individuals to display attitudes that are consistent with a rights-based approach. Where practitioners don't have values and beliefs inherent to a rights-based approach to working with children, it can be difficult to advocate for children's rights.

Sometimes your role will be in championing children's rights and making sure they are not discriminated against for being children. One of the key challenges for the early education and childcare practitioner is to make sure you explore your own values so that you feel you can provide the level and type of support required to take this approach to working with children.

What are values?

The values you have lie at the heart of your beliefs, and affect both how you view things and your day-to-day motivation. Values are what is important to you. Smith ('Children's rights') considers values to comprise fundamental beliefs that don't rely on other factors, including race, gender or disability. Essentially, a person's humanity is the important factor when dealing with children and families.

Activity

You may want to think about some of the values you have. Examples include honesty, integrity, freedom, privacy, commitment, compassion and perseverance, but there are many more.

In small groups, list the values that you and the other members of your group have. Discuss how you think these values will affect the ways in which you work with children. Make a poster to show the values of all the people in the group.

The right to privacy

The importance of being valued

> You've worked really hard at finishing that. Well done.

Case study
Disrespecting Ragar

Ragar is 3 years old. He is brought into nursery by a man the staff have not met before. One practitioner says to Ragar in a loud voice, so that other staff can hear: 'Oh, is that another uncle you've got bringing you into nursery today? Don't you have a lot of uncles?' She then turns to another practitioner and says, 'What is that woman like! She doesn't seem to care who brings Ragar in. She's disgusting.'

By inference these remarks are directed at Ragar's mother through Ragar.

1   How do you think Ragar has been treated?

2   How does the practitioner value Ragar's dignity?

3   What do you think of the practitioner's professional conduct?

In your day-to-day work you need to be able to show how you put your values into practice. An example of this would be: if you value the child's right to dignity, you would make sure you did not humiliate the child in any way.

Values determine the way you think about things and the actions you are likely to take. They are at the heart of what you believe. Values can be, though are not always, determined by attitudes you may have grown up with. Some children are taught to respect others and the property of others; other children are not given those parameters to work within. Sometimes, governments tell us we need to refocus society's values. One example of this is when governments say they want to promote 'family values' or the value of 'community', though they aren't always clear about what these values actually are.

Consider this

Think about the values discussed in your group that you consider important for an early education and childcare practitioner to have. Why do you consider these values to be important? How might you promote these values to colleagues who don't consider them important?

The values essential to a rights-based approach to children include:

- respect
- dignity
- choice
- freedom from discrimination
- independence
- individuality.

These are also the values you are asked to consider in the National Care Standards.

Sometimes you will need to challenge people's values if you think children or their families are being treated inappropriately or if particular comments make you feel uncomfortable.

Case study 1 *Tackling inappropriate behaviour*

The Pier Centre is a school for children with multiple and complex learning disabilities. Jack works there as a practitioner. He is on duty feeding Janet, a 12-year-old girl with severe disabilities who has no speech.

Janet soils herself and very obviously needs to be changed. Jack says, 'Don't worry now. I'm just going to call Ruby over. She'll make you nice and comfortable and you can get on with your lunch when you get back.' When Ruby comes across she says, 'Oh, not again,' and starts to push Janet away without talking to her. Jack says, 'Just a minute, Janet. We'll just clear this food away first. Let me speak to Ruby for a minute.'

He takes Ruby to one side and reminds her that Janet can hear perfectly well and to treat her with respect. Later in the day when all the children are gone, Jack talks to Ruby about the scenario again and tells her how he feels about the way she approached Janet.

1. What does this scenario reveal about Jack's values?
2. How do Jack's actions support his values?
3. Consider the repercussions for how Janet might be treated in future.

Case study 2 *Challenging offensive remarks*

Jenny, Sandra and Ross are the only three members of staff at a centre located in a culturally diverse area of Scotland. Jenny gets on well with all the children and with their parents and has made good community links. Sandra is polite but doesn't feel at ease with this diversity. Ross is quiet and doesn't say a great deal to the parents but is always amiable with the children. Jenny hears Sandra make some offensive remarks about parents in the centre. Ross doesn't challenge this. Jenny talks to Ross

about it but he says, 'Oh, that's just Sandra. She doesn't mean anything offensive by it.' When she talks to Sandra about it, Sandra says, 'Listen, I'm too old for that politically correct stuff.' Jenny lets it go and doesn't say anything else.

1. Is it fair to say that Ross and Jenny are equally in the wrong in this situation?
2. How might they have dealt with the situation more effectively and in a way that might have made Sandra rethink her position?

Exploring your own attitudes and values

Your own attitudes and values affect the way you perform your day-to-day work with children and their families. You need to be able to acknowledge what those values are in order to recognise where your values might be different from those of others. Any difference is not necessarily a bad thing, but you need to ensure that your values are consistent with being able to do your job well and treating children and families respectfully. An example of this would be if one of your personal values was politeness in the way you treat people and in how you wanted others to treat you; you may find you become upset or angry if parents, children or colleagues are not polite with you.

You may also hold particular attitudes about children's rights. It is important to think about what they are and why you hold those views. Do your views need to change? It may be that you need to read more about children's rights in order to take a more informed position, or you may need to really listen to others who have a different view from your own. Listening and reflecting are important skills when understanding values that others may hold.

When you conduct research with children, you will be asked to consider how your values, beliefs and actions affect your research. This is called taking a reflexive approach. If you choose to study children by observing them, you will be describing things as you see them. If you construct questionnaires or design interviews, you will be doing this from your own perspective. While you will try to be as objective as possible, it is impossible to completely shut yourself off from what you already know or how you feel when doing research. You need to be able to acknowledge your thoughts, views, opinions and feelings and take account of them in anything you say or write.

Sometimes the way you interpret things comes about because of your own values and experiences, as the following case study shows.

Case study *Home visit*

Darrowfield Nursery arranges home visits to children and families before they start at the centre. Jane, a mature student at the local college, has a placement at Darrowfield.

Jane has two young children of her own. Her home is very tidy, her meals are prepared in advance and she is very well organised with the children so that she is able to attend college.

Jane has accompanied an experienced practitioner, Fiona, on a home visit to the Jacksons. Mrs Jackson also has two children, Cherry and Alice, who are the same age as Jane's. Her younger daughter, Cherry, is due to start nursery. Mrs Jackson's home is disorganised, with piles of ironing on the available chairs. The house doesn't look as if it has been cleaned for some time. The children are sitting on the floor eating their breakfast of biscuits and a fizzy drink when the two visitors arrive. The family have a dog for which Mrs Jackson shows great affection during their stay.

Fiona and Jane explain about the nursery and try to find out as much as they can about Cherry to help her settle in well. Mrs Jackson seems quite distracted about this.

On leaving the house, Fiona asks how valuable Jane found the experience. Jane agrees it was helpful as a way of getting to know the children, but comments on the mess of the house and how disorganised Mrs Jackson seemed to be. She says that she thought they might have got more out of Mrs Jackson if they had been discussing the dog.

1 In what way do you think Jane's comment may have been affected by her own values and attitudes?

2 Consider what your own response might have been to Jane's comments and the reasons for your response.

How adults can support a process of children's participation

Children in Scotland describe participation as the opportunity for people to express their views effectively and for those views to be listened to and taken account of. Participation is also described as 'being involved in and influencing decision making on matters that affect you' (*Source*: www.childreninscotland.org.uk).

Tokenism describes the process by which children and others are seen to have a say in a matter, when in fact decisions may already have been made and children may be asked so that organisations can say they have 'consulted with' them. Tokenism can also occur when children's views are sought but not considered in any way.

Children's participation occurs when children are active agents in decision making that will affect them and their views are listened to. Often children are regarded as being passive in decision making processes as some adults consider them unable to make judgements.

> **Key term**
>
> **Active agent** is a term used to describe someone who is actively involved in and actually doing something rather than sitting back and allowing something to happen.

Researchers who spend time trying to actively engage with children's views consider it is important to:

- give children enough time to become fully engaged with a process
- make sure children are able to understand what is being asked of or proposed to them
- make sure children are given different vehicles for having their say, non-verbal, written or verbal
- listen and respond to children's views.

Many organisations are committed to children's active participation but don't always know how to put that commitment into practice. Some find participation particularly hard to achieve with younger children without it being tokenistic. Organisations and people that deal with children on a day-to-day basis are encouraged to develop a culture of participation. This means that in the centre in which you work, encouraging participation should be as important to you as caring for or planning for the children.

In England, the Department for Children, Schools and Families (DCSF) has issued useful guidance on the process of children's participation and, in Scotland, Children in Scotland and the Children's Commissioner point out some useful strategies on their websites.

Encouraging a culture of participation

The reasons behind developing a culture of participation in an organisation may be that it is:

- making decisions that affect children's day-to-day lives
- providing services for children, such as play services and community services
- developing policies or processes for children – on a practical level this might mean, for example, organising a new outdoor play area or a wildlife garden in a nursery
- seeking feedback about existing services or processes; for example, feedback on the quality of experiences for children.

Different organisations will need different approaches to involving children through active participation, so the way you might encourage this in a nursery will be different to the way you might involve older children in an out-of-school club, for example. In an out-of-school club, the children may be able to take over the organisation of a particular issue; in a nursery, it is more likely that you will be looking for the children's views or feelings about these issues.

Case study _Encouraging children's participation_

The Sail Centre is a centre with a 20-place nursery and a 10-place out-of-school care club. The average age of children in the out-of-school care club is 9.5 years.

The centre has just been given lottery funding to improve their out-of-doors area. Staff would like to see a wildlife area included in the plans. They go about involving the children in the planning process.

One member of staff sits down with the children and explains how much money they will have to spend. They ask them what they would like to see developed outdoors. Two of the older children say they want to produce a plan then show it to the others. Some of the other children say they want to have a race track, while others want somewhere they can set up a hide to see birds. The older children suggest a committee meeting to discuss what they want to achieve and the staff member says she will make sure they have space to do that. She reminds them it will be a shared space with the nursery.

Meanwhile, in the nursery, one of the staff sits down with small groups of children and explains what is happening and asks them what they enjoy doing best out of doors. One child says gardening and others say riding their bikes and playing on swings and tyres. The centre manager invites a landscape architect into the centre to listen to the suggestions the children have made. The process carries on over a few weeks and he comes back with drawings which the older children discuss. They also put up

notices for the other children and parents. After some disagreements they manage to agree the plan. They go back to the manager and make some suggestions about how they could have the 'hide' incorporated in the design. The architect goes back and does this. Some of the other children remind the centre manager they need space just to 'mess around'. She assures them there will be and says she has listened to their suggestions.

Staff working with the younger children sit down with them again and remind them about what is happening. They look at some books they made up when it was first spoken about, where their ideas are recorded. The new proposal is explained in this way: 'You could have a garden and some swings. You could also have some space to run about and a quiet area for the garden birds to come and feed.' The practitioner takes time with individuals to show them where they can play.

Finally, the practitioners report back to the manager.

1. Was this an example of active participation by:
   - the older children?
   - the younger children?
2. How effective do you think this process has been in getting the end product that the children wanted?
3. Do you think this process is too time consuming? Explain your answer.

Encouraging participation

Sometimes it isn't easy to encourage participation. Some practitioners think it is too time consuming and others think children are too young to resolve differences or make decisions. Observation of children at play as they self-select activities, or negotiate and learn to

Consider this

Describe some of the ways you have seen very young children encouraged to participate in a nursery placement.

How might this differ from the way older children can actively participate?

compromise, shows this isn't the case. However, participation will take more time than making decisions for children would.

Organisations that work with children, including schools, nurseries and out-of-school care, can encourage participation by:

- identifying advocates to make sure there is a culture of participation
- identifying ways that proposals can be presented to children or young people in an understandable way
- identifying ways that children and young people can have their views heard and acted upon
- finding ways of implementing change that children can recognise as being informed by their views
- finding ways of feeding back to children where views haven't been acted on, with clarity on why decisions have been made.

Participation and citizenship

One of the priorities for the Scottish Government and Curriculum for Excellence is the promotion of citizenship amongst children. One of the features of citizenship is being able to articulate views and opinions that help to effect change. As end users of services, children should be encouraged to make their views known about the services they receive. This is why children's opinions are sought during inspections by agencies such as HMIE and the Care Commission.

Among the benefits to children from active participation listed in a report for the Department for Education and Science (cited in *Building a Culture of Participation*, P. Kirby et al., 2003) are:

- increased knowledge and self-belief
- feeling valued and respected
- motivation
- development of group social skills
- the promotion of pro-social behaviour
- future active involvement and greater responsibility

- gaining practical skills
- gaining presentation and language skills
- learning to make decisions and conveying those decisions to others.

Hart's ladder of participation

This is a tool that was devised by Professor Roger Hart as a method of considering different levels of participation by young people. The ladder is explained as eight steps. With each step there is a description of the level of participation by the child and the level of adult intervention (adultism). Where there is no 'adultism', Hart's model moves towards greater autonomy for children and real participation. The levels are described below.

Level 1: Manipulation (adultism): where adults manipulate children into supporting issues and causes inspired by children.

Level 2: Decoration (adultism): children are used to help promote a cause or issue indirectly but don't pretend this has been derived from children.

Level 3: Tokenism (adultism): children are apparently given a voice but don't really have a lot of choice about what they do or how they participate.

Level 4: Children are assigned a specific role and told how and why they are being involved.

Level 5: Consulted and informed: when children give advice on issues or programmes run by adults. Children are told how their input will inform the decisions made.

Level 6: Adult initiated: shared decisions with children. This is where programmes or issues are initiated by adults but the decision making is shared with young people.

Level 7: Child initiated and directed: this is where programmes or issues are initiated and directed by the young people. Adults only have a supporting role.

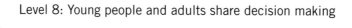

Level 8: Young people and adults share decision making

Level 7: Young people lead and initiate action

Level 6: Adult initiated, shared decisions with young people

Level 5: Young people consulted and informed

Level 4: Young people assigned and informed

Level 3: Young people tokenized

Level 2: Young people are decoration

Level 1: Young people are manipulated

(Note: Hart explains that the first three levels are *non-participation*.)

Hart's ladder of participation adapted from *Children's Participation: From Tokenism to Citizenship*, R. A. Hart, UNICEF ICDC 1992.

Level 8: Child initiated, shared decisions with adults: where projects and programmes are initiated by children and decision making is shared amongst children and adults. Hart's view is that this empowers children and allows them to learn first hand from the life experience and expertise of adults.

(Source: *Children's Participation: From Tokenism to Citizenship*)

While Hart's ladder of participation was developed to describe the participation of older children, there are significant messages in this model that practitioners working with children in their early years or with additional support needs can use to achieve better participation.

Consider this

Think of examples where you may have seen participation by children at all stages of the 'ladder'. Discuss these examples with your colleagues, particularly the successes or weaknesses of any decisions made at each level.

Using the grid below, insert details of participation you have seen at each level in Hart's ladder of participation. You can use examples from your placement or from your own experiences of working with children.

Level 1	
Level 2	
Level 3	
Level 4	
Level 5	
Level 6	
Level 7	
Level 8	

The importance of listening to children

The child's right to express their view and to be heard is enshrined in Article 12 of the UNCRC, but this can only be effective if children are listened to. Listening to children is an active process. This means creating an environment in which children feel safe and able to communicate freely with an adult who they know will listen to and respect their views. Even the youngest children communicate and it is important to learn to listen to all children. When a baby is crying, he or she is trying to communicate an important message to the mother or carer, whether 'I'm hungry', 'I'm tired' or 'I want to be picked up and comforted'. As a practitioner you must be aware of the messages children are sending and, however they are received, they need to be listened to.

Learning and Teaching Scotland (*Let's Talk About Listening to Children: towards a shared understanding for early years education in Scotland* (Perspectives; 2, 2006) suggests some key benefits derived from listening to children. They are:

- it aids personal and social development
- it enables children to feel empowered
- it helps to develop a sense of responsibility
- it helps to improve decision making and independence
- it increases children's confidence and self-esteem
- it helps to develop cooperation and sharing skills, and it reinforces discussion, debating, listening to others, planning, negotiating and problem-solving skills
- it promotes child protection by developing avenues of dialogue between adults and children/young people
- it leads to a heightened awareness of democracy and human rights.

You will see that some of these benefits are the same reasons why participation is important. This is because participation and listening are inextricably linked.

Local authorities in Scotland now have children's committees that help to inform the work of the councils' children's services. In Scotland there is also a Children's Parliament that has been set up to look at the links between children's rights and family life in Scotland today. It is intended for 9–14-year-olds and has a website that you may want to investigate (see www.childrensparliament.org.uk). The Children's Parliament holds meetings across Scotland that inform its work.

Supporting participation when doing research with children

When carrying out research with children, you need to ensure you are working within ethical guidelines and that the view the child wants to express is the view you are recording.

Some of the methods that Alderson and Morrow (*Ethics, Social Research and Consulting with Children and Young People*, 2004) recommend include:

- gathering children's own views by talking to them and asking them to take photographs or keep video diaries, thereby involving the children as researchers (remember the ethics of using video or photographic evidence when researching with children and make sure all the appropriate permissions have been sought)
- using children as experts in the field with a valid contribution to make to research; this can include children recording other children's views or conducting interviews in situ with children.

Other more usual methods of research that you will read about in Chapter 10 include: doing individual or group interviews with children; questionnaires specifically designed for children; observations.

One of the critical issues of using children in research is ensuring you have informed consent from the child. With very young children this may mean consent from both the child and a parent. As a student you will also need to seek permission from the centre before doing any research with children.

Research involving surveys (asking for views), for example about proposed changes to an area in the centre, may only require the child's consent. However, you must clarify with your placement the protocols for doing *any* research with children before you start. The first case study gives an example of a research project that required only the children's permission and permission from the centre. The second case study gives an example of research that is likely to need both children's and parents' permission.

Case study 1 *The quiet room*

Sally, the nursery practitioner, wanted to change the layout of the quiet room to make it a calm place for the children. She wanted to use a different type of lighting. She set up the room with coloured lights and asked the children if they could give her some help and explained what she was going to do. The children spent five minutes in the room listening to a story.

In the afternoon, Sally repeated story time with the children, but this time had only low white lights on. At the end she asked the children which they liked better. They all said the coloured lights were best.

1 In what ways do you think Sally's research was effective?

2 Can you think of any research you could do that might be helpful to your practice?

Case study 2 *Supporting children with HIV*

Jacquie is a practitioner working in a voluntary organisation that supports children infected and affected by HIV. The children are aged from 3 to 12 years and there are various services offered to them in the centre. She is trying to improve some of these, but first of all feels she needs to find out if the centre currently offers enough emotional support to children living with the condition.

1 Why do you think this research will need permission from children and parents?

2 How would you approach the parents and children to get this permission?

Ethics and gatekeepers

People who do research with children often talk about gatekeepers to their research – those adults who provide some protection for children who are research subjects or who are being used in research. The gatekeeper may be the parent or another adult whose role is to provide access to the child where this is appropriate.

The ethics of research describe what is right and what is wrong when doing research. Ethical considerations when carrying out research with children include:

- making sure you have informed consent from children to do the research

- making sure you are not exploiting children in any way by doing the research

- giving children time to decide to say 'yes' or 'no' to participating in the research

- making sure you answer any questions about the research truthfully and fully

- making sure children can stop being involved in your research project at any time and withdraw their consent

- making sure you don't use the research findings for any purpose other than the one you explained at the start of the research project.

Child protection, policies and issues

All adults who are involved in caring for children and young people have both a personal responsibility and a legal duty to ensure children are safe and secure while in their care. In the previous section you explored children's entitlement to human rights that include their right to be free from abuse. You know from the Children (Scotland) Act (1995) that the welfare of the child is paramount when working with children and their families. Your role while working in early education and childcare requires that you must have a good understanding of how to create an environment where children feel that they will be listened to, respected and supported if they ever need your help.

Many aspects of your work with children and young people should contribute to trying to keep them safe. Creating an environment that is safe, nurturing and secure helps children to feel that they are valued and important. Teaching children to respect each other gives messages about their own and others' right to protection from, for example, being hit, called names or left out by others. When you encourage children's participation in your service you will show them that you want to really listen to and understand their experiences. By building open, trusting relationships with children and their parents and carers, you will encourage them to seek support when, and if, they need it. Early intervention in minimising and identifying risks to children and young people is a key aspect of child protection work. The Report of the Child Protection Audit and Review (Scottish Executive) in 2002 highlighted joint responsibility for children's welfare in the report's title, which reminded professionals and carers 'It's everyone's job to make sure I'm alright'.

In this section on child protection you will read about:

- the importance of listening to children – through their play, their behaviour and their language
- children's rights and practitioners' legal responsibilities regarding child protection

- how the Children's Charter (see pages 58–59) and local child protection guidelines inform practitioners' responses when they are worried about a child's safety
- features of a comprehensive child protection policy and procedure
- how and when you should record any child protection concerns, and what information you should include
- the different types of abuse that some children and young people may experience and some of the effects that this may have on them in both the short and long term.

What is child protection?

Child protection is a term that covers a lot of different responsibilities and areas of work that practitioners have when caring for children. It involves:

- understanding the different types of abuse that some children and young people may experience
- thinking about how you respond to a child who reveals by their behaviour, their play or discussion that they are not being cared for appropriately
- being clear about the legal duties and policies that are in place regarding children's well-being.

In some other roles, child protection may also describe the tasks involved in investigating child protection allegations, interviewing children or providing specialised support to families where abuse has taken place.

Further research

Every local authority has a local child protection committee. This is an inter-agency forum where representatives from all of the different agencies meet together regularly to ensure a high quality response to children who are considered at risk.

Try to find out some information about your local child protection committee. Make a list

of some of the agencies, such as the Social Work Department, who would be members of this committee. What benefits do you think there would be to agencies meeting regularly to discuss child protection issues?

What is child abuse?

From your previous studies or your own life experience, you will be aware of many things that you consider harmful to children. Individuals' views about child abuse vary depending on their attitudes and values towards children and childhood. As you will see from looking at children's rights, these ideas change over time. In the past, what may have been seen as an acceptable form of discipline would today be regarded as cruel and harmful given current perspectives on children and their emotional well-being.

There are many different definitions of child abuse, but government documents and local authority guidelines give definitions for practitioners to use in their professional and personal lives. It is important to understand these categories of abuse as these are shared definitions for all professionals working with families. The definitions ensure that staff do not have to rely on their own attitudes about what is or is not harmful to children. It is important to have a shared understanding with your staff team of what is and is not acceptable, as this will give you confidence when taking action to get support for a child in difficulty.

Protecting Children and Young People: Framework for Standards (Scottish Executive, 2004) defines child abuse as 'A deliberate act of ill treatment that can harm or is likely to cause harm to a child's safety, well being and development'. As society develops a better understanding of children – their development, needs and rights – so views and attitudes about children's rights develop.

Child abuse is a term that covers different types of harm that a child could experience. These are referred to as categories of abuse; these are the areas that police, social workers, healthcare staff, education staff and others would use to define the different types of abuse. Having a shared understanding across agencies will help to ensure consistency and make dialogue between staff more effective. Child abuse is a complex issue and often involves a child being ill-treated and manipulated by someone known

Further research

Whether or not parents should smack children can be a very emotive issue. This can be influenced by an individual's own experience of discipline and their views about children and their rights. What is your opinion? The Scottish Executive held a consultation in 2002 with the people of Scotland to find out their views towards the physical punishment of children.

1   Research the issue of whether smacking should be a permissible form of discipline with children. Find research which has been carried out from a child's perspective. What do children think of this issue?

2   Record the arguments for and against smacking children. Where do you stand on this issue? How does the legislation on the physical punishment of children in Scotland relate to the UN Convention on the Rights of the Child?

Documents and websites which may help you to begin to research this issue can be found in the reference section at the end of this chapter.

to them. Where an adult uses their additional knowledge, physical strength or authority to bully or hurt a child, they are taking advantage of the child and this is clearly unacceptable.

The Care Commission explains the element of power that adults can have when they state that 'all forms of child abuse involve the elements of a power imbalance, exploitation and the absence of true consent, whether they relate to deliberate acts where the predictable outcome would include harm to the child, or acts where the outcome is a failure to protect the health, safety or welfare of a child' (*Procedure for Care Commission Staff in Respect of Child Protection*, Scottish Commission for the Regulation of Care, 2006). Adults who work with children need to be aware that they are in a very important position of trust and responsibility when caring for a child.

Activity

Who else works with children and young people who would need to have an understanding of the different types of child abuse? Complete the spider diagram below with some of the other agencies and professionals you can think of who are involved in supporting children and their families. Remember to include support staff in your diagram.

means and what to do if they were concerned about a child. People have different experiences of family life and different attitudes towards what is acceptable and unacceptable when looking after children. While working in an early education and childcare setting it is essential that staff discuss the categories of abuse and their legal responsibilities so that there is a shared understanding of how to respond consistently to any concerns about a child.

The recognised categories of abuse which children and young people may experience are described in the chart overleaf. Some children may experience more than one type of abuse.

Many people are involved in supporting children and their families who would need a basic understanding of what child abuse

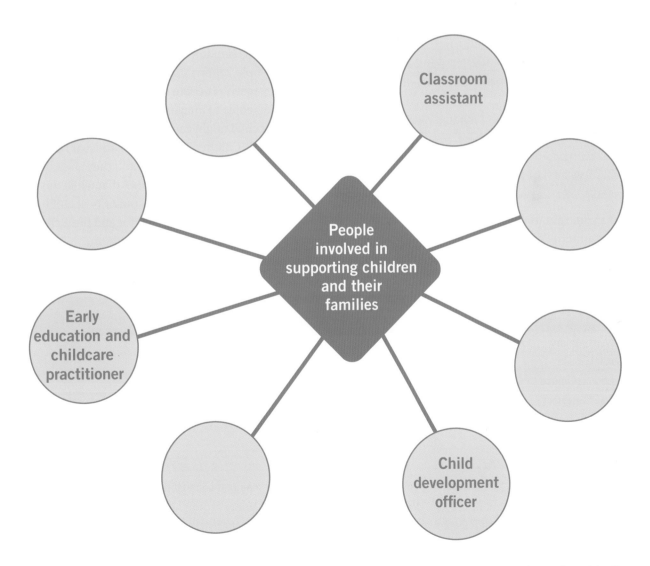

Physical neglect	The failure to attend to a child's essential needs, such as those for adequate food, sleep, cleanliness, shelter and warmth. This might include not accessing appropriate healthcare for a child. At 31 March 2007, 49 per cent of children who were on child protection registers were registered because of physical neglect.
Physical abuse	The actual or attempted physical harm to a child where the injury was inflicted deliberately or knowingly not prevented. For example, punching or kicking a child.
Non-organic failure to thrive	When a child fails to meet their expected developmental milestones and there is no medical or genetic reason for this. For example, a child who is failing to put on weight and develop where all medical reasons have been ruled out for this delay.
Emotional abuse/ emotional neglect	Not meeting the child's basic emotional needs. For example, rejecting or ignoring a child, name-calling or scapegoating them.
Sexual abuse	Where a child under the age of consent (16 years) has deliberately or by neglect been involved in any activity which might lead to the sexual arousal or gratification of any other person. Sexual abuse also includes situations where there may not have been genital contact – such as taking photographs or videos of children.

The categories of abuse

Further research

If you are a direct entrant to the Higher National Certificate in Early Education and Childcare and are new to the issue of child abuse and child protection, it would be useful for you to do some further reading on the different types and categories of abuse. A useful book for further reading on child protection is Jennie Lindon's *Safeguarding Children and Young People: child protection 0–18 years* (London, 2008).

As you train to work with children in environments that seek to nurture young children's all-round development, you may wonder how many of the children you are going to work with may experience abuse.

Childline, the organisation that provides a free, confidential telephone helpline for children and young people, reports that almost one in five of the calls they receive is about abuse. It can be difficult for some people to imagine that people who are close to a child might cause them harm or put them at risk. Children are, however, most at risk of abuse from a trusted adult whom they already know. It is important to remember that while this is a vital area of your practice, the majority of children you work with will be well cared for and protected by their families and those around them.

Category of abuse/risk	As at 31 March...		% of total 2007	% change 2006–2007
	2006	2007		
Physical injury	626	585	23%	−7%
Sexual abuse	266	240	9%	−10%
Emotional abuse	371	472	18%	27%
Physical neglect	1,020	1,275	49%	25%
Failure to thrive	*	7	0%	N/A
Unknown	*	14	1%	N/A
Total	**2,288**	**2,593**	**100%**	**13%**

Note: Cells containing * represent small numbers that are suppressed to maintain confidentiality.

Number of children on child protection registers 2006–2007, by category of abuse/risk identified (A National Statistics Publication for Scotland, Crown Copyright)

Now that you are aware of the different types of abuse that children may experience, it is important to look briefly at the ways in which staff members may become aware of a child protection issue. Again, if you have not previously studied the SQA unit *Child Protection: An Introduction*, you may wish to do some additional reading and study on this topic.

What practitioners can do to help protect children

There are many laws and policies which impact on your work with children. For example, health and safety regulations affect the type of equipment used in centres; the National Care Standards for Early Education and Childcare Up to the Age of 16: Annex A stipulates staff/child ratios; and there are laws and policies which direct you in how to care for and respond to children. This unit requires you to understand and critically evaluate child protection policies and reflect on their implementation in practice.

Children and young people express feelings through their behaviour. It can be a complex and demanding task to know when and why a child undergoes a change in their behaviour or appearance, or to establish how a child sustained an injury. The most important thing that you can do in practice is to develop appropriate caring, trusting relationships with children so that they know that if they need help you will support them.

The *Safe and Well* handbook is produced by the Scottish Executive (2005) for schools and education services, and discusses how to build an ethos which safeguards and responds appropriately to children who need help. This handbook lists ways in which staff may discover that a child needs help or support. The following list describes some of the ways staff may become aware of a concern about a child, although it must be stressed that this is not a checklist to 'diagnose' abuse. These same concerns could have different medical or environmental explanations, so it is important not to jump to conclusions. Causes for concern include:

- concerns over the child's appearance
- a change in the mood of a child
- a significant change in the child's behaviour
- a child not attending the service or being consistently late
- physical signs of bruising, cuts or other injuries
- a child using sexual language or behaviour that is inappropriate for their age, often observed with young children in their play
- a direct statement by the child to a member of staff.

The way a child communicates any difficulties they may experience is affected by their age, stage of development and any additional support needs they might have. Choosing to tell an adult that you are experiencing abuse is a huge risk for any child.

When children choose to tell someone about their problems, they want to be taken seriously, to be listened to, and look for someone who can offer help. Often children are too young or have an additional support need or are just too embarrassed to tell you directly that they need help. Staff who know the child well will notice other indications that they may be experiencing abuse.

A key area of this unit is to understand what you as a member of staff should do if you have a concern about a child. By exploring the child protection policies and guidance in your centre you should develop confidence in when and how you should respond to any concern, worry or even 'niggle' you have about a child's safety.

Protecting children and young people

Framework for Standards

Protecting Children and Young People: Framework for Standards is the government's statement to children, young people, their families and staff working with them. It indicates what every child in Scotland can expect to be put into place to protect and support them. This forms the basis of local authority child protection policies and procedures, as well as those of individual settings. Its four main functions are to:

1 specify what children and families can expect from professionals and agencies

2 set out practice required from these agencies and professionals

3 identify a framework for agencies and their staff to evaluate their performance in this area

4 help to inform the development of multidisciplinary inspections of child protection services.

Further research

There are eight standards that apply to keeping children safe. Three of these are highlighted below:

- Standard One: 'Children get the help they need when they need it'
- Standard Two: 'Professionals take timely and effective action to protect children'
- Standard Three: 'Professionals ensure children are listened to and respected'.

Write down all eight standards and consider the responsibilities they place on your placement. Information on the eight standards is found on the Scottish Government website (www.scotland.gov.uk/publications).

Every centre should have a clear policy which identifies for staff the procedure for responding to concerns over a child. It should list the types of abuse so that staff are clear about what is acceptable and unacceptable. As these areas are sometimes updated and changed it is important for staff teams to discuss their interpretation of the policy and to take up training opportunities regularly on this issue.

The Scottish Social Services Council (SSSC) Codes of Practice also define employers' and employees' responsibilities to ensure children are kept safe. If a member of staff observes or is told directly about something that concerns them about a child, you need to be clear about what the next steps in the process are. Policies should give clear guidance about the correct processes and procedures to follow.

Well-written policies should help you to establish some of the following:

- who to tell and what to do
- what to say to the child
- what happens next
- what to record and how issues of confidentiality will be dealt with
- what effect this will have on what to say to staff and parents.

The Children's Charter provides some messages from children and young people about how to deal with these questions (see below).

Putting it into practice: policies and procedures

Protecting children and young people: the Children's Charter

The Scottish Government wants to ensure that children in Scotland are as safe as possible and that services work together to ensure the protection of children and young people. Where staff are unsure of their responsibilities or of who they should talk to and what action to take, children might not be getting the service they need or deserve. The Children's Charter is made up of thirteen statements which have come from consultation with children and young people about what they would expect and like from services working to protect them. These messages are:

- get to know us
- speak with us
- listen to us
- take us seriously
- involve us
- respect our privacy
- be responsible to us
- think about our lives as a whole
- think carefully about how you use information about us
- put us in touch with the right people
- use your power to help
- make things happen when they should
- help us be safe.

These statements have been incorporated into a framework of standards which should be met by everyone working with children. It is your responsibility when working in early education and childcare to know the child protection guidelines and local policy of your service.

Some of the key aspects of child protection policies that you should put into practice in your work with children are described below.

Protecting Children and Young People: **The Charter**

pr⦿tecting
SCOTTISH EXECUTIVE

The Children's Charter

Reporting concerns

When you have a concern about a child or when staff share information with you, the setting's child protection policy should identify the person you should then share this information with. Usually this will be the manager or a senior member of staff in the setting. You *must* report your concerns to the person name in the policy.

Sometimes staff worry they may have made a mistake or are concerned about what parents will say. Despite this you have a professional responsibility to always report any concern. Remember, it is not your role to investigate the concern – this will be done by staff with specialist training in the role. However, if you do not share information with the appropriate person you could put a child in further danger or send them a message that adults don't believe or cannot help them.

The UNCRC, the Children's Charter, the Children (Scotland) Act (1995) and your own local child protection policy are all in agreement that you should listen carefully to what children tell you about their lives. If a child or young person decides to tell you directly about abuse they are experiencing, this is referred to as disclosure. Preparing yourself to respond appropriately to disclosure of abuse is very important and should form a key part of your workplace policy on child protection.

Handling disclosure

Children and young people may often choose a time or activity where they feel comfortable to talk to you about something that is worrying them.

Consider this

Think of some examples of places/times in a play session where children may feel comfortable enough with a member of staff to talk about how they are feeling.

The following points are common in most child protection policies regarding disclosure.

- Listen carefully, let the child or young person know he or she is believed and will be supported. Most children will be anxious when talking about a difficult issue like abuse. They may have been threatened about what will happen if they tell, or have been warned that people will not believe them. It is important that you pay attention, take them seriously and reassure them that they were right to talk to someone about this.

- Ask only enough questions to gain basic information without asking leading questions. It is very important that you remember you are not conducting an investigation. Concentrate hard on what the child is saying and allow them to talk. Open questions do not suggest an answer or what you think about what has happened. This is a key point as other *trained* staff will investigate any allegation of abuse and any leading questioning at this stage could affect a later investigation.

- Make no judgements or promises. Tell the person who has confided in you what you are going to do with the information. You cannot promise a child to keep this information to yourself. The child has taken a risk opening up and sharing information and you need to follow procedure and report this to the appropriate person. It is important you explain in a way the child will understand, that you need to get some help with this issue and that other adults will talk with the child about what might happen next.

Legislation that supports child protection

UNCRC

The United Nations Convention on the Rights of a Child states that each child has the right to protection from all forms of abuse, neglect or exploitation. Which Articles in particular do you think direct member countries to put into place laws to protect children from abuse?

Children (Scotland) Act (1995)

This is the main legislation that details how children should be protected in Scotland. You will read more about the Children (Scotland) Act (1995) in Chapter 9. It includes the powers and responsibilities of the Children's Hearings system, which is a distinctive system of children's protection and justice in Scotland (see below).

Children's Hearings system

The purpose of a Children's Hearing is that children who have offended or who are in need of care, protection or a place of safety should be dealt with by a system that puts their welfare first. The principles of the Children (Scotland) Act (1995) are that the welfare of the child is paramount; there should be minimum state intervention in family life unless it is necessary to protect a child; and children's views should be taken into account when important decisions are made about them. The Children's Hearings system came about as a result of the Social Work (Scotland) Act (1968). Further information about the Children's Hearings system can be found at www.childrens-hearings.co.uk. The diagram below shows how referrals take place.

Within the Children's Hearings system, Children's Hearings are the legal tribunals that are called to discuss any serious issues affecting the child. The hearing consists of three lay (public) members who have been specially trained. A representative from the Scottish Children's Reporter (the legal representative) will advise hearing members on how children can

The Children's Hearings system: how it works

Incident	Investigation	The Hearing*	Outcome
An incident occurs – for instance, a child may have suffered abuse or neglect, or a child is the perpetrator of an offence.	The Reporter investigates the child's case by requesting information from different sources; social work, police, school, health and voluntary organisations.	Each Hearing comprises three panel members, all trained volunteers from the local community.	The most common outcome from a Hearing is a supervision requirement, ranging from supervision at home to secure accommodation.
Referral to the Reporter	**Reporter decision**	The child and family – or carers – are central participants in the Hearing.	Temporary emergency measures will sometimes be necessary, such as child protection orders.
A referral of a child or children to the Reporter should suggest that there is a need to intervene on a compulsory basis.	The Reporter evaluates the information and decides whether there is a need for compulsory intervention. If there is, the child is referred to a Children's Hearing.	The role of the Reporter is to attend the Hearing to support fair process. The Reporter takes no part in the panel members' deliberations and decision making.	Local authorities have a statutory obligation to implement the decisions made by a Children's Hearing.
		Decisions are made openly during the Hearing.	Hearings may also decide that formal supervision measures are not required and discharge the case.

* Hearings will only go ahead once the grounds for referral are accepted by the young person and their parent(s) or, if necessary, once the court has decided they have been established on the basis of evidence presented by the Reporter.

The Children's Hearings system: how it works (*Source*: Scottish Children's Reporter Administration (SCRA)) be supported. Children and their families are also present, as are any agencies such as police, social workers or teachers that are involved with the family. The informal nature of the panel is intended to put children and families at ease.

The volunteer hearing members must listen to the child's views, consider reports and views by the adults involved and make a decision about what action would be in the child's best interests. Decisions taken by a Children's Hearing are legally binding on the child, their parents/carers and on the local authority, who have a legal duty to provide the relevant services.

Activity

What is your view of the Children's Hearings system? Do you think it is a helpful way of supporting children and families? You could carry out some research on the system in your area.

How do you see the Children (Scotland) Act (1995) principles being implemented in your child protection policy?

Regulation of Care (Scotland) Act (2001) and the National Care Standards

The National Care Standards direct staff to the types of service they should provide for children and young people. Can you see any links between the principles that the National Care Standards are based on and the child protection policy in your centre?

Physical Punishment of Children (Scotland) Act (2003)

What types of discipline by a parent would this Act direct you to report?

Protection of Children (Scotland) Act (2003)

This Act requires Scottish Ministers to keep a list of people who have been deemed unsuitable to work with children in order to safeguard children and young people by preventing such people from working with them. It also makes it against the law for people who are on the list to work with children.

Disclosure Scotland is the current service established by Scottish Ministers to manage the list. Checks are now made to ensure that people who are unsuitable to work with children are identified and that employers can check their employees' suitability. This is also designed to make sure records are shared about people who are not suitable to work with children. The Act puts a requirement on services to inform the Scottish Social Services Council (SSSC) if anyone is not suitable to work with children. What information should an employer check before you are employed to work with children?

Protection of Vulnerable Groups (Scotland) Act (2007)

This Act resulted in a new vetting and barring service to safeguard children and adults. This will be managed and operated by a (shadow) Scottish Government agency (formed in October 2007) of which Disclosure Scotland forms a part. How is this law different from the previous laws about checking police records for staff?

Data Protection Act (1998)

This Act is relevant to child protection as it details how personal information about a child must be recorded, stored securely and accessed appropriately. What section of your child protection policy gives staff in your centre information about where and how information about families that you work with should be stored?

Local area child protection committee

Each local authority has a child protection officer and an inter-agency child protection committee.

Further research

Can you find information on this committee for your own local area? Does this group have any link to the child protection policy in your area?

Evaluating child protection policies

You have read about the types of concerns that may arise when working with children and how to respond to these. You also need to consider how you can evaluate policy from a centre you are working in, a placement you are on or a sample provided by your tutor. You may want to ask your tutor if there is a local authority policy available or go to one of the local authority websites.

An effective policy needs to tell you the following:

- that the agency takes the protection of children seriously and that all staff, children and visitors are expected to also

- a shared understanding of what child protection and child abuse are (which agrees with the law)

- a clear description of staff and managers' responsibilities

- what would happen if there was a concern about a child – who the centre would inform and when they would do this

- what staff should do if they have a concern about a child

- who staff should report any concerns to and guidance on confidentiality

- what staff should record and how they should do this (by recording factual information rather than their own views)

- training and support available for staff to update their knowledge and improve their skills

- contact details or where to access these for other agencies.

A policy is only as effective as practitioners' understanding of it and the way they implement it. The Framework for Standards guidance details the areas of policy which staff need to receive guidance on. Use the Framework to see if the policy you would use in your placement meets all of the criteria in this document.

Conclusion

When working with children and young people it is important to remember that it is a minority of children and young people who are subject to abuse. Some key steps you can take as a professional to help safeguard children are described below.

- Be committed to respecting and listening to children – develop relationships where they know they will be taken seriously and protected.

- See yourself as someone who has the power to act on and change things – if your workplace does not seem to listen to children's opinions, talk to your colleagues and your manager and try to change this.

- Find the child protection policy in any placement or workplace you are in. Read it. Discuss it. Compare your interpretation of it with your team members. Question it. Go on training to update your knowledge and develop your skills.

Activity

How might you respond to the following situations?

1 As a registered childminder you notice bruises on a toddler's leg as you help him use his potty.

2 As member of staff in an after-school care service you are increasingly worried about the change in behaviour of one of the girls in the group. Previously sociable and friendly, she is becoming more and more withdrawn and secretive. Other friends of the girl tell you she is trying to avoid going home and that they are worried about her. They don't want her to know that they have discussed this with you.

3 As a student on placement you are concerned about the way a key worker talks to the children. She frequently raises her voice and ridicules the children when other staff members are not in earshot. While helping with an outdoor play activity you observe the staff member restraining a child from joining the other children on the bikes.

4 While observing some children playing in the home corner you observe a child playing with dolls. The child seems to be recreating a scenario of two parents angry and fighting with each other.

- Report any concern to your mentor, key worker, supervisor or named person in the child protection policy.
- Listen to your own feelings and reactions – if you have a gut instinct, a niggle or a concern about a child's welfare, you must share this with the appropriate person in your centre.

Safe and Well: A handbook for staff, schools and education authorities (Scottish Executive, 2005) says that in your job and while cooperating with other agencies and professionals you should:

- share information to protect children
- minimise disruption to other parts of children's lives
- work together effectively on children's behalf

- be competent, confident, properly trained and supported
- work to continually improve how and what is done to help children.

As an early education and childcare practitioner, the most important thing that you can do for a child or young person is to respect them and listen to them, to encourage those you work with to do the same, and to act to get children support should they ever need it. You may need to work with other agencies and the type of relationships you may have with them or need to develop are explained in other chapters in this book, in particular Chapters 1, 6 and 7.

Check your progress

1. Explain why the United Nations Convention on the Rights of the Child is important for children.

2. Which two other charters have supported a rights-based approach to children?

3. Explain how three key pieces of legislation have been affected by the UNCRC and how this has benefited children.

4. Explain how adults can involve children in research and describe the safeguards that need to be put in place.

5. How can an early education and childcare practitioner ensure children are able to fully participate? Explain some of the advantages of this participation.

6. How does Scotland's Commissioner for Children and Young People help to support children's rights?

7. What are the key policies supporting child protection in Scotland?

8. Explain four indicators of possible abuse in children.

9. Explain how children's rights are violated when they are abused.

10. Explain what is meant by 'It's everyone's job to make sure I'm alright'.

References

Alderson P. and Morrow, V. (2004) *Ethics, Social Research and Consulting with Children and Young People,* Ilford: Barnardos

Department of Health and Social Security (1974) *Report into the Committee of Inquiry into the Care and Supervision Provided in Relation to Maria Colwell,* London: HMSO

Hart, R. (1992) *Children's Participation: From Tokenism to Citizenship,* Innocenti Essays No. 4, Florence: UNICEF International Child Development Centre

James, A., Jenks, C. and Prout, A. (2001) *Theorising Childhood,* Cambridge: Polity Press

Kirby, P., Lanyon, C., Cronin, K. and Sinclair, R. (2003) *Building a Culture of Participation,* London: Department for Education and Skills

Learning and Teaching Scotland (2006) *Let's Talk about Listening to Children: towards a shared understanding for early years education in Scotland* (Perspectives; 2), Glasgow

Lindon, J. (2007) *Understanding Child Development,* London: Hodder Arnold

O'Brien, S. (2003) *Report of the Caleb Ness Inquiry Edinburgh and the Lothians Child Protection Committee,* Edinburgh and Lothian Child Protection Committee

Parker-Jenkins (1999) *Sparing the Rod: Schools, Discipline and Children's Rights,* Stoke-on-Trent: Trentham

Scottish Commission for the Regulation of Care (2006) *Procedure for Care Commission Staff in Respect of Child Protection,* Dundee

Scottish Executive (2002) *It's Everyone's Job to Make Sure I'm Alright,* Edinburgh

Scottish Executive (2004) *Protecting Children and Young People: Framework for Standards,* Edinburgh

Scottish Executive (2004) *Protecting Children and Young People: The Charter,* Edinburgh

Scottish Executive (2006) *Getting it Right for Every Child,* Edinburgh

Scottish Executive (revised 2005) *National Care Standards: Care Homes for Children and Young People,* Edinburgh

Scottish Executive (revised 2005) *National Care Standards: Early Education and Childcare up to the Age of 16,* Edinburgh

Scottish Executive (2005) *Safe and Well: A handbook for staff, schools and education authorities,* Edinburgh

Scottish Office (1998) *Protecting Children – A Shared Responsibility: Guidance on Interagency Cooperation,* Edinburgh

Scottish Social Services Council (2005) *Codes of Practice for Social Services Workers and Employers,* Dundee

Smith, C. (1997) 'Children's rights: have carers abandoned values?', in *Children & Society* 11/1, April 1997, National Children's Bureau

Social Work Services Group (1997) *The Children (Scotland) Act (1995) Regulations and Guidance: Volume 1: Support and Protection for Children and their Families,* Edinburgh

Tisdall, E. (1997) *The Children (Scotland) Act 1995: Developing Policy and Law for Scotland's Children,* Edinburgh: TSO

United Nations Committee on the Rights of the Child (1995) *Concluding Observations of the Committee on the Rights of the Child: United Kingdom of Great Britain and Northern Ireland*; see also www.unicef.org.uk

Woodhead, M. (1990) 'Psychology and cultural construction in children's needs', in James, A. and Prout, C. (eds), *Constructing and Reconstructing Childhood: New Directions in the Sociological Study of Childhood,* Basingstoke: Falmer Press

Useful websites

Information leaflet 'Children, physical punishment and the law: a guide for parents in Scotland' is available from www.scotland.gov.uk/Publications

North East of Scotland Child Protection Committee: www.nescpc.org.uk

Children First: www.children1st.org.uk

Children in Scotland: www.childreninscotland.org.uk

Child Protection Statistics 2006/7 are available from the Scottish Government website: www.scotland.gov.uk

Save the Children: www.savethechildren.org.uk

Save the Children Report 'A Generation without Smacking': www.savethechildren.org.uk/en/54_2326.htm

Scottish Executive report 'The physical punishment of children in Scotland: a consultation': www.scotland.gov.uk/library2/doc11/ppcs-02.asp

Scotland's Commissioner for Children and Young People: www.sccyp.org.uk

The Joseph Rowntree Foundation: www.jrf.org.uk

Chapter 3
Theoretical approaches to development and learning

Introduction

This chapter gives you an insight into the theories that underpin your work with children and young people. It explains the developmental, learning and play theories that you need to know if you are to achieve the unit theoretical approaches to development and learning. Sources are suggested for further research into current thinking in children's development, learning and play.

Theories can be useful to help you understand why children behave in the way they do, and can give you ideas for improving your practice as an early education and childcare practitioner. Use this chapter as a starting point when you think about which theories you could use to inform and guide the topic you choose for your graded unit project.

Learning how to evaluate theoretical approaches to development and learning can help you to understand the practices of your workplace and the roles of other key workers. In this chapter you will be shown how to evaluate, so you can relate different theories to your working practice and current thinking.

Theories applied to different stages of development

Children progress through many stages of development. When you understand this progression, you will be able to recognise the stages individual children have reached. As a result, you will know how best to work with them to promote and support their play, development and learning. You will see how the theory is linked to the practice, and this in turn will help you to plan your graded unit

Children in the age range covered by HNC Unit DF52 34: Theoretical approaches to development and learning (from birth to 12 years) will attend a range of childcare and education settings. Very young children and babies may attend a childminder or a nursery; older children, before the start of formal schooling, may attend the same settings or they may go to a nursery school or class; primary school children may attend out-of-school settings around the edges of the school day; in the holidays, school children may attend holiday play schemes. Different theories inform the work in each of these settings, yet they all share certain key elements; the main differences between them are in their approach.

Linking theory to practice

Look for the 'Linking theory to practice' features found in this chapter. From these you will learn how to apply a range of developmental and learning theories in your own work and on your placement.

In this chapter you will learn:

- The useful skill of critical evaluation
- Theories of how children develop
- The role of play in children's development
- The contribution made to children's development by different play types and experiences
- Playwork theories – how to evaluate and apply them

The useful skill of critical evaluation

It's not enough to know the theory of child development. You also need to exercise your critical judgement to decide what works, and what is appropriate in different situations.

> **Key term**
>
> **Critical evaluation** is an objective look at theory and research. It identifies the strengths and weaknesses of a theory, and the usefulness and limitations of a piece of research.

Linking theory to practice

When you critically evaluate a theory of children's learning, development and play, you should relate the theory to your own experiences and observations. Consider the following:

- How valuable is the theory to your practice and have you been able to use it in your own work?

- Do you agree with the theory?

- If you agree with the theory, what do you find persuasive about it?

- If you disagree with the theory, what points do you disagree with and why?

Your explanations need to be supported by examples from your practice. These examples may include instances where you understood certain behaviours even if you were unable to apply the theory. You can also include your own ideas about how you would like to apply the theory, or describe specific situations or work settings where you think the theory would improve working practices.

The changing role of theories

Research is an ongoing process. Theories are devised and tested over time, and then further theories are developed from the original ones. Everyone who works in child development with an awareness of current theory and a willingness to use their critical judgement has a part to play. By comparing and contrasting different ideas, you will be able to work out which theories or parts of theories may be useful. You can make your own assessments by referring to current thinking then considering your own opinion of recent ideas and theory.

It is important that you keep up to date with current thinking in your early education and childcare practice, so that you can bring the most recent ideas to your work. It is equally important that you develop the ability to critically evaluate new theory and research findings.

Make sure you keep up to date with current theories

Why learn a skill like critical evaluation?

Before any theory is considered useful it needs to be evaluated. As you learn more in this chapter about theories and how these are related to the different aspects of development, learning and play, you will also learn why these theories are important and how some of them have been critically evaluated. Practice in critical evaluation will help you develop good judgement, and this will be crucial to success in your graded unit project.

As you carry out primary and secondary research for your project, you will find the skill of critical evaluation has a useful part to play. In primary research (research data gained from interactions with people, for example via observation and interviews) it will help you evaluate your methods and whether you collected the data you wanted. In secondary research (research data gathered from articles and other media) it will help you decide what information and data is valid, reliable and relevant to your topic.

Theories of how children develop

Children's development is holistic, which means that all aspects of children's development impact on each other and blend together. The age of a child can give you some idea of what they may be able to do, but in practice there are wide variations in children's development.

As children grow and develop physical skills, they are also developing socially, emotionally, cognitively and linguistically. At the same time their personality is developing, and all these elements interact throughout childhood.

For example, when children play ball together, they are not only developing eye–hand coordination and large motor skills by using their arms to throw and catch, they are also developing their social skills and possibly their language and communication skills, too.

More than just throwing a ball around

Exploring developmental theories

If we divide developmental theories into different aspects, they become easier to grasp. These are the elements you will be investigating:

- cognitive
- language
- emotional/social
- personality.

We can divide play theory into two aspects: play and playwork theory. Within this area you should consider:

- play types
- free-flow play
- structured play
- life skills.

Cognitive developmental theory

Cognitive development relates to the development of skills of thinking, reasoning, understanding and learning, memory and recall. The five senses of sight, hearing, taste, touch and smell also have a part to play, as we use them to learn about our environment.

Ivan Pavlov (1849–1936) investigated animal behaviour, especially in dogs. He noticed that dogs begin to salivate when they are about to be fed. Pavlov then incorporated ringing a bell into the feeding process. The dogs soon learned that the sound of a bell meant food. He discovered that eventually the dogs would begin to salivate when the bell was rung even when no food was produced. Pavlov called this learning process classical conditioning.

The theory of classical conditioning has contributed to the understanding of children's emotional responses. Children will develop positive responses to situations and people who make them feel safe and secure. They will also develop negative responses to situations and people who have given them cause for fear or inflicted pain on them. As a result, some doctors treating children refrain from wearing a white coat as they do not wish children to associate a white coat with pain. Some enlightened dentists encourage early visits from children before any treatment is necessary, so that they can become familiar with the treatment room before it acquires negative associations.

> **Key term**
>
> **Classical conditioning** is learning in which a certain response is brought about through its association with a particular stimulus (signal or trigger).

Case study 1 *A learned response*

Ravi is 4 years old and Sugi, his brother, is 10 months old. They live with their parents above the shop that their parents own and run. Many of the goods sold in the shop are delivered in very large cardboard boxes.

Ravi enjoys laying out his train set and enacting various scenarios with it. Now that Sugi can crawl he regularly pulls the train track apart and disrupts Ravi's game. Ravi's parents have given him some large cardboard boxes to play with. Ravi soon discovers that if he puts a cardboard box over his brother it stops him interfering with the train track. Sugi, understandably, cries and protests when this happens and is rescued by one of his parents. Very soon Sugi bursts into tears as soon as he sees a large cardboard box.

- Explain how Pavlov's theory relates to Sugi's response to the sight of a large cardboard box.

Case study 2 *The clapping procession*

Bianca is a nursery practitioner. Each week the children go to the hall for gym activities. Trying to bring together all 20 children to pay attention and follow the nursery staff to the gym hall takes rather too much time. Bianca decides to try using a signal to attract the children's attention that they will recognise as 'time for gym'. When it is time for the next gym session, Bianca stands in the middle of the nursery and starts to clap. Gradually all the children stop what they are doing and look at her. She then says: 'It's time for gym. Let's clap our way to the gym hall.'

The children and nursery staff all begin to clap and follow Bianca.

The following week as gym time approaches Bianca begins to clap. The nursery staff do the same and gradually all the children join in and form a clapping procession. Over the next few weeks the children learn the response and moving from nursery to gym hall is accomplished more quickly.

- Explain how knowledge of classical conditioning informed Bianca's idea.

Jean Piaget (1896–1980) is an influential theorist who contributed a great deal to our current understanding of children's cognitive development. There is some debate now about Piaget's findings because of the numbers and types of children he did his research with. Recent research suggests that Piaget's conclusions were not wholly accurate, and his methods have been criticised, but he is still credited with providing the basis for the current theoretical approach to children's cognitive development.

Some of the conclusions Piaget drew were:

- babies are born with reflexes, which are involuntary responses to the environment

- cognitive development occurs as a result of active exploration and discovery of the world by children

- cognitive development consists of four main stages (see chart below).

Piaget thought that it was impossible for children to understand unless they were operating at the appropriate stage of cognitive development. He also believed that children had to progress through each stage consecutively. Others have challenged this and have put forward other theories that will be discussed later in this chapter.

According to Piaget, at the sensory motor stage, the very young child explores and investigates the environment through the use of the five senses, and defines objects in terms of taste, shape or colour. As children grow older they begin to develop mental schemas and to compare objects, for example, in terms of size, or to classify them into categories, such as 'farm animals'. As cognitive development progresses, schemas become increasingly complex, until they include analysis and logical reasoning.

Piaget's four stages of cognitive development

Sensory motor stage	Birth to around 2 years	Babies progress from initial reflexes to developing schemas
Pre-operational stage	2 to 6 or 7 years	Children are egocentric in that they cannot easily see things from another person's point of view
Concrete operational stage	7 to 11 years	Children begin to develop the skill to think logically
Formal operational stage	11 to 18+ years	Children and young people develop abstract thought

Piaget described the progress from the formation of simple schemas in infancy to the complex schemas of later childhood and into adulthood as following the three processes of adaptation: assimilation, accommodation and equilibration.

An example of a transporting schema at work

Key terms

Accommodation is the way in which existing schemas must change in order to incorporate new information.

Assimilation is the incorporation of new information into existing schemas.

Equilibration is the balance achieved between accommodation and assimilation.

Thus, when a child is confronted with new information, for example an escalator in a shopping centre, he or she will experience disequilibrium – a sense of uncertainty about the new information with which he or she is presented. The child may be unable to assimilate the new information into an existing schema for 'stairs', for example, so may need to create a new schema for 'escalators'. Once these processes of assimilation and adaptation have made sense of the new information, equilibrium is restored.

Chris Athey in the 1970s Froebel Nursery Research Project pioneered study into schemas in young children. Athey considered that children develop patterns of behaviour (or schemas) which lead to the assimilation and coordination of experiences. As experiences are coordinated, schemas reach a higher level. She noticed that schemas have both biological and socio-cultural aspects.

Athey identified a wide range of schemas that children use in their development and learning. These schemas include transporting (moving objects from one place to another), positioning (understanding whether something is above, below or beside), trajectories (movement such as kite-flying, launching model aeroplanes or playing football or tennis), enveloping (hiding under a blanket or cloth or wrapping presents) and ordering (placing objects in order, for example by size). (Scripts and Schema, Chris Athey, www.rsc-sw-scotland.ac.uk)

Linking theory to practice

Observe the children in your workplace setting and record examples of schemas they might be developing.

Further research

Do some research on schemas by reading the book *Extending Thought in Young Children: A Parent–Teacher Partnership* by C. Athey, 2007, listed in the references section at the end of this chapter. You may also wish to refer to *Early Childhood Education*, T. Bruce, 1997.

Graded unit idea

Could you use observations of children's schemas to extend aspects of their learning and development?

Piaget's pre-operational stage

Piaget concluded from his investigations into the cognitive processes of young children that they could not see things from another person's viewpoint. The best known example of this is his 'three mountains task'. He showed young children a model of three mountains of different sizes and colours and gave them a selection of pictures of the mountains. The children were asked to choose the picture that showed what they could see. Most could do this easily but when they were asked what someone on the other side of the model could see, most young children chose their own view again.

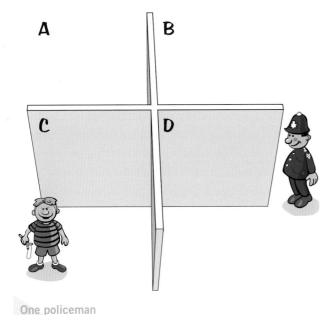

One policeman

Martin Hughes, researching in the department of psychology at the University of Edinburgh, developed a task (described in *Children's Minds*, M. Donaldson, 2006) that was similar to the 'three mountains task'. He presented two walls in the form of a cross and two dolls representing a policeman and a small boy. The task was then explained carefully to the child: the doll was moved to each section and the child asked if the policeman could see him. The policeman was then moved to the other side of the cross, looking at sections A and C, and the child was asked

to hide the doll so that the policeman couldn't see him. The majority of 3½–4-year-old children succeeded in providing the correct answer. Hughes then made the task more difficult by introducing a second policeman. Again, the majority of children succeeded in providing the correct answer.

Hughes' experiment showed, in contrast to the findings of Piaget's 'three mountains task', that young children *are* able to see things from another person's perspective. Donaldson (*Children's Minds*) argued that Piaget's original experiment had not worked because it was too abstract for them. The policeman/doll test was easier for young children to understand and answer correctly because it involved a simple game of 'hide and seek' that they were likely to be familiar with.

Conservation

Piaget also studied young children's ability to conserve. Children shown two parallel rows of counters with the same number of counters in each will agree that there is the same number in each row. If one row is then spread out by the experimenter so it appears longer, the pre-operational child is likely to say that there are now more counters in the longer row.

Two policemen

> ### Key term
>
> **Conservation** is a term for the ability to recognise that although the configuration (outward appearance) of something may have changed, it remains the same in essence. For instance, if two identical glasses of liquid each hold the same amount and the liquid from one glass is poured into a taller, thinner glass, the child who can conserve will recognise that the situation of the liquid has changed but the amount stays the same.

James McGarrigle, a researcher in psychology, developed a conservation task for young children (described in *Children's Minds*) based on the rearrangement of two rows of counters. In McGarrigle's version, the spreading out of one of the rows of counters appeared to be accidental: 'Naughty Teddy' appeared briefly from his hiding place and rearranged the counters. McGarrigle was able to show more children demonstrating the ability to conserve than in Piaget's original experiment.

Critical evaluation of Piaget's theories

Piaget's theory and research methods have been criticised on several counts. However, there is no doubt that much of his work has provided early education and childcare practitioners with valuable insight into children's cognitive development, and many of his observations are valid and reliable.

Criticism of Piaget's methods has focused on lack of objectivity and 'experimenter bias'. A lot of his experimental work was carried out on his own children, which would have made it hard for him to be objective. It is also felt that he asked leading questions which produced the very answers the experimenter was expecting. His clinical interviews included both pre-prepared questions and spontaneous ones, which differed according to the answers of individual children, with adverse effects on standardisation. Modern research favours structured interviews in which all the questions are the same each time.

The most significant criticism of Piaget's theory is that some of the tasks he gave the children did not make sense to them. In conservation experiments, for instance, Piaget asked the same question before and after the change. Young children may have thought that, as the question was repeated, a different answer was required. Other researchers have discovered that young children are able to conserve if they understand what they are being asked (*Applying Psychology to Early Childhood Development*, C. Flanagan 2004).

Piaget has also been criticised for his rigid division of children's cognitive abilities into age-related stages. There is no doubt that children's cognitive abilities progress with their increasing age and maturity. Current thinking accepts some of Piaget's terminology in relation to children's thought patterns, such as 'egocentrism' and 'moral realism'. However, it is now recognised that the stages of cognitive development merge into each other in an ongoing pattern, rather than appearing separately (*Child Development: A first course*, K. Sylva and I. Lunt, 1990).

Another point to consider in relation to Piaget's ages and stages, and the errors more recent researchers have found, is the fact that today's children are more able: cognitive ability has increased, as has physical maturity. This makes it likely that today's children can achieve tasks at an earlier age than children could 40 years ago (*Applying Psychology to Early Childhood Development*).

Lev Vygotsky (1896–1934) is another influential theorist of cognitive developmental theory. Vygotsky's views were similar to Piaget's in that they both saw children as active participants in their learning, rather than the products of passive conditioning. However, Vygotsky considered that social and cultural influences, particularly the use of language, made a significant contribution to children's cognitive development. Thus, to make cognitive developmental progress, children need adult intervention and social interaction.

When adults intervene they expand children's understanding by building on their interest. Smith and Cowie (*Basic Psychology*, 1991) describe a nursery school activity where children were given cardboard tubes to play with. The children used the tubes as trumpets. The nursery teacher then followed up the interest in making noise by providing other things that can be used for noise-making and by intervening to encourage experimentation. Later, the teacher recorded the sounds the children made and asked them to try to identify what made which sound and to classify the sounds into deepest or highest. Through this series of activities the teacher helped children to develop listening and categorising skills.

Vygotsky described the distance between a child's current cognitive skills and his or her potential ability as the zone of proximal development (ZPD). An individual's ZPD will vary according to the task or subject involved. For example, a child may have developed some mathematical skills but be a beginner in the use of a digital camera. Children need social interaction with adults or more capable peers to develop their current knowledge and skills.

Consider this

Do you agree with Piaget's ideas about children's ability to conserve at the pre-operational stage of cognitive development? Explain why you agree or disagree, with reference to the views and investigations of other researchers.

Can you identify different zones of proximal development (ZPDs) that you have? Do you have some knowledge and skills you have brought to your study for this HNC? Are there areas where you will need tutor instruction and support to develop your knowledge and skills?

Case study *Zone of proximal development – peer support*

William, aged 7½ years, and his 6-year-old brother, Sam, are sitting together on the bed. William is now in a P4 class at primary school. Sam has just started P2. They are reading a *Thomas the Tank Engine* early reader book together. Sam is having difficulty with the word 'now'. William turns back a few pages to where Sam has already read the word. 'Look, here it is, Sam,' he says. 'What did it say here?' Sam looks carefully and triumphantly says: 'Now'. William turns back to the page where Sam had his difficulty. Sam now reads the page fluently with the word in a new context.

William has built on Sam's previous achievement to help him reach the next step.

Jerome Bruner (born 1915) has helped to bring together some of the competing theories of Piaget and Vygotsky. He proposes a theory of skill acquisition based on age which links to Piaget's stages but still holds good for adult thinking and skill acquisition.

Bruner's theory of skill acquisition

Enactive mode	Between birth and 1 year	Learning from doing. Babies learn physical skills at this stage. This mode of learning continues throughout life.
Iconic mode	Between 1 and 7 years	Children develop thought through mental images often based on the five senses.
Symbolic mode	From 7 years onwards	Thought makes use of symbolic systems such as language, number and music.

Scaffolding

Like Vygotsky, Bruner recognises the importance of language and social interaction in children's cognitive development. He builds on Vygotsky's ZPD concept, which focused on the importance of adult intervention, introducing a new concept of 'scaffolding'. Scaffolding learning means providing a framework that helps children progress by providing activities that are increasingly complex, or by providing opportunities to consolidate current learning until they are ready to move on. The child makes progress with the adult as facilitator. This requires skills on the adult's part to ensure that demands made of children are within their ZPD, so they can be guided to the next step rather than being told what to do. They are thus encouraged to develop their own problem-solving skills. To further develop understanding of appropriate adult intervention, read *Applying Psychology to Early Childhood Development*, which contains good examples of appropriate adult intervention which you may find useful.

Children need the provision of age-appropriate activities and books so they can practise their skills and learning and gain confidence in their abilities. More advanced toys and books will allow them to make developmental progress. When a child is attempting a more challenging task, an adult can support them by scaffolding. Scaffolding requires the adult to withdraw as soon as the child is able to regain control of the task.

The child makes progress with the adult as facilitator

Case study *Scaffolding learning 1*

Ann (aged 2½ years) is playing with sand. She tries to make the sand stick together so that she can 'make mountains' for the dinosaurs to climb over. Each time she tries to make the sand stick together it breaks up. She is starting to get upset. The practitioner has observed this and has suggested that she adds a little water, 'Just a little at a time.' As each splash of water is added, Ann can see that the sand is getting more malleable and sticking together, until at last she can say: 'That's a mountain'.

Shamita, aged 9 years, attends an after-school club. She was given a digital camera for her last birthday and used it to take photographs at a recent school outing. She wants to use a computer program to edit and print her pictures and asks one of the practitioners, Hamish, for help. Hamish asks Shamita if she has done this before and she tells him that her mother has helped her with a few photos on the family computer. Hamish sits down beside Shamita and says, 'How does your home computer work?' Shamita says that the family computer has a slot for memory cards. Hamish suggests they look at the computer instructions and offers to help. He fetches the manual and together they identify the different slots and connections, with Hamish reading the terms aloud. They find the location of the slot for a memory card. Hamish asks Shamita if she knows what sort of card is in her camera. She is delighted to tell him. They confirm that her memory card will fit the computer slot and push it in.

Immediately a window appears on the screen and Shamita tells Hamish that she doesn't know what to do next. He suggests they close the window and use a computer program to open Shamita's card. Shamita says, 'Yeh, that's what we do at home,' and uses the mouse to close the window. She hesitates and Hamish talks her through the steps, leaving Shamita to make all the manoeuvres with the mouse, which bring her pictures up on the screen as small thumbnails. Hamish shows Shamita how to open a photo so she can edit and print it. He oversees her first edit when she uses 'click and drag' to crop her photo and cut out unwanted detail.

Very soon Shamita has edited and printed her first two photos. Hamish leaves her at the table, telling her to call him if she needs more help.

1 Explain how Hamish established Shamita's ZPD at different stages in the activity.

2 How did Hamish use scaffolding to support Shamita's learning and development?

Linking theory to practice

Take time to consider your interaction with the children in your workplace setting. You are probably using scaffolding to support their development and learning.

Reflect on your practice and describe a situation when you supported a child using scaffolding.

Graded unit idea

Investigate your role in the use of scaffolding to support children's development and learning.

Critical evaluation of Vygotsky's theory

Both Vygotsky and Piaget shared the view that children's cognitive development depended on their active participation in, and so making sense of, the acquisition of knowledge and skills. This is called constructivism. However, Vygotsky differed from Piaget as he considered social and cultural influences, especially language, to be the most significant in children's cognitive development.

Vygotsky extrapolated from the work of a colleague called Schif, in which children aged between 7 and 9 years were asked to complete statements that finished with the words 'because' and 'although'. Vygotsky (1987; cited in *Applying Psychology to Early Childhood Development*) deduced from Schif's findings that children found it easier to finish statements that referred to scientific concepts than those which related to everyday concepts. His conclusion was that the children showed more understanding of scientific concepts because they had learned them from more knowledgeable adults. For everyday concepts the children had relied on their own experience without support from others.

Vygotsky considered that an understanding of ZPD should encourage better teaching methods which would support all aspects of children's development and learning.

Other investigations support Vygotsky's ideas and demonstrate that children can be motivated to learn through adult understanding of ZPD that expands their opportunities to discover and explore. Children working together can also benefit, as different specific aspects and levels of knowledge can be shared.

Language developmental theory

One of the most interesting aspects of child development is the complexity of communication skills that children acquire in the first few years of life. They not only develop a rapidly increasing vocabulary but also replicate conversational tone and facial expressions. Language is a means of communication. It can be in spoken, written or sign form.

Language development involves the development of all communication skills and includes verbal and non-verbal communication. Children's language development relates to hearing and reproducing the speech of others. Also involved is turn-taking in conversation and the development of listening skills, hand gestures and facial expressions such as smiling and frowning.

Children use language to reason and to solve problems. Young children will talk to themselves as they play a game or attempt a task, giving a running commentary on their progress. As children become older, they are able to internalise their thoughts and reasoning processes.

Vygotsky and Bruner stress the importance of language and social interaction to children's cognitive development progress. Piaget, on the other hand, considers language development to be part of general cognitive changes. Language results from the child's interaction with the environment and relates to existing schemas or generates new ones.

B.F. Skinner and language development

Skinner (1904–90) considered that language was a form of learned behaviour. Skinner's belief focused on:

- reinforcement
- shaping.

> ### Key terms
>
> **Reinforcement** is when behaviour elicits a positive response, thus encouraging repetition. For example, if a child makes a sound that can be recognised as a desired word, the adult will respond with smiles and encouragement. This reinforces the child's effort and encourages repetition. Similarly, if making a certain sound results in a reward like a drink or biscuit, the child will be encouraged to replicate the sound.
>
> **Shaping** is the refinement of the reinforced sound to ensure that words are eventually pronounced correctly.

Communication can be verbal and non-verbal, and includes taking turns and developing listening skills

The child makes random sounds which are selectively reinforced when the child receives something she or he wants, such as a drink. Through the process of shaping, the child gradually refines the sound.

Children also learn through imitating sounds they hear from adults, which are reinforced by the adult response.

Noam Chomsky and language

The theory of Noam Chomsky (born 1928) focuses on the innate aspect of language development, which he believes is genetically programmed. In Chomsky's view, language acquisition must be innate because of its sheer complexity – it would be incredibly difficult for an adult to learn a new language as well as a child does in the first 5 years. He sees the way all children appear to follow the same sequence in their development of language as further evidence of genetic programming. If language were purely learned, then children would acquire speech in a different order depending on their experiences.

Some of Chomsky's conclusions were:

- children possess an innate programme to acquire language
- all children seem to follow the same sequence of language acquisition
- children acquire language when they are provided with input of their native language ('bathed in language')
- children acquire language by constructing the rules (or grammar) through hearing their native tongue
- children could not learn language as well just by imitation or reinforcement.

Chomsky viewed the ability to develop language within a grammatical framework as a capacity of the human brain similar to the acquisition of other skills such as walking. Chomsky described this capacity as a Language Acquisition Device (LAD) or Language Acquisition System (LAS). Children have an inherited predisposition to develop linguistic skills in their native language. The particular language a child learns passes through the LAD and the child learns the appropriate set of rules for that language.

Bruner (1983) suggested that children require social interaction to develop linguistic skills, rather than just exposure to language. He proposed the existence of a built-in Language Acquisition Support System (LASS) through which children develop linguistic skills, and which depends on social interaction. Children experience language in familiar social contexts and this is how they develop their understanding of language and grammar. Trevarthen (1993) has shown, through his work with babies, how babies communicate through 'interactional synchrony'. If babies are given space to reply when adults talk to them, they will make noises and facial movements as their part of the conversation.

Key term

Interactional synchrony is a characteristic of communication that includes imperceptible movements as two individuals talk to each other. As people talk together they follow each other's movements and coordinate movements with breaks in the conversation; they will lean slightly towards each other or move back as the conversation flows.

Interactional synchrony

Peter is communicating with his pre-term baby, Zak. You cannot see Zak as he is tucked inside his father's shirt. You can just see Zak's feeding tube which is poking out. Peter speaks to Zak, then pauses. In a little while there is a very faint sound from Zak. Peter waits to be sure Zak has finished and then speaks again and pauses. Again, a little grunting sound comes from the hidden baby. In this way Peter is helping Zak to develop his communication skills.

1 If you have the opportunity to work with young babies, try having a 'conversation' with an infant.

2 Note the responses you receive to your words. Can you recognise any interactional synchrony between you and the baby?

Katherine Nelson (1973; cited in *The Developing Child*, H. Bee and D. Boyd, 2006) was an early researcher who noted different styles in children's early language, which she described as 'expressive' and 'referential'.

These findings suggest there is more to the sequence of language acquisition than Chomsky realised. Children do seem to develop different styles in early language, and Nelson's referential style and expressive style have become recognised elements in the acquisition of language.

Key terms

Expressive style: a style of language that focuses on social interaction with people and follows their grammatical inflection and flow of words.

Referential style: a style of language that focuses on names of objects and seems to be very cognitively orientated; interaction with others is usually around objects.

Critical evaluation of theories about language development

Skinner's theory explains to an extent how children develop language and communication skills. Reinforcement, shaping and imitation all have a part to play as children learn speech sounds and vocabulary. However, Skinner's theory does not explain why children use over-generalisation in their speech. A child who says 'I doned it' after achieving a task, or talks about 'foots' rather than 'feet', is applying a learned grammatical rule, not imitating anything said by an adult. Neither can Skinner's theory be used to explain the speed with which children acquire language.

On the other hand, there are studies of children's language acquisition which have questioned Chomsky's conclusions. For example, if language is innate, why does it take as long as it does for children to acquire it? If the construction of grammatical rules is innate, why do children make so many mistakes as they develop linguistic skills? If language development is innate, why are there such massive differences in children's linguistic abilities?

Various researchers have proposed a critical period for the development of language. Lenneberg (1967; cited in *Applying Psychology to Early Childhood Development*) believed the ability to learn words is present in humans throughout life, but the capacity to develop grammatical language would seem to be restricted to a critical period before puberty. It is possible that the development of grammatical language is biologically programmed and that the area of the brain responsible may degenerate if not utilised within the critical period.

Halliday (1975) criticised Chomsky's theory for focusing on structure and ignoring function, and failing to give sufficient weight to early linguistic skills, such as crying and smiling, gestures and eye contact.

You will read more about language development in Chapter 5.

Neurological development

One of the things we now know about babies that we weren't aware of even 20 years ago is the huge, and often untapped, potential each child's brain has to make connections and to learn. We are now aware of this because of recent work around children's neurological development. Neurological development describes the development of the brain and the body's nervous system.

The Science Museum's website (www. sciencemuseum.org.uk) describes the brain and the number of brain cells each human has as being like the number of leaves in the Amazon jungle. The brain has around 10 billion nerve cells connected to 10,000 other cells. This makes a total of around 1,000 trillion possible connections each person's brain can make. Clearly, each individual's brain has huge potential, but sadly few people really maximise this. Much of the physiological development goes on before the child is born and connections continue after the child is born.

An important principle of neurological development is that the brain has growth spurts as do other aspects of physical development. Each growth spurt is followed by a period of stability. In young babies brain growth spurts are frequent, occurring at intervals of about 1 month, until around 5 months old. Then growth slows down and growth spurts occur at around 8 months, 12 months and 20 months. Between ages 2 and 4 years growth is slow. Then at 4 years there is another significant growth spurt.

Many of these brain growth spurts focus on a specific area or areas of the brain and studies have related these to aspects of cognitive development ('Dynamic development of coordination of components in brain and behaviour: A framework for theory and research', K. Fischer and S. Rose, 1994). The growth spurt at around 20 months is related to the young child's ability to work out how to attain a goal such as moving a chair to climb up to reach a desired object. At 4 years the growth spurt relates to a significant development in language and communication. Other growth spurts linked to specific development aspects are at around 6–8 years when fine motor skills improve significantly and at around 10–12 years when logic, planning and memory make significant progress (*Developmental Psychology*, O. Spreen, A. Risser and D. Edgell, 1995).

Messages in the brain are transmitted via synapses, which can be compared with junctions on a railway line. They allow different neurons to communicate and connect with each other, sending messages across pathways. Once connections are made, individuals remember and can accommodate this for future use. One example of this is that every time a child encounters a new sensation, visual stimulus, taste or smell, pathways are created that help the child recognise it again. Other examples of brain development include the development of visual acuity and hearing, where children gradually develop depth of vision and recognise the directionality of sound.

An important process in neurological development is myelination, which is the creation of sheaths which insulate neurons from each other. This process helps to improve the efficiency of brain functions.

Myelination continues from infancy through to early adulthood. The process relates to cognitive abilities such as selective attention which allows children to focus on the important features of a task. For example a child may be faced with a mathematical problem that asks them to calculate how much 6 articles will cost when one costs 24p. A younger child may feel unable to complete the sum because they do not recognise the word article. An older child will recognise that it is irrelevant what the item in the sum is called and be able to complete the sum.

Myelination also affects the speed at which information is processed. A child aged 6 years and a child aged 12 years may both have sufficient vocabulary to identify several everyday objects. However, due to myelination the older child will name such items more quickly than the younger child. It is likely that such improvements in speed of processing information lead to improvement in memory functions (*The Developing Child*).

Learning to communicate is a key brain function. If a child has a bad road traffic accident where the brain is injured, the pathways that control speech can be destroyed or interrupted and the child may have to learn language again. Similarly, pathways that have been created that help children remember basic physical movements can be damaged. Sometimes movements can be relearned; at other times the damage is so catastrophic that the child can never regain the ability they had before. Something very similar happens with adults who have strokes. Pathways need to be made and repeated for movements and actions to become successful – the more you do it the better you become. This principle is true for every process we do and not only for physical movements.

Chemical factors also affect the brain, and diet is thought to affect how the brain works. For example polyunsaturated fatty acids, which are present in breast milk and have been added to some formula milk, have a significant effect on the development of visual acuity and the development of language in babies. Some scientists think that diet can have an adverse affect on the way children's brains function. Others are more concerned with water and dehydration and think dehydration makes children less effective at thinking. This is sometimes disputed, but many nurseries and schools now provide children with easy access to water throughout the day (www.wateriscoolinschool.org.uk).

Consider this

What is your view on children's performance before or after drinking water? Does it make a difference?

Consider the baby who is hot, tired and is crying. Does providing a baby with water help to calm him or her?

The brain

The human brain is separated into two hemispheres or parts. The left side is concerned with the development of logic, language, mathematics and analytical thought, while the right side is concerned with creativity, intuition, the ability to see likenesses, art and musical ability. As an early education and childcare practitioner, you need to encourage children to use both sides of their brain and to help them make connections between the left and right hemispheres. Brain Gym is a system some practitioners use to help children concentrate and remember; it focuses on tasks and is said to support children's physical coordination and movement.

Further research

Investigate whether your placement has used Brain Gym to support children's neurological development and whether they found it successful. You can find out more about the system at www.braingym.org.uk.

Children's brains and language development

Children have the potential to learn other languages and to develop a wide vocabulary. This is a left brain function, which you can read more about in Chapter 5. However, when children are not in a language-rich environment, the opportunities to make connections and develop vocabulary are lost. A good example of this is the ease with which very young children can become bilingual; however, if language use isn't sustained the child soon loses the capacity for the second language.

Unfortunately, people seem to use only a fraction of their brain potential. If children aren't helped to make and use connections, the pathways won't be used. One of the key requirements of people working with very young children is the ability to provide enriching opportunities, including language-rich opportunities, for the children.

Emotional and social developmental theory

The study of emotional and social development relates to how children feel about themselves and others, and how they interact in society.

Psychologists have tried to find out what makes each child unique, and what kinds of things affect children's emotional and social development. They have also looked at why some people have a positive self-image, while others feel less happy about themselves.

Some children seem confident and willing to try new things, while others are insecure and afraid to make mistakes. Children in the same family can often demonstrate very different characteristics in relation to self-confidence. Children interact in different ways: some children make friends easily while others are shy or aggressive and seem to have difficulty in relating to others. These kinds of issues are all part of the study of emotional and social development.

Consider this

Can you think of events or people who have affected your emotional development as you have been growing up? Was there someone who made you feel valued and important? Can you explain why?

Did anything happen to you that made you feel uncertain or insecure? Can you explain why?

John Bowlby and the theory of separation anxiety

Bowlby (1907–90) was a psychoanalyst who researched the effects on children of separation from their primary carers in their early years. His theory emphasised the importance of the bond established between infants and their primary carer – usually the mother. From this bond comes attachment between infant and mother. Bowlby claimed that a person's future mental health depended on the establishment of successful attachment in the first few months of life. He considered that maternal attachment was as vital to healthy mental development as a balanced, nutritious diet is to healthy physical development.

Bowlby's theory described the effect on infants when separated from their primary carers. The effects of separation become evident as infants approach 5–6 months old. When separated from their attachment figures, infants become distressed and anxious. Bowlby referred to the separation of an infant from its mother as 'maternal deprivation'.

When separation is prolonged in the first 2 to 5 years of a child's life, the child will experience separation anxiety, followed by a feeling of loss and grief. The child will initially cry and protest, but as the period of separation continues will despair and withdraw, eventually becoming detached from relationships with people.

Key terms

Attachment is the process (also termed 'bonding') through which young children form close relationships with a small number of well-known individuals, for example, parents, grandparents, siblings, their childminder or nanny and their key worker in an early education and childcare setting.

Separation anxiety is the difficulty experienced by children when separated from people and places that make them feel secure. Although usually applied to children under the age of 2 years, separation anxiety may occur at any time in life.

Case study *Separation anxiety*

Alice is 3 years old. She has just started to attend the morning session at the local authority nursery. Her mother settles her with play in the water tray. However, as soon as her mother says she is leaving Alice becomes very distressed. After talking to nursery staff, Alice's mother arranges to stay with Alice at nursery for the next few weeks. Gradually, Alice begins to relate to the nursery staff and to allow her mother to leave her for longer periods of time, until her mother can leave her with the nursery staff at the beginning of the session.

Attachment in infancy

Mary Ainsworth (*Patterns of Attachment: a psychological study of the strange situation*, 1978) developed a method of measuring attachment through the 'strange situation' procedure. This involved young children and their parents experiencing eight 3-minute events, as described below.

1   The child and parent enter a room.
2   The child is left to explore while the parent watches but does not participate.
3   A stranger joins the parent and child.
4   The parent leaves the room.
5   The parent returns and the stranger leaves.
6   The parent leaves and the child is alone.
7   The stranger returns and tries to interact with the child.
8   The parent returns and the stranger leaves.

From this experiment three types of behaviour were identified.

- Children assessed as 'anxious/avoidant' made no protest when the parent left and ignored their return.
- Those children assessed as 'securely attached' protested mildly when the parent left, welcomed the parent's return and were quickly comforted.
- Those children assessed as 'anxious/resistant' were very distressed when the parent left, and alternated between clinginess and rejection when the parent returned.

The majority of the children were in the middle category of 'securely attached'. They were found to be more independent and cooperative than children showing the other types of behaviour as they grew and developed.

Bowlby's theories have been studied and followed up by many other researchers, who have expanded on his views to provide further aspects and considerations. Michael Rutter (born 1933, in *Maternal Deprivation Reassessed*, 1972) found that conflict in the home was as significant a factor in disturbed behaviour patterns in children and young people as maternal deprivation. Rutter considers that 'maternal deprivation' is more likely to be the result of other contributing factors, such as divorce, which preceded the separation.

Rudolph Schaffer (*Mothering*, 1977) identified three stages of attachment in infancy.

Stage 1   Infants are attracted to humans in preference to other objects and will smile in response to faces and voices.

Stage 2   From a very early age infants can differentiate between different people. They recognise their mother's voice from a few days old and by 2 weeks can match their mother's voice to her face (*The Perceptual World of the Child*, Bower, 1985). At this stage they do not object to being held by strangers.

Stage 3   At around 5–6 months old, infants develop firm attachments to the significant people in their lives. They seek their attention and show distress if separated from them. They also show fear of strangers, and will become distressed and cry if approached by a stranger.

Socialisation

Emotional and social development are closely linked. If you think about the findings of different researchers on the subject of children's emotional development, you will recognise that much of the theory relates to the relationships children have with others. Relationships and interaction with others is how we make social developmental progress. We learn appropriate behaviour initially from our family relationships and later from relationships outside the home, in nursery and school environments, in clubs and social gatherings.

Sociologists use the terms primary socialisation and secondary socialisation to describe how we learn the rules of conduct in the culture and society in which we grow up.

Social development depends to a great extent on a child's environment. The only child in a small nuclear family will initially develop different social skills from the child in a large extended family who is surrounded by siblings, cousins and grandparents. The only child may be very comfortable playing alone and find it difficult to share toys and space with others. The child who has siblings is more likely to develop negotiating skills in sharing toys.

Children learn gender roles and social behaviour from observing and imitating adults and their peer group. Social learning theory refers to the way children learn behaviours through observing and imitating those they perceive as having power or status. If a behaviour pattern is seen to be rewarded, children are more likely to imitate it. Albert Bandura (born 1925) and colleagues (1961 and 1963) cited in *Applying*

Psychology to Early Childhood Development) found that children copied role models they perceived as having status and power, such as adults.

There are close links between the emotional and social development of children and the development of personality.

Personality developmental theory

Personality is the term used by psychologists to describe the different ways people behave towards others and to events and situations they encounter. For example, some people enjoy socialising with strangers, while others prefer to socialise only with people they know well. Some people welcome new situations and are adventurous, while others are frightened by unknown situations and are more comfortable in familiar surroundings. There are those who seem to enjoy danger and taking risks, while others prefer safety and security. These are all character traits that define personality and affect behaviour.

You will read more about how personality affects behaviour in Chapters 7 and 8.

The table below shows five main personality traits that have been identified by Digman (1990) and McCrae and John (1992; cited in *The Developing Child*).

Five main personality traits

Trait	Qualities of an individual scoring high in that trait
Extraversion	Active, assertive, energetic, enthusiastic, outgoing, talkative
Agreeableness	Affectionate, forgiving, generous, kind, sympathetic, trusting
Conscientiousness	Efficient, organised, full of plans, reliable, responsible, thorough
Neuroticism (also called emotional instability)	Anxious, self-pitying, tense, touchy, unstable, worrying
Openness/intellect	Artistic, curious, imaginative, insightful, original, wide interests

These personality traits were first identified and used to describe adults. Further studies have shown that the same traits can be identified in children, from pre-school to adolescent, and in girls and boys. Most people will display more than one trait but it is likely that one will predominate.

The nature versus nurture debate

There are various theories about how personality is determined and the question of nature versus nurture is hotly debated.

The nature approach to personality development considers that children are born with a genetically programmed response to other people and their environment. Rose (1995; cited in *The Developing Child*) found that identical twins have personalities more similar than those of non-identical twins. This finding would seem to support the view that nature is the predominant influence.

Further research

If you find this topic interesting, you may want to read more about genetic influences on children's personalities. One recommended title in the reference section at the end of this chapter is *The Developing Child,* Bee and Boyd, 2006.

The nurture approach to personality development recognises the influence of the social environment in which the child grows and develops. Children's personalities can be influenced by a wide range of experiences. The nurture view of child development holds that children who live with adults who are thoughtful and considerate to others are likely to grow up thoughtful and considerate also, while children who live in homes where anger and violence are the norm are likely to develop personalities with these characteristics. Children's self-perception is closely related to how they think others view and value them.

Personality development is often linked to sex-role concept, which in turn is likely to link to self-concept.

Key terms

Sex-role concept: the way females and males are expected to act.

Self-concept: the way people perceive and define themselves; it includes self-esteem.

There have been many studies into gender role development and behaviour. Parents who try hard not to sex-stereotype their children can be surprised and dismayed when their children display gender-related preferences. For example, Smith and Dalglish (1977, cited in *Applying Psychology to Early Childhood Development*) found that boys aged between 1 and 2 years preferred to play with cars and lorries, while girls of the same age preferred soft toys and dolls.

Case study *Nature or nurture?*

Olga, aged 7, and Anna, aged 10, live with their parents, Boris and Ludmilla. Ludmilla is a quiet person who loves to read and swim. She has taught both her daughters to swim. Anna enjoys swimming alone and with her mother. She is happy to practise and seems to be showing a clear talent. Anna also loves to read and visits the library at least once a week to change the books she has read for new ones. She likes to be alone. Olga only swims when her mother takes her to the pool. She reads a little but is not often immersed in a book as her sister is.

Boris is a keen sportsman and a member of a pub football team. He takes his daughters cycling every week. Both girls are proficient cyclists. Anna joins in the activities when invited, but sometimes asks if she can stay with her mother and read instead. Olga has joined a cycling club and has begun to gain awards and to enter competitions and win medals. She has an outgoing personality and enjoys mixing with others.

1 How do you think these children's personalities have developed?

2 Explain the differences and why you think they have occurred.

3 Do some research into theories of personality development in relation to the birth order of children in families – that is, the characteristics of the eldest child in comparison to younger siblings.

However, it is likely that adults unintentionally influence what may be perceived as gender-appropriate behaviour even when they believe that their behaviour is gender-neutral towards children.

Smith and Lloyd (1978; cited in *Applying Psychology to Early Childhood Development*) carried out an experiment where they observed mothers playing with a 6-month-old baby. They told the mothers that they were investigating play. The toys provided were 'girl toys' (doll and squeaky Bambi), 'boy toys' (squeaky hammer and rabbit wearing trousers) and general toys (squeaky pig, ball and rattle). When the baby was dressed as a boy and given a boy's name, the mothers offered the 'boy toys' and encouraged more physical activity.

Activity

Look in shops that sell birth congratulations cards. How are the two sexes differentiated? How easy is it to find a 'neutral' birth congratulations card?

A similar experiment was conducted on a BBC TV programme *Baby Monthly* in the early 1990s. The researcher discussed gender bias with a group of mothers, and all stated emphatically that they treated girls and boys alike. They were then introduced to a mixed group of babies and told the sex of each baby, some accurately and some not.

Can you tell the sex of these two babies? Two girls? Two boys? One of each?

The interaction was then filmed and the mothers who thought they were playing with boys engaged in 'rough and tumble' play. Those who thought they were playing with girls had a softer, more interactive language-based approach.

The researcher then showed the mothers the film and confessed the deceit. The mothers were all surprised at the behaviours they observed in themselves. It seems that we unconsciously expect different behaviour from boys and girls from a very early age.

Other studies have found differences in the way babies are treated from birth in relation to their gender. When fathers were asked about their baby's behaviour 24 hours after birth, Rubin, Provenzano and Luria (1974; cited in *Becoming a person: a reader edited*, Woodhead, Carr and Light (eds), 1991) found that fathers described their daughters in terms associated with femininity, such as 'soft' and 'delicate'. They described their sons in more masculine terms, such as 'well-coordinated' and 'strong'.

Consider this

Do you think people have different expectations of girls and boys? If so, how do these expectations affect the ways in which children are treated? Explain your views, giving examples to support your answer.

The development of identity

Erik Erikson (1902–94) considered the development of identity to follow a series of stages. His view was that at specific ages children experience psychosocial crises or cultural challenges and need to develop social skills that will affect their future self-concept and personality. Each stage is defined by an aspect of personality to be developed.

Key term

Identity is a complex concept. It can be defined as your concept of self, shaped by your experiences through life from which the personality develops. Your sense of identity is also shaped by the way others react to you and is linked to the different roles you play.

Erikson believed that identity continues to develop throughout life and he identified eight life stages to this development. As the unit this chapter deals with covers the age range birth to 12 years, the following table only includes Erikson's first four stages.

Erikson's development of identity stages

Age	Psychosocial crisis	Favourable outcome
0–1 year	Basic trust versus basic mistrust	Trust in others and optimism
2–3 years	Autonomy versus doubt, shame	Sense of self-control and adequacy
4–5 years	Initiative versus guilt	Purpose and direction; ability to initiate own activities
6–12 years	Industry versus inferiority	Competence in intellectual, social and physical skills

The development of personality cannot be separated from children's emotional and social development. At the beginning of this section (pages 83–4) you learned about Bowlby's theory of attachment and its influence on children's emotional development. Attachment also contributes to the development of children's self-concept: if children are to develop a positive sense of self, they need to have confidence in their carers so they can feel secure in themselves. Carl Rogers (*On Becoming a Person: A therapist's view of psychotherapy*, 1961) described the terms of such a secure relationship as 'unconditional positive regard'. Children who receive unconditional positive regard from their carers/parents are confident of their self-worth and social acceptability and develop healthy personalities.

Children learn sex-appropriate behaviour through observing same-sex adults and through feedback from parents, other adults and peers. From the age of 3 years most children have very clear perceptions of sex-appropriate behaviour, though this will relate closely to their experiences in the home.

Linking theory to practice

Take time to observe the children in your setting. Are they demonstrating evidence of learning social roles from watching and copying others?

Is there any sex-role stereotyping? For example, are any children playing at being TV characters? If so, which ones?

Children's gender concepts contribute to their self-concept as a whole. Self-development depends on social interaction with others.

Four social factors in the development of self-concept

Argyle (*The Psychology of Interpersonal Behaviour*, 1978) considers that there are four important social factors that contribute to the development of self-concept and which, in turn, reflect a child's self-esteem.

The first factor is the way others react to us, which gives us a picture of ourselves. If we are told we are 'pretty' or 'clever', we accept that view of ourselves and believe in our attractiveness or intellect. If we are told we are 'stupid', then that will be how we see ourselves. In other words, children who have positive feedback from others will have high self-esteem and self-confidence, which is likely to lead to their fulfilling the expectations of others. Children who receive negative feedback about their abilities will be less confident and have lower self-esteem.

The second factor in the development of self-concept relates to comparison. Children compare themselves with others so they can judge how they rate by the standard that exists in that group or situation. Descriptive words such as 'short', 'tall' and 'sporty' invite comparison. Children will rate themselves against their peer group and gain a perspective of themselves in a particular social setting.

Case study *Angus's self-concept*

Angus is 8 years old and a high achiever at school. He is the youngest in his class. His reports from his teachers are glowing as he is an enthusiastic worker who enjoys writing and maths. He is aware that he can complete tasks more easily than some of his peers who are older.

However, Angus does not play football with the other boys at break time as he knows he is shorter and less sporty than his peers. This means he has little social interaction out of the classroom. He is very conscious of his height and compares himself favourably with his siblings and cousins – at present he is the eldest and the tallest.

1 Describe how Angus thinks of himself. How would you rate his self-esteem?

2 As his key worker in an out-of-school setting, what could you do to support Angus's social development?

Linking theory to practice

1 Observe the children you are working with. Assess how individual children show their self-concept:

  • in terms of self-esteem

  • when interacting with others.

2 Explain how you could support children in developing a positive self-concept.

The third factor in Argyle's theory relates to social contact. This is when children meet others with different personalities and may model themselves on those they admire and want to imitate. The role-taking stages identified by Robert Selman (1980, cited in *BTEC National; Children's Care, Learning and Development*) which are described in the table below, lead towards an understanding of the roles of others which, in turn, help children to become more self-aware.

The fourth factor in Argyle's theory is learning social roles which influence how we interact with others in different social situations. For example, a child may be a daughter, granddaughter, school pupil and friend, and behave differently in each relationship. All these roles become part of the child's self-concept.

Selman's table of role-taking stages (see below) describes the ways in which children progress as they mature and begin to understand how others act and what may motivate particular actions or ideas. As role-taking skills develop, children become more aware of how the society around them is constructed.

Selman's role-taking stages

Stage	Age	Description
Stage 0: Egocentric role-taking	3–6 years	Children assume that everyone will be the same and feel the same as they do.
Stage 1: Social-informational role-taking	6–8 years	Children see that others act differently and do not appear to have the same feelings, but do not understand the reasons behind this.
Stage 2: Self-reflective role-taking	8–10 years	Children accept that others have different points of view, but find it hard to bring together the different perspectives.
Stage 3: Mutual role-taking	10–12 years	Children can understand two points of view at the same time and realise that other people can do the same.
Stage 4: Social and conventional system role-taking	12–15 years	Adolescents are beginning to have a more detached view of how other people may be feeling and are able to understand their behaviour in the light of it.

Critical evaluation of personality development theories

Bowlby's research was based on 44 juvenile thieves and he only studied children who were behaving delinquently. There was no control or comparison group of other children who had been separated from their mothers, which means the sample selected for research was biased. He also used Harlow's studies of rhesus monkeys ('Love in infant monkeys', H.F. Harlow, 1959) to support his theory of maternal deprivation. Bowlby's methods are thus open to criticism because there is no clear correlation between the ways animals and humans react to experiences.

Bowlby has also been criticised for his narrow focus on the baby's relationship with the mother. He ignored the importance of other relationships and the possibility that children could develop a number of attachments. Other researchers have found that children deprived of their mothers can make very strong attachments to siblings, for example.

Schaffer and Emerson (1964; cited in *BTEC National Children's Care, Learning and Development*) studied 60 babies in Glasgow over a period of 18 months. They found that these infants formed multiple attachments and that the primary attachment figure was not always the person with whom the infant spent most time. Ainsworth (*Patterns of Attachment*) studied how secure the attachment between mother and child was. She suggested that the quality of the interaction, rather than the quantity of time spent with the carer, will dictate the nature of the primary attachment.

Michael Rutter (1981; cited in *Applying Psychology to Early Childhood Development*) found that separation from a parent was not a strong cause of juvenile delinquency. He looked for further reasons for anti-social behaviour patterns in family backgrounds and suggested that emotional disturbance and anti-social behaviour can be influenced by home circumstances (for example, conflict in the home) rather than separation from a parent; the influencing factor may be the cause of the conflict which led to the separation. Rutter also investigated adopted children and found they could form strong attachments.

Amato (1993; cited in *The Developing Child*) believed that variability in children's personalities was the main reason for differences in the effects of parental separation on children's emotional and social development.

The role of play in children's development

Play is generally considered to be an important element in children's development. Article 31 of the United Nations Convention on the Rights of the Child (1991) affirms:

1. Parties recognise the right of the child to rest and leisure, to engage in play and recreational activities appropriate to the age of the child, and to participate freely in cultural life and the arts.

2. Parties shall respect and promote the right of the child to participate fully in cultural and artistic life, and shall encourage the provision of appropriate and equal opportunities for cultural, artistic, recreational and leisure activity.

Over the years, all serious theorists have identified play as important to children's development and learning. The following list shows how ideas about children's play have developed.

- Friedrich Froebel (1782–1852) felt that play helped children bring their experiences of life together. He believed that children needed to find order in the complexities of life and that play was the mechanism that enabled them to make sense of it.

- Herbert Spencer (1820–1903) suggested that children play to release surplus energy.

- Karl Buhler (1879–1963) believed play was for pleasure and had no planned end result.

- Erikson (1902–94) considered that children develop life skills through playing alone and with others. He believed play helped children to take the initiative and to cope with disappointment and failure. He considered that play encouraged children to take a purposeful approach to life.

- Piaget considered that play was how children brought together their experiences, knowledge and understanding.

- Bruner believed that play is a preparation for life and needs rules.

More recent research has identified two further themes. The first regards play as education because it prepares children for later life. Play helps children to develop skills they will need in the future at the appropriate developmental stage, so it needs to be planned by adults and structured proactively. This approach concentrates on preparing children for future life.

The second theme also considers play as learning in the broadest sense but takes a different line. Here play is perceived as the way children work through their thoughts, emotions and relationships. Through play they become self-aware and come to terms with their knowledge, understanding and experience.

Each idea has merit for the early education and childcare practitioner: play is at the heart of how we work with children and how we support children's well-being and development.

The contribution made to children's development by different play types and experiences

Linking theory to practice

Can you think of a play activity you have used to encourage a child to develop a specific skill? Describe the activity and explain the skill you hoped the child would acquire.

Graded unit idea

Carry out further investigations into providing play activities to support a child's development and learning of a specific skill. Consider a link to scaffolding.

Play that is likely to lead to learning is described as 'epistemic' play, and play where children are 'just playing' is described as 'ludic' play (*Time to Play in Early Childhood Education*, Bruce, 1991). Ludic play is unstructured and free. The term most often used to describe this sort of play is free-flow play.

Key term

Free-flow play is play in which children are free to pursue their own ideas and investigate and explore emotions and relationships, practising the skills they have developed in their own way and bringing together different aspects of their knowledge and understanding.

Advocates of free-flow play date back to the nineteenth century and include Friedrich Froebel. Other early pioneers of free-flow play were Margaret McMillan (1860–1931) and Susan Isaacs (1885–1948).

Tina Bruce (*Time to Play in Early Childhood Education*) extrapolates 12 elements in free-flow play:

1. It is an active process without a product.
2. It is intrinsically motivated.
3. It exerts no external pressure to conform to rules, pressures, goals, tasks or definite directions.
4. It is about possible, alternative worlds, which involve 'supposing' and 'as if', which lift players to their highest levels of functioning. This involves being creative, original and innovative.
5. It is about participants wallowing in ideas, feelings and relationships. It involves reflecting on and becoming aware of what we know ('metacognition').
6. It actively uses previous firsthand experiences, including struggle,

manipulation, exploration, discovery and practice.

7. It is sustained, and when in full flow, helps us to function in advance of what we can actually do in our real lives.

8. During free-flow play, we use the technical prowess, mastery and competence we have previously developed and so can be in control.

9. It can be initiated by a child or an adult but, if by an adult, particular attention must be paid to features 3, 5 and 11.

10. It can be solitary.

11. It can be in partnerships or groups of adults and/or children who will be sensitive to each other.

12. It is an integrating mechanism, which brings together everything we learn, know, feel and understand.

(*From Time to Play in Early Childhood Education*, T. Bruce, Hodder and Stoughton, 1991. Reproduced by permission of Hodder and Stoughton Ltd.)

Graded unit idea

Investigate links between children's schemas and their free-flow play.

Play is not an isolated occurrence and it is not something that only children do. As adults we frequently engage in play, and go on doing this until we die.

Consider this

Can you think of an occasion when you have played since you became an adult?

Explain what you were doing and why you think you were playing.

Playwork theories – how to evaluate and apply them

More recently, a growing number of playwork theorists are building on the work of the early pioneers of play. These theorists support the view that play is freely chosen by the child as well as intrinsically motivated. They think it is so important, they have devised an acronym for it: Play, they say, is the *SPICE* of life – it concerns children's *S*ocial, *P*hysical, *I*ntellectual, *C*ultural and *E*motional development. Current playwork theorists include Gordon Sturrock, Penny Else, Bob Hughes and Stuart Lester.

Playwork theory has built on the concept of ludic play and is bringing in new terminology to explore and refine the idea. One innovation is the study of psycholudics – the cognitive processes used by children when playing.

Playwork theory explores the relationship between play and human development and describes play as a basic human instinct. This instinct can is described as the 'play drive' and is what inspires children to play. Psycholudics refers to the play process as the 'play cycle' which follows a child's initiation of play through to its conclusion. The play cycle begins with the child's internalisation of thought processes that lead to a play idea, referred to as the metalude.

Key term

Psycholudics is the study of the way our minds are involved in play.

Metalude is the source of the play process and the contemplation that precedes the initiation of play.

From the metalude the play cycle proceeds to the 'play cue'. This is the child's initiation of play, and may be subtle or overt. The child will offer a 'play cue', which is an invitation to play. A very young child may begin a game that involves handing a toy to be handed back. An older child may invite other children to 'play pirates'. The response to this play cue is termed the 'play return'.

In the first instance, it is usually an adult who will respond to the play cue and hand the toy back to receive it again, and so the game continues. In the second example, the response will depend on the children who receive the play cue. If the idea to play a pirate game is appealing, the play return will be positive and the play will proceed.

Other people are not a necessary component of satisfactory play

It is important to remember that play is more than an experience for children, it is an integral part of their lives. Play allows children to detach themselves from an adult-constructed world, and has rules that adults are unlikely to understand because the rules belong to the child's world. Children also need to take risks and to develop the skills that enable them to assess risk.

It is the view of playwork theorists that children's play should be unhampered by adults

Further research

Find out more about supporting children to take risks in their play. You may want to read the document *Managing Risk in Play Provision: A position statement*, published by the Children's Play Council in 1992. The document can be downloaded from the National Children's Bureau website (www.ncb.org.uk).

For more information about the play cycle and psycholudics see www.ludemos.co.uk.

A 'play frame' will then be created which contains the play. The child or children may alter the play frame to adapt other circumstances or include other children and this will contribute to maintaining the 'play flow'.

Other people are not a necessary component of play. Children can be involved in the play cycle alone and in that situation the play return may come from the environment that has aroused the child's interest.

This theory has resonance with the psychology of communication, which also refers to cues and returns. The play flow will continue for as long as children are involved and absorbed. The timescale may be minutes or days. When the children lose interest and the game comes to an end, the term to describe this is 'annihilation'.

unless there appears to be a need for adult intervention. Adult intervention that is unaware of children's needs, or disregards them, may destroy the child's play frame. Sturrock and Else ('*The Colorado Paper*' – *The playground as therapeutic space: playwork as healing*, 1998) identify different levels of intervention which should always be responsive to children's needs.

- 'Play maintenance' ensures that children's play is not disrupted by inappropriate intervention.
- 'Simple intervention' is an adult's response to a play cue when they facilitate the play by perhaps providing required materials.
- 'Medial intervention' is also a response to a play cue, but on this occasion the adult is involved in the play frame. When the play flow moves on, the adult withdraws to return control to the child.
- 'Complex intervention' is when the adult shares the play with the child and becomes part of the play frame.
- 'The integrity of intervention' is when the playworker is involved in a number of disputed

Linking theory to practice

Take time to observe children at play in your setting. Can you identify the play cycle?

Explain the process of the play cycle in your observation. Did you notice any play cues? Was there a play return? If so, what was it?

or conflicting frames, narratives, themes and games, and there is pressure on their time and involvement. The playworker is required in these circumstances to become involved with a measure of self-awareness and subtlety, aiming at all times to meet the play needs of the individual children by responding as necessary.

Intervention as described above is supportive of children's play at the required level. However, there are situations where adult intervention is necessary because the child is in serious danger.

Stuart Lester previously proposed the nine processes of playwork (*The 9 Processes of Playwork*, 2004, www.playworklondon.org.uk/index.php?document_id=24):

1. *Communication process* involves talking with, listening to and empathising with children and their parents/carers, and communicating with colleagues within an organisation.

2. *Developing relationships* follows on from the first process to establish responsive, respectful relationships with children. It recognises the importance of children's active participation in their environment.

3. *Facilitating the play process* uses the first and second processes to support children's play. It recognises the need for a play environment where children are empowered to develop their own ideas.

4. *Observation process* uses professional skills to observe children's play and assess their progress and needs.

5. *Intervention process* follows on from skilled observation underpinned by professional values, and informs decisions on intervention or non-intervention so that children's play continues unimpeded. Children will get the message that their play is accepted and valued.

6. *Evaluation process* gathers evidence to assess the effectiveness of the work of the play setting and the quality of the provision. Children should be involved in this evaluative process and their opinions considered.

7. *Creative process* requires the development of an analytical approach to playwork, which includes problem solving and creativity.

8. *Organisational process* ensures that all appropriate available resources are used effectively to provide a positive play environment.

9. *The 'safety' process* ensures that children's physical, social and emotional safety is maintained, while enabling risk-taking and challenge in their play. Children have the right to explore and express their emotions, opinions and ideas.

Graded unit idea

Use your knowledge of the processes of playwork to contribute to supporting children's play.

Observe the play cycles in your setting and assess children's needs. How did you support the play? Was any intervention required?

Consider this

How does planning take place in a playwork setting to ensure maximum freedom for children's play instincts while at the same time ensuring the setting is child friendly?

Irrespective of children's age, the following types of play should be made available.

Three-year-old engrossed in drawing at an easel

Imaginative play

This is where children use their imagination to develop role/fantasy play, socio-dramatic play, pretend and symbolic play. Imaginative play may also be used for children to deal with situations they meet in their lives. It should generally be uninterrupted by adults.

Creative and expressive play

Creative and expressive play includes play with natural and malleable materials. Creative play encourages children to express themselves and allows them to bring their own ideas to the use of the materials and tools they have been provided with (*BTEC National Children's Care, Learning and Development*). This might include play with paints and clay. It is likely to allow play with materials that provide a sensory experience. Babies enjoy sensory and messy play and should be encouraged to do this using a range of materials. Older children may create paintings, collages or models that reflect their own ideas and inspirations.

The playwork perspective defines creative play in a similar way. Creative play allows children to discover new connections between materials and to relish creativity using a range of materials and tools (*A Playworker's Taxonomy of Play Types*, B. Hughes, 2002).

Mastery play

Mastery play relates to the achievement of skills such as building a tower, riding a sit-and-ride toy, a tricycle or bicycle (*BTEC National Children's Care, Learning and Development*). Mastery play includes practising and perfecting skills. As children achieve the skills they aim for they will then exult in the achievement and practise and build on the skills. An example of this is when a child develops the skill to ride a tricycle. The child masters the skill to pedal the tricycle, then progresses to steering and stopping under control.

The playwork definition of mastery play focuses on controlling the environment. An example of this aspect of mastery play is when a child or group of children build a sandcastle on a beach. They want to create a moat around the sandcastle that fills with water so build the castle close to the sea. If the tide is coming in

This child is involved in deep or risky play. She cannot see where she is going, so there is an element of risk in her choice of descent of the slide.

their moat will fill and they will achieve their aim. However mastery play, from the playwork perspective, includes the recognition that the environment may not allow control. In the above scenario, if the tide is going out then the moat will not fill with water.

Adventure play and deep play

This is where children are given freedom in an outdoor environment to express themselves through building camps, digging gardens or 'just playing' in the outdoor space.

Deep or risky play is where children begin to take risks as they play. It often involves height or speed such as jumping off a swing at the highest point or climbing trees (*A Playworker's Taxonomy of Play Types*).

> **Graded unit idea**
>
> Observe children's play and identify the play types. How could you support children's learning and development through supporting their play?

Critical evaluation of theories of play

Theories of play discussed in this section date back to the nineteenth century. There have been many who believed that play should have a purpose and that children should learn and prepare for adult life through play. However, there were also – and still are – many who believe that children should be encouraged to play freely with no determined end.

Today's playwork theorists have built on the ideas dating back to Johann Pestalozzi (1746–1827) via Froebel, McMillan and Isaacs. 'Ludic' play is not a new concept. Children involved in ludic play are also involved in exploring feelings and relationships. Playwork has developed the term 'psycholudics' to bring together the thought processes that underpin free-flow play. Free-flow play encourages children's autonomy in play. It allows them to practise skills they have developed in their own way rather than with adult intervention and bring together different aspects of their knowledge and understanding.

Sturrock and Else believe that the play drive in all individuals is linked to their well-being and that this understanding is the bedrock of therapeutic work with them. Piaget (*Play, Dreams and Imitation in Childhoood*, 1951) considered that children have an innate curiosity which leads them to explore and investigate. Bruce (*Time to Play in Early Childhood Education*), Sylva (*Child Development: A First Course*, K. Sylva and I. Lunt, 1990), Sturrock and Else (*The Colorado Paper*) believe that children have an innate drive to play which leads them to experiment and explore emotions, relationships and their environment.

Playwork has provided a terminology that aids understanding of the process of play. This in turn should allow early education and childcare practitioners to develop skills of observation and assessment when watching children playing. The recognition of different levels of intervention can enable the practitioner to support children's play and understand when, or if, intervention is necessary.

Congratulations on reaching the end of a complex chapter

Conclusion

Well done! You have reached the end of a complex chapter. Theorists and their theories are always quite difficult to understand, especially as they use very complicated language to express what are often simple ideas.

As you will discover through your reading and research, there are many more theorists and theories related to children's development and learning than are explained in this chapter. I hope this account will stimulate you to carry out further research. You will need to know and understand the theory that underpins childcare practice if you are to master unit DF52 34: Theoretical approaches to development and learning. Having insight into the way children develop will also help with your achievement of other units and, of course, your graded unit project.

Check your progress

Now you are at the end of the chapter, take a look at the following questions and consider how you might answer. These questions will help you to prepare for your assessment.

1. Describe a theory of cognitive development and explain how it relates to children's learning and development.
2. Critically evaluate the theory described in 1.
3. Describe a theory of language development and explain how it relates to children's learning and development.
4. Critically evaluate the theory described in 3.
5. Describe a theory of social and emotional development and explain how it relates to children's learning and development. Also describe the development of personality.
6. Critically evaluate the theory described in 5.
7. Describe a theory of play or playwork and explain how it relates to children's learning and development.
8. Critically evaluate the theory described in 7.
9. Select a theory of cognitive or social and emotional development and give an example of how this theory has influenced your practice.
10. Select a theory of play or playwork and give an example of how this theory has influenced your practice.

References

Ainsworth, M.D. Salter (1978) *Patterns of attachment: a psychological study of the strange situation*, New Jersey, New York, London [distributed by Wiley]

Argyle, M. (1978) *The Psychology of Interpersonal Behaviour*, 3rd edn, Harmondsworth, Eng; Baltimore: Penguin Books

Athey, C. (2007) *Extending Thought in Young Children: A Parent–Teacher Partnership*, 2nd edn, London: Paul Chapman Publishing

Bee, H. and Boyd, D. (2006) *The Developing Child*, 11th edn, London: Pearson International

Bower, T. (1985) *The Perceptual World of the Child*, London: Fontana

Brown F. (ed.) (2003) *Playwork Theory and Practice*, Buckingham: Open University Press

Bruce, T. (1991) *Time to Play in Early Childhood Education*, London: Hodder & Stoughton

Bruce, T. (1997) *Early Childhood Education*, London: Hodder & Stoughton

Donaldson, M. (2006) *Children's Minds*, London: Harpers Perennial

Fischer, K. and Rose, S. (1994) 'Dynamic development of coordination of components in brain and behaviour: A framework for theory and research', in K. Fischer and G. Dawson (eds), *Human behaviour and the developing brain*, New York: Guilford (pp. 3–66)

Flanagan, C. (2004) *Applying Psychology to Early Childhood Development*, London: Hodder & Stoughton

Harlow, H. F. (1959) 'Love in infant monkeys', Scientific American, 200 (6), 68–74

Hughes B. (2001) *Evolutionary Playwork and Reflective Analytic Practice*, London: Routledge

Hughes, B. (2002) *A Playworker's Taxonomy of Play Types*, 2nd edn, London: Playlink

Lester, S. (2004), The 9 Processes of Playwork, www.playworklondon.org.uk/index.php?document_id=24

Light, P. and Perret-Clermont, A-N. (1991) 'Social context effects in learning and testing', in Light, P., Sheldon, S. and Woodhead, M. (eds), *Learning to Think (Child Development in Social Context 2)*, London: Routledge

Piaget, J. (1951) *Play, Dreams and Imitation in Childhood*, London: Routledge & Kegan Paul

Rogers, C.R. (1961) *On Becoming a Person A therapist's view of psychotherapy*, Boston: Houghton Mifflin

Rutter, M. (1972) *Maternal Deprivation Reassessed*, London: Penguin

Schaffer, H.R. (1977) *Mothering*, London: Open Books

Smith, P. and Cowie, H. (1991) *Basic Psychology*, 2nd edn, Oxford: Basil Blackwell

Spreen, O., Risser, A. and Edgell, D. (1995) *Developmental Psychology*, New York: Oxford University Press

Squire, G. (ed.) (2007) *BTEC National Children's Care, Learning and Development*, Oxford: Heinemann

Sturrock, G. and Else, P. (1998) 'The Colorado Paper' – The playground as therapeutic space: playwork as healing. A paper for Play in a Changing Society, Research IPA/USA Triennial National Conference June 1998 (www.ludemos.co.uk/colfulla4%20final%2007.pdf)

Sylva, K. and Lunt, I. (1990) *Child Development: A first course*, London: Basil Blackwell

Woodhead, M., Carr, R. and Light, P. (eds) (1991) *Becoming a person: a reader edited*, London : Routledge

Useful Websites

National Children's Bureau: www.ncb.org.uk

Playwork Partnerships: www.playwork.co.uk

Play Scotland: www.playscotland.org

Skills Active: www.skillsactive.com

Regional Support Centre Scotland South and West: www.rsc-sw-scotland.ac.uk

Chapter 4
Curriculum, play and transitions

Introduction

When you are working in an early education and childcare setting, you will often hear staff talking about the curriculum. The practitioners in nursery schools and nursery classes in the education sector consult the curriculum when planning learning experiences for children. Childminders who care for children in their own house are encouraged to offer a curriculum. Play leaders who work in play groups plan play experiences for children with reference to the curriculum. In privately owned nurseries, practitioners follow a curriculum when working with babies, toddlers and children aged 3 to 5 years. In primary schools, teachers refer to the curriculum. As a student, you will develop an understanding of how to provide learning opportunities for children. When you suggest a play experience, you will be asked by your supervisor to explain how your suggestion fits into the curriculum.

In Scotland, the curriculum offers advice and support to practitioners who have a degree of freedom to provide for the children in their care. Different settings approach the curriculum in a variety of ways, but the usefulness of having a curriculum is widely accepted.

It is clear that in every early years context, as an HNC student and as a practitioner, your knowledge of the curriculum and how to use it will be one of the essential professional skills. This chapter will help you to develop the necessary expertise in working within the curriculum and will assist you to become familiar with the different forms of curriculum currently being used in Scotland.

In this chapter you will learn about:

- The curriculum in Scotland
- The importance of play in the curriculum
- How the curriculum supports the work of the practitioner
- How Curriculum for Excellence supports the work of the practitioner
- The importance of play in Curriculum for Excellence
- Transitions
- Influences on the changing curriculum
- Values and principles in the curriculum

The curriculum in Scotland

The curriculum in Scotland

The main curricular guidelines that early education and childcare practitioners work with are:

- *Birth to Three: supporting our youngest children*, Learning and Teaching Scotland, 2005
- *A Curriculum Framework for Children 3 to 5*, Learning and Teaching Scotland, 1999
- *A Curriculum for Excellence*, Scottish Executive, 2004

You may also work with *The Structure and Balance of the Curriculum: 5–14 National Guidelines*, Scottish Executive, 2000 (5–14 Curriculum).

Consider this

What do we mean by the term 'curriculum'?

A curriculum is often defined by listing the subjects studied. You would find it easy to describe the curriculum that you are following in HNC Early Education and Childcare by listing the units that you are studying. The same is probably true of the curriculum you followed in secondary school; you would be able to list the subjects that you studied at standard 'O' level and Higher grade. You may even be able to recall some of the curriculum you followed in primary school.

Key term

A **curriculum** is a programme of study, a course or the subjects included in a course of study in a school or college.

Further research

Check the meaning of the word 'curriculum' in any dictionaries available to you and find out if the definitions vary between different dictionaries.

What does the curriculum in Scotland contain?

When you examine the main curricula used by early education and childcare practitioners, you will find that they contain much more than a list of subjects. The dictionary definition does not adequately reflect the curriculum in Scotland, particularly as it is applied to young children.

How the curriculum helps maintain high quality care and education for children

The various guidelines in Scotland help maintain high quality care and education for children by promoting the view that what is valuable in children's learning extends beyond subject boundaries.

When you are in the early education and childcare setting, you do not see children engaged in a 'course of study', nor do you see them studying 'subjects', but you do see them following a curriculum. The children are busily engaged in experiences that are *educational* in a wider sense.

All the guidelines that you will work with promote high quality education and care for children and share a view of curriculum that emphasises the development of the whole child, not just as a learner but as a fulfilled individual.

Curriculum for Excellence applies to children and young people aged 3 to 18 years: 'the curriculum is more than curriculum areas and subjects: it is the totality of experiences which are planned for children and young people through their education' (*A Curriculum for Excellence: Progress and Proposals,* Scottish Executive, 2006).

The concept of curriculum as being far wider than a list of subjects is also indicated in *A Curriculum Framework for Children 3 to 5*). This gives guidance on what children should be learning in an early education and childcare setting, but it also refers to values and attitudes and the quality of relationships as important components of the curriculum. Even while discussing the importance of pre-school education, it acknowledges that 'many of a child's most valuable experiences will continue to take place in the home and the community'.

The curricular guidelines for children aged 5–14 include much information on subjects and courses of study but also describe the dispositions that pupils should develop as part of the education process. These learning dispositions are described as being 'a fundamental basis for a personally rewarding life and an effective contribution to society', and include a commitment to learning, self-respect and care for the self, care and respect for others, a sense of social responsibility and a sense of belonging (*The Structure and Balance of the Curriculum: 5–14 National Guidelines*, Scottish Executive, 2000).

The framework of guidance offered to practitioners in Scotland who work with our youngest children, *Birth to Three: supporting our youngest children,* makes no mention of areas of learning. This document prioritises the relationships, respect and responsive care required to support the personal, emotional, and social development of young children and to work successfully with their families.

The learning and development of young children does not fit neatly into separate subject areas, but practitioners value a shared understanding and guidance on how to support children's education and development.

The importance of play is widely recognised in the three curricula that you will use in your work as an early education and childcare practitioner.

A Curriculum Framework for Children 3 to 5 recognises that one of the important ways in which children learn is through *playing* and it refers to the 'powerful contribution' that play makes to the learning process.

Curriculum for Excellence emphasises the importance of spontaneous play and planned, purposeful play as opportunities for active learning. The importance of play is also highlighted in the document for practitioners working with children aged 0–3 years.

There is broad agreement amongst practitioners that children's play is valuable and must be supported. The emphasis on the value of play helps maintain high quality education for children and at the same time supports the work of practitioners who provide a developmentally appropriate play-based curriculum. The concern for the whole individual and the importance of play leads to a definition of curriculum that emphasises how children learn as much as what they learn.

The importance of play in the curriculum

Why is play seen to be so important in the early education and childcare curriculum?

Key term

The **early education and childcare curriculum** is a broad range of planned and unplanned experiences, often play experiences, which support children's learning and development.

One reason is that play is important in children's lives. When you spend time with young children, you notice that children will almost always play if given the opportunity to do so. It seems to be a natural activity for children and they will use their own ideas and imagination, the ideas of others and any available equipment to create and invent. This tendency for children to play is something that practitioners value and can use when planning the curriculum.

Imagine a group of children playing with a tea set, some soft toys and dolls' clothes. It's likely that they will make tea for the teddy bears and serve it to them. The teddies will become

Time spent on playing is time well spent

You might admire the way in which children can take forward their own learning through situations of their own invention and by following their own purposes.

Practitioners value play in the curriculum because they understand and respect the energy and concentration that children invest in their play. By basing much of the curriculum on play, you can ensure that children continue to learn enjoyably in a developmentally appropriate way.

'children' and the children will become 'parents'! There may be adult style conversation about the children needing their tea and being put to bed. The teddies will be dressed and undressed as part of the game.

Children can spend a great deal of time playing in this way, but if you look at what a *Curriculum Framework for Children 3 to 5* says about the importance of play, you see that this is certainly time well spent. It states that, through play, children may learn to:

- make sense of real-life situations
- explore, investigate and experiment
- collaborate with others.

You can see how this is happening for these children. They may be developing an understanding of the real-life situation of caring for others when they feed their play 'children' and put them to bed. They may have investigated a number of ways of dressing the teddies and finding clothes that fit. They will have solved this problem in collaboration with others in the group and collaboration will continue as children take on the roles of parents in the game. When you analyse the children's play you can see that it is varied and complex and that it is helping them to develop and learn.

Consider this

Why do you think when studying play, HNC students who have children often make comments such as: 'I wish I had known more about play when my own children were small! I would have let them spend more time doing it' and 'I wouldn't have been so anxious for them to grow up and start doing serious things. I would have recognised that play *is* serious!'

How else could young children learn the complex and high-level skills of collaborating, problem solving and making sense of real situations if not through play? Could they learn these things by being told about them?

Practitioners attach great importance to play for another reason: play allows children to learn at their own level. Respect for children's play helps the practitioner to see learning from the child's point of view. When asked what they have been doing at nursery, children will often answer: 'Just playing.'

Learning experiences should be enjoyable for the children and they should feel that they have been playing, but you must be aware of how every experience that a child has in the setting should be of value to the child's learning and development. The curriculum helps you to do that.

Nasreen is studying for her HNC at a local college. Today she has been observing Finlay playing with Lisa at the water tray. At lunchtime, Finlay's mother comes to collect him and Nasreen listens to them chatting while Finlay is getting his coat on.

His mother asks, 'What have you been doing today, pet?'

'Playin.'

'What did you play with, Finlay?' asks his mum.

'Ah played wi' Lisa.'

'Whereabouts were you playing?'

'At the water,' answers Finlay. 'Lisa an' me squeezed the sponges. It was splashy.'

Finlay smiles as he chats to his mother and Nasreen smiles as she thinks about her observations. She has detailed notes about what Lisa and Finlay may have been learning and how their development will have been supported by this happy time at nursery.

1 How might Finlay answer if his mother had asked, 'What did you learn today, Finlay?'

2 Why would this question not have much meaning for Finlay?

How the curriculum supports the work of the practitioner

A Curriculum Framework for Children 3 to 5 conveys a wealth of useful information for educators, including a description of the main areas of learning that it is hoped children of this age will gain while in nursery, play group or with a childminder.

A Curriculum Framework for Children 3 to 5 is arranged in four main sections, as described below.

Section 1 This contains a general discussion on the importance of early education and some of the values and principles which underpin the curriculum's approach.

Section 2 This describes the broad curriculum that is appropriate for children in their early years, with many practical and helpful examples of how to achieve this in practice.

Section 3 This discusses aspects of the practitioner's role in providing the curriculum.

Section 4 This gives additional advice on working with children and families, emphasising the important values which ensure a high quality educational experience for young children.

Knowledge of this curriculum framework will help you be an effective member of the early education and childcare team.

The five key aspects of *A Curriculum Framework for Children 3 to 5*

A Curriculum Framework for Children 3 to 5 arranges the learning and development that it is hoped children will gain into five areas called *key aspects*. These relate to important areas of development and knowledge. The key aspects are:

- emotional, personal and social development
- communication and language
- knowledge and understanding of the world
- expressive and aesthetic development
- physical development and movement

Each broad key aspect is explained and then broken down into a number of smaller learning or development goals, called *features of learning*. These represent opportunities for the child's learning and development that staff can plan for. The trained practitioner who observes children carefully and who has a good knowledge of the curriculum framework will be able to plan very worthwhile play experiences for children. This is one of the ways in which we provide a high quality curriculum in the early years.

A Curriculum Framework for Children 3 to 5 allows us to plan flexibly and creatively for children's learning. This also provides a structure that staff can use when they evaluate play experiences in the nursery.

The features of learning within the key aspect of emotional, personal and social development indicate that children should have the opportunity to, for example:

- develop confidence, self-esteem and a sense of security
- care for themselves and their personal safety
- develop independence, for example, in dressing and personal hygiene
- form positive relationships with other children and adults, and begin to develop particular friendships with other children
- make and express choices, plans and decisions
- play cooperatively, take turns and share resources.

(Source: *A Curriculum Framework for Children 3 to 5.*)

Nasreen was able to identify some learning and development when Finlay was playing with Lisa. The diagram below offers some suggestions.

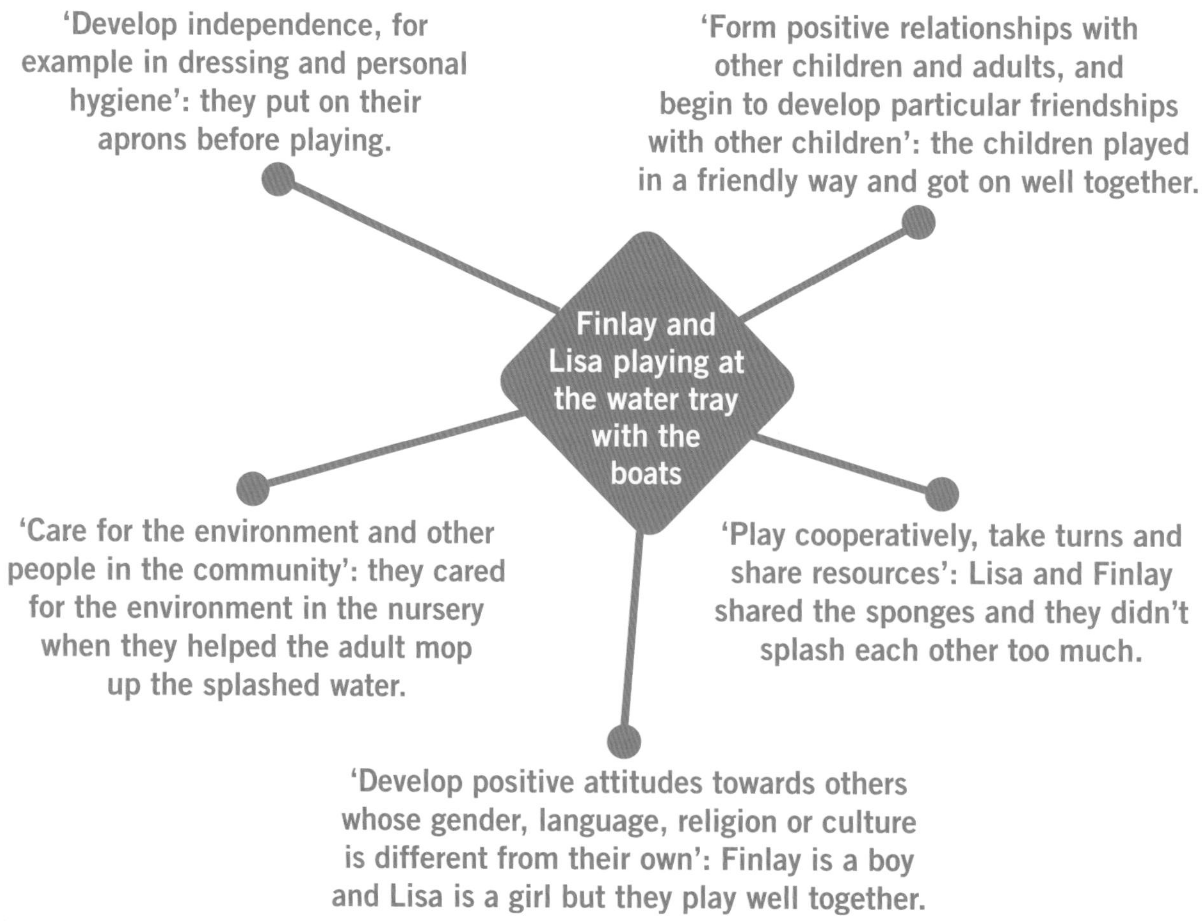

Case study *Water play*

Finlay and Lisa were both quite new to the nursery and the nursery team were not sure how the children were settling. One day they were seen washing their hands before snack time, evidently enjoying the water.

This led to Nasreen being asked to set out the water tray with warm water, some bubbles and sponges, and to observe Finlay and Lisa with particular reference to their emotional, personal and social development.

- Why do you think Nasreen was asked to do this?

'Develop independence, for example in dressing and personal hygiene': they put on their aprons before playing.

'Form positive relationships with other children and adults, and begin to develop particular friendships with other children': the children played in a friendly way and got on well together.

Finlay and Lisa playing at the water tray with the boats

'Care for the environment and other people in the community': they cared for the environment in the nursery when they helped the adult mop up the splashed water.

'Play cooperatively, take turns and share resources': Lisa and Finlay shared the sponges and they didn't splash each other too much.

'Develop positive attitudes towards others whose gender, language, religion or culture is different from their own': Finlay is a boy and Lisa is a girl but they play well together.

Emotional, personal and social development: Finlay and Lisa

Emotional, personal and social development

Activity

What are they learning?

Analyse and evaluate the possible learning that these children are experiencing in this activity.

You can see how the children are developing a number of useful features of learning within one planned experience while they were 'just playin'. The curriculum framework contains many useful examples from practice such as this one, all of which show how practitioners provide a high quality curriculum for children.

The examples from practice indicate a variety of ways in which practitioners can carry out their role sensitively to provide the curriculum. They are valuable aids to learning because they do much more than indicate what the content of the curriculum should be.

The key aspects in the curriculum help to ensure that children have a suitably broad education covering all areas of their development.

By placing emotional, personal and social development first, the curriculum draws our attention to this most important key aspect, stating that 'Children's emotional, personal and social development is linked closely with other aspects of their learning' and 'The way that children feel about themselves affects the way they approach all learning and the way they behave towards others' (*A Curriculum Framework for Children 3 to 5*).

The features of learning help to ensure a curriculum at differing levels to match the needs of children who may well be at different stages. In expressive and aesthetic development, for example, some children may already be learning to 'use instruments by themselves and in groups to invent music that expresses their thoughts and feelings'. Some children may be at a stage where they are just learning to 'listen to sounds, rhythms, songs and a variety of music'.

In physical development and movement some children will be at the stage where they are learning to 'enjoy energetic activity both indoors and out and the feeling of well-being that it brings', whereas children who are more advanced in their development may be learning to 'cooperate with others in physical games and play'.

The key aspects together with the features of learning describe the curriculum that all children aged 3–5 years are entitled to while in an early education and childcare setting in Scotland. You can see that all children, whatever their abilities and needs and wherever they live, can have access to the curriculum at a level that is right for them. This, together with the emphasis on play, maintains high quality education and an appropriate learning environment for children.

How Curriculum for Excellence supports the work of the practitioner

Curriculum for Excellence is being implemented from 2007 and is the name given to new guidelines for the education of children and young people in Scotland. It frees practitioners to promote learning in imaginative ways that will ensure that the relevance of what is being learned is clear to the learner. It also encourages all practitioners to reflect on the ways in which they provide the curriculum to ensure that children are learning in the best way possible. This curriculum also supports the work of the practitioner by indicating subjects and learning outcomes that practitioners can use when planning learning experiences for children.

Curriculum for Excellence suggests a structure for learning in eight subject groupings, as follows:

- health and well-being
- languages
- mathematics
- sciences
- social studies
- expressive arts
- technologies
- religious and moral education.

The outcomes of learning describe areas of knowledge that children should acquire and also the levels of increasing complexity that children will work through as their skills and knowledge develop. For example, part of the new science curriculum is concerned with the study of energy in the environment, including learning about energy in food. The outcomes that the learner will work towards are stipulated for the different levels of complexity as described in the table below.

> **Further research**
>
> Use appropriate Internet sites to learn more about the outcomes for science in Curriculum for Excellence.

Curriculum for Excellence, Science outcomes for 'Energy in food'

Energy in the environment	Early	First	Second	Third	Fourth
Energy in food	I have had the opportunity to taste and enjoy a range of healthy foods and can talk about how I need food to help me grow.	—	I can investigate the burning of different foods. Using my results, I can conclude which foods release the most energy and can evaluate my methods.	—	I can carry out chemical tests to distinguish between different energy-giving foods. I can use experimental techniques to compare the energy released from different foods in a quantitative way. I can evaluate my methods and the reliability of my results.

(*Source:* www.curriculumforexcellencescotland.gov.uk, 2008)

How Curriculum for Excellence helps to maintain high quality education for children

The table on page 106 indicates how quality in children's learning will be maintained through developmentally appropriate goals that ensure progression in children's learning. The subject groupings indicate a wide curriculum for children.

By placing 'health and well-being' first on its list, the curriculum acknowledges the prime importance of personal, emotional and social well-being as a requirement for learning in other areas, similar to those in *A Curriculum Framework for Children 3 to 5*. Health and well-being will be covered in a range of subject areas including science, physical education and home economics.

The new curriculum indicates a concern for all aspects of individual development by emphasising not only *what* children are learning but also *how* they are learning. It aims to develop four capacities within the learner by encouraging young people to become:

- successful learners
- confident individuals
- responsible citizens
- effective contributors.

The characteristics of these four capacities are expanded in the chart below. Here we see a focus on the *kind of person* the curriculum is nurturing and developing as well as the *subjects* that the person should learn.

successful learners

with:
- enthusiasm and motivation for learning
- determination to reach high standards of achievement
- openness to new thinking and ideas

and able to:
- use literacy, communication and numeracy skills
- use technology for learning
- think creatively and independently
- learn independently and as part of a group
- make reasoned evaluations
- link and apply different kinds of learning in new situations.

confident individuals

with:
- self-respect
- a sense of physical, mental and emotional well-being
- secure values and beliefs
- ambition

and able to:
- relate to others and manage themselves
- pursue a healthy and active lifestyle
- be self-aware
- develop and communicate their own beliefs and view of the world
- live as independently as they can
- assess risk and make informed decisions
- achieve success in different areas of activity.

To enable all young people to become:

responsible citizens

with:
- respect for others
- commitment to participate responsibly in political, economic, social and cultural life

and able to:
- develop knowledge and understanding of the world and Scotland's place in it
- understand different beliefs and cultures
- make informed choices and decisions
- evaluate environmental, scientific and technological issues
- develop informed, ethical views of complex issues.

effective contributors

with:
- an enterprising attitude
- resilience
- self-reliance

and able to:
- communicate in different ways and in different settings
- work in partnership and in teams
- take the initiative and lead
- apply critical thinking in new contexts
- create and develop
- solve problems.

The four capacities and purposes of the curriculum 3–18

(*Source:* www.curriculumforexcellencescotland.gov.uk/essentialinformation/purposes.asp, Learning and Teaching Scotland, 2008)

Case study *A tale of two snack times*

Read the two descriptions of snack time in two different nurseries. Both groups of children were given a snack, but the quality of the experience was very different in each nursery. When you have read the accounts of two different nurseries, answer the questions which follow.

Nursery 1

A group of children went out of the room and came back carrying apples, cheese and two boxes of crackers.

One little girl was asked to bring two knives from the drawer and one of the boys fetched the apple-cutter. The practitioner encouraged the children to wash their hands and they then set about preparing the snack.

The children carefully cut the cheese into cubes and used the apple-cutter to cut the apples into segments. As they were working they chatted about the cheese. One child said, 'They're kind of squarey things.' Another said, 'Aye, like wee boxes.' Jamie said, smiling, 'Ah've made bigger cubes than you.'

They also chatted about what they were doing while using the apple-cutter. 'How many bits does it make?' 'One, two, three, four, five,' was slowly counted out.

Kylie said, looking at the apple segments, 'They look like wee boats!'

The children had to press down hard on the cutter and it was quite an effort. The practitioner helped them quietly without taking over.

The children and the practitioner laughed when one of the apple segments flew off the table and landed on the floor. The children talked about this with the adult and, as a group, decided that this couldn't be eaten because it might be dirty.

The children arranged the snack on three plates, one of apple, one of cheese, and one of crackers. 'Cheese and apple's nice,' said Kylie. 'Yeah, it's good for you,' answered Jamie.

The practitioner said that each person could have two pieces of apple, one piece of cheese and one cracker, and asked Charlie to choose the numbers.

He took down a tray of number cards from a nearby shelf and he chose cards with '1', '1' and '2'. A card with '3' was put back as being, 'Not the number we need, today.' The numbers were placed correctly beside the plates of food.

The four children left the room with the practitioner. When they returned they were carrying a clean towel, a jug of water, some cartons of milk and a stack of plastic cups.

'Hey, that milk's got a cow on it, same like the cheese paper,' said Charlie. There was then some talk about cheese being made from milk. The apple segments were stored in a bowl of cold water and the children talked about the reasons for this. One apple segment was left out of the water to see what would happen to it.

The practitioner asked one of the children if he would like to take down the box of morning names. The other children reminded him that these names were kept in the red box and he placed it on the table.

The children had their own snack and when they were ready quietly invited a friend to the table. Throughout this whole activity, the children were involved in their task while the bustle of the nursery carried on around them.

Nursery 2

The children were all asked to come and sit in a circle. One of the adults encouraged the children to make a good circle. 'You sit back a bit, Mark. Chana, you come forward a wee bit. That's a nice circle now.'

There was an interruption while a teacher from another class came to discuss something with the nursery team. The children became a bit restless and the adults gave some instructions about their behaviour.

'Ashley, you *must* sit quietly.'

'Leah, you were told to sit on your bottom NOT on your knees.'

When this was achieved, the HNC student gave a carton of milk with a straw in it to each child and then handed round a plate of biscuits. One little girl squeezed her milk carton too hard and milk spurted out and dribbled down her dress and on to the floor.

'Oh, Melanie,' said one of the practitioners, 'you have made a mess! Never mind, we'll soon clear it up.'

The student wiped up the mess while the children watched.

1 Using *A Curriculum Framework for Children 3–5* and referring to all five key aspects, analyse and evaluate these two experiences to show how one group of children are having a much richer curriculum than the other.

2 Analyse and evaluate the experiences with reference to the four capacities using Curriculum for Excellence. In your analysis, think about the characteristics within all four capacities.

3 Evaluate the experiences with reference to the science outcome relating to food at the early stage of Curriculum for Excellence.

4 Curriculum for Excellence and *A Curriculum Framework for Children 3 to 5* both encourage practitioners to reflect on how they have carried out their role. Evaluate how the practitioners have carried out their role in each nursery.

Consider this

A Curriculum for Excellence: Progress and Proposals describes the early years curriculum as having 'real strengths', stating, 'the existing guidance for the curriculum 3–5 is working well'.

Why do you think the writers of the new curriculum hold this opinion?

Curriculum for Excellence helps to maintain high quality education by expressing broad and very positive aims for the education process in seven important principles for curriculum design. These principles can help practitioners to evaluate the curriculum they provide. The principles are described below.

Challenges and enjoyment

Young people should find their learning challenging and motivating. This principle also refers to active learning and high aspirations.

Breadth

All young people should have a broad range of educational experiences and this breadth should be maintained for younger children. Specialisation should not begin until pupils are in the later years of the curriculum.

Progression

Pupils should experience continuous progression in their learning from 3 to 18 years. This is the first time in Scotland that continuity has been offered for this wide age range within a single curriculum.

Depth

Young people should have the opportunity to develop their thinking and understanding in deeper and more advanced ways as they progress through the curriculum and as they develop increased interest and knowledge in specialised areas.

Personalisation and choice

Pupils should be able to make personal, responsible choices about what they learn and should be supported in this process. This personalisation will happen only when the young person has achieved suitable levels of attainment in the wider curriculum. The curriculum should allow young people to develop their aptitudes and talents.

Coherence

There should be clear links between the different aspects of young people's learning, and the curriculum should include activities which encompass different strands.

Relevance

Within the new curriculum, young people should experience learning activities which have real meaning for their own lives.

It is good to have enjoyment of education recognised as a guiding principle, and the concept of choice and personalisation in the new curriculum may have a deeper meaning than making subject choices in the third year of secondary school.

The principle of progression helps to maintain high quality education by offering a structure to support children as their skills and knowledge develop. This is a simple structure with only six levels covering pre-school to sixth year in secondary school, as shown in the chart below.

Level	Experiences and outcomes for most children or young people
Early	In pre-school and in Primary 1
First	By the end of Primary 4, but earlier for some
Second	By the end of P7, but earlier for some
Third	In S1–S3, but earlier for some
Fourth	Fourth level broadly equates to SCQF* level 4
Senior	In S4–S6, but earlier for some

(* SCQF is the Scottish Credit Qualifications Framework)

One very positive feature of this new progression structure is the joining together of pre-school and Primary 1 into a new unified *early level*. This maintains high quality education for children by promoting continuity between pre-school and Primary 1 and emphasising the importance of play as a curricular approach.

The importance of play in Curriculum for Excellence

In Curriculum for Excellence, the new early level combines nursery and Primary 1 stages and prioritises active learning through play as an approach to learning.

One challenge for practitioners is to maintain the feeling of play in the setting while ensuring that the children experience the whole curriculum, including areas of learning such as literacy and numeracy. These two subject areas are sometimes offered in ways that are too formal for the children. Sensitive practitioners avoid this problem by making sure that children have access to a wide selection of structured play materials.

Key terms

Active learning is 'learning which engages and challenges children's thinking using real-life and imaginary situations' (*A Curriculum for Excellence: Building the Curriculum 2 – Active Learning in the Early Years*, Scottish Executive, 2007). Active learning also includes spontaneous play, planned purposeful play, investigating and exploring as well as focused learning and teaching.

Structured play is play with materials that are designed to promote specific skills such as letter recognition, counting or fine motor skills.

Matching games where the aim is to match a letter to a picture or a word to a picture, perhaps played as a game of 'Snap', can support the child's growing awareness of literacy. Board games where children count squares to move counters, perhaps after throwing a dice, give many opportunities to encourage their developing number skills. When these structured play materials are attractively presented, children will choose to play with them. Adults who involve themselves with this kind of play find that they have many opportunities for informal teaching in the context of the game. For example, baking is a 'real life' situation structured and often led by an adult and greatly enjoyed by the children. When you bake with children you can encourage numeracy, language, scientific and sensory awareness. Beads and laces for threading can develop fine motor skills. Construction sets and building blocks may foster creative design, problem solving and the development of mathematical concepts such as height and area.

Modern structured play materials are often very well designed and one game may encompass a number of learning opportunities such as counting, number recognition and colour matching. Most games can be played successfully by a group of children and so the social skills of taking turns and sharing with others can also be developed.

It is a good idea to investigate the resources for structured play when joining a new setting as a student or qualified member of staff. This might be a useful piece of research for a graded unit investigating aspects of play. (Chapter 10 of this book deals in detail with the graded unit.)

Structured play

Game 1

Game 2

What do you think these children are learning?

Activity

Make a survey of the games and structured play materials available in your workplace. Evaluate them by identifying the features of learning that the children might gain when playing with these materials.

The curriculum can be covered successfully when you provide a wide range of well-resourced play areas and a balance of structured play, adult-led activities and opportunities for free-flow play.

Case Study *Play is a child's work!*

Neelika is an HNC Early Education and Childcare student who is really enjoying her current placement in Primary 1. The teacher in charge of the class is enthusiastically implementing the active learning approach recommended by Curriculum for Excellence.

Having Neelika as a member of the team is a great asset. Every morning the children come in and work in small groups playing with structured play materials, and Neelika is able to circulate around the groups helping the children, supporting their learning and really enjoying the opportunity to work closely with them. The teacher, meanwhile, has the opportunity to work intensively with children as required.

This morning, two groups are engaged in active play related to literacy. One group is playing a picture/word matching game and another group is busy with a sound-lotto game. Two groups are actively engaged in play which has been planned to support their developing numeracy.

At the play dough table, children have been provided with templates of the numerals 1, 2, 3, 4, 5 and an ample supply of play dough for all to share. The children are energetically engaged in rolling out the appropriate number of small balls of dough to match each number. They are also forming the numerals by rolling the dough and using it to copy the templates.

Another group is playing with small coloured elephants that can link together according to size and colour. They are counting the elephants and sorting them into 'families'. There is a red family, a blue family, a yellow family and a green family. The children are forming the families to consist of 'daddy, mummy and two children' elephants. Daddy is the biggest elephant in each family. Mummy is slightly smaller and the two children elephants are the same size. Neelika observes the children discussing their elephant families, making comments such as:

'That one's the dad cos he's the biggest. He goes first. Here's the mum, she's second.'

'This wee green elephant should be with the green family. He's trying to run away. Back you go to your mum and dad.'

'Aw, he only came over to see his pal!'

'Yeah. He has to go to his own house now to have his tea.'

The children at both tables are relaxed and learning in an enjoyable way. The outcomes for numeracy and the number experiences relating to number, money and measure include the following processes which occur as the children play with the materials.

Listed under the 'early' stage you find: 'I have explored numbers, understanding that they represent quantities and I can use them to count, create sequences and describe order.'

Exploring numbers is happening when the children play with the dough. As they roll out and place the correct number of balls beside the numeral, they are developing their understanding of the value of each number. The children are also exploring ways of representing numbers as they model the numerals in dough.

As the children play with the elephants, they are developing their counting skills as they compose each family of four members. They are learning how to create sequences as they arrange the elephants in the order 'Daddy, Mummy, child, child.' They are also beginning to use numbers for ordering when they use the words 'first' and 'second' to describe the position of the daddy and the mummy elephants. You can see that the children are making real gains in their understanding of number and number processes through their involvement in purposeful play.

The way in which these outcomes are expressed is new and interesting. The learning achieved is described from the point of view of the learner rather than from the point of view of the educator or practitioner. This is in keeping with one of the four capacities to be a 'confident individual'. A confident individual is one who is aware of what he or she is learning and who recognises his or her own achievement.

1 Analyse and evaluate the experience described above with reference to the four capacities.

2 Indicate where the children are having the opportunity to become:

- successful learners
- confident individuals
- responsible citizens
- effective contributors.

3 The learning experiences offered to these children demonstrate the influence of some of the seven important principles that form the basis of Curriculum for Excellence.

Look back at the discussion of the principles and indicate where the following principles were being met:

- challenges and enjoyment
- breadth
- coherence
- relevance.

4 Thinking about challenges for the children, what structured play experience would you suggest as a next step in numeracy for these children?

Does free-flow play have a place in Curriculum for Excellence?

Sometimes you will see children engage in free-flow play. This occurs when children are deeply engrossed in imaginative play. The children are not just pretending but seem actually to *live* the events they are experiencing in a very real way.

Free-flow play is not planned or led by the adult. This kind of play seems to arise spontaneously and emerges from the interaction of the children's ideas, knowledge and experiences with the resources they find around them. Free-flow play has value equal to play that has been structured by the adults in the setting.

Free-flow play is deeply absorbing for the children and they develop high levels of concentration, persistence and motivation. These are three characteristics that learners of all ages need to possess if they are to cope successfully with difficult and challenging material. As a student who studies for the HNC in Early Education and Childcare, you will know the importance of being able to concentrate and persist when learning is difficult!

Case study *Free-flow play: fire fighters*

As part of Curriculum for Excellence, the primary school had been working on a cross-school project called 'Our Community'. As part of this a crew from the local fire station visited the school and gave a talk to the children. The nursery class went out to see the fire engine and the children were highly interested although some were a bit nervous. The staff arranged a display of books about fire fighters and fire engines and spent time with the children talking about what they had seen. They also set out fire fighters' hats and yellow jackets from the stock of role-play materials.

Two days later, staff observed a drama unfold at the large hollow blocks. Two of the boys, Ryan and Stefan, both aged 4½ years, were rushing towards the hollow blocks wearing hats and jackets and holding a length of tubing from the water tray. Megan, nearly 5 years old, was crying out in a voice filled with emotion, 'Hurry! Quick! He's still in there!'

'Dinnae worry,' said Ryan confidently, 'I'll go round the back and get him!'

Stefan pointed the length of tube at the blocks and shouted, 'Ah'll keep hosing. Stand back, everybody! The building's gonnae come down.'

Ryan took a small chair from a nearby table and climbed up on it. He brought a soft toy animal from the top of the block and Megan grabbed it and hugged it tightly.

The practitioner watched carefully but unobtrusively, ready to intervene if the children became overexcited or the play became unsafe. She realised that it was time for the morning session to draw to a close. It would soon be time for the children to have lunch but she was reluctant to disrupt their play.

She approached Megan and asked quietly, indicating the toy, 'Is he all right? Maybe you should take him to the hospital for a check-up.' Megan nodded and walked off towards the home corner where she laid the rescued toy on a small bed.

The practitioner said to Ryan and Stefan, 'That was a very brave rescue. You fire fighters must be feeling tired and thirsty now after putting out that terrible fire. I hope you can have some lunch and a rest, back at the fire station.'

'Aye,' said Ryan. 'Come on, Stefan. We'll have our lunch and put out another fire in the afternoon.'

The practitioner wiped up a few water drops from the hose that the boys had been using and replaced the chair that Ryan had stood on. She remembered how Ryan had been one of the

children who had been a bit unsure of the fire engine. She was pleased to have seen him act so fearlessly in his play and made a few notes of what she had observed in order to take these to the planning meeting later in the day.

- Analyse and evaluate the children's play with reference to Curriculum for Excellence. Indicate evidence that the children were becoming:
  o successful learners
  o confident individuals
  o responsible citizens
  o effective contributors.

The role of the practitioner in supporting free-flow play

You can see how the staff in this nursery provided a rich environment which stimulated the children's imagination by offering the new experience of visiting the fire engine. They also supplied a range of resources such as the hats and the jackets.

Safety was maintained by the practitioner, who continued to observe closely and also wiped the floor and replaced the chair. She was very sensitive in her intervention and careful to use the same word as the children when referring to the soft toy. She said 'him' not 'your toy' or

'your cat', both of which might have been at odds with the situation that the children had created together. She helped the children wind down their play by an intervention that was in keeping with the scene in which they had been so absorbed. You will notice, too, how knowledgeable the children were about the role of fire fighters and how they were able to use language that was appropriate to a rescue situation.

By observing the children in their play, the practitioner was able to gain insight into the children's level of knowledge. She was able to assess informally how much they knew by observing them.

The curriculum supports the role of the practitioner by emphasising observation. One essential skill of the early education and childcare practitioner is the ability to observe and this is confirmed by the curriculum.

Curriculum for Excellence includes guidance for practitioners on the importance of observation as part of their role, stating that: 'staff need time to observe children, in order to learn about their understanding and approach to learning. They can then plan next steps and gauge the level of support or challenge required' (*A Curriculum for Excellence: Building the Curriculum 2 – Active Learning in the Early Years*.

A Curriculum Framework for Children 3–5 also emphasises the importance of observation in many of the examples from practice and quite clearly and distinctly in Section 3 of the document. It states in the section on planning: 'It is from *observation and assessment* of children at play that we learn how and what they learn.'

Birth to Three: supporting our youngest children states:

Flexible planning, *close observation* and the ability to reflect on how things have gone all help adults to ensure that the environments children find themselves in are as responsive and thoughtful as possible.

Observations can take different forms depending on the purpose of the observation and the circumstances in which the observation is happening. Often it is a short observation that allows you to further the child's interest quickly. It is important to see observation as an integral part of your ongoing work with children and not something separate and apart from your daily support of their learning and development.

The planning cycle

The planning cycle is the recurring sequence of observe, evaluate, plan, implement, observe, evaluate, plan, implement. Planning was covered in Chapter 1, and you may find it helpful to read pages 10–20 again.

Activity

OBSERVE

Leanne notices a child (3 years, 6 months) playing at the dough table. She observes him making patterns with the rolling pins, spatulas, etc. He tends to be a very quiet child but today he is talking about stripes and spots. He also mentions snakes as he rolls the dough.

EVALUATE

Leanne makes a mental note of the child's interest in patterns and decides to take the opportunity to develop this.

PLAN

Leanne finds an assortment of pattern-making and printing sticks to press into the dough. She finds a book about animals and some fur fabric with interesting patterns for the craft table.

IMPLEMENT

At the display table, Leanne displays the animals and a poster illustrating patterned animals and camouflage. She includes the book opened at the relevant page. She places a wooden log with snakes hiding inside. Then she places fur fabric at the collage table.

OBSERVE

Day 1: Child looks through the book and names the animals.
Day 1 (later): he goes to the display table and role plays with the materials. He names the animals. He mentions their patterns. He acts out that the tiger is eating the zebra.
Day 2: Child walks past the display area, looks at and touches the log and the snakes.
Day 2 (later): The child is seen at the gluing table examining the fur fabric. He picks up some striped material saying, 'That's like Zebra.'

EVALUATE

The child shows interest in the material provided. His interest continues to develop as he plays with the materials. He is developing his language and his knowledge and understanding of the world, naming animals and talking about patterns. His imagination, sequencing and storytelling abilities are being extended. This experience allows the child to learn through play, learn at his own pace using his sense of touch and his manipulative abilities. The provision successfully develops the child's capacity to be a successful learner and a confident individual.

PLAN NEXT STEPS

The staff team discuss Leanne's observations and they agree to give the child and others who are interested more time with the materials provided. They include in the plan for the week to set out the Noah's Ark and to look for an opportunity to work with the child pairing and sequencing the animals and allowing more opportunity for language development, perhaps through role play.

Analyse and evaluate the child's learning shown in the diagram above, with reference to Curriculum for Excellence.

In which of the subject groupings is the child learning? Your analysis will not identify every subject area but will certainly include a minimum of four. You will probably use *A Curriculum Framework for Children 3 to 5* to help you, bearing in mind the correspondence between Curriculum for Excellence subject groupings and the key aspects in *A Curriculum Framework for Children 3 to 5*.

Following Leanne's observations, the child's key practitioners made a note of his interests and achievements. She included this information with some of Leanne's observations in the records that were used to compile the child's profile.

Photographs were taken of the child at play with the patterned animals and included in his 'All About Me' book, which contained a statement in the words of the child: 'I enjoyed playing with the animals and I learned a lot about the patterns on their coats.'

There is a strong connection between profiles, 'All About Me' books and transition documents. They are all used as a means of communicating with parents and other significant people in the child's life. Practitioner observations supply much of the evidence.

The 'All About Me' book is very much a celebration of learning from the child's point of view.

Types of observation

Sometimes there is a requirement for a longer observation to focus on a particular child, group of children or area. As a student you will need to practise some of the observational techniques in common use in the early years.

Narrative observation is one of these techniques. It is fraught with difficulty when you are observing a group actively playing. You can never note down on paper the full detail and complexity of children's learning processes, but you can do your best. Practitioners often say, 'There is no such thing as a perfect observation and there is no such person as a perfect observer!'

This is important as it reminds us to be cautious and non-judgemental when we evaluate observations.

Consider this

What are the differences between individual observers that might influence the quality of an observation?

What are the factors in the nursery or classroom that might influence the quality of an observation?

You need to remember that the value of observation lies in its gradual nature and the way in which you can accumulate information about children by observing them on many different occasions in a variety of situations.

Everyone who attempts observation finds it challenging but we all improve with practice. There is agreement that it is the best way to get to know the children and to find out about their needs, their interests and how to support their learning.

Often you observe as part of your interaction with the children (participant observation). You can make notes as quickly as you can and including as much accurate detail as possible of what the children are saying and doing.

Key terms

Participant observation is an observation made while you are interacting with a child or children. It can be a useful way of assessing a child's understanding while supporting the child's learning.

Narrative observation is an observation in which practitioners record everything that children say and do as it happens before them.

Case study *The water tray*

Halima, the HNC student, is working with two children aged 3 years 10 months and 4 years 2 months at the water tray. They have an assortment of objects and are sorting them out into those that float and those that sink. One of the children blows hard on a small plastic boat with a sail and it moves across the surface of the water. The other child watches and does the same with an identical boat. The children blow harder and their boats move faster. They notice that they need to blow on the sails of their boats and they chat with Halima about having a boat race.

They then notice that their boats stop moving forward when they stop blowing and Halima asks them why this might be. The children answer that it is their 'puff' that made the boats go. By interacting with the children, Halima has practised participant observation and observed that the children are developing one of the outcomes in the early stage of science in Curriculum for Excellence, which states in the words of the learner, 'Through everyday play with toys and from other experiences, I can describe the effects of simple forces.'

Halima has been able to assess the children's level of understanding using 'evidence from day-to-day activities' as recommended in *Assessment is for Learning* (Scottish Executive, 1007).

Sometimes you will be able to observe without interacting, when children are absorbed in their play. This is more straightforward than trying to observe at the same time as interacting.

As a student you are expected to complete a number of narrative observations. Below is a short example of one student's useful narrative observation.

Type of observation: Non-participant narrative

Date: 12 March 2008

Children involved: E. (4 years 5 months), F. (4 years 8 months), A. (4 years 3 months)

Area: the three children are in the construction area. There is a plentiful supply of bricks and some small-world figures

Starting time: 9.20 a.m.

Finishing time: 9.40 a.m.

Aim: To find out how the children interact with each other.

Key term

Non-participant narrative is a type of observation where you do not interact with the children and you note down everything they say and do.

Line no.	Activity	Vocalisation
1	E. looks at others and says:	'Look, F! Look, A, a brick wall!'
2	A. looks at E. and, holding a small-world figure, says:	'Yeah. He's gonnae go over the wall.'
3	A. places his figure on top of the wall. (R.H.)	
4	E. watches and says:	'He's gonnae fall. He'll get hurt!'
5	A. (lifting the toy man and raising him up and then placing him down on other side of the wall of bricks) (R.H.)	'Neeeeeeyaaaaaah! No! Cos he's amazing flyin' man!'
6	F. looks up holding some bricks connected together. (L.H.)	'An enemy's tryin' to shoot him!'
7	A. picks up man. (R.H.) puts some bricks on top of him.	'No! He can hide!'
8	E. starts fitting bricks together using both hands.	'He's goin' to central control.'
9	A. and E. carry on building, working together.	
10	F. leaves the area.	
11	F. returns holding small van in his R. hand.	'Here's his 'scape car!'
12	A. looks up from building.	'Put it round the back.'
13	F. places van on other side of wall and says:	'OK, I'll hide it there.'

The student has observed the rules for an effective narrative observation. She has:

- included the date
- given starting and finishing times
- provided detail about the area
- numbered the lines
- matched action and vocalisation appropriately
- included detail about which hand the children use
- transcribed actual language used by the children, not corrected in any way
- written in the present tense
- avoided any evaluation within the observation
- maintained the children's anonymity by using only the initials of their names.

Social play with construction and small-world materials

Activity

1 Discuss with colleagues why each of these points is considered to be important when writing an observation.

2 What did the student find out about the children's social interactions?

3 Evaluate the observation with reference to the features of learning in the key aspect of, emotional, personal and social development in *A Curriculum Framework for Children 3 to 5*.

4 With reference to Curriculum for Excellence, what evidence is there to indicate the development of any of the four capacities – effective contributors, successful learners, confident individuals or responsible citizens?

Other types of observation

When you want to find out *how often* something happens, you can conduct a frequency sample. This is particularly useful when you are interested to find out about aspects of a child's behaviour. For example:

- How often does Jenni play cooperatively?
- How often does Simon sit by himself reading in the book corner?
- How often does Calum display difficulties in sharing?

Key term

A **frequency sample** is a method of observation in which you record how often something happens.

A frequency sample can be usefully done over the course of a day or a week, depending on the aim. Sometimes it is useful to repeat a frequency sample at a later date to assess the effect of intervention by practitioners. For example, there has been some concern in the nursery that F. has difficulties in playing cooperatively with other children. One of the practitioners does a frequency sample to ascertain how often this occurs, with a view to providing support for F.

Time	Monday	Tuesday	Wednesday	Thursday	Friday
a.m.		/	/	/	//
comments		With C. and D., at dough			Board game with C.
p.m.	/	/	//	///	///
comments	In house corner		In house corner	With C. at board game	In house with C. and D.

Dates of frequency sample: 3–7 March 2008

Aim: to note down every time F. (4 years 10 months) displays difficulties in cooperating with others over the course of one week. (Examples of difficulty in cooperating: snatching toys from other children; not waiting his turn when playing games; shouting and becoming angry at other children.)

The results of the observation are shown in the table above. When the practitioner evaluated her observation, she began this way: 'F. displayed difficulties in cooperating on 15 occasions.' When she shared her observation with the whole team, they felt they had found some other information that might be useful in helping F. to manage his behaviour. What do you think they discussed?

Sometimes you may want to gain an overview of how a child spends his or her whole day. A good way to do this is by doing an observation called a time sample. This is also explained in Chapter 8.

Key term

A **time sample** is a series of brief observations made at regular, pre-set intervals throughout the day.

Case study *A time sample of Carrie's day*

Mrs Wilkinson is worried because her daughter Carrie says she plays at the sand every day and never mentions any other play area. The practitioner prepares her format and does a time sample of this little girl's day in order to gain some evidence of what Carrie actually does at nursery.

The aim of the time sample was to find out how Carrie spends her day. The practitioner observed Carrie for 1 minute every 15 minutes. A small part of her observation is shown in the chart at the bottom of the page.

1. Evaluate the observation, stating any objective information you have gained about Carrie (remember to refer to times). In what ways was this observation useful?

2. The practitioner took two photographs of Carrie that day and displayed one with the caption 'Responsible citizen' and the other with the caption 'Effective contributor'. Why do you think this might have been done?

Time	Play area	Comment
9.15	Sand tray	Filling bucket, singing quietly. No one else present.
9.30	Story corner	Listening to Mrs F. reading story with two other children.
9.45	Sand tray	Digging energetically. No one else at area.
10.00	Snack	At table. Talking to Mrs F.
10.15	Outside	Watching other children on climbing frame.
10.30	Garden	Digging earth to plant lettuces with Mrs M. and two other children.
10.45	Garden	Sweeping earth from path and returning it to vegetable plot.

Part of time sample observation dated 01.05.08

Responsible citizens

Transitions

When practitioners and parents discuss transitions they often express concern that such times will cause problems or difficulties for the children in their care.

Children vary greatly in their ability to cope with transitions. As practitioners we must be observant of any signs of difficulty and be aware of all that we can do to ease the process.

Young children may experience a number of transitions in the course of one day, depending on family circumstances. This represents a change in childhood experience compared to a few decades ago, when the first major transition for most children occurred at the onset of Primary 1.

Case study *Just an ordinary day*

Iain (3 years and 2 months) gets up in the morning and has breakfast with his big sister Lorraine (5 years and 8 months). At quarter to eight, Iain's mother, Tessa, drives Lorraine, Iain and his favourite toy dog, Buster, to their childminder and drops them off. She kisses them both goodbye and drives off to make her 8.30 start at work in the city centre. Iain and Lorraine spend half an hour with Maggie the childminder. She knows that Iain loves his toy dog and she always has a toy dog's basket ready so that Iain can give Buster a rest in case he got up too early! Maggie then walks Iain and Lorraine down to school with her own two children. Iain says 'bye to Lorraine and Maggie's children, and then clutching Buster he walks with Maggie to play group where he spends the morning playing happily with the other children while Maggie goes to her part-time work.

At the end of the play group session, one of the play leaders takes Iain and Cathie, who is also 3 years old, down to the nursery class in the local primary school attended by Lorraine and Maggie's children.

Iain and Cathie have afternoon places at the nursery and their parents have paid extra for them to have lunch there. Iain sometimes sees Lorraine in the playground and she waves to him as he walks into the nursery. In the afternoon session the nursery practitioners have observed that Iain is sometimes very tired and even inclined to be a bit tearful. They are very sensitive to the needs of younger children and Iain's key worker is always there to welcome him. She and her colleagues are very understanding if Iain wants to spend time in the partially screened quiet area equipped with soft cushions, colourful quilts, soft toys and picture books. Iain's key worker always makes sure that there is a 'Spot' book for Iain to look at with Buster.

At the end of the nursery day, Maggie is there to collect Iain. She takes him to the local shop and does a few errands before returning to the school gate to collect Lorraine and her own two children. They all walk back to Maggie's house and have a snack and play and watch children's television

until Tessa arrives to take Lorraine and Iain home after greeting them both with a big hug. Iain is sometimes very sleepy on the drive home but he livens up when Tessa gets the tea ready and enjoys his meal chatting with the family.

Tessa is aware that Iain is really tired by the end of his day. She is looking forward to next year when Iain will have an all-day place at nursery and Maggie will be able to collect him and care for him in the afternoons.

1 How many transitions does Iain experience in his day?

2 Who are the adults who have responsibility for Iain?

3 Explain possible reasons why Iain might feel tired and tearful when he goes to nursery in the afternoon.

4 What are the adults doing well to support Iain? (The lower half of page 4 of *A Curriculum Framework for Children 3–5* is helpful in answering this question.)

5 What might be the difficulties in achieving the best for Iain's all-round development in this situation?

6 Analyse and evaluate Iain's experience with reference to attachment theory.

The curricular frameworks and guidelines all have something to say about transitions.

Further research

Read pages 11, 12 and 41–7 in *Birth to Three: supporting our youngest children* guidelines. Make a note of the main strategies suggested to support children during transitions.

Birth to Three: Framework for Practitioners (City of Edinburgh Council, 2000) is designed to offer practitioners practical advice on how to implement the 0 to 3 guidelines. It states on page 17: 'As with all transitions in a child's life, a well planned settling in process is crucial in building the foundation of emotional security for children'.

Activity

1 Discuss with your supervisor or manager the arrangements in your setting to support children at times of settling in and other transitions.

2 Compare your findings with those of other HNC students in your group.

A Curriculum Framework for Children 3 to 5 also indicates a clear awareness of the importance of effective transitions. It discusses on page 55 the importance of settling in procedures and the vital need for a 'positive and supportive climate for both the parent and child' as well as the importance of good 'two-way' communication between early education and childcare practitioners and families.

It suggests a number of useful occasions when practitioners and families can talk and listen to each other, such as home visits, information evenings and visits to the nursery to build confidence and communication gradually.

When describing transition from nursery to Primary 1, *A Curriculum Framework for Children 3 to 5* includes a discussion on the importance of 'good liaison with the receiving primary school' (page 56). It also contains a useful chart showing the links between the early years curriculum and the subject areas in 5–14 Curriculum (page 57), stating that 'staff in both sectors should be aware of these links'.

This general awareness of the need for good communication and effective transition from one stage of the education process to the other has resulted in the development of transition documents which practitioners complete for children as they leave nursery to progress into Primary 1. Early education and childcare practitioners have devised very useful transition documents designed to inform parents and Primary 1 teachers of the achievements of children when leaving nursery to embark on their primary schooling. The transition documents often reflect curricular design and this is helpful to practitioners in structuring their comments. They are supportive of the child's progression, ensuring that all aspects of the child's learning receive attention. They are also highly informative for the parents and primary teachers as an overall picture of the child's achievement, indicating reasonable expectations for the children as they begin their next stage in the education process.

A transition document should include comments by the child in recognition of the importance we attach to the right of children to be consulted and be active participants in their own education. Recognising the important role of the parents in the educational process and their right to be involved, a good transition document also has space for comment by the parent who signs it.

Despite much good practice, transition remains a concern in Scottish education. In a recent paper published by the education inspectorate (HMIE), the Senior Chief Inspector refers to 'serious concerns about effective continuity and progression in pupils' learning at key points of transition' (*Ensuring Effective Transitions*, HMIE, 2006). He refers particularly to the transition from pre-school to Primary 1.

> **Activity**
>
> Design a transition document that would cover all areas of the curriculum based on the subject areas in Curriculum for Excellence or the key aspects in *A Curriculum Framework for Children 3 to 5*.

How Curriculum for Excellence facilitates transition

Part of the rationale for Curriculum for Excellence was to address what was seen as 'an abrupt transition for children which can prove damaging for some children's confidence and progress' *A Curriculum for Excellence: Building the Curriculum 2 – Active Learning in the Early Years*.

The new curriculum unites the pre-school year and Primary 1 into one new 'early' stage in which children will be working towards the same outcomes of learning within one level and will of course be developing the four capacities to become:

- successful learners
- confident individuals
- responsible citizens
- effective contributors.

The blending of pre-school with Primary 1 and the promotion of active learning through play in the new early stage will give young children a continuous educational experience, free from stress.

Here are some examples of supporting transitions in the 'early' stage:

- children and staff from nursery and Primary 1 working together to plan an early years garden
- older nursery children and Primary 1 children playing together with structured play materials in an 'active learning room'

- pre-school children accompanied by a member of nursery staff spending time in Primary 1 in May and June.

The 5–14 Curriculum

Before the introduction of Curriculum for Excellence, 5–14 Curriculum was the dominant curriculum in Scotland for children in their primary school years and in the first two years of secondary school. There have been revisions to 5–14 Curriculum in response to societal changes and changes in the use of technology.

5–14 Curriculum has six main subject areas (English Language, Mathematics, Environmental Studies, Expressive Arts, Religious and Moral Education with Personal and Social Development and Health Education) and shares some of the principles of Curriculum for Excellence.

Where is play in the 5–14 Curriculum?

There was no mention of play in 5–14 Curriculum guidelines and this caused play to diminish in importance, even in the early stages of primary school. It was therefore difficult for children to adjust to a very different style of education when moving from nursery to Primary 1. Children often found it difficult to cope with whole class teaching methods and lengthy, sedentary sessions devoted to literacy or numeracy.

How the curriculum supports the work of the practitioner in child-centred planning

A Curriculum Framework for Children 3 to 5 supports the work of the practitioner by giving many illustrative examples of how adults can provide worthwhile and relevant learning for the children by following a child-centred or learner-centred approach to planning.

Further research

Consult *The Structure and Balance of the Curriculum: 5–14 National Guidelines* (Scottish Executive, 2000) to learn how it differs from Curriculum for Excellence.

Key terms

Child-centred approach and **learner-centred approach** are approaches to the curriculum that begin with the child or the learner and place the learner at the centre of curricular planning. This means that the curriculum is flexible and adaptable according to the changing interests of the children.

How does a child-centred or learner-centred approach work in practice?

It is essential that practitioners observe children carefully to identify their interests, needs, aptitudes and stages of development. This allows for provision of appropriate resources in the play area.

Sometimes *physical* resources may be required, such as floor space or large pieces of equipment; sometimes the need will be for *material* resources, which are smaller pieces of equipment, sometimes the need is for *human* resources – an adult or other children whose involvement can take the play and learning forward.

A Curriculum Framework for Children 3 to 5 offers many examples of responsive child-centred planning and sensitive resourcing. The example from practice on page 33, where the children have been interested in dancing, gives a good illustration of how the appropriate resources allow the children to take their learning forward. Initially the children have adequate space to work and large blocks with which to build a stage (physical resources). In response to the children's continuing interest in dancing and performing, the adults provide fabric and a variety of music and the children are taken to the library to find books about dancing (material resources). To further encourage the children's interest and expertise in dancing, a parent who is a dancing teacher is invited into the nursery to teach some dance steps (human resources). In this way, the adult provides a natural and relevant extension to the children's experience within the key aspect of expressive and aesthetic development. You can see that the children are helped to make progress and to broaden their understanding of music and movement.

A Curriculum Framework for Children 3 to 5 and Curriculum for Excellence support the work of the practitioner by offering a structure and terminology to assist planning. By using the structure and terminology of the curriculum, practitioners can engage in planning that is clear and efficient. This is immensely helpful to staff as planning meetings take place when the children have left the nursery and time is often limited.

The key aspects and features of learning are useful tools for evaluating your observations of the children's learning and interests *today* and for building on these interests to extend the children's learning *tomorrow*. By referring to the curriculum, you can evaluate the effectiveness of the resources and interactions you gave the children and this allows you to answer the question 'How successful is our curriculum today?' Section 3 of *A Curriculum Framework for Children 3 to 5* describes staff responsibilities and planning.

No adult can observe all the activity in a busy nursery and no member of staff has a monopoly on good ideas to extend the curriculum. Staff need to share information with colleagues and they benefit from the opportunity to bounce ideas off one another and work collaboratively to devise effective curricular experiences. This team-based approach ensures a varied curriculum to which everyone has contributed as well as a shared responsibility for its success.

Case study *Opportunities for learning*

Some of the children have been playing with the nursery bikes and they have been heard chatting about different sizes of wheels. Other groups of children have been playing at the traffic mat on the floor, choosing and talking about different types of toy car as they move them around on the mat. At the art area, children have been using various objects to make printed patterns and some children have been painting with small rollers.

Working together, the staff analyse their observations. They use the curriculum framework to identify a number of features of learning from the following key aspects:

- communication and language
- knowledge and understanding of the world
- physical development and movement.

They also see opportunities in their planned provision to develop each of the four capacities in Curriculum for Excellence.

Melanie, the centre manager, says: 'It would be good if we could take as much of the curriculum as possible out into the garden now that the weather looks settled for a few days.'

After some discussion, the manager enters the features of learning that the children will gain into the planning sheet and indicates where the four capacities might be developed. Staff responsibilities for supporting play are also indicated.

Next day, the staff set out a variety of equipment in the garden. There is a climbing frame, a large sand tray with spades and buckets, a water tray, a basin and a clothes stand with plastic aprons that the children can use when playing at the water. There are three boxes of pine cones of different sizes, a number of magnifying glasses, some paper, paint and paint brushes. Sandy places some car tyres quite close to the bikes. His colleague Natasha and the HNC student, Laura, are all in the garden with him to observe, supervise and support the play.

At the car wash

The children come and go freely and play actively and purposefully with all the equipment. Some children wash the bikes and the tyres with water from the water tray. There is conversation about 'clean cars and dirty cars' and 'queues of cars waiting to be washed'. The tyres then make marks when moved across the ground and the children notice this with interest.

Some children play at 'garages' and ask Janine to bring her car in to 'get it mended'.

Luckily this possibility was discussed at the planning meeting the previous day and Natasha is well prepared for a conversation with the children about cars that might need to be repaired.

There is a lot of interest in examining the pine cones with the magnifying glasses and two children take a magnifying glass each to look closely at the bark of the trees growing in the area. Three children working together decide to paint some of the cones. One child presses her cone down gently on to paper and is pleased with the print that results.

At all times, practitioners are ready to become involved with the children's play.

That evening the team evaluate the day and are able to identify a number of features of learning that the children have gained, as well as clear evidence that the four capacities were being developed. They go home feeling very pleased that they have provided a high quality curriculum for the children that day.

1 Analyse and evaluate the curriculum that day. Identify the likely features of learning experienced by the children from the three main key aspects that the staff had planned for.

2 Indicate how the children might be developing the four capacities in Curriculum for Excellence.

3 *A Curriculum Framework for Children 3 to 5* emphasises that the adults have a vital role in supporting children's play. Analyse and evaluate the ways in which you think the adults have carried out their role.

Planning across different timescales

Clearly there are longer-term plans which take account of the seasons, major cultural festivals, educational initiatives and events in the local community. Children observe and pay attention to seasonal changes and this forms an important part of the Science curriculum and knowledge and understanding of the world.

Many settings will follow a year-long plan that includes experiences relating to festivals such as Christmas, Eid, Hannukah and Diwali. St Andrew's Day may provide a focus for some curricular development as might Shrove Tuesday (Pancake Day), Hallowe'en or Mother's Day. National book and poetry days may be included in the plan as a focus for extra attention to literature within the curriculum.

Early education and childcare teams are usually expert in achieving a balance between short- and long-term planning. It is also important to plan for babies and toddlers where the planning may be focused on developmental milestones for individual children rather than on group aims.

The Birth to Three guidelines

The word curriculum with its overtones of subjects and content areas is rarely mentioned in *Birth to Three: supporting our youngest children*. This important document is intended as 'valuable guidance for all those involved in caring for babies or very young children'. As Andreski and Nicholls (*Managing Your Nursery*, 1996) note:

Case study Adapting plans in response to the Scottish weather

Good planning and preparation is never wasted.

Easter was approaching and the signs of spring were apparent in the nursery garden. The children had been showing interest in the flowers that were beginning to bloom. The team had been involved in discussions with children about the colours that were visible in the garden including the pink of some early cherry blossom, the yellow of the daffodils and the purple of the crocuses. The idea of a spring frieze made by the children had been written in to the year plan and the time seemed right to resource the art area with large pieces of green frieze paper and pots of paint in the appropriate colours.

Overnight there was a sudden change in the weather and the children arrived at nursery having walked through the snow. Some children had not seen snow before and there was huge excitement. There was little interest in the art area and the staff supported the children in their play and exploration of the snow. One of the practitioners, Jamie, replaced the green frieze paper with grey sugar paper and filled some tubs with thick, white paint. The tubs of pink, yellow, and purple paint were carefully covered with lids so that the paint remained fresh.

When the children became too cold outside, they were encouraged to come in. Throughout the day, many children visited the art area and made paintings of snow scenes. Some children wanted to take their paintings home at the end of the day to show their families how they had played in the snow. Other children chose to hang their snowy paintings on the wall.

By the next day the weather had changed again. The temperature rose, the snow melted and when the children were in the garden, they noticed that the spring flowers were still there. The colourful paints and green frieze paper were back on the art table and a number of children made flower paintings.

There was much interesting discussion with the adults about how it was warmer today and colder yesterday. The flower paintings were displayed next to the snow paintings and interesting comparisons were made. Knowledge and understanding of the world was extended as the children became aware that the flowers had been under the snow and that they were still growing. Awareness of time and the language for discussing it was reinforced through the use of the words, 'yesterday', 'today' and – as the children and adults speculated about the weather – 'tomorrow'.

1 In what ways does the longer-term planning support the immediate child-centred planning?

2 How did the children benefit from the approaches to planning used by the adults?

3 As curricular planners, what useful characteristics did the staff display?

Curriculum might seem a rather grandiose word and its application to children before their first birthday, somewhat pretentious. However as it simply means the activities and experiences which we plan and that children initiate for themselves, it is perfectly reasonable to consider it in relationship to babies.

The list of practitioners who may benefit from the guidance in this document includes practitioners and students preparing to work in early education and childcare settings.

The connection with curricular thinking is made clear in the foreword, which states that *Birth to Three: supporting our youngest children* 'acts as a foundation for a child's future learning and development', taken forward in *A Curriculum Framework for Children 3 to 5*. Birth to Three prioritises 'emotional personal and social development', indicating clearly to practitioners that it is their major responsibility to promote this. The document then describes how this can be achieved by attention to three 'key features' of practice. These are:

• relationships

• responsive care

• respect.

The document speaks directly to practitioners, asking them to reflect on their own practice with reference to these three key features. It is arranged into six sections. The first refers to research, both national and international, which has emphasised the great significance of early childhood and family life in influencing the development of individual children. Section 1 also spells out the values and principles which underpin its approach and which this document shares with *A Curriculum Framework for Children 3 to 5*.

Section 2 refers in more detail to research into how children learn, reminding us that the period from birth to three years is a time of most rapid development and growth of the brain. Sections 3, 4 and 5 expand the three key features which the document prioritises as being essential if these young children are to achieve a high quality experience.

How these guidelines support the work of the practitioner

Birth to Three: supporting our youngest children aids your work as a practitioner by informing you and encouraging you to reflect on how to be with young children and their families rather than telling you what to do with them. *Birth to Three: supporting our youngest children* is supportive of the practitioner in that it provides a useful list of resources, references and footnotes. The emphasis on sensitivity to the needs of children and their parents helps to ensure a high quality experience for children.

Section 4 describes ways of interacting with children to offer them responsive care. It states: 'Where adults become too focused on adult-led activities and tasks they may be in danger of forgetting about the individual child' and: 'Playful interactions during routines and simple turn-taking also serve as a means of learning and bonding for babies and young children' (*Birth to Three: supporting our youngest children*).

Case study *More hurry, less quality care!*

Ruaridh has completed his HNC course in Early Education and Childcare. He has gained his first job in a nursery working in the room with children aged 18 months to 3 years. The manager in this room, Anita, has been very supportive of Ruaridh and he feels he has learned a great deal from her. In particular she has emphasised the importance of a calm relaxed atmosphere and the need for every child to be treated as an individual.

One morning Ruaridh arrives to be told that Anita has broken her ankle and will be off work for a few weeks. They are just getting used to this news when Veronica, one of the other practitioners, calls to say that she can't come into work because she has a sore throat. The nursery head telephones one of the staffing agencies and by 9.30 am there are two replacement staff members, one who will act as room manager and one who will be a nursery assistant as she has not completed her training.

Ruaridh is sitting on the floor interacting with three children who are playing with cars when the new room manager comes up briskly but kindly and says, 'I'll take this one for handwashing now. It's nearly snack time. Will you get the other two ready for snack?'

Ruaridh says, 'Well, we usually let the children have a drink and something to eat when they let us know they're ready.'

'Oh, I think it's better if we all have snack together,' says the room manager, 'and we have to be sure the children learn good hygiene habits.' She picks up one of the children, saying, 'Put down your car and let's get your hands washed.' The child is leaning backwards looking at the others as he is taken away.

The other two children stop playing and look at Rhuaridh, who asks, 'Do you want your snack just now?' Before the children answer, the manager's voice can be heard calling, 'Come on, everybody, time for snack!'

Later in the morning, Ruaridh opens the French doors to the garden and fastens them back safely. He usually observes the children and as soon as they start to head for outside, he has a chat with them and helps them put on outdoor clothes. The temporary manager comes up quickly and says, 'Right, children, I'll get you into your boots and anoraks. Who's first?' She quickly and efficiently gets arms into sleeves, zips fastened, feet into boots, occasionally saying, 'That's right' or 'Out you go. Everybody out into the garden. Quick, before it rains!'

The children find themselves outside in the garden and Ruaridh is thinking about the rhyme they usually say with the children when helping them to get dressed. 'Tug, tug, tug your boot. Make sure it's really on your foot.' The rain does come on and the children are soon ushered inside by the manager and the nursery assistant, Sonya. The sun comes out later and there is a beautiful rainbow in the sky. Ruaridh is standing with two of the children talking about the lovely rainbow and the puddles outside when the manager calls across the room loudly and cheerfully, 'Come on, Ruaridh, make yourself useful and help get the lunches ready. Sonya and I will do the handwashing!'

At the end of the day there is a brief planning meeting. The new manager thinks they should change some of the equipment in the room because 'some of the children have played with the same things all day'. Ruaridh feels uneasy about the way the day has gone and says so. 'What do you mean?' asks the manager. 'We've got to use the opportunity to get set up for tomorrow.'

'I think we need to talk about the opportunities we've missed today,' says Ruaridh. 'We usually talk about our observations of the children at the meeting and we often use "Birth to Three" to help us. I'll get us all a coffee and then we can have a chat.'

'Oh,' says the manager, 'I've seen that in a few nurseries but I've never really read it.'

'Pages 26 and 27 are *really* interesting,' says Ruaridh.

1. Analyse and evaluate what happened that day with reference to the quotations from the Birth to Three document at the start of the case study.

2. What opportunities were missed for supporting the children's learning and development that day?

3. Explain why Ruaridh felt uneasy that day.

How does *Birth to Three: supporting our youngest children* help maintain high quality care for children?

Birth to Three: supporting our youngest children describes the quality of sensitive care that young children must have. Children of this age are not always able to express their wishes or preferences clearly. The document places this important responsibility on the shoulders of those who work with young children. It emphasises the need for developmentally appropriate care and makes the point that practitioners cannot make a distinction between care and education.

Activity

Design a chart for new trainee members of staff to help them understand that every care situation is an opportunity to develop the children's emotional, personal and social development and to develop their learning. An example is shown below.

Routine task	Make it fun – build in some learning
Nappy changing	Play 'This little piggie' with the baby's toes. Talk to baby about the mobile above the changing table.
Handwashing	
Setting the table for lunch	
Helping children get coats and boots on	
Toothbrushing after lunch	

Case study *Tuning in to baby*

Miryam is a student on the HNC course in Early Education and Childcare. She is delighted to have been given a student placement in a private nursery where she has the opportunity to work with babies from 9 months to 2 years. She enjoys spending time with the babies and loves to see how they respond when she sings with them, plays with them, carries them round to look out of the windows and takes them for short walks in the garden. She is observant and one day notices Simon touching a soft fluffy chicken toy by stroking it backwards and forwards on his cheek. Later she notices him crawling towards the brick area where there is a wide selection of wooden blocks in various sizes. Simon sits in the area picking up bricks and feeling them with his hands. He touches his leg with one of the bricks and then bangs two bricks together, then puts some bricks into a small box, tips them out, puts two bricks back into the box, picks the box up, shakes it, laughs, shakes it again and looks around the room. Miryam catches his eye, smiles, and Simon smiles to her. Miryam sits down on the floor beside Simon and he passes her a brick. She puts it in the box and rattles it. Simon puts a brick in the box and shakes it. He laughs at the noise. He then tips the bricks out and looks at Miryam. She picks the box up. She shakes it. She holds the box up to her ear and says, 'Oh, no noise!' Simon puts a brick in and looks at Miryam. She smiles, shakes the box and says, 'It rattles!' Simon puts another brick into the box and shakes it. He vocalises the sound, saying 'Aht aht.'

They carry on playing in this way until Simon begins to rub his eyes then starts to whimper slightly. Miryam says, 'I think you're a little bit tired, Simon.' She holds her arms out to Simon and he reaches out to her. She picks him up and walks slowly down towards the quiet area where the babies' cots are placed. Simon lays his head against Miryam's shoulder and makes small noises with his mouth. Miryam notices that he feels quite warm. 'Would you like a drink, Simon?' she asks.

'Mmmm, mmmmm,' Simon seems to answer. Miryam carries Simon down to the food preparation area where she finds Simon's own cup and fills it with cooled boiled water. As she hands Simon his cup she sings, 'Do you know what I think? Simon really wants a drink' (to the tune of 'Twinkle twinkle little star'). She sits quietly with him while he enjoys his drink. He still seems sleepy and so Miryam takes him to his cot and tucks him in gently with his own teddy.

Miryam waits near the sleep area to make sure Simon settles and then writes in his record sheet that he has had a drink of water and has lain down to sleep at 2.30 pm. At 5 pm Simon's father comes to collect him. 'How's he been today?' he asks. The room supervisor smiles and says, 'Miryam, our student, has been working with Simon today.' Miryam tells Simon's dad about the game they played and how Simon had a drink and a sleep. 'He really enjoyed playing with the bricks and rattling them in the box.'

Simon and his dad leave and Miryam says, 'Bye, bye, Simon. See you tomorrow.'

Evaluate this case study with reference to the following:

1   What evidence can you see here that the importance of *relationships* is observed?

2   Where do you see evidence of *responsive care*?

3   Where do you see evidence of *respect* for individuals?

4   Where is there evidence that Miryam is 'tuned in' to Simon?

These all indicate a high quality curriculum for children in the age range birth to 3 years.

Make the connection with Chapter 3 and HNC Unit DF52 34: Theoretical approaches to development and learning. Aim to analyse and evaluate Miryam's interactions with Simon with reference to the work of Colwyn Trevarthen Professor (Emeritus) of Child Psychology and Psychobiology at the University of Edinburgh and a leading researcher in the field of infant–parent communication.

Birth to Three: supporting our youngest children insists on the importance of play as a most valued and natural way for children to learn. It states that 'play is a very powerful tool that promotes children's development and learning'. At this point we can see the connection with *A Curriculum Framework for Children 3 to 5* and the effort to maintain continuity in high quality care and education.

Young children need plenty of opportunities to engage in exploratory play. There should be appropriate play materials available to the children, such as sand, water, play dough and paint. These materials all allow for exploration using the senses and the children will benefit from these opportunities. For these youngest children, the document makes some very important points about play, as follows:

- Babies and young children often benefit most from being able to concentrate on something in depth, rather than being surrounded by many different objects and choices.

- Children like to return to and revisit things that were important to them that morning, the day before, or the previous week.

One particular kind of play of an intensely exploratory nature is treasure basket play. This is also known as heuristic play, which means play that allows the making of discoveries and is based on the work of Elinor Goldschmied. Treasure basket play should happen in a quiet, calm environment free from other distractions. Some settings are so convinced of the value of treasure basket play that they have set aside a special room for this purpose.

Key term

Heuristic play is play that allows children to make discoveries by using their senses to investigate and explore objects.

The idea of treasure basket play is that babies should be given the time to explore the contents of the treasure basket using their senses. Their basket should contain an array of interesting objects. These are usually made from natural materials and can include found objects and everyday objects rather than toys. For example, a treasure basket might contain a sponge, a smooth wooden carving, empty tins of different sizes with rounded rims, no sharp edges, some cotton reels, some pieces of string of different thickness, a pine cone, some plastic bangles, a piece of chain such as a security chain, a hard ball, a soft ball, a small bell, a piece of velvet material, a wooden spoon, a colourful piece of cellophane paper, a plastic tub. Clearly all these materials need to be scrupulously clean and carefully checked with the children's safety in mind.

The children are given time to explore the contents of the basket and they can make discoveries about size, shape and texture. They can find out which objects can fit inside others. They can discover the difference between hard and soft objects.

Activity

1   Make the connection with Chapter 3 and HNC Unit DF52 34: Theoretical approaches to development and learning. Think about the value of treasure basket play with reference to the theories of Piaget.

2   Describe how play with a treasure basket would allow children in the sensori-motor stage of development to construct their understanding of the world.

Making discoveries through treasure basket play

To facilitate treasure basket play, the practitioner needs to provide the materials, carry out all safety checks, ensure that there is sufficient space and time for the activity and ensure that babies are accompanied by a member of staff who knows them well and with whom they feel secure and relaxed. The adult should be quiet and still, ready to reassure the babies if necessary and always watchful of safety. This is an ideal opportunity to observe babies and it may be a good way to involve parents in the nursery community if they are free to do so; they might enjoy observing quietly while their children play in this way.

The nursery team have just introduced the idea of treasure basket/heuristic play into the nursery and they have been pleased by how well it has been going. They have set aside a small attractive room and have collected an impressive range of objects which they have organised into five baskets. They have used their key worker system and from time to time each key worker takes two key children through to the heuristic play room. Some of the parents have asked about the new room when they have been dropping off or collecting their children, but these times are very busy and the parents are often in a hurry. As a result there really has not been time for explanations.

One morning, one of the mothers, who is usually very rushed, approaches Marie and says: 'Can I speak to you for a moment?' 'Of course,' answers the supervisor. She is very surprised when the mother goes on to say that she is really disappointed to hear that the babies have been playing with 'baskets of junk' instead of 'proper toys'. The mother says she doesn't think this is right, especially as the fees for the nursery are quite high!

Marie tries to explain about the value of treasure basket play but the mother doesn't have time to concentrate as she is running late for work. Mary recognises that things should have been handled better.

1 Analyse and evaluate what has gone wrong here. Read page 16 of *Birth to Three: supporting our youngest children* to help your thinking.

2 Marie and her team need to find a way of explaining heuristic play to the parents. What are the main points to include in the explanation?

3 What method of communicating with parents should they use?

4 Design a leaflet to inform parents about the use and value of heuristic play.

Influences on the changing curriculum

The recent introduction of Curriculum for Excellence is an example of change in response to a number of different influencing factors.

The effect of political and social influence is clear on the increased focus on health and well-being. This reflects awareness that the health issues of concern in the Scottish population need to be addressed early in an individual's life. Knowledge of the human body and awareness of what constitutes a healthy lifestyle will allow people to make informed choices about their own health.

Economic, technological and scientific factors have also influenced the formulation of the new curriculum to raise the profile of science at all levels. As stated in the paper *A Curriculum for Excellence: Progress and Proposals* (Scottish Executive, 2006), this is to 'enable young people to develop as scientifically literate citizens, able to hold and defend informed views' on issues related to science. This is seen as good preparation for 'future lives and careers in the 21st century'.

Global issues such as sustainability and biodiversity have shaped the content of the science curriculum. Many nurseries are working towards raised environmental awareness by including such activities as recycling, gardening and composting in the curriculum.

Legislation is a significant influence on the curriculum

The Education (Scotland) Act (2000) confirms the position of children as active participants in their educational experience by stating that 'due regard, so far as is reasonably practicable should be paid to the views of the child or young person in decisions that significantly affect them, taking account of the young person's age and maturity' (cited in *A Curriculum for Excellence*, Curriculum Review Group, 2004). Care and education settings are responding to this by building into the curriculum opportunities for children to participate actively, make choices and express preferences.

The move towards increased participation is in keeping with the four capacities in Curriculum for Excellence. In particular, the capacity to be a responsible citizen mentions as desirable characteristics 'commitment to participate responsibly in political, economic, social and cultural life' and the ability to 'make informed choices and decisions' (*A Curriculum for Excellence: Building the Curriculum 2 – Active Learning in the Early Years*. Children can be helped to develop these dispositions from a young age.

European influences on the curriculum in Scotland

The effort to increase levels of participation reflects influences from outside Scotland. Scotland is a member of the childcare and education community in Europe and is open to influences from European countries, particularly the Scandinavian countries where children's participation is at an advanced stage.

The Danish curriculum also encourages as much learning as possible to take place out of doors and in forest schools. In Scotland this has led to an interest in the establishment of forest kindergartens, where the potential to develop independence, self-reliance and enjoyment of nature is widely recognised. Many Scottish nurseries are developing this aspect of the curriculum. Children are taken out to woodland areas where possible, the outdoor environment surrounding nurseries has been adapted and greater use is being made of urban natural spaces.

The pre-schools of Reggio Emilia in northern Italy have influenced the curriculum. In Reggio the curriculum is based on a view of children as highly competent and talented. The practitioners in Reggio value all the arts as expressive languages and encourage children to take their own learning forward by using their investigative, expressive and cooperative abilities. The learning is often shaped by long-term projects where children follow their interests, related to a particular theme such as 'Our City'. The school buildings are important as they contain ample studio space where children's artistic and investigative efforts can be freely pursued. The practice in Reggio has encouraged many nurseries in Scotland to increase the time and space available for creative and investigative learning with a wide range of materials.

Increased attention to creativity in the curriculum may be given further impetus if the Culture (Scotland) Bill, first published in 2006, becomes law. This bill proposes cultural entitlements for children, particularly in rural areas.

The curriculum in Scotland is also influenced by the ongoing communication with colleagues in England, Wales and Northern Ireland.

The influence of educational figures from the past on the curriculum in Scotland

In the early nineteenth century, Robert Owen set up his school for the children of mill workers at New Lanark, providing a workplace nursery, often seen as a modern idea.

Friedrich Froebel (1782–1852) pioneered the view that play is important in the development of children when he wrote that 'Play is the highest expression of human development in childhood' (www.froebelweb.org). The influence of Froebel's thinking is acknowledged by many practitioners and current play theorists, notably Tina Bruce.

Rudolf Steiner (1861–1925) and Maria Montessori (1870–1952) are pioneers of early education whose influence on the curriculum is very evident.

The Montessori approach is based on a view that children are active learners motivated by their curiosity. Montessori education acknowledges that children progress developmentally through stages of thinking and that children do this at their own pace. This curriculum respects children and believes in fostering learning through freely chosen play with well-constructed materials. These are designed to help the children develop conceptual understanding through using their senses. Montessori practitioners lay great importance on a carefully and attractively prepared environment with rich opportunities for independent learning. Another prime role of the Montessori practitioner is observation in order to judge when to intervene sensitively in the child's play. This will occur only when necessary to move the child's understanding to the next level, perhaps by offering an appropriate piece of equipment.

The Rudolf Steiner approach to the curriculum is concerned with the development of the whole child at the child's own pace. The philosophy of Steiner education proposes that formal teaching should be delayed until children are aged 7 years and that the child's progress should be unhurried through the early stages. In the kindergarten there are familiar daily routines and opportunities for free play within a homely setting. Great value is attached to contact with nature and play with natural materials. Singing, poetry, dance, movement and other modes of creative expression form an important part of the curriculum.

> ### Consider this
> Montessori, Steiner and other European approaches delay the start of formal teaching until children are 6 or 7 years old. The Scottish Commissioner for Children and Young People has included 'Raise the compulsory school age to six or seven years' as point five on a recent wish list. What do you think?

Montessori, Steiner and European approaches have contributed to the introduction of an integrated early stage in Curriculum for Excellence, extending the period during which children learn through active play.

The High Scope approach, which originated in the United States in the 1960s, has exerted an influence on the early education curriculum. Children in a High Scope setting are encouraged to plan what they wish to do, including what resources they might need. They then have a period in which they implement their idea, perhaps making a model or painting a picture. The group come together later in the session to discuss what they have achieved. This is known as 'Plan-Do-Review'. High Scope practitioners often employ direct, very interactive approaches with children.

High Scope, Steiner and Montessori education are all international organisations with a worldwide network of schools and support for their practitioners. You may encounter these curriculum models or their influence as you work in early education settings.

Playwork

Playwork is an approach to working with children that is growing in significance in Scotland. Playwork practitioners are involved with a wider age range of children than the early education and childcare practitioner, and playwork has its own body of theory. As the name for the profession implies, playworkers work with children to support play and they share with early education and childcare practitioners a conviction that play is of immense value in children's development.

Playwork happens in many different settings, often outdoors in free and informal spaces. Sometimes playworkers are involved with children in out-of-school and after-school clubs. Although playwork does not have a written curriculum, the practitioners are guided by similar principles and values to those that underpin early years practice. These include children's right to have choice and control and the requirement to develop independence, self-esteem and respect for others.

One of the key objectives of playwork is to foster 'the child's well-being, healthy growth and development, knowledge and understanding, creativity and capacity to learn' *Best Play. What play provision should do for children*, National Playing Fields Association, 2000.

Values and principles in the curriculum

The curriculum in Scotland in all its forms is shaped by a number of values and principles. These maintain high quality care and education for children and also support the work of the practitioner by setting standards that you always try to achieve in your work with children.

Respect for the individual is fundamental and every curriculum recognises that young learners are unique in their interests and aptitudes as well as the rates at which they develop. Concern for the individuality of the learner leads to learning and teaching approaches that offer 'the right blend and balance for each young person for their particular stage and circumstances' (*A Curriculum for Excellence: Building the Curriculum 2 – Active Learning in the Early Years*).

Both *A Curriculum Framework for Children 3 to 5* and *Birth to Three: supporting our youngest children* value 'the individual child' and 'the best interests of children', while *The Structure and Balance of the Curriculum: 5–14 National Guidelines* refers to individual children's 'preferred learning styles'.

As well as the young person's individuality, *respect for the child's family* is an important guiding principle in the curriculum. Curriculum for Excellence describes parents as 'the first and most influential educators of their children' and recognises the importance of 'the interests and experiences children bring from home' (*A Curriculum for Excellence: Building the Curriculum 2 – Active Learning in the Early Years*). This reminds practitioners of the necessity to work with parents and families at all times and of the positive effects on children's care and education when this is achieved. *A Curriculum Framework for Children 3 to 5* and *Birth to Three: supporting our youngest children* both emphasise the requirement for sensitive approaches to working in partnership with parents and carers, bearing in mind that families vary a great deal in structure and culture.

Consider this

Make the connection with Chapter 9 and HNC Unit DF56 34: Contemporary issues for children and families. Consider what you have learned about family diversity.

What factors within staff teams or families might be a barrier to effective partnerships?

Successful partnerships between practitioners and families require effective two-way communication and collaboration. This means that practitioners and families must be open in communicating and listening to each other, resulting in real benefits for the children.

Parents can pass on valuable information about their children and practitioners can convey detail about the curriculum and what they hope to achieve with the children in the setting. This increases the likelihood of a beneficial continuity between the life of the setting and life at home.

The right of parents and carers to be involved and informed is paramount. The important contribution that they have to make in the care and education of their children has been formally recognised in the Scottish Schools (Parental Involvement) Act (2006).

Children belong to families that differ in ethnic origin, cultural customs and religious beliefs. The recognition and celebration of

The principle of inclusiveness ensures that all children are welcome in the setting

this diversity is supported by the principles of *inclusiveness* and *equality of opportunity*, which are of prime importance in the curriculum.

The principle of inclusiveness ensures that all children are welcome, valued in the setting and feel part of the nursery or school community. This means that curriculum design must include experiences to develop awareness and celebrate aspects of different cultures. *A Curriculum Framework for Children 3 to 5* clearly upholds this principle when it states that: 'Children's self-image is enhanced when their cultural heritage, gender, beliefs and lifestyles of their families are respected (and) acknowledged.'

The principle of equality of opportunity supports the right of every child to access the curriculum and the opportunities for learning and development that it offers. This is a right for all children regardless of ability, gender or cultural heritage. This reminds you of your responsibility to adapt the curriculum where necessary to ensure that it is accessible to all children in your care.

The practitioner's commitment to equality of opportunity and the other values and principles will meet the aims of Curriculum for Excellence and ensure that the early years setting is a place where 'every child matters, where every child, regardless of his or her family background, has the best start in life' (*Vision for Children and Young People*, Scottish Executive; quoted in *A Curriculum for Excellence: Building the Curriculum 2 – Active Learning in the Early Years*).

Check your progress

1 Describe what is meant by 'curriculum' in general terms with reference to the curriculum in Scotland.

2 Consider Curriculum for Excellence, *A Curriculum Framework for Children 3 to 5* and *Birth to Three: supporting our youngest children*. How does each curriculum uphold the quality of education and care for children?

3 Describe how Curriculum for Excellence would help you to plan experiences for children.

4 How would *A Curriculum Framework for Children 3 to 5* help you to plan experiences for children?

5 Describe where you see similarities between Curriculum for Excellence and *A Curriculum Framework for Children 3 to 5* with reference to personal, emotional and social development.

6 Discuss two ways in which the early stage in Curriculum for Excellence is of great importance.

7 Give three reasons why play is the best way for young children to learn.

8 Describe two ways in which you might use observation to support children.

9 Describe two current and two earlier influences on the curriculum in Scotland.

10 Why are values and principles important in early years practice? Discuss this with reference to two of them.

References

Andreski, R. and Nicholls, S. (1996) *Managing Your Nursery*, London: Nursery World

Brown, F. (ed.) (2003) *Playwork: Theory and Practice*, Buckingham, Philadelphia: Open University

Bruce, T. (2004) *Developing Learning in Early Childhood*, London: Paul Chapman

Bryce, T.G.K. and Humes, W.M. (eds) (2003) *Scottish Education Post Devolution*, 2nd edn, Edinburgh: Edinburgh University Press

Children in Scotland, Issue 70 (April 2007)

City of Edinburgh Council (2000) *Birth to Three: Framework for Practitioners*, Edinburgh

Curriculum Review Group (2004) *A Curriculum for Excellence*, Edinburgh: Scottish Executive

Drummond M.J., Rouse, D. and Pugh, G. (1992) *Making Assessment Work*, London: National Children's Bureau, N.E.S. Arnold

Fidler, W. (2006) Montessori Education Supplement, *Early Years Education*, Volume 7 Issue 9.

HM Inspectorate of Education (2006) *Ensuring Effective Transitions*, Livingston: HMIE

Lindon, J. (2007) *Understanding Child Development*, London: Hodder Arnold

Macintyre, C. and Mcvitty, K. (2003) *Planning in the Pre-5 Setting*, London: David Fulton.

National Playing Fields Association (2000) *Best Play. What play provision should do for children*, London

Scottish Executive (2007) *Assessment is for Learning*, Newsletter No. 10

Learning and Teaching Scotland (2005) *Birth to Three: supporting our youngest children*, Dundee

Scottish Executive (2007) *A Curriculum for Excellence: Building the Curriculum 2 – Active Learning in the Early Years*, Edinburgh

Scottish Executive (2006) *A Curriculum for Excellence: Progress and Proposals*, paper from the Curriculum Review Programme Board

Learning and Teaching Scotland (1999) *A Curriculum Framework for Children 3 to 5*, Dundee

Scottish Executive (2000) *The Structure and Balance of the Curriculum: 5–14 National Guidelines*, Dundee

Valentine, M. (1999) *The Reggio Emilia Approach to Early Years Education*, Glasgow: Learning and Teaching Scotland

Watt, J. (ed.) (1994) *Early Education: The Quality Debate*, Edinburgh: Scottish Academic Press

Useful websites

Curriculum for Excellence website: www.curriculumforexcellencescotland.gov.uk

High/Scope Educational Research Foundation: www.highscope.org

Freedom in Education website on Rudolf Steiner: www.freedom-in-education.co.uk/Steiner.htm

Froebel Web, an online resource about Friedrich Froebel: www.froebelweb.org

Learning and Teaching Scotland: www.LTScotland.org.uk

Website about Robert Owen: www.robert-owen.com/quotes.htm

Website about treasure baskets: www.surestart.gov.uk/-doc/P0000207.pdf

Website on the work of Colwyn Trevarthen: www.perception-in-action.ed.ac.uk/PDF-s/colwyn2004.pdf

Chapter 5
Promoting language, literacy and numeracy

Introduction

You may wonder why language, literacy and numeracy are being studied together in this unit. The answer is a simple one: the earlier stages of becoming literate are very similar to the corresponding stages of numeracy development. They both involve the understanding and use of symbols, and children develop much of their early understanding of the processes within the context of their own families and early play experiences. Understanding of mathematical terms and concepts is strongly related to an understanding of language.

Reading and writing are essential requirements for participating fully in our society and culture. Failure to achieve these skills can severely limit an individual's opportunities in life.

As an early education and childcare practitioner, you will have responsibility for motivating children to make the huge effort involved in becoming literate. Your support and input will be vital to their chances of achieving this.

In this chapter you will learn about:

- The development of language
- The development of literacy
- The development of numeracy
- Children's language, literacy and numeracy development through self-directed play
- The importance of working in partnership with the family to develop children's language, literacy and numeracy

The development of language

Language – receptive, expressive and written – is part of communication, and as such is one of the most important human processes. How can we define language? Probably one of the most crucial aspects is that it is something which is not shared by any other species. Although some would argue that certain animals use language, what other species participate in is merely communication.

What makes human language unique? It involves communication by means of symbols, written or spoken, which have to be learned.

Key term

A **symbol** is something which can stand for something else. Words are symbols which are used consistently to represent actual objects, actions, feelings and so on.

Communication through language is dependent on shared understanding. For example, the word 'table' would be understood by all those speaking English. Written words are symbols which represent spoken language.

The following are some of the features of language.

- It is bound by rules – generally, speakers know these rules even though they may not be able to state what they are.

- It is highly creative and open-ended – we are continually forming and understanding sentences which we have never encountered before.

- It enables us to communicate about events which are past, present and in the future. We discuss ideas, memories, feelings, beliefs and so on – things which are abstract or invisible, as well as things which are concrete or visible.

(Adapted from *Language and Literacy in the Early Years*, 3rd edn, M. Whitehead, 2004.)

Consider this

If you apply the above characteristics to the ways in which animals communicate, can you argue that they truly use language? Explain your answer.

Activity

Investigate the communication systems employed by the following animals:

- honey bees
- dolphins
- gelada baboons.

Find out:

1. to what extent each particular system is similar to language

2. what the features are of each system which indicate that it cannot be considered a language.

Nativist approach to language development

The nativist approach to language development assumes that we are all born with an innate ability to learn language. In other words, the brain has been 'hard-wired' to be highly sensitive to language.

In the 1950s the linguist Noam Chomsky (born 1928) put forward the idea of a Language Acquisition Device (LAD), which consists of the parts of the brain associated with language together with the physical characteristics (voice box, tongue, teeth, lips) which allow us to articulate and combine certain sounds to make words. Chomsky stated that the only thing children needed to trigger this pre-programmed ability to learn language was to be born into an environment where language was used. The LAD would allow them to develop a deep understanding of the rules of language, which they would begin to use soon after they became able to utter their first words.

Chomsky's view is supported when you consider the way in which young children use language. It seems clear that they are applying grammatical rules when they make early 'mistakes' with words, for example 'Yesterday I *goed* to the petshop to look at the *mouses*'. How can these mistakes be explained using the nativist view? It would appear that the child has understood the general rule that adding *–ed* to a verb forms the past tense. Similarly, the general rule for forming plurals involves adding *–s* or *–es* to the noun. Unfortunately, English has many exceptions to grammatical rules, so while the child has understood the general rule and applied it appropriately, this is grammatically incorrect. We know that this is not something which adults teach children at this stage in their lives, so it seems as though there is some truth in the notion that language development is innate.

Another example of evidence which would support the nativist view that language development is innate is that the progress of language development appears to follow a similar path in all children, no matter which spoken language environment they are born into. For example, babbling is part of the process of language acquisition and is observed in all babies. The fact that even babies whose hearing is severely impaired or not present also begin to babble (albeit at a slightly later stage) is a strong indicator that this is not learned behaviour. Also, people do not usually instigate interactions with a baby by babbling to them. Therefore, we may conclude that babbling is likely to be an innate process.

However, critics of the nativist theory ask why, if language is innate, it does not develop more quickly, for example as soon as the child develops full control over the voice, at approximately 1 year old?

Behaviourist approach to language development

In 1957, B.F. Skinner (1904–1990) proposed the behaviourist view of how language develops. He said that language development follows the same principle as any form of learning and he rejected the idea that any element of language was inherited or innate. Skinner proposed that the infant's primitive sounds are reinforced by the parent/carer and eventually are shaped into recognisable words. These words then become shaped further into phrases and sentences.

It is clear that certain elements of language development are learned in the way Skinner described. For example, the development of a single-word vocabulary is learned through reinforcement. In addition, how else can we explain accent and dialect? If we return to the emergence of babbling, whilst this is clearly not learned, what is equally clear is that in deaf babies it ceases fairly soon after its onset. This is probably explained by the fact that the baby is not only unable to hear the sounds he or she is making, but also does not experience verbal reinforcement from the parent/carer. This is strong evidence to support the behaviourist theory, at least in part.

Further research

Find out more about the nativist and behaviourist theories of language development.

You are likely to have books containing this information on your particular college's booklist. In addition, you can do an Internet search.

However, the behaviourist theory does not begin to explain the complexities of the process of language development. For example, if language is entirely 'learned', how do you explain the following case study?

Important 'holes' in the behaviourist theory of language development centre mainly around the way in which children combine the words they have learned, firstly into two-word utterances (telegraphic speech) and then into longer and more complex sentences. If this ability to combine words was dependent on reinforcement only, we would never be able to create the consistently original sentences which are part of our everyday interactions.

Social interactionist theories of language development

You read about Bruner and Vygotsky in Chapter 3. They both emphasised:

- the importance of the linguistic environment into which the child is born (it is not sufficient for the child to experience language around him/her as the quality of the interaction is vital)
- the role of the adult
- the existence of inbuilt language structures which are present at and before birth.

The social interactionist view is simply that nativist and behaviourist theories are both valid, in that each *partly* explains how language develops.

Infant-directed speech

In infant-directed speech the adult:

- uses a warm, affectionate tone
- uses a sing-song voice which is pitched higher than usual
- speaks more slowly
- uses a lot of repetition
- uses exaggerated facial expressions.

An important factor to consider is that this way of interacting is not learned; it appears to be instinctive and can be found worldwide, irrespective of language and culture (see, for example, *Baby It's You*, A. Karmiloff-Smith, 1994). From around 2 months, infants can be observed in two-way interactions with caregivers which involve prolonged eye-contact, turn-taking and mirroring of facial and body movements. Trevarthen ('Learning about ourselves from children': why a growing human brain needs interesting companions, 2004) has described these interactions as 'proto-conversations', which he explains as being like 'conversations stripped of words'.

As a result of research into newborn babies, it is known that infants actively respond to and seek human interaction even minutes after birth. Trevarthen ('Learning about ourselves, from children') cites numerous instances of babies being able to imitate facial expressions such as tongue poking, an open mouth and widened eyes.

Babies actively seek interaction

Stages of language development

Spoken language develops along the same lines in all children (with the exception of those experiencing some level of disability which would prevent or interfere with the process). Those of you who have studied child development previously are probably familiar with these stages, although you should revise your knowledge of this from time to time. A good understanding and familiarity with the approximate ages by which children may have achieved the language milestones is important, so that your expectations of children are realistic.

However, ages given in any developmental checklist are not written on tablets of stone. There is usually a timescale during which you might expect a child to have achieved a particular milestone, for example their first recognisable word (any time between 10 and 18 months). This will vary depending on which checklist you consult, and is partly due to a recognition that each child is an individual and development happens at a different pace in each child. Often, children who are a little slower in their language development are noticeably advanced in physical development, particularly their large motor skills.

Numerous research findings have revealed that babies show an 'intentionality' in their behaviour. In other words, they do not just respond to others, they actually invite interaction.

Further research

You may wish to investigate further about early adult–child interactions. The work of the following researchers may be of interest:

- Colwyn Trevarthen
- Daniel Stern
- Lynne Murray
- Alison Gopnik

Case study *Early communication: a two-way process*

Ishbel (aged 3 months) is cared for five days a week in a private nursery, which she attends from 8 am until 6 pm Her key worker, Kamila, has only been working in the baby room for a few weeks; previously she had worked in the pre-school room, which she much preferred.

Ishbel's physical needs are well cared for. Kamila is kind and gentle and happy to give Ishbel lots of cuddles and time, other children permitting. During changing or feeding time, Kamila enjoys the opportunity to chat with colleagues about life outside the nursery. Ishbel used to be quite 'chatty' during these times,

and occasionally Kamila would interrupt her adult conversation to make a comment such as, 'Listen to little Miss Chatterbox!' Just recently, Ishbel has become quieter and more withdrawn. She smiles less, cries more and is apparently less inclined to engage in any interactions in the nursery.

1. Relate this situation to what you have understood about the social interactionist view of language development, especially regarding adult–child interactions.

2. What can Kamila do to improve Ishbel's experience of being in the nursery?

Activity

In 1994, Channel 4 produced a series of six programmes depicting children's development from birth to 3 years. The episode 'Word of Mouth' provides an excellent summary of language acquisition, presented in an engaging and interesting way. The entire series is available on video/DVD, and your college is likely to have access to this.

Watch the episode 'Word of Mouth'. Notes of the main points can be found below.

- Speech allows us to talk about what we are doing and thinking: we can discuss things which are visible/invisible; speech even shapes the way we think.

- At birth, the brain is particularly receptive to speech above all other sounds.

- A child's ability to learn language is greater than that of an adult.

- Learning to speak is a complex task; the child must learn to recognise words, understand their meaning and be able to produce the necessary sounds.

- At 6 weeks, the child is unable to speak because the 'voice box' is not yet in the right position for speech; it is in the correct place to allow the baby to breathe at the same time as feeding, which makes it less likely for the newborn to choke.

- Although the child's anatomy is not yet ready to *produce* speech, hearing is well developed and the brain is ready to *receive* speech.

- At 6 weeks, the infant can already hear all the sounds required for speech in any language – some 150 separate sounds. Adults lose this facility as they focus only on the sounds within their own language.

- Babies are born with the potential to speak any language.

- At around 3½ months, the voice box is in position and the infant begins to gain control of the 100 pairs of muscles in the lips and tongue that will be used in making speech sounds.

- The baby can take part in 'conversations' and responds to the sing-song character of speech sometimes known as 'motherese' (infant-directed speech); this type of speech holds the infant's attention.

- From this stage the child begins to 'babble', which is practice for making more complicated speech sounds.

- Babbling is not learned, it is pre-programmed; all babies do it and at first it sounds the same, no matter what the nationality of the child.

- Gradually, babbling becomes more organised, and sounds not used in the child's first language fade away.

- An English-speaking child makes sounds which sound like English and are interpreted as such by the carers, and in that way they are reinforced.

- The baby begins to use words in a restricted way, for example, he or she may say 'lala' for 'banana' but will only use this 'word' for a banana which is being fed to him or her, and will not use this 'word' for a banana in a picture. This is because the child does not know yet that a word is used for a category of things.

- The child then begins to point to objects, for example, when out shopping; by pointing, the child is asking for the name of the thing.

- Gradually, the infant recognises that all 'things' have a name, which helps the child to organise and classify the world.

- Accurate classification by words develops gradually. For example, the child may call all fruits 'apple' and may know that there is a category of things called apples, but may apply that word to *all* roundish fruits.

- The child learns increasing numbers of 'words' for things; the 'words' may not be said accurately as it is still difficult for the child's tongue, teeth and lips to form the correct sounds, but the child does use the 'words' consistently and understands their meaning.

- The infant begins to combine words in simple, two-word sentences. As with a telegram, words which are not so important are missed out, for example 'Dinna Damie', means 'It's time for Jamie's dinner'.

- Although the child's sentences may not sound like those of an adult, they do show some awareness of the rules of grammar in that the child uses words in much the same order as an adult.

- Around this time, the child may mimic speech just for the sheer pleasure of talking, which also allows the child to become familiar with and analyse phrases and words.

- The infant learns to say 'What's that?', which is an excellent strategy for increasing vocabulary. At this stage, as many as 60 new words are learned per week.

- By around 3 years, the child may be able to use three- or four-word sentences.

(Based on 'Word of Mouth' from the Channel 4 series *Baby It's You* and on the corresponding chapter in the accompanying book *Baby It's You*, Annette Karmiloff-Smith, published by Ebury. Reprinted by permission of The Random House Group Ltd.)

The development of literacy

What do we mean when we talk about literacy? Generally, people recognise literacy as relating to reading and writing. Nowadays, the definition might also include using new technologies, word processing and texting.

Today, it is generally accepted that literacy, in its most basic terms – that is, the ability to read and write – is an emergent process in the child, one which begins at birth and is dependent on a combination of factors. One key factor is the holistic development of the child; in other words, certain processes cannot take place until the child is developmentally ready. For example, mark-making depends on the ability to hold a pencil or crayon and the fine motor control required to manipulate it. In addition, the child needs to be part of an environment which is print-rich, and benefit from sensitive support and appropriate intervention from an adult.

The skills of reading and writing are dependent on the child being able to understand spoken language. As we have mentioned previously, spoken words are *invisible* symbols, whereas written words are *visible* symbols.

A 3-year-old starting nursery will have had experience of seeing both reading and writing in the home. Whitehead (*Developing Language and Literacy with Young Children*, 2007) describes children aged 2 years asking important questions about print, such as 'What does that say?' and 'Will you write my name?' Examples of where children will experience the written word include:

- bedtime stories
- newspapers/comics/magazines/books
- timetables/directories/recipes
- the Internet
- phone texting
- writing shopping lists, cards and emails.

Even in homes where children have not experienced a print-rich environment, it is highly likely that they will have some experience of the written word.

There is now a general understanding that reading begins when children show an awareness of environmental print. (For example see *Key Concepts in Early Childhood Education and Care*, C. Nutbrown, 2006).

One of the ways in which children develop a concept of print is by sitting with an adult who is reading a book, perhaps at bedtime. The adult may trace the words with a finger as they read. The child will conclude that the black squiggles on the page represent words and begin to recognise that print is different from pictures.

Although most children will learn to speak without being actually taught to do so, the same is rarely (if ever) true with learning to read and write. Children seem to be impelled to communicate through speech, and their efforts to speak are rewarded by the attention of their carers and, most importantly, by having their needs met.

The 2-year-old child who is hungry may say, 'Sophie dinner now?', or 'Need biccit'. A 3-year-old child who wishes to go out to play will ask, 'Can I go into the garden?' A 4-year-old in nursery who wants to mix paint while at the art area may ask you if she can have the yellow and blue paints to mix green and you will assist her to achieve this. None of these children need to write a note in order to carry out their purposes! Throughout infancy and the pre-school years, children can function efficiently and cope with the demands of life by using only spoken communication. Why, then, should children make the great additional effort to learn to read and write when life goes pretty smoothly without these skills? It may be true that the brain is hardwired for speech, but this seems less likely to be the case for reading and writing.

Recognition of environmental print on cereal boxes

You will probably think of practical instances of using these skills, as well as reading and perhaps writing for pleasure.

Supporting children's early literacy skills

If reading and writing are not natural in the same sense as speaking, practitioners must find ways of indicating to children how useful and advantageous these skills are. This can be accomplished in part by modelling to children the many uses of writing and reading.

> **Key term**
>
> **Modelling** means carrying out an action or behaviour in order to provide an example that is followed or copied.

Children are very observant of adult behaviours and they will imitate their actions. Children are more inclined to copy adults who are important to them, and as an early education and childcare practitioner *you* will be a highly significant person in the lives of the children in your care. As such, you must take every opportunity to let the children see you writing and reading for as many different purposes as possible. In this way you will be modelling the desired behaviour for them.

> **Consider this**
>
> What events in an average week require you to write, apart from the writing involved in your studies?
>
> Apart from the reading necessary for study, when do you read and why?
>
> When do the children in your setting see the practitioners writing? What are the purposes of their writing at such times?

Opportunities for visible writing include filling out the register, writing labels for displays and posters, writing menus for snack times, writing the description that a child gives of his or her painting, writing notes home for parents and, of course, writing observations. The inventive practitioner can find many opportunities to demonstrate to the children the usefulness of writing.

> **Case study** *Modelling writing*
>
> It is Iain's first day in his new work placement. He enjoyings working with the children and is keen to get on with his work for college. In the afternoon he sees an opportunity to observe a group of children who are building a large construction with blocks. Following the advice he has been given at college, Iain sits not too close to the children, hoping that he will be able to see and hear them without influencing their play.
>
> Iain is a bit nervous as this is the first observation he has made in a nursery. All goes well initially but then one of the children, Sami (4 years, 8 months) comes up to Iain and asks, 'What are you doin'?' 'Oh, just writing,' says Iain, standing up and putting his notebook and pencil away. Sami looks at him.
>
> When Maggie, Iain's supervisor, asks him how his observation went, Iain says, 'Well, I had to stop because Sami came over and asked me what I was doing.' 'You should have tried to continue,' says Maggie. 'It would have been a good chance to let him see writing in action. It might encourage his literacy skills. That's an important part of what we do.'
>
> Iain gives this some careful thought and two days later, feeling much more confident, he observes some children who are working with some clay. Once again, Sami comes up and asks, 'What are you writing?' This time Iain says, 'I'm very busy writing about the interesting work that these boys and girls are doing. Here's a pencil and paper for you, too.'
>
> Sami accepts the offer and sits down at a table nearby, looks carefully at Iain and starts to make marks on his paper.

It is important that children see adults reading a variety of texts. These may include letters, newspapers, timetables, telephone directories, catalogues, recipes and menus.

Linking theory to practice

Make the connection between modelling reading and writing for children and the social learning theory of Albert Bandura.

Turning the setting into a print-rich environment

The early years setting should be a print-rich environment. This means that the children should be surrounded by print and allowed to experience print and texts of different kinds. There ought to be signs and labels to give the children information and strengthen their concept of print, and to support recognition of reading as a useful skill in life. Print should be accompanied by illustrations to aid the children's understanding of the printed words.

An example of a useful sign might be found at the gluing area, where the cardboard shapes and cartons are stored. In order to encourage the children's autonomy, they can have responsibility for storing materials if storage areas are clearly labelled. There might be signs indicating, for example, cylinders, cubes, cuboids, circles, paper and tissue, and the children can be involved in organising the area.

Consider this

When do children see practitioners reading? Is it only at story time?

How does this simple strategy of nursery organisation combine aspects of literacy, numeracy and personal and social development?

In some settings, a reversible 'vacant/engaged' sign is made for the toilet doors and children are encouraged to turn the sign to the appropriate word. This builds the idea for children that printed signs are useful and that reading is a valuable skill which will help them to live independent lives.

Activity

1 Take note of any printed signs used in your setting.

2 Do you draw children's attention to the signs and encourage the children to read them?

3 In what ways do the signs in your setting promote children's independence?

4 How do the signs assist in the smooth running of the setting?

5 Think of a sign that could be added to those already in your setting. Design and make this sign using an appropriate illustration to assist children's understanding.

6 Make the connection with Chapter 4: Curriculum, play and transitions. Consider the four capacities that Curriculum for Excellence seeks to develop within the individual. How does the promotion of literacy by the appropriate use of signs assist children to become:

- successful learners?
- confident individuals?
- responsible citizens?
- effective contributors?

Within an early years setting, one of the ways in which children's print awareness can be fostered is by providing opportunities for them to become familiar with their own names. We all know how interested children are in anything which focuses upon themselves, and recognising their own name appears to be relatively straightforward for most children. Most settings offer opportunities for this to happen as part of the nursery routine. Some examples may be:

- children pick up their names on cards as they come into nursery, perhaps putting them on a board or posting them into a box
- children going for a snack select their names as above
- children's coat pegs are named
- a page of names for each child can be found inside a folder; when children wish to label something they have made, they find their page, cut out one of their names and use it as appropriate.

Often, children not only become quick at picking out their own name, they soon start to identify the names of other children in the setting. This is something which can be encouraged further, with children taking it in turns to 'do the names at snack time' and so on. Frequently, children will try to write their own name, or perhaps ask you to write it for them so that they can copy it. Such attempts should be received positively; in this way, the children will be encouraged to continue.

Linking theory to practice

Which developmental theories do the above examples bring to mind?

The computer can be a useful tool at this stage, as children may enjoy writing their names on it. Picking out the correct letters on the keyboard may be simpler than actually forming them, a task which children's fine motor skills may not be prepared for as yet. However, this method will familiarise them with the letters making up their name, and of course all the others in the alphabet.

The development of writing

Children as young as 2 years will enjoy 'making marks' in many different ways, for example

drawing in sand, making marks in spilt juice, smearing lipstick across a mirror, pouring nail varnish on a carpet – the opportunities are endless!

The process from mark-making through to recognisable writing follows a similar path for all children, which indicates that it is linked to development. Even the grasp of the implement used to make the marks develops from the primitive 'palmar' grasp through the 'dagger' to the 'tripod', which is the ideal grasp for controlled mark-making/emergent writing (see box overleaf).

Another important element in writing development is hand dominance. Usually there are definite signs of preference by the age of 2½ years, but it is not uncommon for this process to take longer. Clearly, the hand favoured by children is going to have a knock-on effect on their emergent writing: because English is written from the left-hand side of the page to the right-hand side, right-handed people have the advantage.

Activity

Try this if you are right-handed: using a pen/pencil in your left hand, try writing this sentence:

Those who are right-handed are at an advantage, as the world is geared towards right-handed people.

What did you notice about the experience? Do you agree with the sentiments expressed in the sentence?

Further research

Find out more about being left-handed. You may want to visit the following websites: www. lefthander.com and www.anythingleft-handed. co.uk. You may be surprised about some of the things you discover.

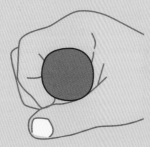

Activity

Read pages 7–8 from *Writing It Right? Children Writing 3–8* (Hughes and Ellis, 1998). This gives excellent examples of the pattern of children's emergent writing.

How practitioners can support children's emergent writing

1. Make sure that children see adults in the setting engaged in the process of writing in as many contexts as possible.

2. Treat children as writers and praise their efforts, giving them opportunities to talk about their writing.

3. Offer as many opportunities for children to engage in writing as possible.

4. Let the children see that writing has results, for example, write a letter with the children inviting someone to come and visit the setting for a particular purpose (which will have been pre-arranged by both parties). The response letter will then be read out to the children.

5. Create a particular area in the setting which is devoted to writing. This should be as quiet as possible, preferably in a corner so that it is not used as a thoroughfare by other children.

6. Provide a variety of materials for children to write with and to write on.

7. Remember that other activities in the setting will also help children to develop the fine motor skills necessary for writing, for example:

   - painting using brushes of different sizes and finger painting
   - playing with dough, clay, plasticine
   - threading, weaving, sewing
   - gluing and using scissors
   - using the computer keyboard and mouse
   - jigsaws, puzzles, small-world and construction toys.

Mairead, an HNC student, is on placement in a child development centre. She is working in the pre-school room and has been asked by the manager to develop the writing area, which is in need of some refurbishment as the children are showing very little interest in using it. Mairead decides that the first thing that needs to be done is to move the writing area into a more appropriate part of the playroom.

Case study 2 *Literacy play*

Janice told the children the story of Goldilocks and the three bears this morning. She has left the props from her story as part of a display, which includes two different versions of the story, a large book and a small one that can easily be held by tiny hands. She observes Katie and Sadie playing with the props and acting out the story with the three bears that Janice has provided. Katie goes to the home corner and returns with a doll that takes on the role of Goldilocks. Using the bears and the doll as actors, the two children dramatise the story including most of the important points of the action and inventing some dialogue as they go. Holding the medium-sized bear in one hand, Sadie says in a cross adult voice, 'Now that's very bad! You're not 'posed to sit on nother person's chair!'

Meanwhile, Katie has taken the smallest bear and the small story book to the home corner. Tucking

1. What might Mairead do next?
2. What resources might she decide to stock the area with?
3. How might the resources be organised?
4. How will Mairead know whether her changes have been effective?

the little bear up in bed, she says, 'Ye dinnae need tae cry. Be quiet and Ah'll read a nice story.'

1 Marian Whitehead states that, 'Narrative is the backbone of all the stories we hear and tell. Narrative is a telling which selects and orders events in time and speculates on life and human behaviour' (*Developing Language and Literacy with Young Children*). Analyse and evaluate the children's literacy play with reference to this comment.

Later in the day, a new parent approaches the lead practitioner with a query about how the nursery promotes children's reading development. The manager gives many examples from the work that Janice has done that day and the children's literacy play.

2 Give a list of important points that the lead practitioner may have included in her explanation.

Processes involved in the development of reading

Reading with an adult and interacting with books, perhaps with other children, is an important element in learning to read. Children can often be seen 'reading' a well-known and loved book to a teddy or to other children. These children have remembered the sequence of events which have taken place in the story, and can reproduce it supported by the pictures which may accompany it.

Understanding narrative and supporting children's reading skills

An understanding of narrative is another of the important elements concerned with the acquisition of reading skills. One of the ways of encouraging this in children is, again, by making activities personal to children. For example, they can be encouraged to write stories about their families, toys, pets and friends, which can be illustrated by their own drawings or photographs. These stories can be done by individual children and supported by an adult, either at home or in the setting. Alternatively, class or group stories can be dictated by the children and scribed by the adult. Of course, often children will want to 'write' for themselves, and they should be encouraged to do so.

Some of these processes can be gained by reading books with children in large groups, but the language value is greatly diminished, as is the warmth and pleasant informality of reading with one or two children. In general, the younger the children, the smaller the reading group should be, and the smaller the group the more pleasant and valuable the experience.

When you have no choice but to do story time with a large group, it is important that you know the book well enough so that you do not need to read it but can tell it. Clearly, then, the first technique of storytelling is to practise and become very familiar with the story. This means that while you look at the printed page from time to time, you are free to make positive eye contact with the children and use facial expression to illustrate the meaning of the text. This is an excellent way to help children develop their understanding of word uses and meanings.

It is good to be able to change your voice slightly for each character in the story, to lower your voice to build a sense of excitement or tension, and to raise it for surprise or shock. You really need to have rehearsed your story to be able to do this well. Knowing the story also allows you to use the book as a prop and hold it up facing the children, so that all children can benefit from the illustrations.

There will be times when you can tell a story without a book because you know the story well. Without a book, you are free to use props to enliven your story and to develop the children's ability to function with symbols. Simple glove or sock puppets, finger puppets, paper plate puppets and real objects can all be used to great effect. The props can be left in the reading area as part of an interactive display, whereby the children are free to continue telling the story themselves. This will improve their memory, their sequencing skills and their ability to enjoy narrative. It may also be an opportunity for children to use the vocabulary they have heard. They may be encouraged to dramatise the story using the props you have provided.

It is important to include in your repertoire some books and stories that deal with everyday events. Shirley Hughes's books are wonderful in their depictions of ordinary families and the adventures experienced by their children. Stories about your own setting can be particularly enjoyable for children, allowing them to reflect on events in the life of the nursery and their own part in the narrative.

Props can help to dramatise stories

Case study *An interactive story*

Julie, the practitioner, had her key children for group time: Bob, Carlie, Ferdie, Morag and Neema, ranging in age from 3 years 8 months to 4 years 5 months. She began to tell them a story that began: 'Once upon a time in the Rowans' Nursery, the children came in and found that the nursery was all in a muddle! All the children and grown-ups looked round the nursery and they found lots of things that were in the wrong place! Look what they found in the sand tray, boys and girls. (*She held up a picture book all covered in sand.*) The children all knew that was the wrong place but Carlie was a good helper and dusted the book and took it back to the...' (*Julie paused and looked enquiringly at the children who answered in a chorus, 'The Book Corner. Yes.' She handed the book to Carlie who went over to the book corner and placed it on the shelf. She then continued with the story.*)

'We've got a good idea,' said Morag, Neema, Ferdie, Bob and Carlie. 'We'll go and look for things that are in the wrong place and we'll put them back.' 'Let's do that, children.'

At this point the story became very interactive as the children walked round the nursery finding misplaced articles and adding them to a pile on the carpet. Each child then became the protagonist by turn and returned things to the correct place.

The key group's story eventually became a book by the children and staff working together, using the camera, the computer and printer. 'Tidying Up' by Bob, Carlie, Ferdie, Morag and Neema became a nursery favourite, which was shown with great pride to parents and other nursery visitors.

The main focus of this group session had been to encourage the children to adopt more responsibility for their own environment, using non-authoritarian approaches with the intention of raising the children's self-esteem. However, the advantages to the children's developing literacy skillls are clear as they developed the narrative and became part of the story, ultimately making a book.

1 Choose a story, or make one up. Design a few props to make your story interactive.

2 Working with a small group of colleagues tell your stories to each other.

Activity

1 a) Make a detailed survey of the picture books in your setting, paying particular attention to the illustrations, the language and the plot line.

b) List five books that seem to you to be of high quality with a strong appeal to children.

c) Describe each book briefly and offer some ideas as to how you might use it with a child.

d) Indicate clearly what you think a child might gain from sharing each of the five books with you.

e) Compare your list and comments with other students in your group.

2 Visit the children's section in a public library and review some of the books for younger age groups. Then visit the children's department in any bookshop and survey some of the books. Find three books that you would rate highly from library and bookshop.

The importance of the reading area

The sign that reads 'Book Corner' or 'Library' is one of the most significant in the setting. It may be illustrated by pictures of books and of children reading. It may also have a sign to remind children to be quiet in order to allow everyone to enjoy the books. The library should be as distant as possible from noisy areas like the woodwork bench or the wooden blocks.

Book areas foster reading for pleasure

The reading area should be equipped as attractively as possible and should be as large as room allows. At the same time, a book area should feel cosy and welcoming, for it is here that the idea of reading for pleasure and relaxation should be fostered. Some settings have colourful rugs, comfortable cushions or small chairs for children. Some areas contain a large chair or sofa to encourage friendly, secure reading sessions where an adult and child, or small group of children, can sit comfortably together. Walls can be hung with posters relating to favourite stories or rhymes. Books should ideally be displayed with their front covers facing outwards, so that children may be attracted by the illustrated covers.

It is part of your role to monitor the reading area and to ensure that the books are well maintained and in good condition. Never ignore books dropped on the floor or left lying on a chair, but tidy up unobtrusively and always encourage the children to do the same. By showing care for books and signs of enjoyment when looking at them, you are modelling behaviours which hopefully children will follow.

Michael Rosen, the Children's Laureate, has spoken of the early stages of education as being 'the very area where the book-loving culture begins' (speaking in The Patrick Hardy Lecture: The Bigger Picture, 2007, www.michaelrosen. co.uk/articles).

Consider this

As your role is to promote the uses and pleasures of literacy by modelling reading behaviour, do you think you would feel comfortable sitting in the book area and reading alone? What might be the difficulty in doing this?

Adults should be available in the reading area at regular intervals, as children are likely to spend longer with the books if there is an adult present. The selection of books in the area should include well-illustrated storybooks covering a variety of subjects which will inspire children's interest.

The library area in your setting should, from time to time, include special displays related to particular themes or centres of interest in the nursery. When you are involved in ordering books, always add to the library bearing in mind the seasonal themes and festivals, as well as those areas that are always of interest to children such as pets, holidays, current films, TV series, animals, dinosaurs or transport. You should also consider storybooks which promote equality and inclusion, for example books which include non-traditional gender roles, a wheelchair user taking a central role in the story, stories about children from a range of cultural backgrounds and so on.

Books to include in a reading area

A library area that contains a wide range of informative and factual books allows the children to experience one of the great reasons for learning to read: it allows them to find things out. Through reading, children can learn from others who are more knowledgeable than themselves. They can build their knowledge and understanding of the world freely and independently following their own interests. Factual books are sometimes the attraction into literacy for young readers whose interest has not been captured by fiction.

It has been said that the best answer you can give a child who asks you a difficult question such as, 'Where does the water go when you water the plants?' might be 'Good question. Let's look in a book to find out.' This approach supports the child's independence and awareness of the uses of literacy as well as easing away from the idea that adults are the holders of all knowledge. Simple pictorial encyclopaedias and dictionaries are therefore vital inclusions in the book area.

Books written in the scripts of other cultures should also be included in the book corner. It is important for children who have English as an additional language to see books in the script of their first language. It is equally of interest for Scottish children to see books written in the scripts of other languages, as this helps to build an awareness of the wider world of literacy. In this way, English may not be viewed as having higher status than other languages.

A well-stocked book corner should also contain a varied selection of rhyme and poetry books. (The usefulness of poetry and rhyme for the development of phonological skills is described later.) However, the unique appeal of poetry to children does not rest in its practical help in learning to read, but in its humour, its rich vocabulary of interesting and quirky words, its rhythm and often the great sense of fun that is part of many rhymes and poems. There will certainly be a place for a collection of Scottish nursery rhymes giving children the opportunity to enjoy verses such as:

Me an ma Grannie,
An a great lot mair,
Kickit up a row
Gaein hame frae the fair.

By cam the watchman,
An cried, 'Wha's there?'
'Me an ma Grannie
An a great lot mair.'

© Norah Montgomerie 1985. Reproduced by permission of Chambers Harrap Publishers Ltd.

With its humour and use of Scots dialect, this traditional nursery rhyme gives a child's eye view of a happy boisterous event.

Children who find stories too long, who have difficulty concentrating and very young children may all gain valuable literacy experiences and fun from a few short rhymes, especially if they are interactive. Of all the forms of literature, poetry and rhyme is the closest to playing. Children's interest in poetry and rhyme begins in babyhood, with simple finger plays and gentle jogging games, such as:

To market to market
To buy a fat pig
Home again, home again
Jiggety jig.

To recite this rhyme with a smile and good eye contact while bouncing the toddler gently and safely provides fun and the beginning of the enjoyment of poetry. Rhymes exercise the child's brain gently, too. The rhythmical, rhyming structure makes them easy to remember and this is a source of confidence and pride for the child.

The best poetry and rhyme books contain colourful illustrations often set in past times.

Through this, and in partnership with an adult, the child can begin to build a sense of passing time and historical and cultural changes. There is also the opportunity to build knowledge of things that can only be experienced through books. Through encounters with poetry, many children will learn to love books and make their first steps in reading as they begin to recognise an old familiar rhyme on the page. As Michael Rosen reminds us 'book-reading and book-loving children do well at school' (The Patrick Hardy Lecture: The Bigger Picture, www.michaelrosen.co.uk/articles).

Phonological awareness

> ### Key term
>
> **Phonological awareness** relates to the ability to recognise sounds within words, for example those at the beginning, middle and end of a word.

Phonological awareness, particularly that related to the ability to distinguish the sounds at the beginning of the word (onset/alliteration) and those with similar endings (words which rhyme, known in this context as 'rime'), is considered to be an important indicator that children's literacy is progressing. In that way, children can learn what words say by analogy. To give an example, *s-ad* rhymes with *m-ad, b-ad, l-ad*. If the child understands the rime associated with this, and is able to recognise individual letters of the alphabet, they may be able to read words such as *p-ad, d-ad* and so on.

Poetry, songs and rhymes are an excellent way of encouraging children's ability to recognise onset and rime. In addition, many children's picture storybooks contain alliteration and rhyme, such as *Hairy McLary from Donaldson's Dairy* (Lynley Dodd, 1983) and *Each Peach Pear Plum* (Janet and Allan Ahlberg, 1978).

The three 'Rs' when referring to reading acquisition relate to rhyme, rhythm and repetition.

Rhyme

Even with babies, the rhymes and songs you use can help to develop the child's understanding of the three Rs; for example, the traditional nursery rhyme 'Round and round the garden, like a teddy bear, one step, two steps, tickly under there!'

There is a well-known link between children's familiarity with nursery rhymes and their later achievement in reading (see, for example, *Phonological Skills and Learning to Read*, H. Goswami and P. Bryant, 1990, and *Understanding Children's Language and Literacy*, P. Mukherji and T. O'Dea, 2000).

Traditional and more modern rhymes should be shared on a daily basis with children. Children particularly enjoy some of the funny, nonsense rhymes such as:

The Pobble who has No Toes
The Pobble who has no toes
Had once as many as we;
When they said "Some day you may lose
  them all;"
He replied "Fish, fiddle-de-dee!"
And his Aunt Jobishka made him drink
Lavender water tinged with pink,
For she said "The world in general knows
There's nothing so good for a Pobble's toes!"

(Edward Lear, 1812–1888)

Children also enjoy tongue twisters such as:

She sells sea shells on the seashore
The shells that she sells are seashells, I'm sure.

> ### Activity
>
> 1 Find a selection of:
>   - rhyming stories
>   - nursery/traditional rhymes
>   - funny/nonsense rhymes
>   - songs/finger rhymes.
>
>   As an early education and childcare practitioner, it is very useful to have a number of resources at your fingertips. Begin an anthology of a selection of the above. You can add to these when you have qualified and you will find it an irreplaceable resource which you will use time and time again!
>
> 2 Working as part of a small group, think of play-based literacy experiences which would help children to develop their ability to recognise onset and rime.

Rhythm

The ability to recognise rhythm is also associated with the development of literacy skills in that children will learn about the way words are segmented into syllables. It can also help them to develop later skills such as punctuation and reading with expression. Children can clap the syllables in their name, or perhaps use a variety of percussion instruments (such as drum, tambour, triangle, tambourine) to beat them out. Singing songs where each note represents one syllable (for example 'Old Mac-Don-ald had a farm') can also help children to understand rhythm in language.

Repetition

Repetition is a feature of many children's picture storybooks. It is important for several reasons:

- it helps to focus children's attention if they are having to listen for a particular line or saying
- it makes the story more interactive and therefore more interesting for many children
- it gives children the opportunity to anticipate what may be coming next
- in some cases, children will start to recognise certain words or phrases that are repeated.

Examples of storybooks which include repetition are:

- *Kiss Goodnight* by Amy Hest (2001)
- *The Gruffalo* by Julia Donaldson (1999)
- *Oh Dear!* by Rod Campbell (1983)
- *The Bad-tempered Ladybird* by Eric Carle (1978)

The development of numeracy

Many students, when asked which subject they liked least at school, will admit that maths was something which filled them with differing degrees of fear and loathing. This may be due to gaps in the development of basic mathematical concepts which have led to 'mathematically disaffected adults' (*Mathematics in Nursery Education*, A. Montague-Smith, David Fulton Publishers, 2002, page 162). Why did these gaps occur in the first place? Could it have been due to developmentally inappropriate teaching methods, which led to maths being viewed as something boring and rather meaningless by older children and adults? It is interesting to note that children under school age engage in mathematical experiences enthusiastically and willingly, probably because they are presented through the context of play.

Cathy Nutbrown (*Key Concepts in Early Childhood Education and Care*, 2006) talks about the importance of children actively *doing* something rather than being told or even being shown how to do it. She argues that hands-on experience will ensure that children truly learn the process.

> ### Consider this
>
> I hear and I forget
> I see and I remember
> I do and I understand
> (Chinese saying)
>
> - How does the above saying and Nutbrown's view relate to Piaget's theory regarding learning experiences in the children under the age of 7 years?

There is some evidence to suggest that babies are born with an innate ability to understand certain aspects of numeracy ('Numerical competence in infants', K. Wynn, 1998). However, there is no disputing the fact that numeracy skills, like those of literacy, are an emergent process. The conditions in which children become numerate are the same as those for becoming literate, with an important additional factor: being numerate depends to a large extent on being literate. To explain further, if a child is unable to recognise symbols (letters, words, numbers) the process of becoming numerate is well-nigh impossible.

Children meet numbers, experience counting and hear mathematical language from the earliest stage in their lives, for example:

- in nursery rhymes and songs ('Round and round the garden like a teddy bear, one step, two steps…' and 'One, two, three, four, five, once I caught a fish alive…')
- while dressing and undressing with parents and carers ('One sock on your little foot, two socks, etc.)

- during meals ('Open wide – in it goes!')
- in general interactions ('Up the stairs, one, two', 'Down we go').

Below are some of the ways in which home activities and experiences provide a numeracy context for children from birth to 3 years:

- counting of fingers and toes
- books, counting stories, rhymes and songs
- exploring toys
- exploring the indoor and outdoor environment
- birthdays (cards, candles on cakes, etc.)
- watching television
- games with older siblings
- trips to the beach and play involving sand
- other family trips and holidays
- bathtime, water play, play in the paddling pool and swimming pool.

Numeracy in the early years is a different experience from that which many of us may remember from our school years under the heading of maths or arithmetic. There is some evidence to suggest that awareness of number is a natural function of the brain and this should inform our approach to children's developing numeracy skills. Ability with numbers has real practical advantages in helping us to describe the world, manage our time and organise our surroundings.

Consider this

Think about the number of times that you make use of numbers in an average week.

The case study below is based on the experience of an HNC student working within a particular early education and childcare setting, as reported to her workplace tutor.

Current approaches to teaching numeracy

In line with the theories of Piaget and Vygotsky, the approach to numeracy in the early years is firmly

Case study *The right time to learn numbers?*

Charlene is a new HNC day-release student. She works in an early years setting which is in a fairly affluent area of Edinburgh. She currently works with children between the ages of 3 and 5 years. Recently, she has been assigned a group of around six to eight children aged between 3 and 4 years. Her remit is to develop their number recognition up to five. She has tried to use a number of approaches, but mainly one of looking at numbers as they are written (e.g. four) and having to say the number correctly. They also count out groups of little animals and cars, etc.

One of the children, Finn (3 years 1 month), has been a cause for concern as he does not appear to be learning anything. His attention span is short, he does not cooperate when asked to participate with the rest of the group, and often he just gets up and wanders off to do something else. Some of the other staff in the setting have been talking about Finn as having possible learning difficulties, as

it is apparent that the rest of the group are learning and able to cooperate with group time numeracy. Alternatively, they think that his lack of cooperation may be due to 'bad behaviour and being spoilt'. Finn's mum has been approached and she cannot understand the problem, as there is no difficulty at home.

Charlene feels guilty as she thinks that it may be because she is not handling the situation well, and that perhaps she has not explained the tasks clearly enough. On her next college day, Charlene puts her concern to the tutor and the rest of the group to see if anyone can shed any light on why Finn is not making progress with his numbers.

1 Why do you think that Finn has behaved in the way he does?

2 Is there any indication that he may have learning difficulties?

3 What advice would you give to Charlene?

based on providing experiences involving problem solving, reflection and playful explanation, which are important components of thinking and learning. (For further information see Supporting Children's Learning in the Early Years, L. Miller and J. Devereux, 2004).

This view of the favoured way to develop mathematical skills is shared by Curriculum for Excellence, which emphasises the experiential in its numeracy outcomes in the early stages. For example, children will be expected within the theme of 'number' to arrive at a point when they can say of themselves: 'I have explored numbers understanding that they represent quantities and I can use them to count, create sequences and describe order' (*A Curriculum for Excellence: Building the Curriculum 2 – Active Learning in the Early Years*, Scottish Executive, 2007). This outcome from the area of number, money and measurement emphasises the processes that the child must work through, with the need to explore numbers prioritised initially over getting the right answer.

The ability to use number skills accurately in an abstract way is essential, and evolves with support and practice within a number-rich environment. This develops over time through a variety of experiences in life and in educational settings. Curriculum for Excellence affirms the idea that much numeracy learning will take place through the medium of purposeful play. While exploring and playing purposefully, what are the aspects of numeracy that children should be learning?

There is general agreement that children should be given opportunities to become gradually proficient in the areas of number and number processes, estimation and rounding, money, time, measurement, information handling and fractions, decimal fractions and percentages. There is also understanding that the learning contained in the numeracy curriculum should promote the number-based skills that are required for everyday life.

How can numeracy learning be achieved through play? If you remember the emphasis on enjoyment that was part of the discussion of nursery rhymes (and is also one of the principles of Curriculum for Excellence) this gives an idea of one way you can approach this. Thinking first of number and

counting, how can nursery rhymes assist with this area? Consider the following example:

> Five currant buns in a baker's shop
> Round and fat with a cherry on the top.
> Along came Jenni with a penny one day
> Bought a currant bun and took it away.

By singing this rhyme, children will develop their concept of 'five'. The rhyme can be sung with children taking the part of the buns; at each verse a bun/child is removed. This supports learning of how to 'count back' or subtract by taking one away each time. The children are also learning in a physically interactive way that leads to the number facts being gradually understood. The rhyme can also be used with props to represent the buns, either facsimile buns or items such as small blocks. This encourages children to think symbolically as they manipulate objects that stand for buns. With many repetitions of this kind of experience, children will gradually come to understand and carry out the process of taking away one, without any materials to assist them. They will be able to perform that number process mentally (in the abstract).

Linking theory to practice

Make the connection with Unit DF52 34: Theoretical approaches to development and learning and Piaget's view of the stages of children's thinking.

Activity

Gather as many examples as you can of rhymes that help to develop counting backwards by removing one each time.

Children also need to develop the number skills of grouping or sorting objects according to similarities and differences. Everyday experiences at home can promote these skills in very young children. For example, when a child helps to put away clothes, storing T-shirts separately from shorts. Children are aware of colour, shape and size and it is through observing these characteristics of objects that they can sort things into groups.

Activity

Suggest two other domestic experiences which would allow infants the opportunity for sorting.

When working with young children, you must provide a wide range of materials that can be sorted and grouped, such as small animals in a zoo or farm set. Children can group families of animals together and the practitioner can support this activity by encouraging the children to explain the rationale for their groupings.

Children need to know and be able to explain what the criteria are for the groups they have made. The contribution of practitioners is of utmost importance here. Through showing an interest in what children are doing, 'tuning in' to their intentions and listening carefully to them in conversation, you can find out how the children are thinking and assess their level of understanding.

These activities can be placed in a meaningful context by creating a simple story with the child. For example: 'There was a very strong wind last night and all the fences in the zoo have been blown down. The zookeeper needs to get the animals into their own pens before he feeds them. Let's help him.' In this way, the child is being motivated to engage in the sorting process.

Case study *Sorting the bear from the sheep*

In the play group, the farmyard complete with a big selection of animals has been set out in the small-world area following a visit to the local farm. Children play freely with the animals and at one point the play leader observes two children, Jamie aged 4 years 6 months and Donald aged 3 years 1 month. Jamie pushes the farmyard tractor and trailer across the table towards the farm saying, 'We've got to get these sheep loaded.' Donald is helping and hurries to put the sheep in the tractor, selecting them from all the animals on the table. 'Hey!' says Jamie. '*He* disnae belong.' And he picks out a polar bear from the crowded wagon. 'Look, Donald. He's goin' tae eat a' the sheep.'

'Mrs MacGregor, there's a bear in the farm!' Jamie calls to the play leader.

'Oh dear, I wonder how he got in there,' she answers.

''Scaped from the zoo, I bet,' says Jamie confidently.

'I hope there aren't any more polar bears hiding amongst the sheep,' says Mrs MacGregor. 'Donald, we'd better check before the tractor starts up.'

Donald looks at the polar bear and checks all the sheep carefully. He finds no bears and then he and Jamie walk over to the storage area where there are various baskets. Jamie points to the one labelled 'Zoo' and Donald puts the polar bear away safely.

When she had a moment, Mrs MacGregor made entries into the profiles of both Jamie and Donald. She wrote a comment on their numeracy in the section 'Knowledge and understanding of the world'. She also made a comment on the children's social development.

1 What criterion was Donald using when sorting his group of sheep for the wagon?

2 In what ways was Donald helped to refine his sorting skills?

3 In what ways did Mrs MacGregor 'tune in' to the children's play?

4 Why did she not ask a direct question such as 'What's the difference between a sheep and a polar bear?'

5 What would you have written for entries on the profiles of the two children?

6 What aspect of play group organisation was helping to develop number concepts?

Using number and counting

Children need to learn the numbers and be able to say the number names, in sequence, in the correct order. Children also need to recognise that each numeral always represents a set containing the same number of items; for example, five is always five whether referring to five socks, five ducks or five sweets. Finally, children need to develop the skills of counting accurately to establish the number in any given group or set of items (one-to-one correspondence).

The case study below considers how a practitioner might support children's number and counting skills.

Matching

Matching is an important numeracy process. It is the ability to associate one thing with another on the basis of similarity.

Matching is of great practical significance, although we may take this skill for granted. It allows us to present ourselves in the world wearing a pair of shoes which match, pair of gloves which match and two earrings that match.

Children enjoy matching games such as 'Snap'. Can you think of another matching game in which the aim is to match sets of dots?

Case study *Counting farm animals*

Ross, aged 4 years 11 months, and Kirsty, recently turned 4 years, come to play with the farm set. Tamsyn, the play group assistant, observes their play and hears them talking about how many they have of each animal. She notices that Ross counts his numbers very quickly and in the correct sequence up to ten but, isn't counting accurately. Kirsty counts more slowly while pointing to the animals, but misses out numbers as she counts, saying: 'One, two, three, four, five, seven, nine, ten, thirteen, fiveteen.'

Tamsyn decides to watch for an opportunity to play separately with these two children at the farm set. She makes a set of cards with numerals up to ten in readiness.

1. Analyse the numeracy behaviours of each of the two children.

2. What processes does Ross need support with?

3. What processes does Kirsty need support with?

4. Describe a pleasant play-based number experience that Tamsyn could implement with each child to help develop their emergent numeracy skills. Each child needs a different experience.

5. Give two examples of other materials from your setting that would be particularly useful in developing children's number and counting skills.

Further research

Investigate the array of games in your setting with the potential to foster children's matching skills.

One way of matching is through a process known as one-to-one correspondence. Children can develop this skill in a myriad of practical situations in the early years setting. The following case study gives an example.

Sequencing

Sequencing is the process of repeating a linear pattern, again it is an important aspect of numeracy for children to learn. An example of a sequence would be shapes arranged as follows: square, circle, triangle, rectangle, square, circle, triangle, rectangle. The aim for the child within the context of a game would be for him or her to be able to recognise the sequence and continue it. This kind of experience can be carried out

---

Case study *Counting and matching for snack time*

It's the end of November and the children are going to have a Scottish snack for St Andrew's Day. At the snack table, two children are helping get the area ready. Four children are allowed to come to the snack table at any one time and the four chairs are already in position. Archie and Marta, both aged 3 years and 6 months, are helping. Luis, the practitioner, brings some plastic mugs over. He asks the children how many they will need and they look at him doubtfully. 'Let's count and see. How many people will we have?' Again the doubtful looks. 'We'll count the chairs to find out.' He walks round the table with the two children, encouraging them to touch each chair as they count. 'One, two, three, four. Four chairs for four people. Now, how many mugs?' Again they walk round the table counting one, two, three, four as each mug is set down. 'That's one mug each. Now let's give everybody a plate.'

The children walk round the table with the plates, putting one down at each place and counting one, two, three, four. 'Thank you very much for helping me to set the table. Would you like your snack now?' The children nod and say 'Yes'.

As the children sit down, Luis kneels beside them, saying to Archie and pointing, 'One boy, one chair, one mug, one plate.' He does the same with Marta and the two children join in, saying 'One girl, one chair, one mug, one plate.'

By encouraging the children and modelling the touching of each item as a counting method, Luis supports the children's understanding of one-to-one correspondence.

Luis then brings over the oatcakes, cheese, carrot sticks and shortbread, saying: 'One child, one chair, one mug and one plate. Here comes the snack and it's going to be great!'

A colleague who is interested in music happens to overhear this rhyme. She starts to sing it to the tune of the chorus of 'Bonnie Dundee' and it soon catches on. With time the rhyme becomes a nursery favourite, often sung and clapped at snack time, especially on occasions like St Andrew's Day.

1 How could numeracy continue to be developed at the snack area? Give three examples.

2 Describe three ways in which the nursery song might help to promote aspects of numeracy, language and literacy.

---

by children working together or, more usually, by children supported by an adult. One way in which the concept of sequencing can be developed is through the reading, discussing and acting out of a number of stories, for example, 'The Enormous Turnip'.

Further research

Make a survey of children's stories and find two others that would help develop the concept of sequencing.

Using mathematical language

Children need to be given the opportunity to develop a consistent use of mathematical language to describe relationships within the environment and in daily experiences. This includes the use of positional language, such as in front of, behind, beside and underneath, which is important for later numeracy work.

Appropriate use of mathematical language such as more than, less than and bigger than,

Case study 1 *Resources for developing mathematical language*

Kate is working with a group of 4-year-olds to develop their use and understanding of mathematical language. She has set up a table with a selection of items including a Lego house, a model tree, a toy train, a beach umbrella and a small bridge. She has a squirrel glove puppet and a smaller wooden carved squirrel. She has positioned a chair for a child and one for herself side by side, facing the table.

• Suggest two ways that Kate might use these resources to develop the children's mathematical language.

Case study 2 *Learning by doing*

At the Sunny Braes Nursery, children are involved in as many aspects of day to day organisation as possible, including mixing the paint. Staff are very aware of the opportunities for including numeracy and always use accurate mathematical language with the children.

While the children mix the colours of paint, they discuss the number of teaspoons of paint needed to mix purple and orange. 'I'm going to try two red and one yellow,' says Cameron. He does this and mixes vigorously. 'It's too red' he says, eyeing the result. 'Well, try adding one more spoonful of yellow,' suggests Mrs Duguid.

When the paint is mixed to everyone's satisfaction, Frank goes to the cupboard to fetch the straws. He opens the box and looks inside. 'There's not enough straws in here,' he says.

The practitioners discuss this interaction at the end of the day and they agree to involve the children in making a paint-mixing recipe book to develop their awareness of the use of written numerals.

1 Carefully identify every example of numerical language and process demonstrated by the practice in this case study.

2 Can you think of more ways to develop children's awareness of numerals by using a paint-based activity?

There was a new student in the nursery who was overheard saying, 'What a time that took! They could have all done loads of paintings in the time it took them to mix the paint.' Mrs Duguid had a very interesting conversation with the student, discussing the importance of learning processes for children and the different aspects of the adult role. She referred to Bruner's theory of scaffolding and Margaret Donaldson's view that 'young human beings have a remarkable fitness for the role of novice. They can enjoy accepting new goals and challenges from other people and can experience great satisfaction from the achieving of conscious mastery' (Human Minds: An explanation, Donaldson, 1992, page 257. Quote reproduced with permission from AP Watt Ltd on behalf of Professor Margaret Donaldson; see also *Understanding Child Development: Linking Theory and Practice*, J. Lindon, 2005, page 186).

1 Look back at the case study and identify where you see evidence of scaffolding.

2 Where do you see a child accepting a challenge from Mrs Duguid?

and questions such as how much, how many and how far, all need to be firmly grasped in order for children to make progress in numeracy.

Children also begin to use numbers accurately and start to master the language for adding, subtracting and even dividing through the medium of play.

Activity

Most children love to bake. Observe and then carry out a baking experience in your setting. Indicate all the points at which numerical processes could be included.

Children often need support with the accurate use of terms such as 'bigger than', 'taller than' or 'higher than'. Consider the following case study.

Case study *Mathematical language*

Example 1: Josh and Zac are building together at the construction area. They are building towers. 'Mine's the biggest!' shouts Josh.

'No! Mine's biggest,' says Zac.

'Let's see which tower is taller,' says the practitioner, bringing over a colourful ruler.

Example 2: Emma and Andrei are clambering over the climbing frame outside. Emma has climbed higher and calls out, 'I'm taller than you.'

'I'm comin' up an' then I'll be bigger,' says Andrei, climbing up fast.

1   How would you help to clarify bigger than, taller than and higher than with all these children?

2   Can you think of other games where children could learn about these mathematical concepts?

Learning about money

Children are interested in money and it is often through using coins in a play situation that they begin to count. The reason is obvious in that almost every child will have had the experience of shopping with the significant adults in their life. This is an important adult activity which children often imitate in their role play.

Activity 1

The following role-play situations all provide valuable contexts for meaningful numeracy with children. Think about how you would equip each of the following areas to promote as many numeracy processes as possible.

1   Post office

2   Shoe shop

3   Travel agent

4   Hairdresser

Activity 2

Is your setting a number-rich environment?

1   Carry out a survey to assess how frequently numbers are used in signs and displays in your setting.

2   Look out for role-play materials such as telephone directories, appointments books, maps and rotas of helpers.

Time

This is a fascinating topic for children, who often ask the questions 'When?' and 'How long?' When considering how to support children to develop a sense of time, find out whether calendars, clocks, egg-timers and weather charts in frequent use in your setting. These all assist children to come to an understanding of how we discuss and measure time.

Children's language, literacy and numeracy development through self-directed play

Children are able to drive forward their own emerging language, literacy and numeracy skills in the many ways in which they play freely by themselves and with others. This is particularly so in a richly resourced environment, and there are many play areas within an early years setting that have the potential to assist children's emergent skills. The ability to speak and communicate effectively with others develops gradually, and although there is recognition that children have an innate predisposition towards language, it is also clear that the language environment that surrounds children has a powerful effect on how their language skills develop. This is so from the earliest interactions that children have with each other.

If you analyse this simple interaction you can see that Frieda has been involved in some important processes of emergent language development through self-directed play. Her ability to pick out sounds of different pitch is being exercised as she notices the bird sound and crawls towards it. Her ability to concentrate is being promoted as she stops and listens again. Her ability to identify the origin of a sound is also being developed. The long process of associating words with objects and learning the names of things to build a vocabulary is being assisted when she hears Luke use the word 'birdie' for this toy. Her concept of a bird is gradually being constructed as she sees the object, hears the chirping sound and associates the word with both sound and object. Her understanding of the word 'no' is being developed as Luke accompanies this word with a frown, and through hearing what Luke says, Frieda is being introduced to ways in which we combine words within sentences.

All of the above is happening through the medium of the two children's self-directed play, and such interactions make a vital contribution to the long, gradual and complex processes involved in being an effective communicator. In nine months to a year's time, Frieda may be able to defend her own interests by stating 'No! Frieda's birdie!'

The processes involved in emergent language, literacy and numeracy continue to develop as children grow older, their play becomes more varied and associative play increases in complexity.

In the following case study, try to identify which of the processes involved in becoming literate and numerate are being developed through the children's self-directed play.

Case study *Language development through self-directed play*

Luke (22 months) and Frieda (11 months) are playing contentedly in the child and family centre in a room with other children and adults. Luke tends to be quite a still child who will stay happily in one place when he has something that interests him. He is already developing a range of words and other utterances. Frieda has recently become an expert crawler, and she is active in her explorations of the environment.

Each child has a collection of soft toys in a basket, including teddies and other animals of different sizes and shapes. Some of the animals make sounds. Luke picks a fluffy bird from his basket and grips it tightly with both hands. The toy bird makes a chirping noise. Frieda turns her head towards Luke. He squeezes the toy bird again. This attracts Frieda's attention and she crawls closer to Luke who squeezes the toy again.

Frieda stops, listens, then smiles and looks intently at the bird. Luke puts the toy down and picks up a teddy. Very quickly, Frieda crawls over and takes the bird by the head. It does not make the chirping noise. Luke frowns, pulls it from Frieda's hands and says firmly, 'No! Uke birdie!' He holds it closely, and squeezes it with both hands, causing the toy bird to chirp again.

Case study *Ordering a takeaway*

Annie, Rashid, Greig and Sofia are all in the home corner which has been transformed into a café.

'I'll get the orders,' says Sofia. She starts going round the nursery asking children, 'What d'ye want for your takeaway?' The children she asks respond in different ways. Eilidh asks for pizza, Rami wants chips, Timothy asks for burgers and Max orders kebabs. As each child orders, Sofia uses a pencil from the drawing table to make marks on a piece of paper to write the orders down.

Meanwhile, back at the café, Rashid and Annie are talking about wearing aprons. 'We'll need one each' says Annie and she takes two from the stand nearby, giving one to Rashid. Soon they are opening the doors of the small kitchen units and putting in baking trays. Some don't fit and they are exchanged for smaller ones.

Sofia goes back to the café area and starts to read the orders from her piece of paper. Annie busily opens the cupboard door and takes out play food from the trays. Rashid calls out, 'Who's next?'

'Timothy wants burgers,' says Sofia. 'How many?' asks Rashid. 'Three' answers Sofia, consulting her paper. Rashid pops three plastic burgers into a pan and concentrates as he turns them over with a fish slice.

Greig has taken some sheets of paper from the art table. He wraps some crayons in the paper and says, 'Ah'm delivering the chips to Rami.' He goes over to Rami and hands him the parcel saying, 'It's your takeaway.' He then comes back for Timothy's burgers.

Meanwhile, some other children enter the café asking for food. 'It's too busy now,' says Annie, 'You'll need to wait in a queue.'

'I'm first,' says Joseph. 'And I'm second,' says Katie. Joseph looks at the card with food illustrations, points to the picture and orders pizza. He then says 'I'll read the paper till my order's ready.' He pulls over a plastic stool and gets a book from the library area. Katie orders a kebab and points to the word, saying to Joseph, 'That's like my name.'

In the above case study, various processes are being developed through the children's self-directed play. These are described in the chart below.

LANGUAGE DEVELOPMENT	
Listening to others	This is happening throughout the children's play. They take each other seriously and pay attention to each other's conversation.
Forming sentences and questions	The children are developing these uses of language when Annie states that it is getting too busy and when Sofia asks her customers what they want for a takeaway.
Developing vocabulary	The children are learning and using a variety of words for different foods.
Using language appropriate to real-life situation	The children speak as if they are really involved in this situation. They are practising some of the language interactions necessary for adult life.
READING DEVELOPMENT	
Pictorial recognition	This is seen as the children consult the illustrated card.
Play reading	Sofia is play reading when she consults her piece of paper to read the orders.
Memory and sequencing	Sofia uses these skills when she recounts what her customers have ordered.
Understanding of the uses of print	This is shown in the way the children accept the importance of the 'written' orders that Sofia has taken.
Listening skills	The children take in appropriate and relevant information from each other within the context of this situation.
Awareness of reading for pleasure	This is shown by the way the children read 'the paper' (books) while they wait for their orders.
Recognition of letters of the alphabet	This emergent skill is illustrated by Katie recognising the 'k' of kebab as being the same initial letter as her own name.

WRITING DEVELOPMENT	
Development of fine motor skills	This is happening at a number of points in the case study. • Annie and Rashid tie their aprons. • Rashid turns the burgers over using the fish slice. • Greig wraps the crayons in paper to represent chips. • Sofia grips her pencil to write down the orders. It is not clear which type of grip she is using but this type of play will help to develop a mature tripod grip.
Pretend writing	Sofia is not able to write yet but she is showing awareness that written symbols can convey a message. Other children may be developing this awareness through participating with her in this shared understanding.
NUMERACY DEVELOPMENT	
Spatial awareness	This is being developed when Rashid and Annie are fitting the toy baking trays into the oven. They are learning about relative sizes.
Early counting and developing a concept of number	The children develop these numeracy skills as they order specific numbers. For example, Sofia states that Timothy orders three burgers and Rashid prepares the correct number.
Using numbers to sequence and order things	This is developing where Rashid asks who is next and also when Joseph and Katie organise themselves into first and second positions in the queue.
The understanding of one-to-one correspondence	Annie says that they will need an apron each and she correctly brings two, one for herself and one for Rashid.
Estimating and measuring of size	This process occurs when Greig manages to wrap the crayons in paper to deliver to Timothy. Greig has chosen a piece of paper big enough to hold the crayons.

Activity

Discuss with colleagues the possible processes that might be encouraged by the inclusion of a telephone, a cash machine, some play money and a written menu in the children's play. Think of as many processes as you can.

Suggest one other resource that might develop the processes further. Indicate what you think the children would gain from this.

Resources to develop children's language, literacy and numeracy skills

There are many commercially produced materials to promote children's language, literacy and numeracy skills.

• Matching games encourage children to match pictures with pictures and pictures with words, which may develop the ability to recognise the word independently of the picture. Such games are of value to children at varying stages of emergent literacy.

• Games to promote listening skills include sound-lotto, a game in which children must match sounds, for example animal calls, to the appropriate animal picture. This encourages close listening and concentration.

• Some games help to develop number concepts by matching numerals to cards depicting a set number of objects. Other games are designed to develop number concepts and colour recognition simultaneously.

• Computer programs in wide use in early years settings include games to promote literacy and numeracy.

Language, literacy and numeracy can also be promoted in play where the connection with these areas might at first seem to be less obvious.

Consider the brief case studies below and identify the possible ways in which language, literacy and numeracy might be developed.

Case study 1 *Numeracy through creative play*

There is an area set up as dressing table with a mirror and boxes of beads of various sizes and colours. There are threads and laces of differing thickness.

Cheryl and Chrissie are threading beads carefully and Cheryl says, 'Ah'm making a long necklace for mah party.'

'So'm I,' says Chrissie, 'I'm makin' a green necklace.' They ask the practitioner for help in fastening their necklaces and she does this, chatting to them about what they have made and what their plans are. She supports their language and numeracy through this interaction.

1 What might the practitioner be saying to Cheryl and Chrissie?

2 Give one way in which this play might be extended to promote an aspect of literacy.

Case study 2 *Playing with dough*

Hamish, Ali and Owen are rolling play dough vigorously. Hamish rolls a long 'snake' and makes it into a circle. 'Hey, that's like my name!' says Owen. Meanwhile, Ali is making lots of small balls out of his dough and is placing them in a row while muttering, 'Got to get the cakes ready before they come home.' Neemah, the student, is sitting with the boys and she manages to promote a little numeracy and literacy in an informal way.

1 How does Neemah do this?

2 Can you think of other ways that literacy and numeracy could be taught through this form of play?

Case study 3 *Responding to a child's painting*

Mai, the student, is supervising the painting area. Laura (3 years 9 months), who is usually very quiet, brings over her painting and says, 'Look at my picture.' For a minute Mai is not sure what to say but she tells Laura that she likes the picture very much. She then points to all the colours in the painting and says, 'I like all the colours you have used. There's red, green, yellow and purple. Four colours! This is a very big purple square you've painted in the middle.'

'It's a bus,' says Laura. 'I'm going on the bus with my gran.'

'I think we'll make a sign for your painting and put it on the wall when it's dry. Would you like to find your name label to put on your painting?'

Laura goes over to the book of names but seems very uncertain. Mai helps her to find her name and then they sit together while Mai writes in big clear letters, 'Laura is going on the bus with her gran.' At home time, Laura takes her gran by the hand and shows her the painting on the wall.

1 Identify the language, literacy and numeracy development that is happening here.

2 Give two suggestions for further supporting Laura's learning.

In all three case studies, the adult has supported language, literacy and numeracy by getting alongside the children, listening to them and tuning in to their interests.

Analyse and evaluate the following two case studies (below and overleaf) with reference to:

- curriculum theory
- theories of how children learn
- ways in which adults interpret their role
- the importance of a team approach to literacy.

Case study *Anya's first placement: learning the letter 'C'*

It is a bright, frosty day in February and many of the children in the nursery are outside running around to keep warm. Some are stamping on the ice of a shallow puddle which has frozen over during the night. The nursery supervisor says to Anya, the student, 'Please go and tell the children to come in. It's story time.'

Anya has to make a big effort in order to get all twenty children inside and they are slow to settle down for the story. 'I want you to read them *The Very Hungry Caterpillar* because we're on to the letter "C" in the literacy programme,' says the supervisor. 'Be sure to draw their attention to the "C" as often as you can.'

Anya sits on a chair with all the children at her feet and when she holds up the book she asks the children what they can see on the cover. They do not seem to be very interested, although one or two children say 'a caterpillar'.

Anya repeats that it's a caterpillar and she points to the letter 'C' and says the sound. She does her best with the story, but finds it hard to hold the children's attention. She often has to interrupt the narrative to ask children to sit quietly or to listen. She finds it a very demoralising experience, especially when her supervisor calls across the room to reprimand individual children.

Anya now feels very anxious about her ability to support children's literacy.

It's a sunny day and nearly everyone is outside in the nursery garden. A few children are pointing at something on the ground and calling out excitedly, 'Look, Teacher. Look!'

Anya, the HNC student, goes over to see what is causing all the interest. She finds that the children are gazing in fascination at a large striped caterpillar. She bends right down beside the children and listens to what they are saying.

'It might bite us!' 'It's hairy!' 'It's stripy like a snake.'

'It's not a snake,' says Anya. 'What do you think it is called?'

'A worm,' says one child shyly.

'That's a good suggestion,' says Anya. 'It does wriggle along but it's different from a worm. It's called a caterpillar.'

Some of the children repeat the word and they talk for a bit longer about this interesting find. One of the boys asks, 'Can we take it inside?'

'No,' says Anya. 'A caterpillar needs to stay outside where it can get plenty of green leaves to eat. Maybe you would like to draw it.'

Some of the children want to do this and Anya encourages them to go and fetch paper, pencils and crayons from the drawing area. Anya also fetches some clipboards for the children to lean on and a magnifying glass.

Later that day, Anya pins up the children's drawings with a sign that reads 'Sandy, Joe and Colin drew a caterpillar'. Colin points to the 'C' of caterpillar and says, 'That's the same, like my name'.

'Well done, Colin!' says Anya. '"C" for Colin and "C" for caterpillar.'

She puts out two copies of *The Very Hungry Caterpillar*, one in large format and a smaller hardcovered version. She also sets out a factual book about insects where the life cycle of a butterfly is displayed. Anya positions herself in the book area, to look at these books and to read the story with any children who wish to hear it.

At the planning meeting, the supervisor compliments Anya on the way she has used this experience to develop the children's literacy. The staff decide to cut out large 'C' shapes for the drawing table, so that the children can colour them in if they wish. Each 'C' becomes a segment of the body of a large caterpillar which is displayed on the nursery wall accompanied by a sign that reads 'Curly the caterpillar crunches cabbages and carrots'.

The importance of working in partnership with the family to develop children's language, literacy and numeracy

If you acknowledge that the majority of children already know a lot about language, literacy and numeracy by the time they come into pre-school education at the age of 3 years, then you must also agree that this knowledge has been gained, for the most part, in their home environment.

That being the case, you must also agree that working in partnership with parents and carers is going to provide the optimum level of support for children's developing skills.

The term 'partnerships' has been current for several years now, and it would seem that all the emphasis being placed upon it is beginning to bear fruit. Previously, parents were not always viewed as important and equal partners in their children's learning. We now have a situation where Her Majesty's Chief Inspector, Kenneth Muir, identified the positive relationships between parents and nursery staff as a 'strong element' in ensuring that children's pastoral needs are met (LTS Early Years Conference, 19 May 2007).

Ways to promote working in partnership with parents and carers

Some ideas for activities which can promote working in partnership with parents and carers are described below and on pages 172 and 173.

1. Ted the Bear

This is not an original idea and has been observed in several different guises in different settings.

Dear Parent,

My name is Edward (Ted for short), and I live in the Nursery with the children. During the weekends I get very lonely, and would love to be invited to your house to spend Saturday and Sunday with you. I am very well behaved and promise not to be any trouble. I would love to do whatever you are all doing, especially if you are having an adventure! Maybe you would be able to write down what we did so that we can share it with the other boys and girls on Mondays. You might even want to take a photograph or two.

Thank you,
Ted Bear

On Friday evening, Ted and Rory went to stay with Rory's gran, because she was looking after them while Rory's mum and dad went to a party. Rory and Ted had Gran's special fish pie for supper. Then Gran read Ted and Rory a bedtime story called 'Peace at Last!' Here they are fast asleep after listening to the story.

The aim is to get parents and carers to share their child's weekend experiences with the setting. This is achieved by staff sending 'Ted the Bear' home with a child for the weekend; the child's parents and/or carers then create a record of what the child and Ted did together. The artwork opposite gives an example of the type of letter which could be sent to parents and carers explaining the activity, as well as a sample recording of what Ted got up to when he spent the weekend with Rory.

The resources required for this activity are:

- Ted the Bear
- two changes of clothes
- pyjamas
- toothbrush
- comb or brush
- disposable or digital camera
- diary
- rucksack with Ted the Bear's name on the front, to contain all the previous items listed.

Activity

List the possible benefits of the Ted the Bear activity in terms of:

- promotion of partnerships
- enhancing the child's literacy learning.

2. 'All About Me' books

As the name suggests, this is a book which is created for each child individually. It is put together by the setting staff, parents and the child involved. The reasons for its development include an acknowledgement of the importance of the home and to facilitate good links between home and setting. As well as giving the child a very personal literacy experience, it helps to build confidence and self-esteem. Because the child and his or her family is at the centre of the book, it becomes an extremely valued source of precious memories for child and parents for years to come.

How are 'All About Me' books put together?

Staff at Craigentinny Primary School Nursery in Edinburgh have used 'All About Me' books successfully for several years. As each new group of children starts the nursery, a letter is sent to the parents explaining what the 'All About Me' book is and inviting them to take part. The letter explains that it has been found that the book is an excellent way for staff to get to know the children, for children to get to know each other as they share their books with one another, but above all, for the child to have a lovely record of him or herself to take on to primary school and beyond. Parents are invited to work on the book at home or to come into the nursery to work on it with their child; but if they would prefer, staff will work on the book with their child.

What does an 'All About Me' book contain?

Included in the book are:

- photos of family members and friends, pets, places and special times; each of the photos has a caption, very often dictated by the child – home is very much the starting place
- a record of what the child does at home, favourite toys, games and so on
- a record of what the child does in the setting, – recording activities across the curriculum
- scribing the child's words
- details of favourite songs and rhymes
- a record of achievement, for example: Joe read all these names today/Joe can tell you all these colours
- examples of art work
- the child's own thoughts and reflections
- certificates of achievement
- contributions from parents
- a record of achievements from outside the setting, for example 'Here is a copy of my swimming certificate and I can swim 50 metres'
- details of family/setting outings
- details of family holidays/birthdays.

Feedback from parents about the books has included:

> The 'All About Me' book has helped us as a family to share and to involve each other in making things to go into the book.

> The A.A.M. book has helped me to be aware of all the things that Dylan is learning in nursery.

3. Email initiative

Referring back to the beginning of this chapter, the use of technology was mentioned as an important part of literacy development in the twenty-first century. The staff at Craigentinny Primary School Nursery have also been involved in an email initiative, whereby children and their parents send each other emails. This has been very successful, with the children very motivated by this. One of the concerns was that there would be a problem for children whose families did not have a computer or who were simply unwilling to take part. However, this is a nursery where parents clearly feel valued and included, and the vast majority were keen to take part. Some of the older children in the primary school acted as 'buddies' for those whose parents were not able to participate.

> ### Consider this
> What do you think the benefits of an email initiative might be:
> - for children
> - for staff
> - for parents?

4. Storysacks

Storysacks were first developed by Neil Griffiths, a former primary school head teacher from Wiltshire. A storysack is a bag containing a picture book along with various props to aid storytelling. Griffiths is now the director of the National Storysacks project. During a recent interview (for *Literacy Today*, March 2001 issue), he explained that the idea for storysacks came to him as he had been trying to think of a way to involve parents more effectively with their children's literacy development, and also to motivate the many children who did not really enjoy books and stories.

What is included in a storysack?

A storysack consists of the following:

1 a large, cloth bag with a drawstring (the title of the book is indicated on the outside of the bag)

2 the storybook upon which the sack is based; it should be an enjoyable, engaging story which is attractively illustrated

3 a tape/CD of the story (this can either be commercially produced or home-made)

4 soft toys of the main characters, or puppets or wooden or plastic characters or masks of the main characters

5 a related non-fiction book, for example, if the story is about a dinosaur, then the non-fiction book could be based on dinosaurs

6 a game, jigsaw or puzzle related to the story, for example, for *The Very Hungry Caterpillar* there is a wooden puzzle which shows the metamorphosis of the caterpillar into the butterfly

7 a parent/adult 'prompt card' giving ideas for ways of using the sack, together with other language activities depending on the age and interests of the child

8 a parent/adult feedback sheet/card

9 a list of the sack's contents.

Since the development of storysacks, the idea has been extended to include:

• poetry rhyme sacks

• numeracy sacks

• listening sacks.

Consider this

In what ways do you think that the contents of sacks such as those described above might support children's learning and improve partnerships with parents?

5. Curiosity kits

Curiosity kits were originally devised for reluctant boy readers, especially those experiencing difficulties. They were intended for children around 7 to 8 years, but there seems to be no good reason why these could not be developed for children in P1 or P2, many of whom are already experiencing disaffection and difficulty with reading.

Further research

Find out more about storysacks on the Internet. Details of commercially produced storysacks are available at www.storysacks.co.uk.

Carry out an Internet search to find out more details about curiosity kits. How might these be used in the early stages of primary school? Can you suggest some 'boy-friendly' topics which may be the subject of such sacks?

Activity

1 List the possible benefits to children and parents of using a storysack.

2 Choose a suitable picture storybook which you think would be useful for encouraging children's language, literacy and numeracy.

3 For each of the three areas of language, literacy and numeracy, suggest a suitable play experience which could be provided. Give details of the resources required and how your proposed activity might develop the child's learning. (You should also refer to *A Curriculum Framework for Children 3 to 5*, Learning and Teaching Scotland, 1999 and the key aspects and features of learning.)

4 Suggest how your storybook could form part of a storysack, giving details of what the contents of such a sack might be.

5 List the possible challenges of developing storysacks within an early years setting and suggest how these may be addressed.

Case study 1 *Making the most of bathtime*

'Time for your bath, Charlie!' His mum, Victoria, leads Charlie (3 years 11 months) upstairs into the bathroom, where she has already run the bath and selected some of his bath toys which are floating in the bubbles. She undresses Charlie quickly and pops him into the bath. She sits beside him, leafing through a magazine as Charlie plays quietly with his toys.

You could make the following suggestions:

1 Victoria could have pointed out the time, for example, It's seven o' clock – do you know where the seven is on the clock?'

2 She could have counted the stairs as they went up them together, encouraging Charlie to join in.

3 She could have asked Charlie to choose his own toys, having a chat about which ones he would like to have tonight and why.

4 During Charlie's undressing, Victoria could have made this a fun activity where she was counting the socks as they came off, commenting on the fact that his vest is 'under' his T-shirt, his jumper comes 'over' his head, he is stepping 'out' of his trousers (and other mathematical and positional language).

5 Instead of reading a magazine, Victoria could have chatted to Charlie about the events of the day, what he was going to do tomorrow, what story he would like to have for bed, etc.

6 As he was playing in the bath, she could have observed to see whether there were any opportunities for her to support his play/learning in any way.

Of course, it would be ridiculous to say that anyone could be expected to carry out *all* of the suggested activities with a child, all the time.

Case study 2 *School pick-up time*

Sarah, a childminder, walks to Maggie's school to pick Maggie (6 years 2 months) up. Rowan (3 years 3 months) is with her and stops to pick up a brightly coloured autumn leaf which has attracted her attention. 'No, dirty darling,' Sarah tells her, gently removing the leaf from her hand and dropping it on the ground. They arrive at the school gate several minutes before the bell rings and stand watching as parents' cars arrive. Soon, other adults arrive to wait for their children, and the adults become involved in conversation. Rowan stands quietly for a minute or so, and then starts pulling on Sarah's hand. 'Maggie won't be long, just be patient for another minute, Rowan.' Sarah is so involved in her conversation that she hardly notices the school bell ringing.

Case study 3 *Going to the shops*

Anwar (4 years 3 months) is being looked after by his daddy, Husni, while his mum is in hospital having had a new baby girl.

Husni has explained to Anwar that they are going to visit his new baby sister, and that on the way to the hospital they will have to stop at the shops as they need a few things. 'Can I write a list, Dad?' says Anwar. 'No thanks, pet, we don't really need one.' Anwar looks a bit downcast, but brightens up and says, 'Can I choose a card from me to Mum and write it myself?' Husni replies that Anwar can certainly choose the card, but that he will write it, as Anwar can't write yet. Husni tells Anwar that his new baby sister's name is Amal. 'Oh, that means that she's the same letter as me!' he cries excitedly. 'Yes, darling, that's nice. We'd better go now or we'll be late for visiting time,' replies Husni.

A word of warning – although we are talking about reluctant boy readers specifically here, it is important not to stereotype them. While it is widely recognised that the majority of reluctant readers, and those having problems with literacy in general, are boys, it is equally true that many boys enjoy and readily engage in reading. Similarly, although it is recognised that some subjects and types of book are more appealing to many boys, we should not take too narrow a view as this could lead to reduced opportunities for boys to access a wide variety of reading matter. It is also true that there are girls who experience difficulty in reading and seem to be reluctant to become involved with books. All approaches should be equally available to every child in the setting.

Read through the following case studies, noting where you find missed opportunities for developing the child's language, literacy and numeracy. Suggest how the adult in each case could have used these opportunities in a positive way.

This chapter has covered only some of the issues involved with children's development of language, literacy and numeracy. Perhaps the most important thing to remember is that your role in supporting these processes is vital. If you can be enthusiastic and positive in your approach, and if the experiences are play-based, meaningful and fun, you will have gone a long way towards motivating children to learn.

Check your progress

1. Describe the main theoretical approaches to language acquisition.

2. Why is it said that literacy and numeracy are emergent processes?

3. Why is a print-rich environment considered to be so important?

4. Explain why modelling appropriate activities (for example, writing a shopping list or counting out pieces of fruit) encourages children's literacy and numeracy development.

5. Explain the significance of rhyme, rhythm and repetition in literacy development.

6. What are the features of a good library corner?

7. Why is it preferable to read a story to one child or a very small group of children rather than to a large group of children?

8. Why should children learn about numeracy through play and appropriate practical activities?

9. What is meant by the term one-to-one correspondence?

10. Why has there been so much emphasis placed upon the importance of family in the development of language, literacy and numeracy?

References

Barratt-Pugh, C. and Rohl, M. (eds) (2000) *Literacy Learning in the Early Years*, Buckingham: Open University Press

Bruce, T. (2004) *Developing Learning in Early Childhood (0–8 Years)*, London: Paul Chapman Publishing

Donaldson, M. (2002) *Human Minds: An Exploration*, London: Penguin

Goswami, U. and Bryant, P. (1990) *Phonological Skills and Learning to Read*, Hove: Lawrence Erlbaum

Hughes, A. and Ellis, S. (1998) *Writing It Right? Children Writing 3–8*, Dundee: Scottish Consultative Council on the Curriculum

Karmiloff-Smith, A. (1994) *Baby It's You: A Unique Insight into the First Three Years of the Developing Baby*, London: Ebury Press

Learning and Teaching Scotland (1999) *A Curriculum Framework for Children 3 to 5*, Dundee

Learning and Teaching Scotland (2005) *Birth to Three: supporting our youngest children*, Dundee

Lindon, J. (2005) *Understanding Child Development: Linking Theory and Practice*, London: Hodder Arnold

Makin, L. and Whitehead, M. (2004) *How to Develop Children's Early Literacy: A Guide for Professional Carers and Educators*, London: Paul Chapman Publishing

Miller, L. and Devereux, J. (2004) *Supporting Children's Learning in the Early Years*, London: David Fulton Publishers

Montague-Smith, A. (2002) *Mathematics in Nursery Education*, 2nd edn, London: David Fulton Publishers

Mukherji, P. and O'Dea, T. (2000) *Understanding Children's Language and Literacy*, Cheltenham: Nelson-Thornes

Nutbrown, C. (2006) *Key Concepts in Early Childhood Education and Care*, London: Sage Publications

Nutbrown, C. (2006) *Threads of Thinking – Young Children Learning and the Role of Early Education*, 3rd edn, London: Sage Publications

Palmer, S. (2004) 'Music and memory', in *Child Education*, May 2004 edition

Riley, J. (ed.) (2007) *Learning in the Early Years 3–7*, 2nd edn, London: Sage Publications

Scottish Executive (2007) *A Curriculum for Excellence: Building the Curriculum 2 – Active Learning in the Early Years*, Edinburgh

Trevarthen, C. (2004) 'Learning about ourselves, from children: why a growing human brain needs interesting companions', Research and Clinical Centre for Child Development, Annual Report 2002–2003 (No. 26), Graduate School of Education: Hokkaido University, pp. 9–24. (available at www.perception-in-action.ed.ac.uk/pdf/colwyn2004)

Whitehead, M. (2004) *Language and Literacy in the Early Years*, 3rd edn, London: Sage Publications

Whitehead, M. (2007) *Developing Language and Literacy with Young Children*, 3rd edn, London: Paul Chapman Publishing

Wynn, K., 'Numerical competence in infants', in C. Donlan (ed), *The Development of Mathematical Skills*, Hove: Psychology Press (pp. 3–25)

Useful websites

Learning and Teaching Scotland: www.LTscotland.org.uk/literacyandnumeracy

National Literacy Trust: www.literacytrust.org.uk

Michael Morpurgo website: www.michaelmorpurgo.org

Scottish Book Trust: www.scottishbooktrust.com

Read together: www.readtogether.co.uk

Julia Donaldson website: www.juliadonaldson.co.uk

Eric Carle website: www.eric-carle.com/home.html

BBC Skillswise: www.bbc.co.uk/skillswise

Early years teaching ideas: www.teachingideas.co.uk/earlyyears/contents.htm

Michael Rosen website including the Patrick Hardy lecture: www.michaelrosen.co.uk

Chapter 6
Children and young people with additional support needs

Introduction

In Chapter 1 you recognised that working with children is an interesting and varied career, requiring skills of communication, problem solving and the ability to work with others. This is never more apparent than when working with children and young people who have additional support needs. These are children who are, or are likely to be, 'unable without the provision of additional support to benefit from school education provided (*Supporting Children's Learning: Code of Practice*, Scottish Executive, 2005).

Many people who are embarking on an early education and childcare career express an interest in working with children who have additional support needs. Certainly it is an area of practice which is particularly rewarding, but it can also be challenging.

In this chapter you will learn about children's needs in general and how some children require additional support. You will also learn the correct terminology to use when describing additional support needs. This is an area where many people are confused and do not always know what is appropriate or indeed offensive terminology. This is because society's attitudes have changed, as has its tolerance of the use of certain terms.

In this chapter you will also learn how children and young people with additional support needs are given the necessary support and resources to allow them to fulfil their potential. Earlier in this book you learned that children are unique beings with individual needs and interests; they come from varying backgrounds and have very different experiences of being cared for. All of these factors have an impact on the child or young person which means that an assessment of their needs is essential to give them the individual support plan they require. You will learn about this assessment process and the individuals, organisations and agencies that will provide the appropriate support.

In this chapter you will learn:

- How children's basic needs are met
- How additional support needs are understood (past and present) and the terminology used
- How a range of conditions can lead to additional support needs
- How children and young people with additional support needs, and their families/carers, access support

How children's basic needs are met

We all have basic needs which have to be met to ensure our survival. When studying child development you will have learned that children's basic needs fall into the categories of physical, social, emotional, cognitive and language.

It is necessary for you to understand these basic needs before looking at how children have additional support needs. Some examples of how these basic needs can be met are described below.

Physical needs	Food, water, warmth, shelter, protection from infection, access to medical services
Social needs	Opportunities for social interaction, playing with others, outings, sharing, learning group rules, taking turns, hobbies, interests
Emotional needs	Love and affection, unconditional positive regard, praise, reassurance, security, promotion of self-esteem
Cognitive needs	Opportunities to learn through play, mental stimulation, problem solving, concept development
Language needs	Opportunities to communicate with others, books and stories, listening games, circle time

Some theorists have studied these needs in depth including Mia Kellmer Pringle.

Mia Kellmer Pringle

Today the needs of children and support mechanisms to meet these needs are high on the political agenda, but this was not always so. Mia Kellmer Pringle (1920–83) helped to lay the foundations of what we would now call 'child-centred' practice, highlighting the importance of early intervention to prevent children's needs remaining unmet.

In 1963 Pringle was invited to become the first director of the newly formed National Bureau for Cooperation in Childcare, which later became the National Children's Bureau. The work she is most closely identified with is *The Needs of Children* (1975), in which she acknowledged the research of John Bowlby. She also spent years researching children's needs through her own clinical practice.

Pringle outlined four significant developmental needs which have to be met. These are the need for love and security, new experiences, praise and recognition and responsibility.

The need for love and security

Children need to be unconditionally loved (love with no 'strings attached') and cared for in an environment which is emotionally secure. This need is met, in the first instance, by giving the child the stability of a secure family unit, where the family relationships are solid, attitudes and behaviour are consistent, there is a known routine and a familiar place. All of this provides a firm dependable structure to allow the child to develop relationships with others and have good self-esteem and a strong sense of identity. For young children, where each day may bring new and challenging experiences, this continuity and predictability is essential. Mia Kellmer Pringle agreed that without this foundation the child would not be able to form effective relationships with others later on, or be able to respond to affection. The consequences for the individual and for society are alarming. A child who feels unloved, unwanted and rejected may become the adult who resorts to vandalism, violence and delinquency to unleash his or her anger and hate.

The need for new experiences

For children to learn, they need to have new stimulating experiences which challenge them. In the early years it is largely through play that children learn. Mia Kellmer Pringle argued that new experiences are essential, 'Just as the body requires food for physical development and just as an appropriate balanced diet is essential for normal growth, so new experiences are needed for the mind' (from *The Needs of Children*, M.K. Pringle, 3rd edn, 1986, page 149 published by Hutchinson. Reprinted by permission of The Random House Group Ltd.).

As children explore their world they face problems they need to solve and encounter new unfamiliar objects. Children need to experiment in a safe environment, where they have the freedom to try things out for the first time. Children learn best when the environment is rich with stimulation, and as each skill is mastered, for example a large floor puzzle, another more challenging one should be given.

Praise and recognition

'To grow from a helpless infant into a self-reliant, self-accepting adult requires an immense amount of emotional, social and intellectual learning. It is accomplished by the child's modelling himself on the adults who are caring for him. The most effective incentives to bring this about… are praise and recognition' (from *The Needs of Children*, M.K. Pringle, page 150 published by Hutchinson. Reprinted by permission of The Random House Group Ltd.).

Children love to be praised and respond well to it. Praise is an effective tool to encourage a child to succeed, especially if it is given by a significant adult – someone the child respects and looks up to. Praise can help a child continue with a difficult task or promote positive behaviour. If children's efforts are not recognised they can give up easily or behave in a negative way to gain attention. As an early education and childcare practitioner, it is essential that you praise the process and not the product; for example a child may spend a long time on and put a lot of effort into a drawing although the end product may not be as accomplished as his peers. The important point is that the child must be rewarded for his or her efforts.

The need for responsibility

Children will never learn to take responsibility for their possessions or their actions if opportunities are not given to them to learn how to be responsible. Like every other skill this needs to be practised in a safe environment with adult support, until the child becomes a fully independent adult. During adolescent years many young people rebel against the rules and boundaries parents and carers put into place. It is crucial, at this stage, that these young people know that with freedom comes responsibility and that they need to be aware of the consequences of their actions.

The need for responsibility is sometimes a dilemma for parents of children who have additional support needs. They may feel that their children are somehow more vulnerable and need to be protected from difficult tasks such as negotiating public transport. Nevertheless, it is the ultimate responsibility of every parent to ensure that their child is equipped to live as independent a life as possible.

How additional support needs are understood (past and present) and the terminology used

So far in this chapter you have learned about children's basic needs. You will now look at what are considered to be additional support needs. We defined this earlier and learned that children need extra or additional support (for a variety of reasons) to enable them to benefit from their education. Remember that these children still have 'basic' needs but may require additional support in the way of one-to-one work or specific resources to allow these needs to be met.

All children have a right to be inclusive participants in society and in their education. We are now aware of this right but the history of provision for children with additional support needs shows very different views and approaches were held to be correct. Two approaches considered in this chapter are the medical (or deficit) model and the social model.

The medical model of disability

Up until the 1970s the deficit or medical model of disability dominated the way professionals regarded the provision of services for children with additional support needs. In the medical model the child was seen as 'faulty'. He or she was measured against a set of developmental

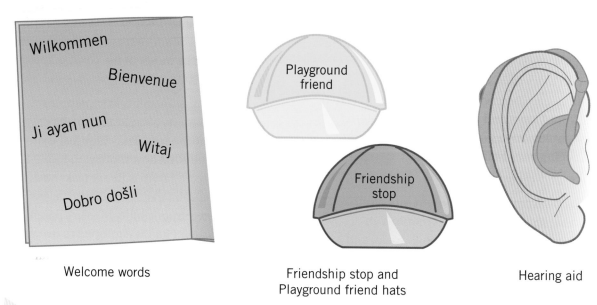

Welcome words

Friendship stop and
Playground friend hats

Hearing aid

Resources to support inclusion

norms and found to be lacking in essential skills and/or growth. All efforts were then made to bring the child up to the point where he or she was within an expected range of development.

The medical (deficit) model of disability therefore required that the child was diagnosed. In other words, because the child was not following the expected pattern of development, he or she was assessed and examined so that an accurate diagnosis of the problem could be obtained. A characteristic of the medical model was therefore labelling.

> **Key term**
>
> **Labelling** is the practice of giving a diagnostic label to a child which may describe the condition the child has, for example cystic fibrosis. Labelling may conjure up a picture of some of the characteristics of a condition but does not give an accurate picture of the individual needs of the child.

Once diagnosis was complete and a label given, the condition became the focus of attention, not the child. Efforts were made to improve or reduce the effects of the impairment while disregarding the 'ordinary' or basic needs of the child (which were described at the beginning of the chapter). Throughout this process the child's impairment would be continually assessed and monitored, and rigorous programmes of therapy or intervention imposed. In certain cases it was considered better at that time for some children to be educated in special schools and not with their mainstream peers; this was done for a variety of reasons. Only if the impairment/disability improved would the child be included with his or her peers. Throughout this process the fixed opinions and attitudes of society remained unchanged, meaning that the child was expected to change (come up to the standard set as 'normal') or remain an outsider.

The social model of disability

The social model of disability allows us to think about disability in a different way. In the social model the child is placed at the centre of provision and is valued as an individual regardless of his or her abilities. Where the medical model regarded the child as *lacking* in skills or abilities (a negative approach), the social model concentrates on what the child *can* do (a positive approach). Where the child encounters

How do we challenge stereotypical thinking about those we consider 'different' from ourselves?

barriers the social model advocates that a solution should be found and resources made available to allow the child to be included. Within the social model, educational programmes are designed which are challenging yet achievable. Also, parents, carers and professionals who support the child are given the necessary information, training and resources to ensure a strong network of care. Within this environment of equal opportunities and inclusion, diversity is welcomed and as a result society evolves.

Moving from a negative to a positive view of disability

The change from medical model to social model has been a slow process. Society's attitudes have had to change, labelling and terminology have been challenged and we have been made to examine what we mean by inclusion. But how do we develop our attitudes towards and challenge stereotypical thinking about those we consider to be 'different' from ourselves?

As individuals our initial opinions and views are drawn largely from the people who we grow up with. We hear their opinions, perhaps share their experiences, and take their views as our own until we come to a point in our lives where we must form our own opinions. It may be

that we are suddenly challenged when faced with new facts and our opinions have to change.

Consider the following example: a child grows up being told by his parents to 'feel sorry for the poor wee crippled boy who lives down the road. He will never drive a car or have a job like a normal person. He'll be in that wheelchair for the rest of his life.'

Never having met the little boy down the road, the child may for years have carried a mental picture of a poor unfortunate soul shut out from the world. Imagine his surprise when years later he applies for a mortgage. The solicitor who deals with the paperwork is none other than the boy who lived down the road. Not only is he enjoying a flourishing career but he is also driving a very smart car!

In the past, attitudes towards disability were often based on ignorance or fear of the unknown. Religious bigotry also endorsed these views as a child born with a disability was sometimes seen as being cursed by God, thereby bringing shame on the child and family. Even as late as the mid-twentieth century it was not unknown for parents of children with profound disabilities to be advised to have them put into care to give them (the parents) a chance to 'try again'.

Attitudes can lead to stereotyping

Key term

Stereotyping means having a general mental image of a group or class of people that is usually oversimplified and fixed, for example thinking that all children who are deaf are less intelligent than those with full hearing. Stereotyping occurs as a result of making judgements or assumptions because of a fixed opinion of how a person or group of people may behave.

For years, people with any kind of disability have experienced stereotyping. Common examples are children and young people with disabilities being seen as:

- helpless and unable to become fully independent
- a financial burden on the state due to their being unable to work
- people to be pitied
- always needing care and supported accommodation
- less intelligent
- infectious
- to be feared/avoided
- always getting more support than anybody else, to the detriment of other children.

Discrimination

Fixed attitudes and opinions based on stereotypes can lead to discrimination.

Terminology and labelling

When talking or writing about disabilities it is important to choose your words carefully. Many terms which were considered acceptable in the past are now deemed offensive and so inappropriate. The table below provides some examples of appropriate and inappropriate terms when referring to people with disabilities.

Inappropriate terms	Appropriate terms
Handicap (the origin of this word derives from hand-in-cap, a reference to the days when a disability meant the individual had to beg to survive)	Disability
Spastic (only appropriate when used as a medical term to describe certain types of cerebral palsy)	Cerebral palsy
Deaf and dumb	Deaf/partial hearing
Mongoloid	Down's syndrome
Cripple	Person who has a disability
Wheelchair bound	Wheelchair user
Suffering from, afflicted by	Person who has
Mental, maniac, insane, abnormal, mentally defective, maladjusted	Emotional disability; poor mental health
Retarded, idiot, imbecile, feeble minded, subnormal, mentally handicapped, backward, dull	People with learning difficulties
The blind	A blind person; someone who has a visual impairment
The deaf	A deaf person; someone who has a hearing impairment
Invalid	Disabled person

Under the medical model of disability, the labelling of people with disabilities was common. Labelling was used to help make sense of an unknown condition and to give a reason why a child was experiencing difficulties. Sometimes, sadly, only with a label would a child fit into a category and then be able to access provision. We know of course that each child is different and that labels do not help to ascertain the particular 'blend' of needs which a child may have. Consider the following case studies, for example.

Case study 1 *Attitudes and stereotypes about disability*

Mrs Colville's son, Alec (10 years), attends Richmount Primary School. In his class is James (also 10 years). James has a visual impairment and gets regular help from his support for learning assistant, Janice. Janice helps James on a one-to-one basis, making sure he can find his table in the class, enlarging some of his worksheets and helping him with his own adapted computer.

Recently, Mrs Colville has been to see the head teacher, complaining that James is getting all the attention and more money spent on him that the other children. She says that she feels sorry for the 'blind boy' but that it was better in the past when people like him went away to the school in Edinburgh where they could 'deal with children like him'. She feels that James is keeping everybody else back and that this is not fair.

- Outline what you think are the attitudes, stereotypical views and the potential for discrimination in this case study.

Case study 2 *Three children with cerebral palsy*

All of these children have cerebral palsy, but their needs are very different.

Ryluka (9 years) has a mild form of spastic cerebral palsy. She has weakness in her arms. One of her arms is prone to strong muscle spasms which she finds painful, but she receives medication for this. Her legs are not affected and she enjoys drawing and painting. Ryluka has come to Scotland from Poland. She sometimes gets stressed because she cannot understand English very well. If she is stressed her muscles can go into spasm.

Nina (12 years) also has spastic cerebral palsy, affecting her arms and her legs. She has a wheelchair but prefers to try to walk as she has been told that the muscles in her legs will weaken if she does not use them. One of her arms is pressed tight towards her body and this makes eating and drinking difficult. Nina is worried about starting secondary school.

Teachers at her current school have noticed that she is quiet and withdrawn. They have tried to reassure Nina that her new school will be supportive of her needs.

Alastair (7 years) has all three forms of cerebral palsy. He has no mobility or use of his arms. His speech is also affected, although his carers understand what he is saying. Sometimes Alastair chokes and this can be very worrying for his mother, as Alastair cannot cough and needs help quickly. As his mother has had long-term mental health problems, Alastair receives regular respite care provision from Barnardo's. Recently the regular carer retired and Alastair does not want to go to his new carer. He has started to refuse to eat at the new carer's house and at home.

1 What are the individual needs of these three children?

2 Does having a 'label' help in meeting these needs?

A continuum of need

The case study overleaf showed below that labelling a child does not help you to get a clear picture of the specific needs of that child. This may help you to understand the concept of continuum of need. A continuum is something that does not stop but continues. All children, whether they have been assessed as having additional support needs or not, lie on this continuum; it is like a road on a map along which they travel. At certain points on the map you would expect children to do certain things, for example by 6 months children should be starting to sit up. Certain factors will change how quickly a child moves from point to point on this journey (for some children, some points will never be reached). These factors are diverse and can include the provision of extra support, or a delay in assessing a child's needs or a change in school or family circumstances. You cannot label a child by the category of disability of condition that he or she has, although knowledge about it will help you understand a little more about the child.

Understanding inclusion

When you looked at the two models of disability, the social model was acknowledged as that which allows the child to be treated as a valued and valuable contributor to his or her education – someone who is not an outsider but who is included. Now let us consider what is meant by 'inclusion'.

Key term

Inclusion means fully including all people irrespective of race, gender, disability, medical or other need. It is about giving equal opportunities, allowing active participation and preventing discrimination. Inclusion is *not* the same as integration, and it is much more than simply occupying the same building.

The Salamanca Statement

Inclusion as an issue in education has been raised at a national and international level. In June 1994, representatives of 92 governments and 25 international organisations formed the world conference of Special Needs Education. The conference was held in Salamanca in Spain, giving the name to the statement which resulted from this conference. The Salamanca Statement recognised 'the need to work towards "schools for all" – institutions which include everybody, celebrate differences, support learning, and respond to individual needs' (*The Salamanca Statement and Framework for Action on Special Needs Education*, United Nations Educational, Scientific and Cultural Organization, 1994). The statement underlined the reasons why inclusion is a necessity:

Regular schools with this inclusive orientation are the most effective means of combating discriminatory attitudes, creating welcoming communities, building on inclusive society and achieving education for all.

Inclusion is important because all children and young people irrespective of their abilities have a part to play in society. Children have a right to be included; indeed, it is part of their human rights. Inclusion is necessary to fully support the social model of disability, but what do practitioners have to do to ensure children with additional support needs are fully included?

Early education and childcare practice has come a long way in recognising and meeting the needs of children with additional support needs. In the UK, much of the legislative changes have taken place since the latter part of the twentieth century. It may be useful at this point to look in more detail at the history of provision in Scotland and the Acts of law which changed the future for disabled children.

The history of provision for disabled children in Scotland

In Scotland, the first provision for children needing extra help relied on support from voluntary and private bodies, as there was no state provision. The timeline below outlines the historical path to additional support needs provision. You will notice that many terms appear which are today considered offensive and inappropriate.

The history of additional support needs provision in Scotland

Date	Provision
1773	Asylum for the Industrious Blind opens in Edinburgh.
1850	Donaldson's Hospital (later school) for the deaf opens in Edinburgh. (Around this time establishments for the education of 'imbeciles' and 'defectives' were opened in Dundee and Edinburgh.) Originally this school was for both deaf and hearing pupils, making it one of the first examples of integration.
1862	The Lunacy (Scotland) Act set up care and training provision for 'imbecile' children.
The education these establishments provided was mainly vocational training in manual skills to support future employment.	
1872	The Education (Scotland) Act establishes a national system of public education making education compulsory for children aged between 5 and 13 years.
1906	Special schooling for blind and deaf children made possible by a 1906 Act.
1907	Education of Defective Children (Scotland) Act. School boards set up special provision for children experiencing difficulties in learning.
1913	An Act is passed in which school boards have to 'ascertain' which children in their area are 'mentally defective'. Under this Act, children were put into institutional care if it was felt that they would not be able to benefit from special schooling.
1945	Education (Scotland) Act. Children categorised into three sections: educable, trainable, untrainable.
1954	Special Educational Treatment (Scotland) Regulations 1954 defines nine legal categories of handicap which will need special education provision. These categories are: deafness, partial deafness, blindness, partial sightedness, mental handicap, epilepsy, speech defect, maladjustment and physical handicap.

Date	Provision
1969	The Education (Scotland) Act changes the terminology from 'special educational treatment' to 'special education'.
1973	A government working party concludes that no child is 'uneducable' or 'untrainable' and in so doing oversees the move of children previously attending day centres or health authority mental hospitals to educational settings.
1974	A committee of enquiry is set up, chaired by Mary Warnock, to report on the education of handicapped children and young people. It is the first inquiry to review educational provision for all handicapped children in the UK since 1889.

The Warnock Report

The Warnock Report (1978) is seen as a milestone in changing provision for children with additional support needs. It changed the previous way of thinking about 'special' provision and resulted in changes in the law. The report came up with the following recommendations:

- the term 'special educational need' to replace the word 'handicap'

- a change in the law to provide for a child's individual needs as distinct from his or her disability

- there should be no distinction between special education and ordinary schools, and as far as possible children and young people with special needs should be educated in ordinary schools

- needs should be recorded for children with severe complex or long-term disabilities

- a child's educational needs should be identified through assessing the child

- there is recognition of the importance of professionals working in partnership with parents.

The Warnock Report saw the term special educational need as applying not only to the two per cent of children who had pronounced specific or complex difficulties but to other children as well.

It recognised that up to 20 per cent of children may be considered as having special educational needs if:

- they had emotional or social difficulties or had behavioural problems
- they had difficulties which stemmed from a range of circumstances but resulted in them needing 'remedial' support
- they had difficulties which were temporary and short-term, such as frequent absences from school
- their first language was not English.

The chart below outlines the key developments in the provision of additional support needs for children and young people in Scotland since the Warnock Report (1978).

1978	The Education of Pupils with Learning Difficulties in Primary and Secondary Schools in Scotland report concludes that remedial education is too narrow a term to describe the wide range of learning difficulties experienced by children and young people, stressing instead that 'appropriate' rather than remedial education is needed.
1980	The Education (Scotland) Act (1980). This enshrines the recommendations laid out in the Warnock Report Act (1978). The term 'record of need' is introduced for children aged 2 years and over. The definition of 'special educational need' is applied to children who 'have greater difficulty in learning than most other children of their own age'.
1994	The report Effective Provision for Special Educational Needs (EPSEN) by HM Inspectors of Schools outlines ten features of effective provision for special educational needs. They are: • understanding the continuum of special needs • effective identification and assessment procedures • appropriate curriculum • provision based on need • effective approaches to teaching and learning • attainment of educational goals • involvement of parents • cooperation between professionals • effective management of provision • young person to be fully involved.
1995	The Children (Scotland) Act. Special consideration is to be given to looked-after children within the education system, and the welfare of the child is considered paramount when making decisions affecting the child. Children's views must be recognised. Children with a disability have a right to live as normal a life as possible.
1995	Disability Discrimination Act. It is unlawful to treat disabled people less favourably than others for reasons related to their disability.
2000	The Standards in Scotland's Schools etc. Act. Mainstream schools are to be considered as the first choice for *all* young people.
2003	Moving Forward! Additional Support for Learning. In this document, the view is taken that inclusive schools 'welcome pupil diversity and develop an ethos and values which promote the educational, social and cultural development of all pupils' (*Moving Forward! Additional Support for Learning*, Scottish Executive, 2003).

The Education (Additional Support for Learning) (Scotland) Act (2004)

Perhaps the biggest change in provision has been the Education (Additional Support for Learning) (Scotland) Act (2004). A national consultative exercise in 2002 focused on finding out what changes would be necessary to improve and update the assessment and recording process of children and young people with additional support needs; the result was the 2004 Act. The changes established by the Act were also to acknowledge the five national priorities in education which the Scottish Executive Education Department had outlined in 2003, as follows:

- achievement and attainment
- framework for learning
- inclusion and equality
- values and citizenship
- learning for life.

The changes brought about as a result of the Education (Additional Support for Learning) (Scotland) Act (2004) include the following.

- a change in terminology: additional support needs are defined as all learning support needs, not just special educational needs
- education authorities have a duty to identify and take steps to meet the support needs for learning for *all* children
- parents can request an assessment of their child's needs
- a coordinated support plan replaces the record of need
- an independent mediation service is to be provided for all disputes with parents
- a new independent Additional Support Needs tribunal will hear appeals relating to the coordinated support plan.

Under the Act, children and young people may need additional support for learning for a variety of reasons, including:

- having a motor or sensory impairment
- having a learning difficulty
- having emotional and social difficulties
- being on the child protection register
- living with parents who have mental health problems
- living with parents who misuse substances
- being 'looked after' by the local authority
- being non-attendees at school
- having English as an additional language
- having a particular talent
- having experienced a bereavement
- being young carers
- being bullied.

How a range of conditions can lead to additional support needs

Short- and long-term support needs

For some children, support will be needed for only a short amount of time because their particular needs may not require long-term support (for example, children who are multilingual may only need support initially when they start in a new school setting). For others, such as children who are on the autistic spectrum, support may be needed throughout the time they are at school.

Shane is in his second year at High School. He moved from England earlier in the year and speaks with a Yorkshire accent. A group of older pupils have started to bully Shane. At first he was subjected to taunting and name calling, but recently the bullying has become physical. In one attack his glasses were broken and some of his books thrown over a hedge. Shane is frightened to tell his guidance teacher as the group have threatened to 'beat him up' if he tells anyone.

1 Do you think Shane has additional support needs?

2 What kind of support would Shane benefit from?

Short-term support needs

You may have wrongly assumed that children and young people have to have an identified medical condition before they can be considered as having additional support needs. As the list of criteria outlined in the Education (Additional Support for Learning) (Scotland) Act (2004) demonstrates, the net has now been cast much wider: children and young people may now access support who would not have been able to do so previously.

Some children may need short-term help. In other words, support and resources may need to be put in place temporarily until the child no longer needs it. An example of this would be a child whose family are Polish and who does not speak English. For a short while the child may need a translator and support from the bilingual services team, which is part of local authority provision.

Other children may need support during the time they are in full-time education. An example of this would be the child who has Down's syndrome. This child may need a coordinated support plan (details of this can be seen on page 207) which will outline the support and services each professional involved with the child will provide.

Bullying as a short-term support need

Let us examine one of the short-term needs you have just read about. In the last case study you learned that Shane would be entitled to support. Bullying is an issue which is taken very seriously by schools and can take many forms. Children who are bullied feel vulnerable and isolated. The bullying may involve name calling, being deliberately left out or ignored, or physical abuse such as spitting, kicking and hitting. Both sexes bully and are bullied. Children who bully may need help just as much as those who are bullied, as their behaviour may be connected to personal problems which they are experiencing.

Sometimes children are too ashamed to admit that they are being bullied. They may go to great lengths to hide the fact; they may be afraid that they will be viewed as a coward. Signs such as not wanting to be at school or frequent unexplained illnesses may indicate that a child is being bullied.

Bullying in schools can only be solved if parents, teachers, other professionals and the pupils themselves work together. Schools have a duty to investigate instances of bullying and their anti-bullying policies will indicate how they will deal with the issue (each school's policy may be different).

Young people are particularly vulnerable to factors which may affect their mental well-being. In 2006 a research project (part of a 'Healthier Scotland' initiative; listed in the references section of this chapter) investigated the link between non-suicidal self-harm and attempted suicide in young people, with the aim of identifying possible ways of reducing the risk of self-harm and suicide among young people. The study involved interviews with 20 young people who had experience of self-harm and attempted suicide (self-harm is defined as an act of self-injury or self-poisoning which is not intended to result in death). The study found that self-harming began around the age of 12 years and suicide attempts started around the age of 16 years. The factors which contributed to these mental health issues were, in the young people studied, very similar. They included complex and chaotic lifestyles, serious family problems including physical and sexual abuse, and neglect. Self-harm methods varied but included self-cutting, overdosing, burning, pulling hair out, drug/alcohol misuse and forms of eating disorders. When asked what the starting point had been to their self-harming, they listed three reasons:

1. being bullied or ostracised at school

2. being abused/neglected at home

3. having a serious argument with a friend or parent.

The young people who took part in the research project described themselves as feeling lonely, isolated, depressed, out of control and worthless. For these young people asking for help is very difficult. Schools may dismiss their behaviour as 'attention seeking'. Negative and judgemental responses by professionals only made them feel that no one cared for them. For those who received help, having someone to talk to, who was able to listen to them and whom they could trust, was a key factor in their recovery.

What kind of support do bullied children need?

Children and young people who are being bullied need:

- to feel that they are listened to and their comments acted upon

- to feel safe

- support to cope with their feelings, such as anger mangement

- peer group support, such as that provided by a 'buddying' system where other children agree to support those who are feeling left out.

Should bilingualism or multilingualism be considered an additional support need?

Much of the world's population regularly uses more than one language as they go about their daily life. This is in contrast to the common perception that the brain cannot cope with learning another language due to a limited capacity. Fortunately this is not true and children have the capacity to learn additional languages while continuing to progress with their 'home' language.

Children may need support for a short time if they are bilingual or multilingual.

> ### Key term
> The terms **bilingual** and **multilingual** indicate that learners already have one language and that English is a second (if bilingual) or additional (if multilingual) language.

Scotland has seen a rise in bilingual and multilingual learners needing support in the last few years, which is not surprising as the demography of Scotland is changing rapidly. The needs of this group of children are diverse and factors need to be considered such as:

- the home language(s) they speak

- their previous educational experience (if any)

- their social/economic background

- their pastoral needs

- the support from home

- their cultural or religious background.

Recent policy statements and legislation have raised the profile of the needs of bilingual learners. *Supporting Children's Learning: Code of Practice* (Scottish Executive, 2005, page 20) states that:

> A need for additional support does not imply that a child or young person lacks abilities or skills. For example, bilingual children or young people whose first language

is not English may already have a fully developed home language and a wide range of achievements, skills and attributes. Any lack of English should be addressed within a learning and teaching programme which takes full account of the individual's abilities and learning needs.

Children whose home language is not English may also experience isolation and discrimination through racism, which may compound any difficulties they experience through their lack of language. Local education authorities are required to identify and tackle barriers to achievement, including institutional racism. The *Report of the Stephen Lawrence Inquiry* by Sir William Macpherson (1999) defined institutional racism as:

> the collective failure of an organisation to provide an appropriate and professional service to people because of their colour, culture or ethnic origin.

Children who are asylum seekers or are from gypsy and travelling families may experience this type of discrimination.

Children of asylum seekers often have particular circumstances to cope with which affect their welfare and learning. Examples of these circumstances may be emotional trauma resulting from dawn raids on their families, repeated moving from house to house and being detained in detention centres. To date there are more than 1,400 families in Scotland awaiting decisions about their future (www.scotland.gov.uk/Resource/Doc/197969/0052908.pdf). Children of such families may not be able to establish a routine of attendance at school or nursery.

Children who are bilingual or multilingual may require the following additional support:

- translators/interpreters
- support from bilingual services (provided by the local authority)
- one-to-one support from classroom assistants
- good home/school communication.

Supporting bereaved children

Children may also need extra support if they experience bereavement. There is evidence that children and young people who have experienced the death of a parent are at a greater risk of developing mental health problems. The adults in their lives may not be in a position to provide support because they themselves are coming to terms with the loss.

Bereaved children may experience a range of emotions including:

- an initial numb phase where the death seems unreal and the child is in shock
- a mourning phase during which the child is likely to be distressed, deeply sad and may be preoccupied with the person who has died
- acceptance of their loss and readjustment to their new life.

There is no set time when each of these phases will be reached, as each child is different, but they are likely to experience these emotions in the same order. In some cases the child may experience physical health problems such as appetite loss and headaches. Children may also display certain behaviours when they are bereaved, including:

- withdrawal
- stealing
- sleep disturbance
- attention-seeking behaviour.

Any bereavement has to be dealt with sensitively. Grief does not 'go away' and children may experience strong feelings when they realise that a loved one will not be with them at significant periods in their life, such as birthdays.

Obviously, responses to grief vary with the age of the child. Young children may not understand the finality of death and the fact that their parent will not be coming back home. Older children may find the idea of impermanence easier to understand but hard to deal with.

What kind of support do grieving children need?

Depending on their age, grieving children may need opportunities to remember and talk about the person who has died, to meet other children who have experienced bereavement, and information about death and what death means.

In the past, children were often excluded from the grieving process. It was believed to be kinder to children to carry on as if nothing had happened, not allowing them to attend the funeral or talk about their loss. In truth, this may have been more about sparing the adult a difficult task in explaining death than protecting the child. Helpful strategies to support grieving children include:

- making time to allow a child to talk freely with a trusted adult

- liaising with the family, especially regarding the child's return to the setting

- being sensitive to the fact that children may not want to separate from surviving family members and may worry about their well-being

- being aware that children may regress to an earlier stage of development; they may not perform academically at the same stage they were at prior to the death

- informing peers of the child's loss.

Short-term need: separation and divorce in the family

Separation from a parent may also occur if parents divorce. In any one year approximately 8,000 children in Scotland under the age of 16 years live in families where parents are divorcing (sources: *All Children, All Ages* (2000), a report on implementation of the UN Convention on the Rights of the Child in Scotland published by the Scottish Alliance for Children's Rights; and *Fact File 2000: Facts and Figures about Scotland's Children* by NCH Scotland). Children may experience difficulties if the separation has been acrimonious. As well as grieving for the loss of the parent who no longer lives in the family home, a child may experience:

- feelings of guilt, somehow believing that they may have contributed to the separation

- stress after witnessing parents' arguments with each other; children may feel torn between both parents.

In addition, a child may have to attend contact sessions to see the parent who no longer lives in the family home.

It is not unusual for children who experience the divorce or separation of their parents to feel anger. This may be shown by displays of aggressive behaviour or by bullying others.

Long-term support needs

We have examined factors which may cause a child to need support in the short term. The tables on pages 192–202 outline a range of conditions which may mean that children need long-term support.

Condition and description of condition	Cause	Incidence	How child is affected	Support requirements
Friedreich's ataxia This condition affects the central nervous system and there is progressive deterioration of coordination and muscle control. Onset of the condition normally happens about age 15 years, but can appear as young as 2 years. There is no cure.	This condition is genetically inherited. Research has tracked the abnormal gene as chromosome 9. When two people who are both carriers have children, the chances of having a child with Friedreich's ataxia are: • 25% chance of child not being affected • 50% chance of the child being a carrier of the gene but being unaffected by the condition • 25% chance of the child having the condition. (Source of statistics: www.patient.co.uk)	Recent studies show that 1 in 85 people are carriers of Friedreich's ataxia and a disease incidence of 1 in 29,000. (*Source: Management of Ataxia: Guidelines on Best Practice*, Ataxia UK http://www.ataxia.org.uk/page.builder/clinical_guidelines.html)	• Clumsy movements • Lack of coordination • Respiratory problems may lead to pneumonia • Slurring of speech • Eventually child may have heart problems Friedreich's ataxia is a progressive disorder, though it may not always be fatal.	• Physiotherapy to support muscles • Occupational therapy to support balance • Medication for lung infections • Child may need appropriate support to deal with feelings of depression, anger and frustration which a progressive condition may generate
Dyslexia Dyslexia may affect the child or young person's reading, writing and spelling. ('dys' means difficulty and 'lexicon' means words).	New research using brain scans shows that there are differences in the brain of a person with dyslexia. This may be caused by the neurological system affecting the processing and transmitting of sensory stimuli. There is also a genetic link, with abnormalities with chromosomes 15 and 6 being the most likely cause.	The British Dyslexia Association estimates that around 4% of the population (over 2 million people in the UK) is severely affected by dyslexia. Recent research shows that reading problems could be just as common in girls as in boys and boys suffering from reading problems to a greater degree is a myth. ('Reflections of research on reading disability with special attention to gender issues' L.S. Siegel and I.Smythe, 2005)	Early indicators that a child could be dyslexic include: • articulation problems • confusion over directional words such as up/down, right/left • mixed-up sentences • delay in speech • delay in fine motor skills • problems with rhythm, e.g. clapping to a beat • delayed development of hand preference • problems with sequencing • 'mirror writing', e.g. letters reversed and/or inverted.	• Assessment of child's writing to identify support needed • Educational psychologist may advise support programme • Specific computer programs and equipment may benefit the child • Toe-by-Toe (a multi-sensory reading programme) • Enlarged print, particular fonts and coloured overlays may help with written work

Condition and description of condition	Cause	Incidence	How child is affected	Support requirements
Duchenne muscular dystrophy This is a condition in which there is a lack of dystrophic – a substance which is necessary for the muscle cells to survive. Children appear normal at birth but by 3 to 4 years may start to show muscle weakness. The lower legs may be well formed but this is fatty tissue. There is no cure for this condition.	This is a genetic condition which is sex-linked (carried by the mother) and mainly affects boys.	About 100 boys with Duchenne muscular dystrophy are born in the UK each year. There are about 1,500 known boys with the disorder living in the UK at any one time. For the general population the risk of having an affected child is about one in every 3,500 male births. (Source of statistics: www.muscular-dystrophy.org/information_resources_factsheets/medical_conditions_factsheets/duchenne.html) (For further information on muscular dystrophy visit www.muscular-dystrophy.org)	• As the child gets older, the muscles weaken – activities needing large motor skills are affected. • Children may develop an unusual gait and start to fall over. • By the age of 9–12 years, a child may lose mobility. • About one-third of boys with the condition may also have a degree of learning difficulties.	• Physiotherapy to keep the child as mobile as possible. This may involve exercises such as swimming and muscle stretching. • Leg callipers may help with balance. • A wheelchair may be needed by the age of 9–12 years. • A back brace may be needed for children who are wheelchair users as they have a high risk of developing spinal curvature. • Some children benefit from steroids which slow down muscle degeneration. • Speech therapy may help articulation. • As muscular dystrophy is degenerative, family support may include counselling.

Condition and description of condition	Cause	Incidence	How child is affected	Support requirements
Spina bifida Spina bifida is a fault in the spinal column in which one or more vertebrae (bones which make up the backbone) do not form properly. There are three main types of spina bifida: • spina bifida occulta (hidden) • spina bifida cystica (cyst-like) which has two forms: – meningocele – myelomeningocele.	The cause is unknown but may be partially hereditary. If a mother has a child with spina bifida, she runs a greater risk of having another child with spina bifida. Folic acid taken in pregnancy can reduce the risk of the baby developing spina bifida. The condition occurs between the 14th and the 28th day of conception.	It is more prevalent in white races and premature babies often have it.	This varies with each type of spina bifida. *Spina bifida occulta* The child may never be aware they have this type as it produces no obvious difficulties. *Meningocele* This is the least common form. A sac or cyst containing tissue is visible on the spine. There may be no damage to the spinal nerves and therefore no disability. *Myelomeningocele* This is the most common and most serious form. The sac or cyst contains nerves and part of the spinal cord. Children may have mobility, bladder and bowel problems. They will also have paralysis and loss of sensation below the damaged part.	• Surgery may be needed for myelomeningocele to close the sac • Strict hygiene to avoid infection, especially when nappy changing • Where a child has paralysis it is essential that carers avoid pressure sores • Physiotherapy and occupational therapy will encourage movement • Primary Health Care team will give advice on the use of catheters; GP may advise medication • Adaptations may be needed to home and learning environment to accommodate wheelchair

Condition and description of condition	Cause	Incidence	How child is affected	Support requirements
Cerebral palsy (CP) This term applies to a physical condition which affects movement. There are three types of cerebral palsy: 1. Spastic cerebral palsy 2. Athetoid cerebral palsy 3. Ataxic cerebral palsy.	Caused by injury to the brain. Genetic factors may predispose a child to CP. Encephilitis and meningitis when a baby is very young can cause CP. Smoking, drug use, alcohol use and toxaemia during pregnancy can increase the risk of a child being born with CP.	Around 1 in every 400 children born in the UK develops cerebral palsy. (*Source*: www.scope.org.uk)	• Control of muscles causing problems walking, writing, eating, talking, dressing • Balance and coordination difficulties • Difficulty controlling posture • Some children with CP also have visual and hearing difficulties as well as learning difficulties • One in three children with CP has epilepsy	• There is no cure for CP • Physiotherapy to ease symptoms such as spasticity • Occupational therapy • Speech therapy • Some children with CP benefit from a programme of conducive education (a programme designed to help the child overcome problems with movement) • Drugs can ease muscle spasms • SCOPE is an organisation which offers information and support to those who have CP, as well as Capability Scotland
Dyspraxia (may also be known as developmental coordination disorder, clumsy child syndrome, motor learning difficulty or perceptuo-motor dysfunction) This is a condition where there is an immaturity of the brain resulting in messages not being transmitted properly to the body. Some children may be mildly affected while others are profoundly affected.	It is thought to be the result of immaturity of the nervous system or damage to the nerve links in the brain which send messages to other parts of the brain.	Dyspraxia affects about 10% of people in the UK. It affects one child in every classroom of children. Males are more likely to be affected than females. (*Source*: Dyspraxia Foundation – www.dyspraxiafoundation.org.uk)	• Large and fine motor skills are affected giving difficulties with PE, dressing, writing, eating; handwriting may be poor • Coordination is affected • Articulation (speech) may be slow • Children find it difficult to remember instructions • They may fidget and hand flap • Some children have difficulties sleeping and sometimes experience migraine-type headaches • Perception may be affected	• Some skills, such as coordination, can be improved with support from physiotherapists and occupational therapists • Tasks broken down into small achievable goals • Speech therapy to aid articulation

Condition and description of condition	Cause	Incidence	How child is affected	Support requirements
Down's syndrome (Trisomny 21) Down's syndrome results in specific physical features, learning difficulties, ear/eye defects, heart problems and an increased chance of having chest infections. Some individuals have the mosaic form of Trisomny 21.	Down's syndrome is a chromosomal disorder. It occurs when instead of two copies of chromosome 21, there is an extra chromosome (three copies). Normally there are 23 pairs of chromosomes, but the child with Down's syndrome has 47 chromosomes instead of 46. In Mosaic Down's syndrome this chromosomal make up is 'patchy', i.e. some cells have 47 chromosomes but some have the normal 46. In a very few cases (3–4%) the condition is inherited.	Down's syndrome affects approximately 1 in every 1,000 babies, which means that about 600 babies with Down's syndrome are born each year in the UK. The condition tends to affect male and females equally. It is estimated that there are approximately 60,000 people with Down's syndrome currently living in the UK. The chance of having a baby with Down's syndrome increases when the mother is over 35 years of age. For example, a 20 year old woman has a 1 in 1,440 chance of having a baby with Down's syndrome, while a 35 year old woman has a 1 in 338 chance. A 45 year old woman has a 1 in 32 chance. (*Source:* http://www.nhsdirect.nhs.uk/articles/article.aspx?articleid=136, Crown Copyright)	Child has physical features which are obvious at birth. They are: • poor muscle tone • the baby may be 'floppy' • flattened facial features • small, low-set ears • epicanthi (fold of skin) over the eyelids gives the eyes an upward an outward slant • feet and hands are short and broad • the mouth is small and the tongue is large • 50% of children will have heart problems • hearing and visual problems may occur • child has a poor immune system • child may have severe learning difficulties (this varies with each child).	• The child may respond well to learning Makaton. • The Portage home visiting service builds on the skills the child already has and may be beneficial. • Pre-school specialist teachers employed by the local authority may work in a similar way to Portage. It is essential that early support is put in place quickly to achieve the maximum benefit for the child. • Support for learning will be needed at school. • Heart problems need close monitoring, with 50% of all heart problems eventually needing surgery. • Regular eye tests are needed to support vision.

Condition and description of condition	Cause	Incidence	How child is affected	Support requirements
Fragile X syndrome This condition is relatively recent in being diagnosed. It is the most common inherited cause of learning difficulties.	The condition is passed on by the X chromosome, which is one of a pair that decides the sex of the child (a boy is XY and a girl is XX). The X chromosome is abnormal.	• 1 in 4,000 males • 1 in 6,000 females (*Source:* Fragile X Research Foundation – www.fraxa.org © FRAXA 1997–2008)	• Child may have a learning disability with difficulties in concentrating • Anxieties and mood swings • Behaviours normally associated with children on the autistic spectrum • Long face, large ears, flat feet • Hyper-extensible joints, especially fingers • About 25% of people with Fragile X syndrome also experience seizures • Children may have speech and language difficulties such as echolalia (repetition of the last word or phrase)	• Language support may be beneficial, including Makaton, sign language, TEACCH, CCH visual structure, PECs (picture exchange communication system). Classroom environment is important: • auditory and visual distractions should be limited • support for learning teachers/assistants should work alongside the child on a one-to-one basis, either behind or beside the child to reduce the need for eye contact • work to be done in 15-minute 'units' • classroom routines need to be consistent, with notice given of impending change.

Condition and description of condition	Cause	Incidence	How child is affected	Support requirements
Autistic spectrum disorder (autism) Autistic spectrum disorder (ASD) is a term used to describe the group of developmental disorders characterised by the following 'triad of impairments': • difficulties in relating to or understanding social situations • difficulties in communication • a lack of imaginative play and displays of obsessive repetitive behaviour. (The autistic spectrum includes Asperger's syndrome, which will be considered separately on page 199.)	The exact cause of autism has not yet been fully established. It has been suggested that there may be a genetic link or a difficult birth may cause slight damage to the brain.	• 1 in every 100 in the UK • About half a million people in the UK have autism • Boys are affected more than girls. (*Source*: The National Autistic Society http://www.autism.org.uk/autism)	• Communication is affected. Children can be silent in play, talk about a fixed topic and not listen to others, demonstrate 'echolalia' (repeating what the other person has said). • Words are taken literally, e.g. 'pull your socks up' would have the effect of making the child literally pull up their socks. • Obsessive and ritualistic behaviours may include always doing the same tasks in the same order. Failure to do so would cause extreme distress. • Autistic children find it hard to socialise and to play. • Eye contact is avoided. • Some children on the autistic spectrum also have digestive problems.	• Specific communication systems such as PECS (picture exchange communication system) or Boardmaker • Clear, consistent routine • An 'uncluttered' environment • Help with social situations • Language which is clear and unambiguous • High-functioning pupils benefit from computer-based learning and individual work stations

Condition and description of condition	Cause	Incidence	How child is affected	Support requirements
Asperger's syndrome This condition was first described by Hans Asperger in 1944. Children with Asperger's syndrome have difficulties with the same 'triad of impairments' as seen with autistic spectrum disorder, but they may be less pronounced. Some, but not all, children with Asperger's may have a specific skill or talent in a specific area.	Asperger's is viewed as a variant of autism. Genetic causes: • a difficult birth • infections in pregnancy or in early infancy.	• 1 in 200 children • More common in boys than girls (*Source:* www.aspergerfoundation.org.uk/what_as.htm)	• Preoccupied with own area of interest • Unaware of social clues such as personal space and body language • May have difficulty in using social language (language may be 'book-like') • Take everything literally • Clumsiness	• A paediatrician can confirm a diagnosis or rule out other conditions • Pupils with Asperger's are visual learners and respond well to visual clues such as those used in Boardmaker • Timetables should be adhered to with prior notice given of any changes • Children with Asperger's syndrome respond well to computer-based learning

ADHD – attention deficit, hyperactivity disorder
There are other names for this condition including hyperkenetic disorder and ADD (attention deficit disorder).
 	
Symptoms will appear before the age of 7 years and persist for at least six months.
 	
The main features of the condition are:
• inattentiveness
• over-activity
• impulsiveness.
	There are several causes:
	• twin studies show a strong genetic link
	• environmental causes include:
	  – maternal alcohol consumption
	  – infections during pregnancy and brain damage
	• intolerance to certain foods.
		• ADHD affects 1.7% of the UK population
		• More common in boys than girls
		(*Source:* NetDoctor – www.netdoctor.co.uk/diseases/facts/adhd.htm)
			• Short attention span
			• 'On the go' all the time
			• Clumsy and disorganised
			• Cannot wait their turn
			• Impulsive
			• Poor concentration
			• If children are on Ritalin, they may experience feelings of nausea and tiredness. They may also lose weight.
				• Child may need medication such as Ritalin
				• New research has suggested that dietary supplements such as fish oils can help
				• One-to-one work with classroom assistant or support for learning assistant to keep child 'on task'
				• Work broken down into small manageable steps
				• Praise for effort
				• Because this condition affects socialisation, strategies to support this may be implemented, such as small group work, teaching a child to take turns or say 'thank you'

Condition and description of condition	Cause	Incidence	How child is affected	Support requirements
Epilepsy Epilepsy is defined as a tendency to have recurrent seizures (fits). A seizure is caused by a sudden burst of electrical activity in the brain, which may disrupt the normal messages passed between brain cells. There are more than 40 types of seizure which need to be managed in different ways. Seizures are usually classified as either general or partial seizures.	There are a number of reasons why a child may develop epilepsy: • brain damage caused by a difficult birth • infection of the brain (such as meningitis) • brain tumour • family history of epilepsy.	There are around 456,000 people in the UK who have epilepsy. That's about one in every 131 people. There are around 50 million people with epilepsy in the world. Tests such as electroencephalogram (EEG), which records brainwave patterns, can help diagnose epilepsy. (*Source*: The National Society for Epilepsy – www.epilepsynse.org.uk)	This differs with each type of seizure. *Generalised seizures:* • tonic-clonic seizures are the type most associated with epilepsy • children may see lights, taste or smell something • body goes into spasms; may lose bladder control • may froth at the mouth • after seizure the child will be drowsy. *Absences:* A brief interruption of consciousness; once known as 'petit-mal'; child may flutter eyelids. *Partial seizures – simple:* Child does not lose consciousness; limbs may twitch. Child may experience 'pins and needles' sensation. *Partial seizures – complex:* Child may lose consciousness or child may wander around classroom unaware of surroundings.	• During a spasm the child should be placed in the recovery position, if possible putting something soft under the child's head • Child may take medication, e.g. anti-epileptic drugs • All staff should be made aware of children who may have seizures and this must inform curriculum planning, e.g. some children have photo-sensitive epilepsy and television viewing may bring on a seizure • A sensitive approach is needed, e.g. children may be embarrassed if they lose bowel/bladder control • Staff may have to recap parts of lesson missed if child has had an 'absence'

Condition and description of condition	Cause	Incidence	How child is affected	Support requirements
Visual impairment There are many reasons why a child may have a visual impairment. These include: • short/long sightedness • squint • nystagmus (flickering of the eye) • glaucoma • tunnel vision • cataract (the lens of the eye is cloudy) • astigmatism (the eyeball has an irregular shape).	Causes vary according to the type of visual impairment but could include: • rubella in pregnancy • a premature birth • family history of blindness • injury to the eye.	There are an estimated 25,000 children with sight problems in the UK, 12,000 of these children also have other difficulties. (*Source:* http://www.rnib.org.uk/xpedio/groups/public/documents/publicwebsite/public–researchstats.hcsp. Reproduced with the permission of the RNIB.)	• Learning – 90% of learning in infancy takes place through visual senses • Mobility may be affected as a child may be unable to clearly see their surrounding physical environment and be uncertain where to go • The child may find it hard to make friends and support may be required (such as fluorescent arm bands for friends to wear in the playground)	• Child may need to attend a school with a specialist sensory unit or a special school • Support from visiting teacher of visual impairment • Pathways must be kept clear • The layout of the classroom must be explained and not unexpectedly changed • Make sure that the child can see the adult's face • Toys and equipment which are tactile • Lighting is important • Child may need to be encouraged to wear glasses • Work may need to be enlarged or an enlarger provided • Braille resources • Regular eye tests from optician

Condition and description of condition	Cause	Incidence	How child is affected	Support requirements
Hearing impairment There are two main types of deafness: • *Conductive deafness.* In this type of deafness, sounds cannot pass through the outer and middle ear into the inner ear. This could be caused by wax build up, glue ear or a small object being placed in the ear. • *Sensori-neural deafness.* This is not a temporary loss of hearing but a condition in which the inner ear does not work effectively. This can be on one side only (unilateral) or both sides (bilateral). Hearing loss is usually described as mild, moderate, severe or profound.	There are many reasons why a child may have a hearing impairment, including: • family history of deafness • rubella in pregnancy • substances taken during pregnancy • severe jaundice at birth • premature birth • meningitis • mumps • infections.	About 65,000 children in the UK have a hearing impairment. About 840 babies each year may be born with a permanent hearing impairment. (*Source: Good Practice in Caring for Young Children with Special Needs*, A. Dare and M. O'Donovan, 2002, page 325. Reproduced with the permission of Nelson Thornes Ltd.)	• Learning may be affected as the child cannot hear verbal input. • In profoundly deaf children the ability to understand language and to vocalise will be affected. • A child's ability to speak may be affected as he/she cannot hear language. A speech and language therapist may need to provide support. • A child may find it difficult to socialise, and opportunities for interaction may need to be planned.	• Child may need to attend a school with a specialist sensory unit or a special school • Support from visiting teacher of hearing impairment • Hearing aids and knowledge of how to use them • Radio loop system: a microphone picks up the speaker's voice and transmits it to a receiver worn by the child • Specialist computer software; some have programs which have British Sign Language (BSL) signing and text onscreen to match this • Assessment from audiologist

How children and young people with additional support needs, and their families/carers, access support

Before you can begin to provide the appropriate support, you need to know exactly what type of support the child needs. For this, you need to assess the child to find out what he or she can and cannot do.

In *Supporting Children's Learning: Code of Practice* it is recommended that local authorities should keep in mind some of the following principles when assessing children:

- a holistic view of children and young people should be taken; this should take into account their personal circumstances
- children's views should be sought
- parents and young people themselves should understand the reasons why assessments are taking place
- assessment should be ongoing, because needs continually change.

The assessment process sounds very formal but in reality many children's needs are assessed informally by observation, as part of the teacher's or practitioner's day to day work. If the child's needs are more complex, then specialists may carry out more formal assessments.

Assessment of children at birth

Assessments start early – babies are assessed after birth. Paediatricians will weigh the child, test for PKU (the Guthrie heel test) and listen to the child's heart beat. The baby's reflexes will also be tested. In response to the Royal College of Paediatrics Health Report *Health for all Children 4* (2005), National Health Boards are introducing Universal Newborn Learning screening. It may be at this stage that a child is found to have additional support needs, for example Down's syndrome or a hearing impairment. The local Health Board will then inform the local education authority, who then establish what support the child will need.

Assessment for children under the age of 3 years

The midwife and the health visitor are key health professionals in the child's early years. The health visitor will see the child at home shortly after the birth and will continue to assess the child against developmental charts to ensure that expected stages of development are reached. At these home visits and any clinic visits the health visitor will check the child's physical development (height, weight, balance and motor coordination) by observing the child playing and asking them to play games such as matching games. The health visitor will perform a simple hearing test, called a *distraction* test, to identify any hearing problems. If any problems are found in any of these areas, the health visitor would then refer the child to the GP or to the community paediatric team, a local specialist clinic or the local hospital to be assessed by a specialist consultant. At this stage, the local education authority may become involved in assessing the child so that nursery provision can be arranged. The professional employed by the education department might include a home visiting teacher for pre-school children and/or the educational psychologist.

Assessment of children of pre-school and school age

In Scotland's schools there are systems in place for identifying which children have additional support needs. Sometimes, other agencies such as voluntary agencies, social work staff and health professionals may also be part of the assessment process. Some local authorities use the Pre-SCAT (Pre-school Community Assessment Team) model of identification and assessment. This has proved to be a very effective way of identifying needs and ensures that all agencies and parents work together (see diagram overleaf).

Early identification of need is usually based on observational checklists which nursery staff would complete. These are linked to *A*

Curriculum Framework for Children 3 to 5 and may indicate any problems a child is having. The Chart below is an example of an observational checklist based on physical developments and movement (one of the five areas of *A Curriculum Framework for Children 3 to 5*).

Since 2003, all pupils in Scotland should have a PLP (personal learning plan). The PLP is an ongoing record of a child's progress and planned action to support the child. Information from observational assessments would be used to set targets on the PLP.

Since 1997 schools have developed programmes as part of the Early Intervention Initiative. These support core skills at the earliest stage. Attempts are made to intervene as early as possible (in the pre-school stage) to support children who otherwise were in danger of falling behind. This can be viewed as a preventative measure – identifying children who may experience difficulties and providing support, rather than allowing them to fail and then putting support in place.

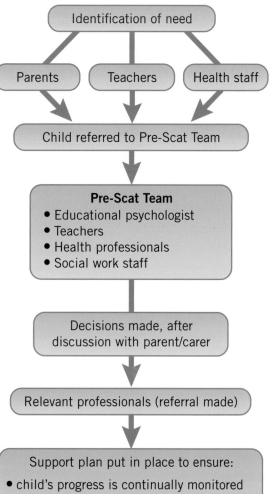

A simple diagram of the Pre-SCAT model (*From Additional Support Needs: An Introduction to ASN from Nursery to Secondary*, P. Hamill and K. Clark, Hodder Gibson, 2005. Reproduced in amended form by permission of Hodder and Stoughton Ltd.

Linking theory to practice

Consider the theories of Vygotsky and Bruner in relation to the Early Intervention Initiative.

Some children may need an IEP (individualised educational programme).

Observational checklist based on physical developments and movement

Name:	Yes	No	Comments
Date:			
Child can hop			
Child can stand on one leg			
Child can catch a ball			
Child can throw a ball			
Child can walk down steps			

PLPs and IEPs

A personal learning plan (PLP) sets out aims and goals for the child to achieve that relate to their own circumstances. They must be manageable and realistic and reflect the child's strengths and abilities as well as their needs. All children who have additional support needs will have a PLP, as set out in *Supporting Children's Learning: Code of Practice*. For many children, a PLP will be enough to plan and monitor their learning. However, if needed, their PLP can be supported by an individualised educational programme (IEP).

Again, observations would be used to help set targets for the IEP. Some of the children's own work, such as their paintings and photographs of the things they have made, may be used to help build up a picture of what the child can do. An IEP does not mean that the child will receive one-to-one individual support; it means that account will be taken of the particular individual needs of the child when work is being planned for the class.

We will look at IEPs now in more detail. An IEP:

- is a plan for a child which is inclusive – it plans for the child in the classroom environment• allows for the strengths which the child has, as well as identifying where further support is needed
- maximises the opportunities for children to achieve
- outlines the steps to be taken to enable a child to achieve specific targets
- may vary, depending on the child's needs – some may be lengthy and detailed, while others may be short.

The IEP is a useful tool. It contains the long and short targets for the child. These may also include recommended tasks that can be done at home, thus aiding partnership with parents. Because targets are clear, it allows staff to plan effectively and then assess how the child is progressing.

Read the case study below which describes the development needs of a 4-year-old girl called Leanne. A possible IEP for Leanne is then given in the chart on the next page.

Case study *Creating an IEP for Leanne*

Leanne (4 years) lives with her grandmother in a small town in the Scottish Borders. Leanne is a 'looked after' child. The local social work department are working with Leanne's mother on a drug rehabilitation programme.

Leanne attends a Child and Family Centre, where she also has contact with her mother, Julie. Leanne's grandmother does not want contact to take place in their home as in the past Julie has been unable to control her own behaviour.

Leanne attends the centre five mornings a week and has a good relationship with her key practitioner, Ashley.

Ashley is concerned that Leanne is very quiet and does not play with the other children. She is very clingy to her grandmother and often sobs when she leaves. She sometimes seems reluctant to go through to the contact session room to spend time with her mother. Leanne's language is difficult to understand, although her grandmother understands her. A referral has been made to the speech and language therapist. Leanne sucks her thumb and carries her blanket with her everywhere. She gets upset if she is parted from it and her grandmother is concerned that when she goes to school she will still have the blanket.

A possible IEP for Leanne might be:

Individualised Personal Programme	
Child's name: Leanne	
Date: 10 January 2009	
Date of birth: 18 April 2004	

Long-term targets – 3–5 Curriculum area	
Communication and Language	
Targets	**Evidenced by Leanne**
1. Listen and respond to others	Listening to peers in play situations and making appropriate response
2. Articulate clearly	Articulating words clearly so that others understand
Emotional, Personal and Social Development	
3. Develop a sense of security	Settle in to centre routine
4. Interact with others	Play cooperatively with peers
The short-term targets are:	**Strategies to support this:**
1. By February Leanne will say her name at circle time	1. Circle time, activities and 'show and tell' session each Monday morning
2. By April Leanne will have 10 or more clearly recognisable words – baby, mummy, want	2. Repeated story time of Leanne's favourite book 'Owl Babies'
3. By February Leanne will allow blanket to be put on shelf during play session	3. Stories about transitional objects, e.g. 'Dogger' by Shirley Hughes Strategy to use water/soap in play area. Blanket washed and put away
4. By March Leanne to share play tasks, e.g. passenger in car/driving car in large area	4. Role-play area: buses, cars, prams, table setting

Leanne's IEP will allow staff to plan experiences for her to give her opportunities to develop in the areas identified. This intervention is a planned process and will be continually monitored. Staff must be aware of the following points when they develop IEPs.

- *Coordination*
  As you saw in Leanne's case study, there may be many members of staff who are involved in compiling an IEP and it is important that one of them takes responsibility for coordinating the work and making sure that parents are part of this process.

- *The support/resources available*
  Any specific resources/professionals needed to support the child should be listed in the IEP, for example an IEP may require a child having one-to-one support from a support for learning assistant to reinforce learning targets set by a teacher, or the child may need specific software for the computer.

- *Monitoring/record keeping*
  The work must be ongoing and regularly monitored. Evidence of targets being reached (e.g. in the case of Leanne, Leanne spending the morning without her blanket) needs to be recorded.

- *Target setting*
  The curricular goals recorded should be developed within the context of *A Curriculum Framework for Children 3 to 5* or 5–14 Curriculum, Standard Grade/Highers. Goals should be 'SMART', i.e. Specific, Measurable, Achievable, Realistic and Time-set.

Local education authorities design their own 'pro-forma' IEP forms but information may include:

- relevant personal details of the child – name, date of birth, class and any medical or health information if this is relevant
- the interests, abilities, aptitudes of the child
- the list of the staff involved and their roles (the role of the coordinator, for instance)
- relevant documentation; some current documents may have relevance for planning, for example, assessments made by the speech and language therapist and the strategies they have identified to support the child.

For some children an IEP will not be enough – they need a coordinated support plan.

Coordinated support plans (CSPs)

According to *Supporting Children's Learning: Code of Practice* (page 47), a child will require a coordinated support plan if he or she has additional support needs arising when:

- there are one or more complex factors or multiple factors
- the needs are likely to continue for more than a year
- the needs require significant additional support to be provided by the education department and other agencies.

(Normally a child would not be eligible for a coordinated support plan unless they were over 3 years old.)

Earlier in this chapter you examined the various factors which could lead to a child having additional support needs. These factors are considered *complex* if they have a significant adverse affect on the education of the child. Examples of adverse affects are described below.

The learning environment

Example: a child has dyslexia but cannot access the curriculum because:

- they do not have a scribe
- they have not been provided with appropriate overlays for written work
- they do not have access to specific software programs to support dyslexia.

Family circumstances

Example: a child is a young carer responsible for looking after the parent and young siblings. They cannot access the curriculum because:

- they have frequent absences from school to look after others
- they are not able to do homework as time is spent looking after brothers/sisters.

Disability

Example: a child with cerebral palsy cannot benefit from their education because:

- they have frequent disruption to their learning because of hospital appointments
- they are frequently exhausted, perhaps because of medication, and this tiredness affects their concentration.

Social and emotional factors

Example: a child with behavioural difficulties cannot engage with the curriculum because:

- they have a poor concentration span
- they frequently avoid school and have long absences.

Multiple factors are factors which by themselves may not be complex but when they are grouped together have a significant adverse affect on the child. An example of multiple factors would be a child who has Asperger's syndrome who is living in a family where there are mental health problems and the family are stressed because of rising debt.

The coordinated support plan (CSP) is a statutory planning document and is for children who need a wide range of additional support from different services. It replaced the old record of needs but it sets long-term targets, rather than focusing on what the child cannot do.

It is the responsibility of the education authority to ensure the coordination of the CSP. Like the IEP, there will be one identified coordinator (though this person need not be employed by the education authority). In most cases, the head teacher of the school or someone from the senior management team will coordinate the plan.

The CSP must contain details of:

- the factors which the local authority feel have contributed to the child or young person needing additional support
- the objectives to be achieved
- how the objectives will be achieved
- who will provide support
- the person who will act as coordinator.

From plan to practice: how the child receives support

So far you have examined the assessment process which allows practitioners (and parents) to get a clearer picture of the type of support which is needed and some of the ways in which this information is recorded. But what does it actually look like in practice? Some of the ways children may get this extra support are as follows:

- adaptations to the curriculum; for example, a child who is very able in ICT may move from Band B to Band C (from 5–14 Curriculum)
- a therapist may come to the school to show the class teacher how to use appropriate strategies to help the child, e.g. a speech and language therapist may show the teacher articulation exercises
- adaptations to the school building; the school may need to make adjustments, such as ramps, lifts or better signage for children with visual impairments
- differentiation of the curriculum, for example a child who has dyslexia may access his or her work online using a specific software program
- individual or small group work; small groups or individuals may work with a support for learning teacher or a support for learning assistant may reinforce work taught by the teacher
- peer group support may be put into place such as paired reading, buddying and circle times where other pupils support their peers
- a visiting teacher may offer support; this could be a visiting teacher of hearing or visual impairment, or someone from bilingual services.

Professionals involved in supporting children with additional needs

When considering the support that may be put into place, you quickly realise the importance of the network of professionals who offer this support. Some of these are listed in the table below.

Professionals offering support

Education	Educational psychologists
	Support for learning teachers/assistants
	Early years practitioners
	Visiting teachers
Health	Speech and language therapists
	Physiotherapists
	Clinical psychologist
	Doctors/consultants
	Orthoptrist
	Paediatricians
	Audiologist
	Occupational therapists
	Health visitors (community nurses)
	Psychologists
Social work	Social workers
	Family centre staff
	Welfare rights team

We will now explore in more detail the role of some of the professionals listed above.

The educational psychologist

Educational psychologists are graduates who have additional qualifications in educational psychology. They work where there may be difficulties with:

- transitions from nursery to primary – they will assess the needs of the child by gathering information from parents, teachers and through direct observations of the child
- education – if the child is having problems with learning, they will observe the child to find the underlying reason

- behaviour – behaviour is challenging and the child is not responding to the usual strategies of behaviour management used in the school or childcare setting

- emotional issues – the child may be withdrawn and not participate at school; there may be personal/family circumstances underpinning this

- bullying – a child may be being bullied, which is impacting on his learning; they may be reluctant attendees because of bullying

- transition from primary to secondary school.

Educational psychologists work in partnerships with parents and teachers. A consultation with an educational psychologist could be arranged if a parent discussed this with the head teacher of the school. Anyone with a formal role in the life of the child could ask for a consultation.

Educational psychologists work at several levels:

- directly with the child or young person

- indirectly through parents and/or teacher

- via trained staff who are in direct contact with the child.

Parental permission is necessary for any involvement and parents are encouraged to be part of the decision-making process about their child. Educational psychologists have a statutory role in the process of assessing children's additional support needs.

Visiting teacher – visual impairment

These professionals work with children and young people, families and other professionals in supporting the child who has a visual impairment. They work with pre-school, primary school and secondary school pupils. Some of the tasks they perform include:

- supporting school staff so that a pupil with a visual impairment can access the curriculum; they might give advice on lighting, where a child should sit or materials to use

- supporting the parents and offering strategies to help them; this might include making home adaptations

- assessing the child to monitor progress and identify future targets to inform an IEP or CSP

- sharing expertise and skills with other staff.

To become a visiting teacher of visual impairment, you would need to be GTC (General Teaching Council) registered and hold an appropriate postgraduate qualification in additional support needs which includes teaching of the visually impaired. A qualification in Braille is also desirable but not essential.

Visiting teacher – hearing impairment

This professional works in the same way as the visiting teacher of visual impairment and would need the same qualifications (relevant to hearing impairment). It is likely that the teacher will be able to use British sign language or be a qualified Makaton user. Teachers of the deaf will have a specialist qualification incorporating audiology, so they would have a working knowledge of hearing aids, but there are usually audiologists available for more complex issues. In the UK it is 'total communication' that is the preferred method of communicating with children who are deaf. This means using speech where appropriate, having good lip patterns and at the same time using a sign support system such as BSL or 'Signed English' to support the child.

Support for learning assistants

Support for learning assistants work in the classroom or unit to support children. The recognised qualification in Scotland at the time of writing is PDA Support for Learning, though many support for learning assistants are recruited who do not have this qualification and undertake training when in post on a day-release basis. Support for learning assistants may:

- work one-to-one encouraging children to stay on tasks

- administer medication

- support mobility around the school

- undertake personal care tasks (changing children, feeding)

- make specific resources (enlarge worksheets)

- collate information about the child.

Support for learning assistants work in nursery schools, primary schools and in secondary schools.

Health visitor

Health visitors have a background in nursing, obstetrics and knowledge of health and the developmental stages (milestones) of the child. They are part of the primary care team. They have particular responsibilities to children from birth to 5 years. The health visitor is usually the first professional to visit the child at home. They offer counselling, advice, information about local support groups and may make referrals to other professionals such as the child's GP or the Child and Family Centre.

Physiotherapists

Physiotherapists are graduate health professionals who must be registered with the Health Professions Council (HPC). They work in nurseries, schools, clinics and with the child at home. A referral to the physiotherapy services may come from a GP.

When a referral is made the physiotherapist will assess the child. This will include assessing the child's:

- strength and coordination
- motor development
- posture and balance
- mobility and movement
- function.

The child may be asked to perform tasks so that these abilities may be assessed. Informal information gathering will also take place through discussions with the child's family, school or other agencies which can help build up a picture of the child. Parents are always kept informed about this assessment and they will be sent a written report.

Some of the ways a child may be supported by a physiotherapist include:

- training other service providers (school, health professionals) to show them specific ways of working with the child, e.g. leg strengthening exercises for a child who has cerebral palsy

- provision of programmes of work, such as daily plans of suggested ways of working with the child or young person, e.g. a child who has muscular dystrophy may need passive movement of limbs (limbs positioned) to prevent the muscles contracting
- provision of specialist equipment
- swimming classes – hydrotherapy is often used as an enjoyable way of a child getting exercise as muscles move more freely in water and are less likely to be strained by over-exertion.

Speech and language therapist

Speech and language therapists work with parents, carers and others who are supporting the child to assess if a child has a speech/and or language difficulty, communication problems or problems with eating and drinking.

Before a programme of support starts, a child will be assessed. This assessment will find out:

- how much spoken language the child understands
- if the child understands and/or uses non-verbal communication skills
- the quality of the spoken language (articulation and expression)
- the child's play skills
- how the child uses language in a variety of contexts: home, school, play areas
- how the child eats, drinks and swallows.

The speech and language therapist may give advice and training for parents and other organisations, work directly with the child or provide communication aids and services (such as Makaton).

Anyone, including parents, can refer a child for speech and language therapy; if other agencies refer the child, parental permission must always be sought. Children who have a hearing loss, cystic fibrosis or cleft palate may need support from a speech and language therapist.

Social work department

The social work department may support a child or young person and their family in many ways. They may undertake an assessment to discover how specific issues in the child's life are affecting their education. This could include family break-up, being a young carer or being excluded from school because of behavioural issues. The type of support the social worker may offer includes:

- giving advice about behavioural strategies
- liaising with staff from welfare benefits to allow families to access funding
- organising respite care
- arranging transport to hospital appointments with volunteer drivers employed by the social work department
- organising practical support at home such as home help for families who need it.

Voluntary organisations

Many voluntary organisations offer support and advice for children and families. A list of voluntary organisations is to be found in the chart overleaf.

Supporting parents and carers of children with additional support needs

Earlier in this chapter you considered the needs of the child – you are now going to consider the needs of the carers and families who support the child or young person.

For parents, coming to terms with the knowledge that your child has additional support needs may be hard and time may be needed to fully accept this. When offering support you need to take into account the feelings of parents and carers. What type of support might the family need? They may need:

- practical support such as adaptations to their home, specialist equipment or someone to help them with housework
- support to help them with finances to provide for any additional support needs (for instance, some children who have cerebral palsy have an uneven gait, meaning that they wear down shoes – sometimes only on one foot – very quickly); for this type of financial help they may need advice about how to access funds or help in filling out forms
- social contact with carers who are in similar circumstances, such as local support groups

- counselling to come to terms with a way of life they had not expected
- advice, information and training about a specific condition or how to use equipment such as hearing aids
- respite care or day care to allow them to spend time with other children or to have a break
- support to attend meetings about their child; being with professionals who may unwittingly use jargon associated with additional support needs can sometimes be daunting.

When working in an early education and childcare setting, you may be the professional who directly meets these needs or who indirectly meets them by linking the parent to another agency. It is important that the practitioner adopts an approach which allows the parent or carer to be part of the support 'package'. Care must be taken to be empathic, not sympathetic (pity does not help anyone). Sometimes professionals can inadvertently hinder this communication process by using jargon, displaying a patronising attitude or assuming that they (the professional) have more knowledge than the parent or carer. When faced with the fact that their child may have a particular condition, many parents make a huge effort to make themselves as informed as possible about it.

> ### Consider this
>
> What role do you feel that parents play in their child's education?
>
> Do you think that the parents/carers of children who have additional support needs have a different role to play?

Practitioners often talk about working 'in partnership' with parents. Good partnership working means having a common goal (in this case both parties wanting the very best for the child or young person), showing mutual respect (recognising that there are things the parent will know about the child that the professional may never know) and being open to changing your approach to meet the needs of the child.

List of organisations providing support

Name of organisation	Type of support offered
AFASIC 1 Prospect 3 Gemini Crescent Dundee DD2 2DG Web: www.afasicscotland.org.uk	Helps children and young adults who have speech and language difficulties
Barnardo's Scotland 235 Corstorphine Road Edinburgh EH12 7AR Web: www.barnardos.org.uk	Runs local projects for children who are disadvantaged, including children who have additional support needs
Capability Scotland 11 Ellersley Road Edinburgh EH12 6HY Web: www.capability-scotland.org.uk	Supports people who have cerebral palsy
Children in Scotland Princes House 5 Shandwick Place Edinburgh EH8 8PJ Web: www.childreninscotland.org.uk	Information about children and young people in Scotland. Website gives a link to Enquire, the Scottish advice and information service for additional support for learning
Down's Syndrome Scotland 158–60 Balgreen Road Edinburgh EH11 3AU Web: www.dsscotland.org.uk	Information and support for children who have Down's syndrome and their families
Dyslexia Scotland Unit 3 Stirling Business Centre Wellgreen Stirling FK8 2DZ Web: www.dyslexiascotland.org.uk	Offers advice and support for children and young people who have dyslexia
Dyspraxia Foundation 8 West Alley Hitchin Hertfordshire SG5 1EG Web: www.dyspraxiafoundation.org.uk	Increases public understanding of dyspraxia and supports children who have dyspraxia and their families
The National Autistic Society Scotland 1st Floor Central Chambers 109 Hope Street Glasgow G2 611 Web: www.scotland.autism.org.uk	Helps those with autism (including Asperger's syndrome) to gain skills to live independently
National Deaf Children's Society Scotland 187–9 Central Chambers 93 Hope Street Glasgow G2 6LD Web: www.ndcs.org.uk	Supports children who have a hearing impairment and parents of such children
Royal National Institute of Blind People Dunedin House 25 Ravelston Terrace Edinburgh EH4 3TP Web: www.rnib.org.uk	Supports those who have visual impairment

Now answer the following questions to see what you have learned in this chapter.

1. Outline the basic needs of children, giving examples of how these needs can be met

2. Name two theorists who described needs. Outline what they said.

3. Give a definition of 'additional support needs'.

4. Describe a continuum of need.

5. What is meant by the term discrimination?

6. What major piece of legislation in 2004 changed provision for children who have additional support needs?

7. Give five reasons why a child may need additional support.

8. What is an IEP? What is a coordinated support plan?

9. Identify the professionals who would work with a child who has a hearing impairment. Which voluntary organisation would work with the child and his/her family?

10. What support is needed by the families of children and young people who have additional support needs?

References

Dare, A. and O'Donovan, M. (2002) *Good Practice in Caring for Young Children with Special Needs*, Cheltenham: Nelson Thornes

Enquire (2005) *The Parents' Guide to Additional Support for Learning*, Edinburgh: Enquire Scotland (available at www.enquire.org.uk/pcp/pub/pcpguides.php)

Hamill, P. and Clark, K. (2005) *Additional Support Needs An Introduction to ASN from Nursery to Secondary*, London: Hodder Gibson

Learning and Teaching Scotland (1999) *A Curriculum Framework for Children 3 to 5*, Dundee

Macpherson, W. (1999) *The Report of the Stephen Lawrence Inquiry*, The Stationery Office (available at www.archive.official-documents.co.uk/document/cm42/4262/4262.htm)

NCH Scotland (2000) *Fact File 2000: Facts and Figures about Scotland's Children*, NCH Scotland

Pringle, M.K. (1986) *The Needs of Children*, 3rd edn, London: Hutchinson Education

Scottish Alliance for Children's Rights (2000) *All Children, All Ages*, Scottish Alliance for Children's Rights

Scottish Executive (2003) *Moving Forward! Additional Support for Learning*, Edinburgh

Scottish Executive (2005) *Supporting Children's Learning: Code of Practice*, Scottish Government Publications

Siegel L.S. and Smythe I., (2005) 'Reflections of research on reading disability with special attention to gender issues', Journal of Learning Disabilities, Vol 38, pp.385–480

United Nations Educational, Scientific and Cultural Organization (1999) *The Salamanca Statement and Framework for Action on Special Needs Education*, Spain: UNESCO (available at www.unesco.org/education/pdf/SALAMA_E.PDF)

Websites of interest

Asperger's Syndrome Foundation: www.aspergerfoundation.org.uk/what_as.htm

British Dyslexia Association: www.bdadyslexia.org.uk

Dyspraxia Foundation: www.dyspraxiafoundation.org.uk

FRAXA: www.fraxa.org

Healthier Scotland research project: www.scotland.gov.uk/Resource/Doc/197969/0052908.pdf

Muscular Dystrophy Campaign information and support service: www.muscular-dystrophy.org/information

NetDoctor: www.netdoctor.co.uk

RNIB: www.rnib.org.uk

Scope: www.scope.org.uk

The National Attention Deficit Disorder Information and Support Service: www.addiss.co.uk

The National Autistic Society: www.autism.org.uk/autism

The National Society for Epilepsy: www.epilepsynse.org.uk

Chapter 7
Team working and communication

Introduction

Key to working in an early education and childcare setting is the ability to work and communicate well with colleagues. This is because in this sector you will almost always be working as a member of a team that may include external as well as internal personnel.

One of the core objectives of an early education and childcare team is to provide care and learning for children. Not all teams will go about this in the same way and not every member of a team will have the same characteristics or attributes. Sometimes you will work with people who are from different backgrounds and who have different skills to your own. On occasions their approach may be at odds with the way you would have tackled the same issue. Understanding how others work, learning when and how to compromise, and communicating well are important for effective team working. Learning to work as a successful team member will help you to understand your strengths and to see the strengths of others. It will also help you to have a better appreciation of the challenges colleagues may face.

Understanding how your skills blend and complement others is critical to providing the right experiences for children. Establishing good communication is fundamental to ensuring good working practices and an effective service for children and parents.

The Scottish Government, having listened to employers, frequently cite the ability to work with others as one of the key strengths required for any part of the job market. Put simply, if you are not able to work effectively with others it is unlikely you will have a long career in early education and childcare, where there is a high expectation you will be able to do so.

Among the skills you need to work with other people are good verbal and written communication skills; effective interpersonal skills; the ability to deal with conflict; the ability to be self-critical and to accept constructive criticism; and the ability to set goals and to evaluate both your successes and your failures. Understanding why something worked well or how you might do it differently next time is also essential for reflective practice.

In this chapter you will learn:

- How teams work
- How goal setting and performance review can support an early education and childcare setting
- How conflict can be avoided and how conflict resolution can support team work
- How other key professionals contribute to the work of the team
- How communication is affected by the style of language, the intention of the message and the way it is conveyed

How teams work

What is a team?

HNC Unit DG5D 35: Team working in care settings reminds you that working in a team can include working with parents or anyone that has an interest in the child's care and learning. Sometimes people confuse teams with groups of people but they are not the same. Groups are often less well coordinated than teams.

Think of the class you are in. Would you describe that as a group or as a team? It is likely to be a group. Generally, teams are different to groups because teams consist of people who are working *together* towards a *common aim* or *purpose.*

Often when you think of a team it might be a football or other sports team. An example would be the Dundee United Football Club team. All the players in that team will be working together towards a common goal of winning matches. They will also aim to win the SPL, any major trophy competitions and getting a place in a European competition. If eleven individuals perform every week without focusing on the rest of the team, the club is unlikely to win matches and perform well. This is true of work teams as well.

You may have been in a situation where you have been asked to work with others, for example to give a presentation. The generality of the class group becomes a more focused and specific work team who share the common goal, albeit for a short time, of giving a presentation. If everyone in the team is clear about the common aim and works towards achieving it, it is likely you will be successful. You will have worked out, in your team, what you need to do, who will contribute what and when it will be done by. However, if no discussion takes place and each person works independently of the others, the team effort is likely to be disjointed, lack focus and fail to achieve the common goal.

A group is less focused than a team. It represents a number of people who may have something in common but who are not working with a common purpose. Joining an HNC Early Education and Childcare class gives you something in common but this isn't a common aim or goal. Each person in your class group is likely to have a different reason for being there and so will have different individual goals. Some may want to do the HNC course for interest; others may want to do this because it will help them in their career; others may want to do it because they think it will give their day-to-day practice added value.

When you are working in a nursery or out-of-school care club you will be working in a team with others. One of your main goals will be to provide care, play and learning to children in an environment that supports children's physical, language, cognitive, emotional and social development. Another may be to provide support to families.

Everyone is important in a team

Your overarching goals will be broken down and each day, week or month the goals will be more specific and less general, in the same way planning goals were described in Chapters 1 and 4. How you go about achieving your goals and the level of communication and interpersonal skills you use to achieve these will contribute to the success of the team. Where teams are unsuccessful it is usually because communication is poor and ineffective teams are operating.

Consider this

Have you ever been a member of a team?

What was the common goal of that team? What do you think the likely outcome would be if someone didn't share the same goal?

Characteristics of a good team

In any setting you are likely to find teams that are effective and others that are less effective. For a team to work well it needs to show certain key characteristics. These have been described by a range of researchers but the description used by Sadek and Sadek (*Good Practice in Nursery Management*, 2004) sums it up well. In any organisation a good team will:

- work together
- share common aims
- cooperate with others
- share with, communicate with and support its members
- be motivated for the task in hand
- develop relationships that allow new things to happen
- be committed
- be made up of people who know where they fit in the team and who understand their role
- be reliable
- complete what has been asked of them. (Reproduced with the permission of Nelson Thornes Ltd. From *Good Practice in Nursery Management*, Elizabeth Sadek and Jacqueline Sadek, 978 0 7487 7548 4, first published in 1996.)

Consider this

Spend some time discussing these features in your class group. Do you agree with all of them or do you think there are others that may be added to the list?

These features are important outcomes from good team working but they can be achieved by individuals who work alone. However, team work can give added value to a centre, particularly where there is a wealth of individual talent. By combining talents you can produce even better outcomes for children. The case study below gives an example of how this is achieved.

Case study *Working together to bring added value*

Sam, Sukla and Dave all work at the Grove Centre. Sukla was previously a successful childminder and has an excellent rapport with children and parents. She is well organised and is bilingual in English and Urdu. Sam is a new member of the team but brings with her lots of enthusiasm, new ideas and has a really good singing voice. Dave has worked for many years in industry. He is a good communicator, has excellent IT skills and tells stories to the children really well.

Individually they are all invaluable members of the centre. Recently they have started to work together and have replaced the staff that were in the baby room. This part of the nursery had been static and slightly unimaginative and was criticised in a recent inspection report for not offering enough variety to the children. Within a week of them being there, Sam, Sukla and David have introduced a 'singing circle', used puppets and props to tell stories to the children, and established well-organised and well-balanced programme. They have also set up a mother and baby group for parents from the local community, many of whom speak Urdu as their first language. So, by combining their individual strengths, this team has made improvements in the centre.

Being a reflective practitioner

Team work is important, and being able to reflect on what you have done and how well you have met team goals is critical to making ongoing improvement. Included in this self-reflection is the ability to be self-critical. This means acknowledging what you did well and highlighting what you did less well, so that you can consider why and how you might approach the particular issue in future. It is important for the whole team to be able to get together and discuss areas where they have succeeded and areas where improvements could be made. You may be familiar with this approach, having seen it in placement. Most teams use discussion to get to this point but some use performance checklists.

Below is an example of a good practice checklist you might want to use in placement.

Fill it in to help you identify strengths in the team and where you have been able to make an effective contribution to the existing team. It may also help you to highlight some areas where you can make improvements. The first two are done for you as an example.

Why teams are important

A great deal is written about teams and team working and you will find some other useful sources in the references section to this chapter. Teams are important in an early education and childcare setting because they add value to the work of the centre. Team work is collaborative and good teams enable collaboration between colleagues. Colleagues who are less confident can be supported in this way. Occasionally, colleagues who have been working in a centre for some time can become inflexible and lack energy and new ideas.

Area of practice	Examples from your own practice
Share knowledge, ideas and information with others in the team	Darren is going to hospital for a tonsillectomy next week. His mother has indicated he is apprehensive. I suggested we change the home corner into a hospital area and brought out some of the hospital dressing-up clothes.
Make an active contribution to discussions and to planning and solving problems	The team are considering how to organise the Christmas outing for the children. We are short of adults to help out. I suggested putting a request in the bulletin and asking if the two students would be allowed time off college to accompany us.
Show you are open to new ideas and suggestions from others	
Take responsibility for areas of work where you have the skills and knowledge	
Hand over to someone else if they have skills and knowledge that is more appropriate	
Show you are reliable by completing work when and how you agreed	
Show you are flexible and prepared to adapt if circumstances change	
Show you are able to remain professional by maintaining confidentiality about things you hear in meetings	
Show that you respect the views of others in your team	
Thank others for help they have given you and for feedback you have received	
Maintain professionalism by ensuring you don't gossip about others	

Good practice checklist (from *BTEC National Children's Care, Learning and Development*, Squire, 2007)

One of the benefits of team work is that it is possible to refresh a team with new personnel or a change of personnel. This can generate new ideas and approaches. Some will be accepted, others rejected, but the discussion generated will be important to the centre. Teams can support decision making and this leads to enhanced practice. The centre can benefit from teams that work well because there is likely to be a more consistent approach to how childcare is provided and to implementing policies and procedures

For a newly qualified practitioner, the benefits of working in a team come from the support you receive from others and from seeing different approaches used. Teams can facilitate communities of practice to develop.

You have already read a little in this chapter about what makes an effective team and how to make sure you can contribute to team success. You will notice in your placement that some teams work really well together even when people in them seem to be very different. At other times you'll find teams that don't gel. Some researchers think this happens when the wrong mix of personalities is put together and different personalities affect the team dynamics.

Key factors that detract from good team working

When teams don't work well together it can be for a variety of reasons. The table below shows some of these and the impact this can have.

Team work research

Researchers hold different views about what is important in making teams work. One of the most quoted is Meredith Belbin, who suggested the roles that people naturally assume in teams are important in making them work effectively. His view is that a team needs a balance of roles to make it work well. Where there is insufficient variety in the type of personalities employed, this is likely to be less beneficial to a team. Sometimes this can be problematic in an early education and childcare setting because, by the nature of the work, it attracts similar types of people who may have similar personality types. Nevertheless, Belbin's view is that the wrong dynamics produce a less successful team. By including different personality types in a team it is likely they will bring a range of skills and so benefit the team.

> ### Key terms
>
> **Communities of practice** are alliances brought together through a common interest in a subject or area. Communities of practice discuss and innovate to enable changes to occur.
>
> **Team dynamics** describes how the team works together and interacts.

Key factors that impede team work	Their impact	How they can be avoided
Lack of awareness of goals	Lack of consistency of approach; conflict within the team	Clear goal setting; checking and rechecking by team members; better communication
Lack of success in achieving goals	Demotivation sets lower level of expectation next time	Checking progress; setting smaller steps towards reaching the goal; encouragement
Poor communication between team members	Poor performance; lack of clarity; conflict; failure to meet goals	Formal and informal opportunities to meet; good leadership that encourages discussion between team members; checking progress; asking for feedback; performance review
Underperforming staff	Poor performance; resentment among colleagues; lack of focus; failure to meet goals	Performance review and feedback; opportunities to work shadow

Impediments to team work

Other researchers, including Robbins and Finley (*Why Teams Don't Work: What Went Wrong and How to Make It Right*, 2000), identify key strengths that varied teams bring to an organisation. Strengths include:

- improved communication
- being able to do together what individuals can't always do alone
- greater creativity at solving problems and finding solutions
- better use of resources and allowing differentiation.

It is also important for a team to be managed well to bring out the strengths in a team and to find ways of compensating for weaknesses.

Belbin's roles

In *Management Teams: Why They Succeed or Fail* (2003), Belbin identifies three types of roles people naturally assume. He describes these as action-oriented roles, people-oriented roles and cerebral roles. Belbin had noted in research that teams all tend to conform to certain ways of working and believed some people are more focused on doing things or taking action in teams; others are more concerned with relationships, people and getting on along with others; while a third type are concerned with thinking things through and planning for action rather than actually taking the action. He further refined these three main areas of action, people and thinking, and a description is provided in the table opposite. By defining people in this way, Belbin is suggesting that different people have different dispositions and different motivations that affect the way they work.

Key terms

Differentiation means including different people who will contribute a range of skills and attributes.

Disposition means the character you have or the tendency you have to do something; so you may be described as having a sunny disposition if you are usually quite happy or a morose disposition if you are often glum.

Belbin considered all teams are made up of people who conform to these roles and believed if you carefully select the *types* of people you most need, you are likely to have the most successful team.

Further research

What are your views about Belbin's team types? Are you in agreement with his categorisation or do you think Belbin is overstating the case? Do some research to investigate this further.

Think of an example of each type of person that might fit into a) an action role b) a cerebral role; c) a people role and the type of actions they might take.

On a practical level, Belbin's typology would mean that if everyone in an early education and childcare team conformed to the 'cerebral type', the planning and organisation would be excellent but the centre might lose focus on empathy and people skills. If everyone conformed to the 'people-oriented roles', there would be no real innovation or challenge – the centre may keep functioning but staff would not feel challenged to consider new opportunities and approaches; they may take a safe option. Finally, if everyone conformed to the action-oriented roles there may be too much innovation without really considering the potential benefits or the consequences of constant change. It could mean too much disruption and not enough consideration of people's feelings while changes were happening.

In each of Belbin's team roles there are 'allowable weaknesses'. These are thought to be an acceptable risk that attracting that type of person brings. So, the good features hopefully outweigh the less good.

Team role	Type	Contribution	Allowable weaknesses
Plant	Cerebral role	Creative, imaginative, unorthodox. Solves difficult problems.	Ignores incidentals. Too preoccupied to communicate effectively.
Resource Investigator	People role	Extrovert, enthusiastic, communicative. Explores opportunities. Develops contacts.	Over-optimistic. Loses interest once initial enthusiasm has passed.
Co-ordinator	People role	Mature, confident, a good chairperson. Clarifies goals, promotes decision-making, delegates well.	Can be seen as manipulative. Offloads personal work.
Shaper	Action oriented	Challenging, dynamic, thrives on pressure. The drive and courage to overcome obstacles.	Prone to provocation. Offends people's feelings.
Monitor Evaluator	Cerebral role	Sober, strategic and discerning. Sees all options. Judges accurately.	Lacks drive and ability to inspire others.
Teamworker	People role	Co-operative, mild, perceptive and diplomatic.Listens, builds, averts friction.	Indecisive in crunch situations.
Implementer	Action oriented	Disciplined, reliable, conservative and efficient. Turns ideas into practical actions.	Somewhat inflexible. Slow to respond to new possibilities.
Completer Finisher	Action oriented	Painstaking, conscientious, anxious. Searches out errors and omissions. Delivers on time.	Inclined to worry unduly. Reluctant to delegate.
Specialist	Cerebral role	Single-minded, self-starting, dedicated. Provides knowledge and skills in rare supply	Contributes on only a narrow front. Dwells on technicalities.

Belbin's roles, from *Management Teams: Why They Succeed or Fail*, Meredith Belbin (www.belbin.com)

You may recognise yourself in Belbin's descriptions and can do a team roles test to find out which of Belbin's roles you actually fit. Your college tutor may be able to help with this or you can pay to download a test from www.belbin.com. This website will also provide you with more detail of Belbin's roles.

Consider this

Consider how Belbin's team types might be used effectively in a nursery or out-of-school care centre. You may want to think about how the different roles he has identified contribute to team effectiveness in a day-to-day situation.

You might also want to think about the staff dynamics you would select for a centre with eight members of staff.

How personality types might affect team work

When you learn about teams you also hear about the way different personalities affect a team. Personality types affect the roles you are likely to take within a team. You will have read in Chapter 3 about how children's personality develops. Theorists consider this also affects how we work as adults. Some employers regard theories of personality types as important when making sure they employ people whose personalities fit best with specific job roles.

Personality testing

One of the most frequently used personality tests is the Myers-Briggs Type Indicator (MBTI) (1956). This is used as a profiling tool that assesses how different personalities are *likely* to get on with and understand others; how *strongly* or *weakly* motivated they might be; and how *likely* they are to perform well in teams. It doesn't deal in certainties but is thought to be a useful indicator of likelihood. Myers and Briggs developed their inventory of personalities as a result of work done by Carl Jung. His work is explained briefly in this chapter (see below).

The MBTI is used in situations where it is important to understand how people's preferences to perform in certain ways might affect a job role. An example of this would be: you are appointing the managing director of a large firm where decisions have to be made regularly and quickly. Your preferred candidate scores low on decisiveness. The firm may think it is too risky to their business to employ that person. In early education and childcare, if you are low on empathy and people skills you may not be the best choice for working in the sector. For more information on MBTI go to www. myersbriggs.org.

How Jung's work has affected work on personality types

Work carried out by the psychologist Carl Jung (1875–1961) has been used to inform practice in psychology and psychiatry and has been used extensively by researchers who try to categorise individuals by personality types. Jung considered certain traits were inherent in people. This means that people are born with an inclination to behave in certain ways. Jung was of the view that, psychologically, we are born with the ability to perform key functions: namely how to look at the world (perceptions) and how to make decisions. These are further divided into the functions of: sensing, intuition, thinking and feeling. Sensing and intuiting are functions used to gather information while judging and thinking are based on either the use of logic or belief in consequences. Jung thought that people use each to a greater or lesser extent in the way they go about life and make decisions. He believed that an individual's preference for certain functions over others is useful in revealing personality. Personality tests use Jung's ideas to establish different permutations of 'type' and thereby indicate probable behaviour.

Jung based his theory of personality on *introverted* and *extroverted* personality types, with each one mutually complementary to each other.

Key terms

Introverts are defined as naturally shy.

Extroverts are defined as naturally outgoing.

Jung's view was that extroverts are more concerned with the outside world while introverts are more focused on the internal world. So, extroverts in teams will consider external sources to find solutions while introverts would look to self. Extroverts might be more socially adept but need to be at the centre of what is going on. They can communicate well with others and consider what is going on all around them.

Introverted personalities tend to be self-focused and have less need of approval from others; they can work independently and are more likely to concentrate on and finish a task. Introversion does not mean they don't like or get on with other people. According to Jungian theory, it would be important to achieve a balance of both introverts and extroverts because teams require an appropriate range of personality types to ensure there is moderation in behaviours.

Further research

Explore some of Jung's theories further to learn more about how he considered personality types affect the way we see the world and operate as individuals.

Consider this

Would you describe yourself as someone who tends to base decisions on instinct or 'gut feelings', or as someone who thinks things through rationally before making a decision?

When you meet someone for the first time are you affected by your immediate perceptions or do you wait and form a judgement based on tangible facts?

How does this fit with Jung's theories?

Motives

Motives describe the inner drives that allow individuals to go about their everyday work, and motivation is needed by individuals to perform everyday activities. You may have heard people who have been unemployed for a long time and who have applied for many jobs with no success say they have 'lost motivation', or dieters tell you they 'lack motivation'.

Team motives

What motivates performance is important for understanding how teams work effectively. If people within a team have conflicting motives then the team is likely to be less effective or to experience conflict. An example of this would be where a practitioner in a nursery is motivated by the need to be really well organised and prepared. This means she can't comfortably leave the nursery in the evening until everything is carefully planned and organised for the following day and she has had an opportunity to discuss the plans with colleagues. Her colleague is less careful and doesn't think this matters, since she is motivated by getting things done quickly so they are out of the way; she is casual about planning and organisation. This results in conflict between the two.

Team motivation enables good performance. Individuals generally feel motivated if told they are doing something well. Children's achievements and progress often motivate practitioners in this sector and adults like children to respond to success. Teams need motivation to perform well. Other motivators include financial reward or the prospect of promotion, and there are some incentives for career progression in early education and childcare, particularly in the private sector.

Teams that are led well and so communicate well are likely to be better motivated than teams that are unclear about their goals and team roles. You may have noticed in placement that individuals in successful teams with high levels of motivation tend not to complain. Where teams lack motivation this can affect performance in major or more subtle ways, one of which is undermining; the first case study shows some examples of this.

Demotivation can also occur if staff feel they have been treated badly and can cause a disincentive to work. This can happen because staff have not been kept informed or where actions have been taken without any discussion. The second case study gives an example of this.

Case study 1 *Undermining a colleague*

A new HNC student starts Merryweather Nursery where the manager has some concerns about the motivation of a senior member of staff, Mary. She asks another practitioner, Joyce, to supervise the new student instead of Mary, who usually does it. The manager has simply told Mary that Joyce is to be supervising.

When the student is asked to help wash up after lunch, Joyce indicates it would be useful if the children helped. When Mary sees this she shouts over to the student: 'That's not how it's done. I don't know what Joyce is playing at, she should know better.'

Later, Joyce asks the student to help get the children ready for a walk. As she is organising coats and boots, Mary comes rushing along saying: 'It's far too late to be going out now. Just bring them back in and we'll tell a story.' This is very confusing for the student and for the children.

1 Is Mary making her points in a way that undermines Joyce?

2 What might a sensible course of action have been in this scenario?

3 Is this a situation you have encountered?

Case study 2 *Staff demotivation*

Drew, Anna and Asif work together at a local out-of-school care club called 4all. A new manager has recently taken over and has had to tell staff that the club is losing funding and needs to make significant savings to keep jobs. They have been told this includes cancelling the planned trip to the Edinburgh Dungeon.

All three members of staff are angry because the trip had been organised for some time, a lot of effort went into the planning and they had been assured money was available. Additionally, new equipment they had promised the children can't now be ordered. The manager asks them to let

the children know that evening. He also tells them confidentially he is concerned the temporary contracts they have may not all be renewed.

After the meeting Drew says to the others, 'I'm not telling them. That's not my job. It's his.' Asif says, 'That's it. I'm off to find another job. Why stay here with no support?' Anna can see the manager is in a difficult position, but he is also unwilling to make any concessions and Anna is disappointed.

1 Explain how this situation might cause demotivation amongst the staff.

2 Could the situation have been handled differently?

Theories of motivation

Two of the theories used in understanding team motivation are Abraham Maslow's hierarchy of needs ('A Theory of Human Motivation', A. Maslow, 1943) and Frederick Herzberg's 'Two Factor Theory'. (*The Motivation to Work*, F. Herzberg et al., 1959)

Maslow's hierarchy of needs

Maslow's hierarchy considers personal rather than team motivation. Maslow (1908–70) considered people were more alike than different and that key factors that motivate are inherent in all individuals. Those needs are core to motivation.

Maslow described needs as a hierarchy because he believed there was a progression: basic everyday 'needs' have to be satisfied before progress can be made. Where this fails, the individual can't progress because his or her basic needs are overwhelming.

Maslow's needs are presented as a triangle. At the base of the triangle are the *physiological needs* such as food and water. They are basic to all humans. Once they are satisfied there is no longer this need and a higher one takes its place.

On the next level are *security* needs such as being free from pain. Once you feel physically secure you are able to move to the next stage.

Level 3 is the *belonging* stage. This involves being able to love and being able to trust; giving and receiving affection. It includes having stability. Some individuals find this difficult to achieve.

Esteem needs include self-esteem or the ability to feel good about self, being self-confident, having self-respect and feeling adequate. This stage means you are able to take control of yourself and make decisions about your future and what you want. Without being able to do this, Maslow felt you could not move to the final, fifth stage at the top of the triangle: self-actualisation.

Self-actualisation means a person is comfortable with self, can be open to new experiences, and can be creative and comfortable with who they are and with what they can achieve. They can make mistakes and move on from them without being over-critical and can be happy with their success. Maslow didn't believe you could reach this stage if the stages below this in the triangle were unmet.

Herzberg's 'Two Factor Theory'

Frederick Herzberg (1923–2000) examined how motivation affected work situations and how it contributed to job satisfaction. By studying practitioners in situ he was able to determine some factors that were key in judging job satisfaction. He described these as being either motivator factors for job satisfaction or hygiene factors needed to combat job dissatisfaction.

The motivator factors that make people satisfied with their work situations are:

- achievement
- recognition
- the type of work

Maslow's hierarchy of needs

- levels of responsibility
- opportunities for promotion or personal growth
- the organisation itself.

The hygiene factors that help people to feel less dissatisfied with their work situation include:

- pay and benefits
- organisational policies
- relationships with colleagues
- physical environment
- supervision
- status
- job security.

Herzberg concluded that although removing factors causing dissatisfaction was important, it didn't necessarily motivate people to work. He thought this was driven by a different factor called job enrichment and described some of the key features needed to achieve job enrichment. They include:

- removing some control
- giving additional authority for individuals to complete whole tasks, not just bits of tasks
- allowing individuals to become experts
- allowing new work to be done that hasn't been done by the individual before
- making individuals more responsible for the accountability of their work
- increasing autonomy.

Consider this

Consider how Herzberg's factors might apply to motivation in an early education and childcare setting. What are some of the key factors you think are needed to motivate practitioners.

Do you think Maslow's and Herzberg's theories are appropriate to the early education and childcare sector? How can you see them working to the advantage of a nursery owner or manager who is trying to increase motivation in her team?

How goal setting and performance review can support an early education and childcare setting

Why are goals important?

Earlier in this chapter you read about how teams operate. Included in this was recognition of the importance of setting goals. Goals are sometimes called the objectives of an organisation. In some centres you will be working with an organisational plan that will clarify what the core objectives of your organisation are and how you are expected to contribute to achieving these. These are the goals of the organisation.

Goals describe major or smaller aims a service has. An example of major goals are: the goal of Riverview Centre is to be in new premises by October 2010; the goal of the centre is to be a centre of excellence for literacy by 2009. Examples of day-to-day goals are: to embed healthy eating options into the snack in October; to organise a summer outing for all children.

Goals are closely linked in a centre to the plans you have read about in this book. It is important to set goals in an organisation because they clarify for all what the expectations are. Objectives are the steps in the process of achieving these goals. Some describe these as steps to achieving goals.

Features of goal setting: SMART objectives

Goals should be understandable: that means they should be clear and everyone that needs to know about them should. When centres are setting goals they need to be achievable; this means they should be possible. Goals also need to be realistic for the setting you are in: if you are working in a large centre with many resources, it may be possible to do more than if you are working in a two-person playgroup, for example.

You will have opportunities for one-to-one discussions with your manager

equipment in place by the target date, this is well on the way to achievement. If you haven't made any progress by the target date, you may need to reassess and consider setting smaller objectives to reach the bigger one.

One final feature of setting goals is consideration of the resources required to achieve the intended outcome. This requires consideration of whether or not the intended output is achievable with the budget and resources you have been given.

If goals are set collaboratively, with the team discussing and defining some of the goals, it is likely you will feel you have more ownership of them. Goals tend to be unsuccessful if they are imposed without any discussion or collaboration. Sometimes individuals feel they can't achieve goals because they are unclear about what is being asked, and sometimes it is because they feel they don't have the skills or competence to achieve them. A collaborative approach to goal setting means you are able to ask for support in understanding and are able to remind the team of your particular strengths.

You should be able to measure the success of the goals so that you are able to demonstrate achievement. If you were 'introducing healthy eating options for snack in October', then if this has become a reality you know you have met the goal set. If you haven't, you should be able to track progress or say why it hasn't been achieved.

Goals should be time limited otherwise they become irrelevant. Taking too long to achieve an outcome can negate the reason for doing it. In this case you need to reassess the goal to see if it is still appropriate.

One of your goals might be to develop outdoor space in your centre. You will set targets for achievement and if you have 90 per cent of your

Activity

Work with your colleagues to set SMART objectives for the following group activities.

1. You have been asked to provide storysacks for a local playgroup that is short of resources. The playgroup would like to have the sacks by the end of January so they can start to prepare a group of rising 5-year-olds for transition to Primary 1 in August. They have just £100 at their disposal but hope you might be able to get them some sponsorship from local stores.

2. You have volunteered at the special school where you are on placement to provide a crèche for their Christmas bazaar. You need to do this on 3 December, which falls on a Saturday. You need to organise friends from your course to help and make sure the resources are in place for this. You know the area you have available to you. You also know you are likely to have around 15 children in the crèche at any one time, some of whom have mobility difficulties.

This process of looking at goals has been abbreviated to SMART. SMART means:

- **S**pecific — Goals should tell you what you want to achieve.

- **M**easurable — Can you measure whether you are meeting the goals?

- **A**chievable — Are the goals you have set achievable?

- **R**ealistic — Can you achieve the goals with the resources you have?

- **T**ime limited — When do you want to achieve your goal?

A key motivator that helps to keep teams on target is to allow 'small wins' along the way. Setting timelines and targets by which you would like to have achieved key points can often make goals less daunting. Sometimes teams fail to perform because the goals set have been too ambitious.

Performance review and feedback

When you are working with others it is important to be able to receive feedback. This helps you to improve your performance or to look at things you may need to do differently. Some centres do this through an annual performance review, sometimes called appraisal. Different centres and agencies may use different systems for this process.

A performance review provides an opportunity to review your performance, usually with your manager or line manager to determine if you have met the goals that were set for you. It provides an opportunity to think about areas of your day-to-day work where improvements could be made. It also gives you an opportunity to reflect on your personal development needs and indicate aspects of personal or professional development that require help, support or development.

Forms used for performance review will vary from centre to centre. They are usually completed by the person who is being appraised (the appraisee) and the person who is appraising (the appraiser). Although managers or line managers tend to take this role, occasionally all members of staff and other professionals you work with in the centre will contribute to your review. This is called a 360-degree appraisal because it takes note of everyone's view of your performance.

Usually appraisal is done once a year and sometimes it is linked to pay and grading. You should check with an employer if they have an appraisal system in place and how it affects your pay when you go for interview. The performance review process is often also used as an opportunity to discuss and agree your goals for the forthcoming year. It provides you with key targets to work towards and makes the organisation's expectations of you clear.

An appraisal interview should highlight the things you are doing well in the organisation and should set you key areas for improvement or for further development. Examples that might be included are shown in the table below.

Subsequent performance review meetings will look at the areas you were asked to work on and will consider how these have been addressed. Performance review is a two-way process. It means you get feedback from those you work with but also means you can give feedback on how you feel you have been supported.

Providing feedback

Feedback is used in performance review and is an important feature of day-to-day practice and effective team working. When feedback is constructive it can motivate and enhance performance. If it is done badly, team members can feel disheartened and demotivated.

Key strengths	Areas for improvement	Areas selected for development
Observation skills Report writing Planning Communicating with children Communicating with parents	Time management	Time management Play in the outdoors

Examples of areas that may be highlighted by an appraisal

Sometimes feedback is resented and regarded as personal rather than professional. Good feedback should not be personal but should be focused on performance. It allows the practitioner to understand ways to improve practice. Asking for feedback is essential to understanding and you should welcome any opportunity to do this. Once you have finished this course and are working as an early education and childcare practitioner, you will be required to act as mentor to other HNC students. Part of your role will be to provide them with effective feedback and it is important to do this well.

Here are some of the key features of good feedback:

- it has a clear purpose, e.g. to teach the recipient something or to find out something
- it is used for a range of situations both positive and negative; comment on and encourage the recipient to identify things that they did well
- it is only offered when you think it can be of value to the recipient
- the recipient seeks feedback
- the feedback involves asking questions as well as making statements, for example 'How could you have dealt with that situation?' rather than the more blame-ridden 'You should have done it this way'
- it is about a specific issue and doesn't stray into other issues that have been left over
- it is based on observed behaviour rather than impressions, so you could say 'Your voice started to get louder as you were talking to John' instead of 'You were needlessly aggressive'
- it should be constructive rather than destructive.

Receiving constructive feedback

As an HNC student you will find yourself in the position of receiving feedback from a range of people. They are likely to include:

- the children you work with
- your placement supervisor
- the manager of the placement
- other practitioners
- your placement tutor
- lecturers in college
- other students you need to work with.

The purpose of feedback is to highlight what has been done well, to help you improve performance and to reflect on how you might do things differently.

Case study *Receiving critical feedback*

Carrie-Anne is a new HNC student at Thornycross Nursery. She is a mature student with a grown-up family. The staff team are all around 20 years younger than Carrie-Anne.

Carrie-Anne is well prepared and observant with sound ideas which she has tried to share, but she feels she isn't listened to. She also feels awkward at break times and unable to join in conversations. Her mentor has observed that she is reticent but very calm with the children and thinks she doesn't mix well with the rest of the staff. She has also noted Carrie-Anne stands back and observes instead of becoming too involved, but when she does get involved the children respond well to her.

Carrie-Anne's mentor has been asked to give feedback prior to a visit by Carrie-Anne's college tutor. This is what she says: 'You've really got to be more assertive with the children. You're too quiet. We're all quite outgoing here and the children really respond to that. You've got to try to fit into the team better, you know. We're all very friendly here. We won't bite your head off!'

1 What impact might this feedback have on Carrie-Anne?

2 How might Carrie-Anne's mentor provide more constructive feedback?

3 What are Carrie-Anne's key areas of strength?

4 What feedback/observation might Carrie-Anne provide to her mentor?

Case study 1 *The need for a performance review*

Roddy has worked in the out-of-school care club for 15 years. He is popular but tends to do his own thing. There is a staff rota indicating who does what in the club, but Roddy ignores it because he likes 'working on the shop floor with the bairns'. Consequently he doesn't tidy up, order equipment or food, do pick ups from school or help with the accounts for parents (which the club has to do to keep solvent). He is also quite relaxed about health and safety and on a recent outing left a group of children unattended while he went off to have a cigarette. On this occasion, another member of staff had to take the children back to the minibus which then had to wait for Roddy. Roddy didn't understand why the staff were concerned and on the way home was regaling the children with jokes, which they loved.

The others in the team have voiced concerns about Roddy's lack of team work to the manager, but she is reluctant to do anything. She uses two excuses for her inaction: the children really like Roddy and he'll be retiring soon so it isn't worth rocking the boat.

1 What effect do you think Roddy's actions and his manager's inaction might have on the rest of the team?

2 How might a performance review help to support Roddy better?

3 What SMART goals might be set for Roddy by his manager?

Case study 2 *Questioning feedback*

Jack has been told by his manager that his report will need more work. She has given him clear indication of why this is and how it can be improved and has spent 15 minutes reading and talking it through with him.

Feedback 1 – Jack's response: 'I don't agree with you. There's nothing wrong with that report.

Just because you do it that way doesn't mean it's right.'

Feedback 2: 'Thanks for taking the time to go over this with me. I'm still not clear whether it's my style you are unhappy with or if it's the way I've set it out. If it's the style, do you have an example I could use?'

Feedback can be given in a range of ways, including:

- verbal feedback
- non-verbal feedback
- written feedback
- as a mark for a piece of work you have done.

As an early education and childcare practitioner you should regard feedback as essential for professional development and actively seek it. Feedback is not intended as *personal* criticism and should not be delivered in this way – it is a *professional* critique. If those working with you told you everything you did was fine it wouldn't help you to make improvements.

It can be very dispiriting when you have spent time and effort preparing something or doing a piece of work to be told it isn't good enough. However, if the criticism is constructive you should be told:

- what was good
- what was less good
- how you can make it better.

If you are unhappy with the feedback or you're still confused by it, you can politely ask for further clarification. The two scenarios described in the case study below provide different versions of how individuals question feedback; the second scenario is more likely to achieve a result.

The chart opposite gives some practical suggestions of words you might use when you are trying to be assertive and take control of tricky situations in placement. Always remember to thank the person for their help afterwards.

Practical suggestions for difficult situations

Scenario	Possible response
You feel no one is helping you and you don't understand what to do	'Could you help me out please? I've been asked to do — and I'm not sure how you usually do that.'
You've been told to do the same thing two different ways	'Thanks for showing me how to do this. Mary has just shown me how to do it by —. Do you have a preference?'
You are in the staffroom and two members of staff are disagreeing. They are trying to draw you into the argument.	'I really don't have a view about this' or 'I don't think its appropriate for me to comment.'
An irate parent is shouting at you	'Mrs Scott, I can see you are upset. If you would like to come into the parents' room I'll find the manager so it can be sorted out.'

How conflict can be avoided and how conflict resolution can support team work

When you are working in a team it is likely you will work successfully with your colleagues. Occasionally, however, conflict can occur. This happens when people have opposing views or beliefs that may seem irreconcilable. Good leadership can prevent conflict situations and leaders should have strategies to resolve any conflict that has occurred.

You read earlier in this chapter about different personality types and how different people prefer to work in varying ways. Sometimes team dynamics cause conflict. This is because everyone believes their way of approaching something is the correct way and although many practitioners are willing to compromise, some don't.

Conflict can occur over trivial matters or over major issues and can cause negativity in a workplace. This is because:

- people believe their goals are different from those of other colleagues or other professionals they work with
- there is poor communication within the team
- team members are uncooperative
- team members become polarised in their views

- team members distrust colleagues or managers
- the workplace is over-competitive
- little encouragement is given
- there is a perception in the workplace of a lack of equity between members of the team
- managers do not encourage a democratic approach in the workplace.

When conflict occurs, team members can behave in ways that are damaging to the team. This can include:

- blaming others for your own shortcomings
- becoming openly hostile to colleagues
- avoiding communication with colleagues or keeping it to a minimum, and refusing to perform key job functions
- not being fully engaged in the day-to-day activities in the workplace
- sabotaging the efforts of others.

Ways of avoiding conflict can include:

- trying to view an issue from the other person's point of view
- communicating well and listening to others
- stating your position rationally and clearly
- meeting with those involved in the issue together to try to reach a compromise
- ensuring teams have consistent and clear parameters for dealing with areas that may be problematic
- being assertive.

Case study *Conflict in the workplace*

Good4Kids is an out-of-school care club in the east of Scotland. The club has expanded recently and in addition to the two existing members of staff, Jack and Lynne, three new colleagues have started recently, one of whom has been appointed as the new manager. The existing staff had expected the club to run pretty much as it had before but the manager has some new ideas, including asking the children for feedback on the effectiveness of the provision and on the range of activities available to them.

Jack and Lynne are really opposed to this but the new colleagues think it's a good idea and are used to working this way. Jack and Lynne are trying to canvass parents against the idea and the manager has become aware of this happening. They have also said at a recent staff meeting that if this system goes ahead they will leave. Both are good practitioners and the manager doesn't want to lose them. However, she also wants to try out new approaches and feels very strongly that this is best for the centre and for the children.

1   In what ways might this conflict be resolved?

2   Are there ways this conflict might have been avoided?

Conflict is not necessarily a bad thing. Sometimes conflict helps teams reconsider their actions and question why those actions have been taken. If conflict continues you may have to tackle it. The following suggestions for tackling conflict are taken from Squire (*BTEC National Children's Care, Learning and Development*, 2007).

Prepare yourself:

- Write down what the problem is from your perspective and share it with someone in the team you trust, asking them for their views.

- Think of the various ways out of the situation – the pros and cons.

- Have your say.

Be assertive:

- Say how the problem makes you feel and how you think it is affecting you.

- Avoid saying 'You are making me feel' and use the phrase 'When you say/do… it makes me feel…'

- Make sure your body language is not threatening.

Get the full picture:

- Listen carefully to what others are feeling and show you are listening.

- Don't interrupt.

- Ask open-ended questions to clarify what others are saying if you need to.

- Acknowledge what you can agree about and concentrate on where there are any differences.

Aim for a resolution:

- Offer and consider several options for the way forward.

- Be prepared to reach a compromise.

How other key professionals contribute to the work of the team

Multi-agency working

Often team work involves working with external agencies and professional teams, and you read in Chapter 1 about the key professionals you will work with. This included working with educational psychologists, social workers, health visitors and others. In this chapter you will look at some of the ways that, by team work and collaboration, you can support children better.

Working with others is integral to the early education and childcare profession. Sometimes this is called multi-professional working, at other times inter-agency working. There are a number of ways this is expressed but essentially it means collaboration across and between different teams and professions. This happens because children and families can have complex lives and are often being supported by professionals from other sectors. The work you do with children and families can't be seen in a vacuum or as separate or disengaged from the work of others.

One of the main drivers of the Scottish Government is to streamline services that children and families receive to make sure that the systems that support them are more efficient. They also want to make sure those families don't need to repeat their personal stories, which are often harrowing, to multiple agencies. Much has been made of 'joining up' services for children and multi-agency working is one way of ensuring this happens. Working effectively with others helps to ensure services for children and families are well coordinated to provide the support, advice or help that may be required.

Some of the professionals and professional teams you are likely to work with will vary according to the setting you work in. The range of professionals covered in this chapter is not exhaustive and it does not discuss the specifics of external professionals' roles; rather, it looks at how working together can combine specialism and knowledge to ensure the best possible outcomes for the child and family. You can research who these professionals are by investigating those that support teams in your placement.

Further research

When you are next in placement, ask about the range of professionals that support children and families. If there are professional groups that are not indicated here, do some additional research on:

- the key purpose of that professional with the child or family
- how their input enriches the team work of the centre.

Why it is important to work with other professionals

Often the professionals that come into the nursery school or child and family centre are not located there permanently. You will be with the children on a day-to-day basis and will see families on a regular basis. You have the professional skills to observe children, report on what you have observed and make sound professional judgements based on this. Other professionals need to be able to access and interpret your information to make specialist recommendations. At other times they will use your observations to make recommendations about the child's future needs, design specific programmes or undertake further assessments.

Some professionals will carry out diagnostic assessments to make decisions about a need a child may have. They will also advise the centre on specific programmes to support the child better. Supporting assessments will mean you need to know:

- the purpose of the assessment
- the purpose of any programmes subsequently devised for the child
- expectations of you to implement the programme, i.e. what you do and what others need to do
- expectations of how you will report and record information you have observed
- how information about the assessment and any subsequent to it is conveyed to children, families and other interested agencies.

Multi-agency teams

Nursery schools and classes, special schools, mainstream schools and children and family centres are amongst the settings supported by other key professional groups. Out-of-school settings may also have some additional specialist support, particularly when they are operating in holiday times to provide services to children with additional support needs or respite care.

Other specialist voluntary services will also work with other professional staff. An important feature of working with very young children is to make sure the family stay as involved as possible while keeping the best interests of the child at the centre of decisions. Different groups of workers bring different professional skills to the team.

A key feature of multi-disciplinary work is to identify early on which professional is providing what specialism so that there isn't unnecessary repetition for the child or family and to ensure all are clear about their roles.

Some of the key professionals you may find working with teams in early education and childcare settings include the following: health visitors (community nurses); speech and language therapists; physiotherapists; paediatric occupational therapists; educational or clinical psychologists; social workers; bilingual support workers; play, art or music therapists; play specialists; specialist teachers of drama, art, music or languages; teachers; specialist fitness or sports workers. (An explanation is given about some of these roles in Chapters 1 and 6.)

The type of expertise these workers are likely to bring to the centre will vary. Some will have a statutory duty to provide support, while others may be engaged by the centre to provide support to existing teams. Centres should expect external professionals to support the internal team's knowledge and understanding by:

- responding appropriately to requests about the child
- attending internal staff meetings where relevant
- contributing to reports on the child.

A well-coordinated multi-disciplinary approach can ensure consistency and clarity of actions for the child and family.

Multi-disciplinary working in special schools and classes

Special schools and classes are more likely to have a multi-professional mix of personnel contributing to the child's coordinated support plan. One of the reasons for admitting very young children to special schools is to ensure the particular, specialist help that the child and family may require is given at the earliest possible stage. The same range of professionals will be involved with children in special schools as in mainstream provision and include:

speech and language therapists; audiologists; physiotherapists; educational psychologists; teachers, social workers; health visitors (community nurses) amongst many others.

Why multi-agency team working is important

Chapter 2 highlighted the Children (Scotland) Act (1995) and the Children's Hearing system in Scotland. Both support vulnerable children who may be at risk and the Act highlighted the need for collaborative action for those agencies working with children.

Some children are supported in centres because the centre provides a place of safety for the child.

A key requirement of a multi-agency approach is to coordinate information and reports sent back to lead agencies, such as the local social work department, on the progress made by children and families. Another requirement is to inform coordinated support plans to enable consistency of approach and avoid duplication in supporting children and families.

Children who have complex lives and difficulties may need more than one agency to support them. Each agency needs to know what the other is providing so that a coordinated approach is taken. Most child protection tragedies of recent times have reported badly coordinated services as a key factor in the failure to provide adequate care and support.

Further research

Investigate one of the following to establish how multi-agency coordination failed.

1 The O'Brien Report

2 The Herbison Report

Coordinated support plan

Under the Education (Additional Support for Learning) (Scotland) Act (2004), local authorities have a duty to provide a coordinated support plan (CSP) for children who have multiple, complex or enduring barriers to their learning. (You can read more about this in Chapter 6.) It is crucial that the reports are accurate and take the best interests of the child into consideration. This means the practitioner needs to work in close collaboration with other agents that may be involved in writing a report.

The CSP needs to reflect all the support the child may require and will almost always require a multi-agency approach to completing it. If communication between professionals is poor it may be inaccurate and will have a detrimental effect on the child, who may not receive the special support required or may not get it soon enough. This causes anxiety and frustration to families. Clarity between professional groups is required to ensure consistency of approach and to avoid delays.

The following case studies show the type of inter-agency collaboration that may be required.

Case study 1 *Gathering information about children*

Pinegrove Nursery offers full day care to 60 children. Each child has his own profile and at the end of every term parents are given a short report on the key milestones reached. The nursery has recently employed a dance instructor and a Spanish teacher, and each spends one hour a day with the pre-school children. The nursery operates a key worker system. Key workers are responsible for compiling their children's profiles and for making sure all observations are recorded appropriately. The nursery owner has asked the key workers to let her know how successful the additional dance and Spanish lessons are.

- How can the key workers make sure information about the children is accurately gathered to allow feedback to parents?

Case study 2 *Supporting a family in need*

Joanne is 18 years old and her partner Jake is 19 years old. Joanne is pregnant with her second child. Joanne drank heavily while pregnant with her first child, Lewis, and both parents misuse drugs. Lewis is 3 years 6 months. Reports indicate Lewis's slow growth and developmental delay may be because of foetal alcohol syndrome. Following allegations of neglect the family have been referred by their social worker to the local child and family centre for help designed to support their parenting skills. Both parents are attending addiction services for drugs misuse.

Since Lewis has started at the centre, staff note he has more energy and can concentrate for a little longer than before. They observe that Joanne quickly loses patience with him if he doesn't pay attention to her. They have also noticed Lewis has unexplained bruises 'from falling over'. They have observed Joanne can have very high or very low moods.

Jake seldom comes to the centre but when he does he is aggressive with staff. He has started to confide in one of the practitioners that he is concerned about the new baby and how they will cope financially. He says Joanne is under a lot of stress and he has seen her lash out at Lewis. Joanne, on the other hand, is saying very similar things to another member of staff about Jake. Jake and Joanne can either be very aggressive with each other or very close.

1 What range of professionals are likely to be working with this family?

2 As a practitioner in the child and family centre, what information is it important to record?

3 What might you record as important in this case?

Working with other professionals in the primary school

You have read about the importance of working with other professionals who are likely to be external to the organisation you work within. One of the key professionals you will work with who may be internal or external to your organisation is the Primary 1 teacher. Liaison with the Primary 1 teacher is very important for children who make a transition from nursery to Primary 1. In Scotland this happens in the year in which children reach their fifth birthday and is usually in August. Because of the summer holiday between children leaving nursery and entering Primary 1, the liaison has to be done before the end of June each year.

When a child entered the nursery you communicated with parents to produce a profile of the child. This profile helped practitioners understand the child better and allowed appropriate provision of play. The same process takes place when a child is leaving nursery and going into Primary 1. Curriculum for Excellence has helped to make transitions more straightforward because of the need to streamline and embed what is happening in the nursery with the play and learning needs of Primary 1. So the Primary 1 teacher and the nursery staff need to liaise to ensure continuity and progression for the child.

Records that have been passed on from nursery are crucial in helping the Primary 1 teacher make an initial assessment of the child. Good communication between the nursery and the school is key to ensuring the right information is passed on in the most appropriate and helpful way.

Communication with the school is likely to be both verbal and written. It may involve meetings in both establishments to outline the most helpful way of recording and presenting information. It may also involve three-way meetings between the nursery, the child and family, and the school. If the child has a recorded need there is also likely to be a multi-agency approach to providing transition information.

Some of the strategies used to help the transition process include:

- good observation, reporting and recording of relevant information
- planned visits between the nursery class and the school where there will be a verbal exchange of information
- planned visits by the Primary 1 teacher to allow observation of children in the centre
- writing reports or profiles of children that indicate key information including: successes; readiness for reading; understanding of mathematics/number; interests; any specific needs; preferred learning styles
- involving children and parents in the process and other professionals as required.

The nursery practitioner's role in this process is critical. Your contribution will be based on your observations and assessments and your knowledge of the child and family based on fact. It will require high levels of written and verbal skills.

Further research

Find out the policy in your local area for transitions between nursery and Primary 1. What is the role of the nursery in developing transition records?

Starting Primary 1 is a really important transition for a child

How communication is affected by the style of language, the intention of the message and the way it is conveyed

How to communicate effectively with adults

Throughout this chapter a key feature that has emerged is the need to communicate well with others. Communication is at the heart of what you do when you are working with others and covers a range of different forms. These include verbal and non-verbal communication, listening skills, report writing and written communication with parents, colleagues and other professionals. Communicating well with children is a particular skill and is dealt with in other chapters in this book, including Chapters 1, 2, 4 and 10.

Body language is important in effective communication: it can say more than words

Communication is directly affected by the intention of your message, the style of language you use and the way you convey a message. The effectiveness of the communication is also affected by the type of communication you use. This section will look at verbal communication, non-verbal cues and some aspects of written communication. The 'team working' section covered previously in this chapter also emphasises the place of assertiveness in successful communication.

Verbal communication

Talking to others is something you do throughout each day. The messages you convey verbally should be appropriate to the situation you are in. You may have a more casual style when you are with friends and a slightly more formal approach when at work. When you communicate with others it is important that the message you give is clear and unambiguous. That means it shouldn't be misinterpreted.

Talking face to face with someone is often the most effective way to get a message across. Sometimes messages are misinterpreted or misunderstood and this can lead to confusion or conflict. You need to be in control of the message you send. To do this you will need to consider the following.

- Choose an appropriate time for the conversation.
- Choose a suitable location: is there too much background noise to be heard and do you need privacy?
- Speak clearly and try not to speak too fast.
- Always face the listener and make good eye contact.
- Avoid jargon or colloquialisms that the listener may not be familiar with.

Key term

Colloquialism is an informal way or example of speaking that you wouldn't use when writing.

- Provide an appropriate amount of information: not too much but not too little for the listener to fail to understand what you are conveying.
- Check the listener has understood you and allow questions.
- Think very carefully about how anything you say might be interpreted.
- Think about your tone of voice.
- Think about your body language and what it might be indicating.

Barriers to effective verbal communication

When you deliver a message there is an intended target. This is shown in the diagram below.

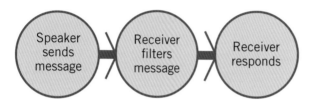

When you send a message verbally you make an assumption the recipient will understand the message and respond appropriately. Sometimes messages are misinterpreted. This can be because:

- the message was confused
- the listener was distracted
- the listener took a different meaning because of your body language
- the message was incomplete.

Consider this

Consider a situation where you have been confused by a message or you have misinterpreted a message. Can you say why that was and how the situation might have been improved?

Here is an example of a confused message: a lecturer walks into the Team Working class. After a few minutes she says: 'When do we finish?' One person calls out 'Half past two', another says 'At the end of January', while a third says 'On the 11th of June'. All three answers to the question are correct but the question is ambiguous. Respondent one thought the lecturer meant 'When does the class finish today?' The second thought she meant 'When does the Team Working unit teaching finish?' The third thought she meant 'When does this HNC course finish?'

You may be very clear about your question or statement when you are communicating verbally but your listeners don't have the luxury of knowing what is going on in your head and may need more information. Recipients have to rely on the message they hear and their understanding of it.

When you are giving verbal information it is tempting to think everyone is in receipt of as much information as you are, but this is seldom the case. Sometimes you are several steps ahead of the listener and so the communication becomes confused.

Usually when you give a good news message you will smile or laugh. If the message is serious you will adopt a more sombre tone. If you are agreeing with someone you tend to nod in agreement. Sometimes when you hear a message that you feel you should agree with but you really don't want to agree with you may say 'yes' but subconsciously shake your head. This gives conflicting messages to the recipient.

Poor communication and the need for assertion

Researchers, including Liz Willis and Jenny Daisley (*The Assertive Trainer: A Practical Handbook on Assertiveness for Trainers Running Assertiveness Courses*, 1995) consider the message you deliver is affected in the following way: 58 per cent of the message received is affected by the appearance of the message giver; 37 per cent is concerned with the voice used; 5 per cent is about the words used. This means that you may think you are saying something in a particular way but your appearance or tone might suggest otherwise.

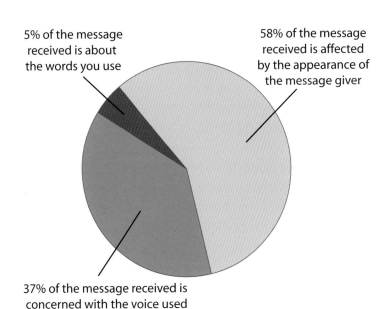

5% of the message received is about the words you use

58% of the message received is affected by the appearance of the message giver

37% of the message received is concerned with the voice used

Body language is important in effective communication: it can say more than words (from *The Assertive Trainer*)

Consider this

What makes you want to listen to someone? Does the tone of voice used make a difference to how you respond to a message?

Being assertive

Assertion can be an aid to communication and lack of assertion a barrier to it. Assertiveness in getting your message across involves your body language, your tone of voice and the content of what you say. Some people are too passive and so don't get their message across, while others are too aggressive. The middle ground you should aim for is assertion. The following provides examples of how assertion helps you to become a better communicator and ways that aggression and passivity prevent good communication taking place.

Your body language suggests you are assertive if you:

- make and retain good eye contact
- stand or sit in a fairly upright position
- are relaxed
- make sure the expression on your face fits the message that is being conveyed
- ensure you leave the right amount of space between yourself and the recipient of the message
- have an open or relaxed hand.

Aggressive behaviour is usually shown by:

- staring
- pointing or jabbing your finger at the recipient

- clenched fists
- clenched jaw
- drumming fingers or tapping toes.

Passive behaviour is often shown by:

- little or poor eye contact
- showing fear or sadness in your expression
- shoulders that are up
- a nervous smile
- legs that are wrapped one round the other.

Assertive comments include:

- 'My experience is that…'
- 'I will do my best to…'
- 'I'm not sure I can agree to do that because…'
- 'How does that seem to you?'
- 'Can we think of some other ways of dealing with this?'

Aggressive comments include:

- 'I don't understand what the problem is – I don't have any difficulty with it.'
- 'You'd better get that done before I get back or there will be real trouble.'
- 'I'd have been much better just doing it myself.'
- 'You need to get on to it *now*.'
- 'Everybody says you're like that.'

Often this type of comment is accompanied by a voice that is sharp, strident, sarcastic, cold, shouting or abrupt.

Passive comments include:

- 'Well, maybe, perhaps I could think about doing that.'
- 'I don't really like to ask you and if you can't its OK, but I was wondering if you could maybe…'
- 'I'm probably wrong about this and you're probably right, but I was thinking…'
- 'Don't worry about me…'
- 'I don't mean to cause a fuss but I was wondering if…'

(Reprinted with permission from Liz Willis and Jenny Daisley, *The Assertive Trainer: A Practical Handbook on Assertiveness for Trainers Running Assertiveness Courses*, London: McGraw-Hill, pages 28–32)

These type of passive comments may be said in a soft or hesitant voice, and the person may not feel able to finish his or her sentences.

Consider this

Consider how an assertive approach might have helped you in a difficult situation. What approach did you take to the situation and how might you have dealt with it more assertively?

Active listening

The art of active listening is important in ensuring that you understand what others are communicating with you. Active listening also shows that you have an interest in what another colleague is saying and so contributes to successful team working. It is also applicable to the work you do with children and parents.

Key term

Active listening involves showing by your verbal and non-verbal responses that you are listening.

Some of the things to remember in active listening are as follows.

- Don't anticipate what someone is going to say.
- Avoid interrupting while someone is speaking or edging into a conversation before that person has finished.
- Show you are following what the person is saying. If you think you are losing the point, find an appropriate time to interrupt and ask for clarification by saying: 'Can I clarify that what you are saying is…'
- Make sure your non-verbal behaviour doesn't contradict, so avoid looking away from or over the shoulder of the person who is speaking to you.

Case study *Poor listening skills*

Terry has two children at the after-school club. He is currently on Jobseeker's Allowance, having lost his job when the local factory closed down. He knows the children love going to the club but is really concerned that he can no longer afford the fees, as it's looking unlikely he will get a job any time soon in their local area.

Terry doesn't feel particularly at ease because the practitioners who run the club always seem to be busy and to ignore him when he comes in. He finally summons up the courage to approach the manager and says tentatively, 'I'm not sure if the bairns are going to be able to come here much more.' At that point the phone rings and the manager turns from him to pick up the phone. She puts her hand over the phone and says, 'Oh, that's a real shame. They both really love it here,' then goes on with her call.

Terry becomes annoyed and shouts: 'Don't you think I'd keep them here if I could; its not easy being on the dole you know! You folk just haven't got a clue what its like,' and storms out.

1 Analyse what has gone wrong with this communication.

2 What could the manager have done differently in this situation?

- Avoid walking away or doing something else when someone is talking to you (while you say 'I'm listening just keep going…').

You have possibly encountered some of the responses described above. The case study below shows how some of these might appear to others.

Asking for feedback

One way of ensuring that the message you intended is put across successfully is to ask for feedback. This means checking what you have said or recapping the message. Two ways of doing this are: checking by asking the recipient to repeat the message; paraphrasing and repeating the message yourself.

Repeating a message can involve the following:

> *Nursery practitioner to student:* 'I'd like you to go over to the craft area and make sure there are six pairs of scissors, some glue, and shiny and black paper available for the children today.'

> *Student:* 'Where is the craft area?'

> *Nursery practitioner:* 'We usually set the craft area up over by the window. Now, would you like to repeat what you need to set out on the table today?'

> *Student:* 'Yes, you want six pairs of scissors, glue, and shiny and black paper.'

> *Nursery practitioner:* 'Yes, that's great… let me know if you need any more help.'

When you are recapping a message it is acceptable to shorten it a little. Here is an example:

> *Practitioner:* 'Samir's mum has just phoned to let us know that he needs to leave by 11.30 today. He has a hospital appointment. She has stressed that Samir mustn't have any snack today as the hospital need to do some tests. He can have a drink of water but no solid food and no orange juice.'

> *Student:* 'OK. I'm on snack so I'll try to remember.'

> *Practitioner:* 'Just to recap: Samir can have water but can't have any food or drink this morning. That's very important. I'll make sure he's ready at 11.30.'

Activity

Look at the following scenarios and consider how you might deal with each one.

Scenario 1

You are having a conversation with someone in college and her eyes start to drift over to someone who is walking down the corridor. How do you feel?

Scenario 2

You are telling someone how you feel when they speak to you in a particular way. The person is now folding her arms and is starting to tap her foot. What is her body language suggesting to you?

Scenario 3

You are explaining to the nursery practitioner that your daughter won't be in next week because you are all going down south to see your sister's new baby. She is attentive and when you have finished the practitioner smiles and claps her hands before saying to your daughter 'What lovely news!'

What impression do you get? Is it likely you are going to give her further information?

Scenario 4

A parent comes into the out-of-school club. She is looking around her and is wringing her hands. She comes over to you and a colleague, but is still looking round for other parents. She says tentatively, 'Can I have a quiet word?' Your colleague says, 'Yeah, shoot.' You say, 'Would you prefer to go somewhere private?'

Bearing in mind this parent's body language, which do you think might have been the better response?

Getting the message across clearly

As an early education and childcare practitioner you may work with people whose first language may not be English. This means you need to make sure you don't use language that is confusing, including too much technical language. In early education and childcare there is a lot of technical language around and sometimes acronyms or abbreviations are used. You probably use them when you speak to friends. An example would be saying to a parent: 'I've just heard that HMIE are coming to the school next week' (HMIE means Her Majesty's Inspector of Education). You will know that HMIE are the school inspectors but a parent may not.

In centres you may have your own acronym for reports or for forms that need to be filled in but you need to remember that not everyone shares the same understanding. You may also have a different understanding of technical words or phrases. An example of this might be risk assessment: in nursery you may talk about risk assessment by describing some of the health and safety implications of an activity; in social work terms risk assessment might be more concerned with the personal risk to the individual child in a child protection case.

You also need to make sure that you are not misinterpreted in what you say. Sometimes local dialects can be confusing to people who have been taught Standard English. Local dialects should be welcomed but some words that are very specific to your area may have to be explained.

Written communication

In an early education and childcare setting you are likely to have to provide written communication for some of the following:

- reports
- letters to parents and others
- newsletters
- email
- notice boards.

The essence of a written report is that it should state clearly and concisely what you want to communicate. Some reports you may need to fill in will have pre-identified categories and you may be required to complete these using a narrative style. Sometimes reports for parents are set out in this way, and you may complete them as a team or be asked to complete them individually. There is likely to be a house style which you will be required to follow; this describes the organisation's standard way of writing a report.

Alternatively, you may simply be given a blank sheet of paper and be asked to fill in some detail about the child. You should always ask for some guidance on the type of detail required and the preferred format. When you are writing a report it is a good idea to have worked out the key points you want to convey first. Most agencies prefer reports that are concise so aim to be economical in what you say.

Make sure your report contains all the important facts:

- the subject and purpose of the report
- who you are writing about
- the key points you want to talk about
- the role of others
- who has compiled the report with contact details
- when the report was written.

You also need to make sure all reports are grammatically correct and with no spelling mistakes. Equally important is that you respect the confidentiality of children and families by making sure all written reports are filed securely and are not left lying around.

Try to practise a style of writing that is concise, grammatically correct and uses plain English. Avoid unhelpful jargon. Think about who will be reading the report and make sure it is appropriate for that audience. When you are writing, stop at the end of each sentence to ask yourself the question, 'Is this relevant to what I am trying to communicate?' If the answer is no then delete the sentence – it isn't adding any value to the report.

It's often a good idea to ask a colleague to read your report while remembering the professional requirements for confidentiality. Another person's view is often useful to pick up on points that are unclear.

Case study *Comparing two reports*

Two different reports are given overleaf – the first on page 244 and the second on page 245. Which do you think is more beneficial to an external colleague about the child, how he is progressing and the next steps in the process? Which do you consider is the more professionally written of the two?

The key points of the case are described below for your information:

- Child: Ruraidh, 4 years 5 months
- Admitted to Mill Lane Child and Family Centre on 15 August 2007
- Ruraidh is on the 'at risk' register following concerns raised by the local social work team
- Health visitor involved with Mrs Scott, Ruraidh's mother, who is living alone with Ruraidh and known to have alcohol addiction problems
- Two older children (12 and 13 years) who Mrs Scott asked to be taken into the care of the local authority because she couldn't cope with their behaviour
- Update on progress to date and any further interventions required

Ruraidh arrived at Mill Lane on 15 August 2007 and had been in two previous nurseries but they couldn't cope with his bad behaviour. Mrs Scott thought they were making matters worse and letting him do what he wanted. She thought Ruraidh's behaviour was 'out of hand'. Ruraidh was showing some signs of anxiety when he came here at first and he was biting and spitting at staff and swore at and often kicked the other children.

The staff are also working with Mrs Scott to try to help her to see she isn't being consistent with Ruraidh. It was difficult to work with Mrs Scott, who has often been drinking when she comes into the centre. She didn't think we were doing Ruraidh much good and she was very critical of the centre in general and some of the staff in particular. Ruraidh kept biting and spitting at other children until one day he seemed to calm down and stop. Mrs Scott has continued to be difficult to work with and thinks the staff here are ganging up on her. That isn't the case because the staff here are trying hard to be calm with her at all times. However, she blames the staff for the swearing, biting and spitting Ruraidh gets up to all the time.

We have spoken with the health visitor about this and she is going to try to visit Mrs Scott at home. The social workers are pleased that Ruraidh has settled in and seems to want to kick and spit less. The staff here think it will be difficult to get Ruraidh to settle in school, however, but are happy to keep working with him.

Signed: Janice Stirling

Report 1

Mill Lane Child and Family Centre

Paisley

Report for Case Conference on Ruraidh Scott (d.o.b. 06 June 2003)

Date of conference: 19 October 2007

Author: Janice Stirling – Child and Family Centre Key worker

Contact: 0141872336 ext21

Admission details:

Ruraidh was admitted to the centre on 15 August 2007 following a request from his social worker John Brown (see attached report).

Key issues:

Ruraidh was displaying behaviours that his mother found distressing and that had meant he was asked to leave two nurseries before admission to Mill Lane. This behaviour included spitting, kicking and swearing at other children, his mother and nursery staff. Mrs Scott's response to Ruraidh's behaviour had been causing some concern given the family history highlighted in the admission report.

Progress:

Key workers have provided focused support to modify Ruraidh's behaviour and are working with Mrs Scott to try to establish a consistent approach to his behaviour management. Sometimes Mrs Scott has been less able to do this, but this has been discussed with Mrs Scott and her additions worker. Mrs Scott has expressed concern at the support she is getting from the centre but staff continue to work with her to progress this.

Next steps:

Ruraidh requires consolidation of behaviour management and one-to-one support. Staff at the centre would like to work with Mrs Scott and Ruraidh to try to minimise his outbursts and support Mrs Scott. This includes showing Mrs Scott effective ways of dealing with adverse behaviours and how to promote positive behaviour.

Proposal:

Ruraidh should remain at the centre until June 2008 when he will be eligible to transfer to the local primary school. Ongoing review of this is essential and a suggested review date is January 2008.

Signed: Janice Stirling

10 October 2007

Report 2

You may want to ask your placement about what contribution practitioners are asked to make to formal reports. You may also want to find out if there is any practical help available to you if you feel unsure of how to write a report.

Check your progress

1. Describe ways that groups and teams differ.

2. What are the key characteristics of a good team?

3. Describe some of the key strengths that can make a team more effective.

4. How do personality type tests support recruitment of effective teams?

5. Describe the different types of roles Belbin thought were a feature of teams.

6. What are the factors that Herzberg thought made people better motivated to work?

7. How can goal setting and performance review support the early education and childcare practitioner?

8. Explain ways that assertive, passive and aggressive behaviour can affect communication between colleagues.

9. Explain why active listening is essential and supports team working.

10. Explain why conflict occurs in teams and ways it can be avoided.

References

Belbin, R.M. (2003) *Management Teams: Why They Succeed or Fail*, Oxford: Butterworth Heinemann

Guirdham, M. (1995) *Interpersonal Skills at Work*, 2nd edn, Hemel Hempstead: Prentice Hall

Herzberg, F., Mausner, B. and Snyderman, B.B. (1959) *The Motivation to Work*, New York: John Wiley

Maslow, A. (1943) 'A theory of human motivation', *Psychological Review*, 50, 370–96.

Myers, I. Briggs, McCaulley, M.H., Quenk, N.L., and Hammer, A.L. (1998) *MBTI Manual (A Guide to the Development and Use of the Myers Briggs Type Indicator)*, 3rd edn, Palo Alto, CA: Consulting Psychologists Press

Robbins, H. and Finley, M. (2000) *Why Teams Don't Work: What Went Wrong and How to Make It Right*, London: Harvard Business Essentials

Sadek, E. and Sadek, J. (2004) *Good Practice in Nursery Management*, Cheltenham: Nelson Thorne

Scottish Executive (2007) *A Curriculum for Excellence: Building the Curriculum 2 – Active Learning in the Early Years*, Edinburgh

Squire, G. (ed.) (2007) *BTEC National Children's Care, Learning and Development*, Oxford: Heinemann

Thomson, R. (1998) *People Management*, London: Orion Books

Willis, L. and Daisley, J. (1995) *The Assertive Trainer: A Practical Handbook on Assertiveness for Trainers Running Assertiveness Courses*, London: McGraw-Hill

Useful websites

The O'Brien Report: the report into the death of Caleb Ness: www.edinburgh.gov.uk/social_work/calebness/calebness.html

The Herbison Report: the independent review into the death of Danielle Reid: www.highland.gov.uk/NR/rdonlyres/E7BA7919-AE72-4F57-AED6-D0A52A39CBBD/0/hc03.pdf

Meredith Belbin's website: www.belbin.com.

Website for the Myers-Briggs Type Indicator (MBTI) personality test: www.myersbriggs.org

Chapter 8

Understanding and supporting children's behaviour

HNC unit covered:
Unit DF54 34

Introduction

This chapter provides you with information on the factors that influence children's behaviour. You will learn about the theories that are used to describe and explain influences on children's behaviour. You will also learn about the strategies that are used to support children's behaviour and how to recognise causes for concern, as well as the roles of other professionals involved in supporting behaviour and the strategies they use.

The contents of this chapter will give you some of the knowledge and understanding that you need to complete and achieve Unit DF54 34: Understanding and supporting children's behaviour. Some of the theories you have already learned about in Chapter 3. The contents of this chapter will help you consider whether you might want to select a behaviour-related topic for your graded unit project.

Sources for further research are suggested to help develop your knowledge and understanding of current thinking in understanding children's behaviour and how to support it. You will also learn how to analyse and evaluate a range of strategies to support children's behaviour. Knowledge and understanding of why children behave the way they do and what influences their behaviour will allow you to recognise how to work with and support them. You will learn how theory is linked to your practice in early education and childcare. This may help with the planning stage of your graded unit.

Children in the age range covered by this unit (birth to 12 years) come from a variety of family and cultural backgrounds and attend a variety of childcare and education settings.

Children's responses to various environments, family and cultural backgrounds will vary. Different temperaments and personalities will respond differently to the same situations and circumstances. Some children will be affected by genetic or health conditions that affect their behaviour and may need additional support. Other children will need the intervention of specialist professionals to understand and support their behaviour.

In this chapter you will learn:

- How to evaluate theories that describe influences on a range of children's behaviours
- Theories describing influences on the development of a range of behaviours
- The importance of recognising age-appropriate behaviour
- How to observe and assess children's behaviour
- Strategies used to support children's behaviour
- Modifying the environment to encourage appropriate behaviour
- The procedures for referring children in need of additional support for their behaviour
- Behaviour policies in early education and childcare settings

How to evaluate theories that describe influences on a range of children's behaviours

The ability to critically analyse and evaluate theory and research is an important skill to develop for the HNC student.

Key term

Critical evaluation views theory and research objectively; it identifies the strengths and weaknesses of a theory and the usefulness and limitations of a piece of research.

If you are undertaking this unit as 'stand alone' for continuous professional development (CPD) you might find it useful to look at Chapter 3, 5 and 10. Critical evaluation requires you to compare and contrast different ideas, theories and research findings. Research is an ongoing process where researchers develop and test their ideas. Initial findings may produce indecisive results that lead to a different approach. Other researchers may take another's idea, test it and have different results or develop the original idea further.

It is important that you keep up to date with current thinking in your early education and childcare practice so that you can bring the most current ideas to your work. It is equally important to analyse any theory you learn and critically evaluate it. When you critically evaluate a theory of children's behaviour you should consider how the theory relates to your experiences and observations. You may find that a theory does not fit with your experience in the workplace or that the implementation of a suggested course of action does not achieve the desired effect. This will lead you to offer an alternative or to do further reading to find out which research supports particular views.

What is behaviour?

Human behaviour can be defined as how an individual responds to a specific circumstance or situation. The focus in early education and childcare should be to promote positive behaviour and discourage unacceptable negative behaviour.

Behaviour is a complex concept and trying to learn acceptable behaviour is often very difficult for a child. For example, shouting, running and jumping is acceptable during outdoor play but is less appropriate in a nursery book corner or an out-of-school setting computer area. A child may also find that behaviour considered unacceptable for him or her is tolerated in a younger sibling.

Generally, positive behaviour describes what is acceptable in the culture and society where you live. This is important to know when working with children and young people who may come from different family and cultural backgrounds. For example, in some cultures it is considered unacceptable behaviour for a child to make eye contact with an adult when being addressed. In Scotland we encourage eye contact when talking.

Negative behaviour is that which is unacceptable, inappropriate or anti-social. Such behaviour may be abusive or aggressive.

Consider this

Do you have examples of younger children 'getting away with' behaviour not permitted in an older child? How would you manage a situation like this?

What behaviours would you describe as positive? Explain your opinions. Are your opinions age-related?

Young children show a range of behaviours including laughing, crying, listening, shouting and sociability. Different children have different dispositions and display different behaviours.

There are many factors that influence children's behaviour. One belief which favours the 'nature' side of the nature/nurture debate is that children are born with their talents and personality. Others believe that 'nurture' plays a greater role and consider the input of parents and carers to exert huge influence on how children behave.

Positive role modelling is one of the key responsibilities of early education and childcare practitioners. Courtesy to others is an example of positive role modelling. Demonstrating patience and listening skills are further examples.

Consider this

Can you think of other ways you could demonstrate positive role modelling as an early education and childcare practitioner? Explain why you think these are examples of positive role modelling.

Children who observe positive behaviour patterns in the practitioners in their early education and childcare settings are more likely to develop similar attitudes and behaviours.

Antenatal factors

Some factors to consider are those that may affect the growing foetus before birth. Research is ongoing into the effects of substances such as alcohol taken by pregnant women on behaviour patterns shown later by their babies and children.

Genetic factors

The study of how genetics contributes to the individual's behaviour has become known as behaviour genetics. In behaviour genetics, psychologists look at how heredity influences aspects of growth, development and behaviour such as height, body shape, intelligence, reading ability, aggressiveness, depression, temperament and sociability.

Genetic factors may lead to conditions such as attention deficit disorders and Down's syndrome. Some medical conditions, such as haemophilia and cystic fibrosis that affect growth and development, are hereditary.

The influence of the family on children's behaviour

The family has an enormous influence on a child's behaviour. If a family doesn't value a particular way of behaving, it is unlikely that the child will. Where a family has consistent ways of supporting children, the child is more likely to develop parameters around behaviour. So where a child is brought up in a calm and loving atmosphere, and where parents or carers explain why they have taken a course of action, it is more likely the child will respond in a calm way. You can read more about how the family influences children and their behaviour in Chapter 9.

Parenting styles

Parents approach child-rearing in different ways. Erikson (cited in *Applying Psychology to Early Childhood Development*) identified two main aspects in the relationship between parents and their children. These are parental warmth and parental control. Children need warmth for their emotional development and their sense of self-worth. Children need control to encourage moral development and the development of self-control. Further studies of parents and their children by Diana Baumrind in 1971 (cited in *Applying Psychology to Early Childhood Development*) identified three parenting styles that are generally recognised: authoritarian, permissive and authoritative.

Authoritarian parents exercise a high level of control over their children and have high expectations of their behaviour and achievement. They are unlikely to recognise or respond to their children's emotional needs

The family has an enormous influence on a child's behaviour

or communicate well with them. Research into behaviour patterns of children from authoritarian families show that they are likely to be low achievers at school and have difficulty relating with their peer group They often have low self-esteem. These children may show subdued, withdrawn behaviour or may have high levels of aggressiveness.

Permissive parents are indulgent and demonstrate warmth and responsiveness towards their children but may not communicate well with them. Any control they exercise is likely to be inconsistent. Children with permissive parents are also likely to be low achievers in school and to demonstrate aggressiveness. They are likely to appear immature in comparison with their peer group and are less ready to take responsibility. These children may also lack the ability to act independently.

Authoritative parents communicate well with their children and demonstrate warmth and responsiveness towards them. They exercise control by setting consistent boundaries and also ensure that children's individual needs are met. Studies of these families showed that children with authoritative parents had high self-esteem and were able to act independently. These children are self-confident and have a high standard of achievement in school.

All the above parenting styles imply a degree of parental involvement in their children's lives. Later studies by Eleanor Maccoby and John Martin in 1983 (cited in *The Developing Child*) identified a fourth parenting style. *Neglecting parents* are uninvolved with their children. They are unaware of their children's needs and have little communication with them. They are unlikely to exercise control or impose any boundaries. Children with neglecting parents often show hostility and have difficulty in developing relationships with their peers and others. These children are more likely to be involved in anti-social behaviour and the misuse of substances such as alcohol and controlled drugs.

> **Consider this**
>
> Do these parenting/child-rearing styles describe those you have observed? Are there other categories? Explain your answer with reference to further research.
>
> Can you think of examples of staff who are authoritarian or permissive with the children in their care? How might this affect the children's behaviour?

Critical evaluation

Baumrind's classification of parenting styles has been criticised as being over-simplified. Most parents will have a combination of styles and

Demonstrating warmth and responsiveness is a characteristic of both permissive and authoritative parenting styles

styles may change at different ages and stages of children's development. Children's personalities will also affect parenting styles. Different children react differently to different approaches from their parents.

Life circumstances may also affect parenting styles. A parent may temporarily become a neglecting parent due to illness or other severe forms of life stress. Very few parents can achieve the 'ideal' status of the consistently authoritative parent.

Further research

Research child-rearing styles. Some helpful titles are listed in the references at the end of this chapter, especially: *Applying Psychology to Early Childhood Development*; *The Developing Child*; Squire (ed.) (2007) *BTEC National Children's Care, Learning and Development*; and Rutherford cited in Taylor and Woods (eds) *Early Childhood Studies: An Holistic Introduction*, 2005.

Cultural factors

Cultural factors may be closely associated with a family's lifestyle, their values and attitudes and beliefs. Some cultural backgrounds focus on gender roles and expectations of behaviour in girls and boys. For example, boisterous behaviour is often tolerated more readily in boys than in girls.

Different cultures value different skills. For example, some may value academic achievement, which may have a negative effect on the self-esteem of children who do not achieve academically. Other cultures focus more on physical sporting ability, which may have a similar negative effect on the child who has no interest in or aptitude for sport.

Cultures have been described as individualist and collectivist.

Key terms

Individualist cultures focus on individual achievement and value winning medals and prizes for outperforming others.

Collectivist cultures focus on group interaction and achievement, and individual contributions from group members are recognised and acknowledged.

Children reared in individualist cultures may experience low self-esteem if they are unable to win but high self-esteem when successful.

Children reared in collectivist cultures are more likely to develop positive feelings of self-worth as their contributions to the group are acknowledged. Non-competitive games such as parachute games, where the children can participate together but there are no winners or losers, are a feature of a culture of this type.

Consider this

Does your workplace setting have an individualist or collectivist culture? Explain your decision.

Theories describing influences on the development of a range of behaviours

Attachment theories

Much developmental theory relates to the development of behaviour patterns. The way people behave often reflects how they are feeling in a particular situation. Behaviour is closely linked to children's social and emotional development. You may want to refer back to Chapter 3 and read Bowlby's theory of attachment and bonding between children and their primary carers, which describes the separation anxiety that results from their being separated.

Although Bowlby focused on the relationship between mother and child, other studies have found that children often develop several attachments. So children can be closely attached to key workers without disrupting the bond with their parents.

Mary Ainsworth (1978, cited in *BTEC National Children's Care, Learning and Development*) considered that the quality of interaction between young children and their carers was of prime importance in the development of attachment. Schaffer and Emerson (1964, cited in the same work) found that infants with multiple attachments did not necessarily have the carer with whom they spent most time as their primary attachment figure.

You need to recognise the behaviour patterns that are expected from children at a specific age and stage of development. For example, a young child who protests and cries when separated from his prime carer will be reacting in an expected way. It is important that practitioners are aware of how they can influence behaviour in early education and childcare settings. A responsive practitioner who is a young child's key worker will ensure he or she is the person who primarily cares for the child in the setting so that an attachment

can form. This approach will allow the child to develop feelings of safety and security and reduce separation anxiety to the minimum.

Case study *Addressing separation anxiety*

Bairns Nursery cares for children from infancy until they enter primary school. There is a carefully designed 'settling-in' policy for all new children. Every child has a named key worker who discusses all aspects of the child's care with the parents and/or carers before the child enters the nursery.

Each child's settling-in period responds to the child's individual needs. Some children settle very quickly whereas others may need several weeks to adapt to the setting. The usual pattern is for the parent to attend the nursery with the child for several sessions while the child is introduced to the key worker. When the child appears to accept and respond positively to the key worker the parent gradually withdraws.

1. How have the staff in the Bairns Nursery used their knowledge and understanding of attachment theory to inform their practice?

2. How could nursery staff reassure parents that their bond with their child will remain strong?

Attachment to key worker

Classical conditioning

Pavlov's classical conditioning theory describes how a certain response is brought about through its association with a particular stimulus (signal or trigger) (see also Chapter 3, page 70). Children in early education and childcare settings often follow a specific routine which includes 'tidy-up time' at the end of a session. Many settings develop a specific signal so that children can recognise when it is time to tidy activities and playthings away.

Case study 'Using classical conditioning in an early education and childcare setting

Lilliput Nursery School cares for children from 2½ to 5 years and also has an after-school club catering for 5–12-year-old children. The staff found that they all were involved in encouraging the children to tidy up at the end of a session. They decided to try introducing a specific piece of music for each group as a signal for 'tidy up time'. They consulted the children on the choice of music for each group. The staff then began to implement the plan. For the first few weeks the children needed reminding of what the tune signalled. Very soon each group responded to their signal and 'tidy up time' was accomplished more quickly.

1 What do you think of this method of using classical conditioning?

2 Can you think of other ways to accomplish a quick and effective clearing away at the end of a session?

Critical evaluation

The theory of classical conditioning has contributed to the understanding of children's behaviour patterns. Children develop positive responses to situations and people who make them feel safe and secure. They also develop negative responses to situations and people who have given them cause for fear or inflicted pain on them. Many doctors treating children will not wear a white coat as they do not wish children to associate a white coat with pain. Classical conditioning can also be used inappropriately to brainwash individuals and has the potential to be both dangerous and damaging.

Operant conditioning

The psychologist B.F. Skinner developed the theory of operant conditioning as an aspect of a behaviourist approach to learning theory (see also Chapter 3, page 78). Skinner's theory focused on reinforcement. Skinner believed that we learn behaviour from the consequences experienced as a result of our actions.

Key term

Operant conditioning is a method of learning that results from the consequences that follow an individual's behaviour.

Skinner divided the consequences of our actions into three groups.

- *Positive reinforcers* encourage the repetition of a particular behaviour. Skinner considered that positive reinforcement encouraged children to learn new skills. Adult attention is probably the most desirable positive reinforcer in response to children's appropriate behaviour.

- *Negative reinforcers* also encourage behaviour repetition but this time the action taken is to ensure that something negative doesn't happen.

- *Punishers* will discourage repetition of behaviour. For example, a child will avoid touching a hot object like a teapot if he or she has been burnt by one previously.

Skinner also identified other behaviour consequences. Unexpected positive reinforcers may result in unwanted repetition of behaviour. For example, children may find that inappropriate behaviour attracts adult attention when behaving well receives no similar reinforcement. In consequence, children may deliberately misbehave in order to receive adult attention even though that attention may result in being scolded.

Linking theory to practice

Take time to consider how you respond when children are behaving in an acceptable way. Reflect on your practice and explain how you promote positive behaviour in your setting.

Social learning theory

Children learn much of their behaviour from observing and imitating adults, older children and their peer group. In Chapter 3 you read about Albert Bandura, who investigated children's behaviour in response to the adult behaviour they observed. He and his colleagues concluded that children copy those they perceive as having power and/or status.

Very young children imitate their parents and tend not to choose gender specific roles. For example, a boy will copy household tasks he observes his mother doing such as ironing or cooking regardless of whether his father undertakes the same tasks. As children grow older they tend to imitate the same sex parent and usually will model themselves on him or her.

In early education and childcare settings, children will view the practitioners in the setting as role models. How you behave with your work colleagues is likely to inform children's behaviour.

Case study *Positive reinforcers*

1 Unexpected positive reinforcer

Jenny's mother is busy preparing the family meal while Jenny, aged 3½ years, plays with her dolls' house. Jenny plays quietly on her own while her mother is busy. Jenny's mother is glad that Jenny is quiet and not requiring attention so that she can finish her tasks. She finishes her meal preparation and sits down with a magazine. After a while Jenny starts to throw her toys around the kitchen. Jenny's mother puts her magazine down and scolds Jenny.

2 Positive reinforcer

Ewan's mother is talking on the telephone. Ewan, aged 3½ years, is making a model with his construction bricks. He plays quietly while his mother continues his phone call. As soon as the telephone call is over Ewan's mother goes to Ewan and says, 'Thank you for being so good and quiet while I was talking on the phone. What shall we do together until I need to make lunch?'

Positive reinforcement

1 Compare the way each mother responded to her child's positive behaviour.

2 Explain why Ewan's mother's approach is more likely to encourage acceptable behaviour.

Later, as children progress through primary school, their peer group becomes more important as role models, and they will imitate behaviour they observe in groups to which they belong or wish to be involved with. As children grow older they may look to more distant figures such as television characters or sports personalities as role models.

Another concept of social learning relates to children fulfilling the expectations of others as identified by Rosenthal and Jacobsen's study of a class of schoolchildren (cited in *BTEC National Children's Care, Learning and Development*). Teachers were informed that a particular group in their class was expected to achieve especially good results during the school year. The children had, in fact, been chosen at random. When results were monitored at the end of the year it was found that those chosen had made significantly better progress than their peers. The term used to describe this result is self-fulfilling prophecy.

The perception of the expectations of significant others in a child's life will link closely to their self-concept, which is discussed in the next section.

Do girls learn about their gender by imitating their mother?

Self-concept

A child's concept of self will influence the development of their behaviour patterns. (Refer back to Chapter 3, pages 86–90, to read about how children develop their views and opinions of themselves.) Social interaction with others gives a picture of how we appear to others based on how they react to us. This, in turn, helps us to develop our self-concept.

Self-concept includes self-esteem. Self-esteem in turn affects self-confidence. Children's behaviour reflects their self-confidence and their self-esteem. A self-confident child is ready for new challenges and is likely to be eager to learn, investigate and experiment. An unconfident child will be less likely to try new tasks and activities for fear of failing.

Carl Rogers

Carl Rogers considers that the development of positive self-esteem is based on secure relationships with significant others where a child receives unconditional positive regard. Significant others in a child's life will include parents, extended family members, siblings and all others involved in their care such as early education and childcare practitioners and teachers.

Children who feel they are only valued for their appearance or achievements may lack self-confidence and a feeling of self-worth. Their behaviour may be withdrawn and subdued as they consider they will never reach the attainment required for approval and acceptance. They may become very competitive and constantly strive for further achievement. This is likely to lead to high levels of anxiety which may result in outbursts of anger and aggression.

The importance of recognising age-appropriate behaviour

It is very important that practitioners working with children are aware of behaviour that is appropriate for their ages and development stages. A chart describing children's expected behaviour by age is found on pages 258 and 259.

As children grow and develop and acquire cognitive, social and emotional skills, they begin to understand acceptable behaviour within their own family. This understanding extends to their culture, environment and peer group as they grow older and their horizons extend.

Understanding children's unwanted behaviours

If, as adults, our state of mind, general health and relationships with others can affect our behaviour, then it's of no surprise that children can be influenced just as strongly by their experiences, feelings and relationships – but they may demonstrate this in different behaviour. Recognising and identifying the factors that influence them is key to understanding and supporting young children's behaviour.

Inappropriate or undesirable behaviour in children can often indicate that there may be underlying causes for concern. For example, a child may display behaviour you would expect from younger children or a child you know well may begin to display uncharacteristic negative behaviour. Any significant changes in a child's behaviour should be observed, taken seriously and recorded. Where you know the child and the family and their circumstances well, you may be able to identify possible factors that are contributing to the child's feelings and behaviour. Sometimes you may identify factors within the environment of the early education and childcare setting that are contributing to undesirable behaviour such as diet, relationships with staff or children or particular activities. There may be times when parents/carers and early years staff will not be able to identify factors and will then consider the involvement of other professionals who may be able to offer specialised support.

Age range	Expected behaviour
Birth–6 months	Until the age of around 4 months most infants will smile and respond to all human faces. They recognise significant others in their lives and often respond to them with greater pleasure.
	They are likely to sleep for long periods but are unlikely to sleep longer than six hours in one stretch in the first two months.
	They will make sounds in response to others' communication and stare intently at human faces.
6–12 months	From about 5–6 months until 15–18 months children are likely to react negatively to unknown human faces and protest strongly if approached.

Stranger anxiety is a normal part of development

If separated from a main carer they are likely to be very distressed and difficult to console.

Between 6 and 12 months children usually become mobile and start to explore and investigate their environment. They have little concept of danger and will pull to stand and climb with no regard for their own safety.

Spoon feeding is a messy occupation for the carer as children will reach for and grasp everything in sight – spoons, food, dishes – exploring with mouth and hands.

Spoon feeding is a messy task for the carer

They love to drop objects for others to retrieve, often at mealtimes or out of prams.

Age range	Expected behaviour
12–18 months	As children of this age become more mobile they have little concept of ownership and will take any toy or object they find attractive. They are, however, easily distracted and often will relinquish an object if offered an alternative. They are investigating and exploring their environment with their senses, which is why they may bite or pinch other people.
18–24 months	Children of this age will explore permitted and forbidden behaviour with parents and carers, testing boundaries. May tease a sibling, especially at times of conflict. May offer comfort to distressed sibling or peer (Dunn, *The Beginnings of Social Understanding*, 1988). Usually plays alone (solitary play) or alongside other children (parallel play) but prefers the presence of a familiar adult. May have temper tantrums when thwarted in their wishes. Unlikely to achieve bladder and bowel control.
2–3 years	No real concept of sharing though some will share if prompted. Tantrums still occur when wishes are thwarted. May show acts of aggression such as kicking or hitting when angry or frustrated. Not fully aware of the consequences of their actions. Solitary and parallel play continues. Some simple games played with others may begin (cooperative play). Offers comfort when they see others hurt or distressed. Daytime bladder and bowel control may be achieved.
3–5 years	Understands how to share though may show reluctance if a favourite toy is involved. Enjoys cooperative play. Beginning to understand when it is appropriate to run and shout and when it is necessary to sit quietly. Will offer to help younger children with tasks and activities. Uses language with increasing vocabulary and fluency to defend a position or action. Capable of aggression when provoked. At 5 years most children have achieved bowel and bladder control day and night. Some children may continue to experience bedwetting (nocturnal enuresis) for another year or two.
5–7 years	Is able to dress, wash and feed self. Shows independence. Is developing self-control and can wait and take turns. Understands and enjoys games with rules and team games. Night-time bladder control may not yet be achieved. Bedwetting at this age is only a cause for concern if a child has previously achieved consistent night-time control. Can carry out simple tasks in the home.
7–10 years	Becomes increasingly independent. May be self-critical about school work and can be easily discouraged. May be able to represent self when visiting the doctor or dentist. Develops the ability to control emotions and can keep opinions and thoughts to themselves. Forms close friendships with peer group – usually with own sex. Beginning to be aware of the feelings of others but often will not fully understand them.
10–12 years	Shows increasing ability to understand the feelings and needs of others. Is likely to be self-conscious and very sensitive to criticism. May have mood swings related to the onset of puberty. Seeks company of peer group and friends and is susceptible to peer group pressure. Seeks increased independence but still needs the reassuring presence of significant adults.

A small number of children and young people have specific behavioural problems which are medical or psychological in origin. However, discipline problems may have their roots in the social and economic challenges faced by families and communities, and sometimes in the way in which the management of learning and teaching is organised. Frequently discipline problems have a variety of causes. Whatever the problems are they are a barrier to learning and teaching and must be addressed for the benefit of our young people and society as a whole (*Better Behaviour – Better Learning*, Scottish Executive, 2001, page 10).

Reasons for unwanted behaviour can often fall into more than one category. There may be physical factors affecting a child's behaviour, social factors in their interactions with others or factors in the environment which are contributing to the unwanted behaviour that they are demonstrating. Children may also behave very differently in an early education and childcare setting than they do at home.

Children may behave differently in different settings and with different carers for many reasons. They may have different relationships with staff compared to those with their parents/carers, they may have different boundaries/limits in different settings, and they may have to interact and cope with other children which can be very different from their experience at home. The behaviour issues that are of concern may be issues that only directly affect the child or they may impact directly or indirectly on the other children and young people that you work with.

Responding appropriately to unwanted behaviours

Common unwanted behaviours include:

- attention seeking
- inappropriate language
- tantrums
- being destructive towards own or others' work, toys, possessions or equipment
- disruption or repeated interruption of activities

- refusing to follow instructions or 'rules'
- biting
- refusing to share or cooperate
- aggression – verbal or physical
- jealousy towards other children or siblings
- refusing to eat or being very selective in eating choices.

Your response to these unwanted behaviours will depend on the age and stage of development of the child you are working with. Your knowledge of any physical, social or environmental factors affecting their behaviour would contribute to your understanding of the child and the selection of an appropriate strategy to modify their behaviour. How you respond to a 2-year-old who is finding it difficult to learn how to share her toys with her peers will be different from how you respond to a confident pre-schooler who exerts controlling behaviour over other children in a group activity. Some behaviour from children which may be regarded as undesirable by adults can actually achieve its desired aim every time – to get your attention.

Where children constantly interrupt activities, stories or conversation, this can be through enthusiasm – not being able to wait their turn – or deliberately in order to get an adult's attention. Where a child constantly says 'no' they may not be directly challenging you but rather trying to establish their own independence and power over their life and choices. Some children may be clingy and lack confidence to try activities or interact with other children without support from a particular adult.

The most important thing you can do for a child in interpreting and responding to their behaviour is to get to know them – to understand their home life, their relationships and their own unique personality. By building a relationship with the child and the people who are important to them you can support a child to gradually become more self-reliant. You will also be more likely to notice when a child becomes uncooperative and challenging that this is out of character for them. It is vital to use your skills in listening to children – in all the ways they communicate with us – and try to identify and understand what other factors may be influencing their behaviour.

Some behaviour could be described as being anti-social. Anti-social behaviour is a concept that is often discussed in the media and is defined in Scottish law as 'Acting in a manner that causes or is likely to cause alarm or distress'. (Guide to the Antisocial Behaviour Etc (Scotland) Act 2004, Scottish Executive, 2004). Some possible examples of anti-social behaviour in children could include:

- lying
- stealing
- swearing
- bullying
- discriminatory behaviour such as leaving another child out, or abusive language towards another child or adult because of their race, gender, disability or any other factor.

Again, your response to these behaviours will depend on the context and your knowledge of the child and family. How you respond to a child who is making up stories will differ from your response and observation of a child who lies about important events or about other children or adults. Any response must be age appropriate, calm and considered, and based on the facts about the situation and not any beliefs or attitudes you may have about a child or their background.

Severe causes for concern

Some types of behaviour will give you serious cause for concern. This behaviour may raise concerns about the child's emotional well-being, physical safety and/or the impact of their behaviour on themselves and others. Families may need support to assess these types of behaviour and to arrange specialised support where this is appropriate.

How to observe and assess children's behaviour

It is part of the responsibilities of early education and childcare practitioners to observe and assess the children in their care. There are many reasons for observing and assessing children, and practitioners use a variety of methods. The methods used will depend on the information that is needed. Chapter 5 covers how children are observed and assessed in their settings to identify their learning and developmental needs and plan to meet these needs. It is extremely important that observers always have stated reasons for carrying out their observations.

Part of these observations and assessments will include how children are behaving. Practitioners will note how children interact and play with each other, which activities attract and sustain their interest and which rarely engage them. Skilled observation will identify individual children's strengths and their needs. In order to support and promote children's development and learning, practitioners need to know which child is confident and ready to try new tasks and which child is reluctant to attempt anything new.

It is very important that children's behaviour patterns are observed to ensure that children are not labelled as having particular behaviour

Activity

Choose one of the following areas of concern:

- the introverted/withdrawn child
- self-harming behaviour
- obsessional behaviour
- children under stress
- depression in children
- attention-deficit hyperactivity disorder (ADHD).

Research your chosen area then prepare a leaflet that would help a parent understand this issue. Your leaflet should describe the types of behaviour that may be demonstrated and how they might best be responded to.

traits. For example, the child who appears to be a 'butterfly', flitting from one activity to another, may be completing each activity very quickly before moving on, rather than lacking the ability to concentrate on a task. The child who appears to show aggression to other children may, in fact, be a child who is easily roused by others and whose aggressiveness only occurs in response to provocation.

Ongoing assessment, often called *formative assessment*, is a technique that informs practitioners about the children in their care. From observing children at different times and in different circumstances a pattern of behaviour can emerge that can contribute to a summary of the behaviour of individual children. This form of assessment is called *summative assessment*.

Key terms

Formative assessment describes how different observation techniques can be used to gain an all-round picture of a child over time, and how these observations can identify situations that seem to trigger a particular behaviour.

A **summative assessment** can be used to provide a 'snapshot' of a child that identifies particular skills he or she has achieved at a specific moment in time. Summative assessment may also be used to draw together all information about a child collected over time to provide a summary of the child's behaviour, often in a written report.

Consider this

What summative and formative assessments have you experienced? For example, if you have taken and passed your driving test, how would you describe the assessment process?

Have you undertaken any assessments as part of the HNC Early Education and Childcare course? Would you describe them as summative or formative?

Observation techniques

You may meet a variety of observation techniques in use in your early education and childcare practice, and these have been outlined in Chapter 4. The following case studies will help you see how observation techniques can be used when looking at different behaviour.

Activity

Investigate the observation techniques used in your workplace setting to gather information about a child's behaviour. Why are these techniques used?

Time sampling

Time sampling is one technique that can be used to establish behaviour patterns in children. The observer is required to decide on and establish a pattern of observing. A time sample will provide information on what a child is doing for a set time at specific intervals during the day.

For example, you may choose to observe a child for 5 minutes every 20 minutes for 2 hours during a Monday morning. You could repeat this observation on different days at different times.

Event sampling

Event sampling is a technique to establish how often a specific behaviour occurs. It may be used to clarify how often a child approaches others to initiate play, for example. The technique may also be used to establish how often a child displays inappropriate behaviour such as aggression towards other children or adults.

Event sampling can be difficult to implement as observations are recorded in response to specific incidents that cannot be planned. It is important that the circumstances of the behaviour are also recorded as well as the consequences.

Key terms

Time sampling is a series of brief observations made at regular, pre-set intervals throughout the day.

Event sampling is a method of observing a child to record an event at the moment it occurs.

There are many methods and techniques for observing and assessing children and you will meet different approaches in the settings where you work.

Strategies used to support children's behaviour

You have read in an earlier section in this chapter about behaviours to expect at different ages and stages of children's development. As an early education and childcare practitioner you will need to develop different strategies to support children's behaviour that are appropriate to their ages and stages of development.

Setting routines

Children respond well to frameworks that establish the behaviour that is expected of them. For the very young child this may consist of established bedtime and mealtime routines. Infants respond well to a structured life. Often before they are born they learn family routines.

Feelings of safety and security can be provided by a consistent framework for children in their early years. It also can help to establish sleep, feeding and play patterns. Very young children require consistency in their daily routines to allow them to grow and develop to their full potential. This consistency includes interaction with significant others. Inconsistency in the care of a young child can lead to the child's becoming anxious and apprehensive.

> ### Case study *Setting routines*
>
> Rohit is now 6 months old. From the time he was born his parents have followed the same bedtime routine for him. He has a bath, a gentle massage and then his bedtime feed. The bedtime feed is given to Rohit in a darkened room with just enough light to see. During his first few months Rohit's mother or father sang to him as he fed. Now they go through a picture book with him, talking about the pictures as part of his bedtime routine.
>
> Rohit has a special blanket he takes to bed with him and a musical mobile that plays a soft tune after his parents have left him in his cot.

Toddlers between 1 and 3 years can display very challenging but normal behaviours. The child who has limited communication abilities cannot explain his wishes and desires and may scream and throw tantrums when thwarted. Supporting children's behaviour at this stage of development requires a variety of different strategies which will depend on the situation.

Praise/positive reinforcement

Most children seek praise and acceptance from their parents and carers. Many early education and childcare settings ensure that children receive appropriate praise and that they are aware what behaviour is being praised. It is important to ensure children understand why they are being praised and this can begin with very young children. To use the phrase 'Good girl/boy' indiscriminately is unlikely to reinforce positive behaviour, however, 'Good girl, you ate all your dinner' will.

Look back at the case study 'Positive reinforcers' on page 251. In each scenario the child was behaving in a positive manner. The responses from their mothers were different, though, and Kirsty's positive behaviour was reinforced while Jenny only attracted her mother's attention when her behaviour became negative.

Children who observe adults offering praise and positive reinforcement to positive behaviour will learn how to recognise positive behaviour in others. The adults will be providing positive role models. Being a positive role model is one of the most valuable roles an adult can take. One way of dealing with this is to be clear about what you are praising, for example: 'You were very clever helping me to clear away.'

Distraction

Young children have an unerring instinct for choosing inappropriate playthings even when they have a range of toys to choose from. Toddlers can usually be easily distracted by the offer of something else in exchange for their chosen object. Sometimes their attention can be drawn to another event as a distraction or the offer of a favourite game or story may provide sufficient distraction.

> ### Case study 1 *Praise/positive reinforcement*
>
> Tomas is 13 months old and constantly exploring and investigating his environment. There is an open fire in his home. Tomas is moving towards the coal scuttle. His mother says 'No, Tomas.' He turns to look at her, smiles and continues towards the coal. His mother repeats, 'No, Tomas. Come away from the coal here to Mummy.' Tomas hesitates and then comes towards his mother, away from the coal. His mother smiles at him and lifts him up for a cuddle, saying, 'Well done, Tomas! You come to Mummy. That was very clever of you'. She then begins to play one of his favourite singing games with him.
>
> ### Case study 2 *Distraction*
>
> Ellie is 2½ years old. Her family are putting on their coats, preparing to go to the park. Ellie does not want to put her coat on and says she doesn't like it. Her mother ignores Ellie's protests and buttons her into her coat. Ellie is screaming and crying loudly. Her mother says quietly, 'When you have your coat on we can go to the park. Do you want to take your new scooter to ride?' Ellie stops crying, waits for her coat to be buttoned and runs off to fetch her scooter.

The older toddler is less easily distracted and can be surprisingly persistent in his or her course of action. Knowledge of the individual child can assist in developing an appropriate distraction strategy.

It is extremely important that children understand that when their behaviour is inappropriate or unacceptable it is the behaviour that is considered undesirable and not them. You may remember reading about positive unconditional regard earlier in this chapter.

Consider this

Are there other strategies you might use in the opposite two case studies? Explain how you could have managed each situation using a different approach.

Why is it important that children receive positive unconditional regard regardless of their behaviour?

Modifying the environment to encourage appropriate behaviour

Adults caring for and working with children observe and assess them on an ongoing basis. If the behaviour of the children is negative or challenging it is important to establish the probable cause. Once the apparent reason for the negative behaviour pattern is identified, adults can develop strategies to modify the situation and circumstances to encourage a behaviour change.

Enabling children to manage their own behaviour

As children grow older and their communication skills develop, it is easier to discuss their behaviour with them. Children should always be involved in setting *goals* and *boundaries* for themselves and their peer groups where this is practicable and possible. Primary and secondary school children interviewed for the report *Behaviour in Scottish Schools* (Scottish Executive, 2006) stressed the importance of involving the children in setting goals and boundaries for behaviour while at school.

Key terms

Goals are aspects of positive behaviour for children to aim for.

Boundaries contribute to the rules that govern behaviour and provide behavioural limits to guide children.

From the age of 5 to 6 years, children develop a strong sense of right and wrong. They also respond to being involved in establishing the ground rules for behaviour in different settings. This is one strategy that encourages children to develop self-discipline and work together to ensure ground rules are complied with.

Case study *Modifying the environment to encourage appropriate behaviour*

Maria is a practitioner in a nursery for children aged 3–5 years. Her observations have shown that some of the children have tantrums or start crying when they are told to put their activities away immediately at the end of the session. Maria discusses the situation with her colleagues and they decide they should give the children 15 minutes' warning to finish activities.

At circle time at the beginning of the next session the new routine is explained to the children. As the session is coming to an end, Maria and her colleagues go to their groups to tell them to be ready to finish in 15 minutes. The children respond positively as they like time to finish what they are doing.

Children and practitioners set Dos and Don'ts

A new after-school club has been established. It is attached to Fern Den Primary School and provides care for children aged 5–12 years. Cameron is the lead practitioner and he wants to ensure that the children are fully involved in setting the behaviour framework for the after-school club.

On the first day Cameron brings all the children together and explains what he hopes to do. He produces a flip chart and asks for suggestions under the headings 'Goal' and 'Boundary'. He emphasises that all suggestions will be considered though he may not be able to include them all. He includes all staff members as well as the children and listens carefully to all suggestions, inviting comments. At the end of the meeting a list of Dos and Don'ts have been agreed.

Other strategies for this age group include discussion with children about how to cope with negative feelings. Children need to be reassured that having negative feelings is acceptable as everyone has them. They need to develop their own strategies for managing their negative emotions. Time spent in group discussion is often helpful and many centres hold circle time sessions where children can explore feelings together. Sometimes one-to-one discussion will be required, particularly with the older child who may be approaching puberty with all the conflicting emotions that accompany this major life change.

Further research

Research ways of supporting children's behaviour. You will find more information in *BTEC National Children's Care, Learning and Development* and in Faber and Mazlish (2002) *How to Talk so Kids Will Listen and Listen so Kids Will Talk*.

Critical evaluation

When different strategies are used to support children's positive behaviour it is important that the evaluation of the effectiveness of strategies includes all those involved. For children who are cared for in early education and childcare settings, there are likely to be several individuals involved. These include the child's parents and/or carers, practitioners, teachers and, of course, the child.

Some studies have shown that rewards are not always effective in encouraging consistent positive behaviour. Lepper et al. (1973; cited in *Applying Psychology to Early Childhood Development*) asked a group of children to draw a picture. Some of the children in the group were told earlier that they would receive a certificate for good drawing. The other children had no knowledge of a certificate. Several weeks later the same group of children was asked to draw another picture. Lepper and colleagues found that the non-certificate children showed more willingness to draw. However, a later study in Scotland (*Behaviour in Scottish Schools*) found that primary and secondary schoolchildren thought it good practice to provide the opportunity to earn rewards for good behaviour.

Bower and Hilgard (1981; cited in *Applying Psychology to Early Childhood Development*) considered that punishment must be prompt and clear to be effective. It is important that punishment is not used too often as children may cease to respond. Punishment may also encourage a desire to rebel or a child may seek the attention that punishment brings. The Scottish study *Better Behaviour – Better Learning* also found that children were in favour of punishment for inappropriate behaviour. Punishment should be appropriate and fair. Children should always know why certain actions are being taken.

All children are unique with individual strengths and needs. A behaviour strategy that is effective with one child may not be effective with another child, although the behaviour patterns may have significant similarities.

Consider this

How was your unwanted behaviour dealt with as a child? Were the strategies used effective? Explain why they worked or did not.

The procedures for referring children in need of additional support for their behaviour

Some children and their parents/carers may require, or already receive, support from a specialised agency or professional. You may be involved in participating in the referral of a child for additional support to manage their behaviour or to try to identify factors that are influencing their behaviour. It is important that you understand the procedures for the referral of children in need of additional support and your role while working with other agencies.

When staff or parents have concerns that require further investigation, initial discussions will often rely on the quality and objectivity or any observations and records you have made of the child's behaviour. When giving your views and experiences of the child it is important to be factual and objective. Where families request a specialist assessment, many different agencies from fields such as social work, education or the health service may be involved. All of these agencies will have their own methods, training and policies but the shared aim should be to work in the child's best interests. A multi-agency approach ensures that information is shared appropriately between staff with the family's consent. This is to try to ensure the family are given the best support possible and that everyone involved approaches supporting the child in a holistic way.

Different settings and local authorities will offer a range of responses to children who require specialised intervention. These could include:

- a behaviour support worker visiting the playroom to observe the child
- the family attending an initial session at a child and family guidance service
- the child going for a period of time to an assessment unit
- an assessment in the educational setting and perhaps in the home by an educational psychologist
- an assessment by the social work department.

There are many services available which offer support to families with children. Some of these services are open to all families with children. So, for example, a universal service would include the National Health Service. Where a health visitor offers support and advice to a parent in managing their child's behaviour then this would be an example of a service which is available to all.

There are also some services which are targeted at children of a certain age who live in a particular area or who have certain specific needs. These will sometimes require an assessment to take place before a particular piece of work can be carried out.

Professionals involved with children requiring additional support for their behaviour

Behaviour support worker (support for learning assistants/one-to-one assistants)

Different local authorities have different job titles for these posts. They involve someone who is specially trained working with an individual child or, more often, in a small group. This worker may support the child by providing them with individual attention they need or may develop a particular strategy at home and/or in the early education and childcare setting to improve or manage a child's behaviour.

Social worker

A social worker can try to work with a child and their family to address some of the issues for the child that are impacting on their behaviour. New community schools may have their own dedicated social worker. Social workers practice in teams, so a child who is experiencing abuse or neglect will meet a social worker from the children and families team, and a child who has a physical or learning need would be assessed by a social worker who specialises in supporting families where children have additional support needs.

Parenting support worker

Parents may work with a professional who has a role which involves supporting parents individually and/or in groups to examine or develop their skills in responding to and managing their child's behaviour. Parenting groups usually last for a limited period. They encourage adults caring for children to examine their own relationship to the child and how they respond to the child's positive and unwanted behaviour.

Educational psychologist

This is a specially trained psychologist who will assess children and then either work directly with the child, their family and the staff involved or who may support staff and the parent to implement a specific plan to modify behaviour. They may identify specific difficulties a child is having with an aspect of their learning which is then affecting their behaviour.

Specialist services

Specialist services are those that families would only access where they have been referred to this service because of a particular concern. These would include services provided to children who have experienced abuse of any kind. There are many examples of specialist services in the voluntary sector as well as those based with Police Family Protection Units. Psychologists, social workers and play therapists could all be involved in a specialised behaviour programme with a child and their family.

Behaviour policies in early education and childcare settings

Most early education and childcare settings have well-established behaviour policies based on the research findings and strategies you have studied in this chapter. Best practice ensures unconditional regard for the child while recognising and responding to behavioural issues. Good relationships and communication between home and setting contributes to meeting the individual needs of the child.

Behaviour policies are shared with all staff in settings and with parents and carers. It is very important that consistency is demonstrated between all adults who are involved in supporting children's behaviour.

Working with parents/carers on behaviour

Your behaviour policy should detail how important it is to work in partnership with families to understand and support children's behaviour. If you accept that many factors influencing children's behaviour come from the relationships they have with adults, then working with the adults in children's lives to identify the contributing factors and develop a consistent positive approach is invaluable.

You will be involved in supporting parents and carers every day in your interactions with parents when they share information on how a child behaves outside the care setting. You will often informally pass on knowledge and reinforce their own skills and confidence as they try to understand what is age-appropriate behaviour and respond in a way which shows clear boundaries without rejecting the child.

Some parents will need more structured support and they may get this by working with a member of staff or by attending a parenting group. Often parents who attend parenting support groups report that this was the best method of helping them understand and respond to their child's behaviour. This is effective as they can discuss with other parents and reflect on strategies and progress.

The setting's behaviour policy will detail how you must keep appropriate, confidential records which parents are entitled to know the contents of.

Linking theory to practice

Consider your workplace practice experience. What is the behaviour policy? Explain how the policy relates to the theory you have learned.

Reflect on your practice and explain how you contribute to implementing the behaviour policy. How effective have you found the policy to be? Explain your reasons.

Check your progress

These questions will help you to prepare for your assessment.

1. Explain a theory related to the development of children's behaviour.

2. Explain the importance of the concept of 'self' in the development of behaviour.

3. Explain the importance of adults as role models in the development of children's behaviour.

4. Evaluate the influences of two different parenting styles on children's behaviour.

5. Explain two methods of observing and assessing children's behaviour and when each may be used.

6. Explain how a setting can work with parents and/or carers to promote positive behaviour.

7. Explain a strategy you have used to influence a child's behaviour and link it to any relevant behaviour policy.

8. Select an age and stage of child development and explain any causes for concern about a child's behaviour. Suggest possible reasons.

9. Explain procedures used for referral of children in need of additional support for their behaviour.

10. Select a professional who might be involved in addressing a child's behaviour and explain their role.

References

Bee, H. and Boyd, D. (2006) *The Developing Child*, 11th edn, London: Allyn & Bacon

Dunn. J. (1988) *The Beginnings of Social Understanding*, Oxford: Blackwell

Fawcett, M. (1996) *Learning Through Child Observation*, London: Jessica Kingsley Publishers

Faber, A. and Mazlish, E. (2002) *How to Talk so Kids Will Listen and Listen so Kids Will Talk*, New York: HarperCollins

Flanagan, C. (2004) *Applying Psychology to Early Childhood Development*, London: Hodder & Stoughton

Harding, J. and Meldon-Smith, L. (2001) *How to Make Observations and Assessments*, 2nd edn, London: Hodder Arnold

Squire, G. (ed.) (2007) *BTEC National Children's Care, Learning and Development*, Oxford: Heinemann

Scottish Executive (2006) *Behaviour in Scottish Schools*, Edinburgh

Scottish Executive (2001) *Better Behaviour – Better Learning*, Edinburgh

Scottish Executive (2004) *Guide to the Antisocial Behaviour Etc. (Scotland) Act 2004*, Edinburgh

Taylor, J. and Woods, M. (eds) (2005). *Early Childhood Studies: An Holistic Introduction*, 2nd edn, London: Arnold

Chapter 9

The impact of government policy on the lives of children in Scotland

Introduction

Every child you work with in an early education and childcare setting comes with their own unique family life. These family structures may seem different to the one you grew up with but for a child they are normal and important. Families are integral to a child's life. Each person's idea of what constitutes a normal family life is likely to be affected by how their family functions. As an early education and childcare practitioner you need to acknowledge every child and family's culture and uniqueness. Sometimes this may present challenges; more often it brings opportunities to get to know the context in which children live and the communities in which they are supported.

Government policy has an impact on the day-to-day lives of children in Scotland. This chapter brings together issues relating to families and the policies that support both children and the families they live in. You will learn about different family types and structures; communities that support children; and different ways children and their families are supported through policies and initiatives by Scotland's devolved government. You will also learn how the UK government's policies ensure there is adequate funding for children and their families.

When children are growing up they need to be strong and healthy and to establish good patterns for eating and exercise. In this chapter you will learn key ways that children and families are encouraged by the Scottish Government, and by those that work with them, to become healthier, active and achieving. You will learn about the effect on children when these conditions are not in place.

This chapter will also be important in shaping your views about families, including families that may have become disorganised or fractured. You will have a chance to explore your own attitudes so that you can effectively challenge others who may hold a prejudiced view. Finally, you will read how a system of regulation is helping to support children's care, learning and development and how this helps families feel confident about the care their children are receiving.

In this chapter you will learn:

- How contemporary family life is affected by a range of factors and social trends
- How changing attitudes and perceptions in society affect children and families
- How policies of inclusion help support children and families in Scotland
- How local and national policies, strategies and initiatives support healthy lifestyles for children and families in Scotland
- How policies affect children's care, learning and development
- How research skills can be used to inform practice and develop strategies

How contemporary family life is affected by a range of factors and social trends

The Scottish Government's vision for Scotland is described in *Social Justice: A Scotland Where EVERYONE Matters* (Scottish Executive, 1999, page 21) as 'a Scotland in which every child matters, where every child regardless of his or her family background, has the best possible start in life'. This is repeated in other key documents and is important to remember as you start to consider what family units may be like for children. An important thing to remember when working with children is that you can never *know* what a child has left behind in their home life when they come to the centre each day. You may suspect life is good or not so good for some children, but no one really knows. Children's home and family lives directly affect them, their ability to play and learn, and their capacity to cope with day-to-day situations. Many children have extremely happy and stimulating family lives; other children may suffer great hardship. It is the role of the early education and childcare practitioner to be aware of the needs of every child in their care and to support them in the most effective way possible. Working with parents and carers is integral to this support.

What is a family?

Defining what is meant by a family is not always easy. It seems most people have a view of what a family is but find it quite hard to define accurately. What is certain is that there are similarities in family types but differences in conformity. So, each family has its own context, may seem to conform to a type of norm, may seem to be similar, but will not be identical. You will find some types of families that fit certain parameters but it is important to remember that what goes on in each family is individual to them.

You may judge what constitutes a family because:

- it's what you have experienced yourself
- it's what your friends' families are like
- it's what you have seen on television
- adverts suggest a certain family lifestyle or conformity
- books or magazines you've read suggest a stereotype
- your particular religious belief suggests a family should conform to a particular pattern
- it's the type of family you may have dreamed about but haven't had.

> ### Consider this
>
> Discuss the following in small groups.
>
> 1. Does a family only become a family if there are children involved?
> 2. If you are married to a person or are living with them, do they automatically become part of your family?
> 3. Is there a person who is pivotal in the family?

> ### Key term
>
> **Norm** is a term used by sociologists to describe a convention that people in society tend to stick to. One example of a social norm is to obey the law; this doesn't mean everyone has to do this but for most people it is an accepted way of behaving.

Sociologists consider families falling into key types. They also describe what makes a family in terms of kinship and social relationship between members.

Kinship is the term used to describe genetic or blood relationship. Kinship relationships in a family would describe parents, children, grandparents, uncles, aunts and other relatives. It would not describe a family member who has joined through marriage or civil partnership. Social anthropologists now consider kinship to include other types of relationships, including children who have been adopted or children conceived through egg donation. Others disagree with this wider view of kinship and in different cultures, including some European cultures, those children are not regarded as having kinship ties. There is often ambiguity or varying opinions about what a family is and what kinship means. So, when describing families and how they are formed, it is important to remember that different cultures have different beliefs in what constitutes a family.

A *social relationship* in terms of a family refers to a close relationship such as marriage, civil partnership or cohabiting. This means that when a person marries or cohabits it is acceptable to describe that person as being part of a family. It is also acceptable to consider children who are fostered as part of a family, as fostering could be described as a social relationship. This means that once couples start cohabiting it is thought to be acceptable to describe them as part of their and the other partner's family.

Often families are able to track their ancestors back through kinship and social relationships. This is the practice of genealogy. Some people will try to find out more about themselves through investigating a 'family tree'. Sometimes in nurseries and Primary 1 class, children work on 'All about me' topics that might include producing a pictorial 'family tree' showing photographs of themselves, their siblings, parents or carers, uncles and aunts, cousins and grandparents.

An example of step-siblings would be: if Mrs Smith has two children and she remarries Mr Jones who also has two children, any child of their marriage would be a sibling to both sets of children. The children by the first marriage are step-siblings but bear no blood relationship to each other. In Scotland today there are increased numbers of reconstituted families such as this and step-sibling relationships.

Key terms

Siblings is a term used to describe a person's brothers or sisters, or stepbrothers or stepsisters – the important feature of a sibling is that they usually share one blood relative.

Reconstituted means 'made again', as in reconstituting a meal when cooking by adding some extra water and a few more ingredients; with families you are adding new people.

In the previous example about siblings, Mrs Smith and her two children have kinship ties. Mr Jones and his two children also have kinship ties. However, Mr Jones's children by his first marriage and Mrs Smith's children by her first marriage have no kinship ties.

Consider this

Is the statement about Mr Jones's children and Mrs Smith's children consistent with adoptive children being regarded as having kinship ties by some social anthropologists? You may want to discuss this or do further research into the subject.

Activity

You may find it helpful to try to construct your own family tree. You can show kinship relationships in blue and social relationships in red. If you really want to trawl further, you might want to access the Scotland's People website, though you will need to pay to use it. It is the official site for the Scottish Government records and you can access it by logging on to: www.scotlandspeople.gov.uk.

Types of family

In HNC Unit DF56 34: Contemporary issues for children and families, you will be asked to look at different types of family and how social trends and cultural variations impact on these. Central government and the Scottish Government supply data to the General Household Survey (GHS), which reports annually on various topics related to households and families in the UK (www.statistics.gov.uk). Among the data is information on households, families and people, and specific family information including the numbers who are cohabiting and married at a given time. Data is gathered annually and you may find this a useful resource.

The GHS advice on gathering data for the survey describes a family unit as 'a married or opposite sex cohabiting couple on their own; or a married or opposite sex cohabiting couple, or lone parent and their never married children (who may be adult) provided these children have no family of their own.' The GHS goes on to say

> the GHS family cannot span more than two generations, i.e. grandparents and grandchildren cannot belong to the same family except where it can be established that the grandparents are looking after the children. Adoptive and step-children belong to the same family unit as their adoptive/step-parents but foster children are not part of their foster parents' family (as they are not related to their foster parents). (www. statistics.gov.uk/ssd/surveys/general_household_survey.asp).

What this means is that when the government are collecting data on families they use those definitions to help them decide what is and what is not a family. This may be helpful to some, but others may find it unhelpful as it excludes key groups of people, including same-sex couples who are cohabiting or who have a civil partnership and who may have children. Also, in some Bangladeshi, Pakistani and southern European households there may be two generations living together. This definition suggests they would not, officially, be regarded as a family unit.

There are different types of family living in Scotland today

Family structures

Sociologists often describe three types of family structure: the extended family, the nuclear family and the lone-parent family. Increasingly there are reconstituted families as well. A brief explanation of this type of family was given earlier in the chapter (see pages 273–74).

There are often different opinions about what constitutes each of these types of family and it is important you read as much as possible to try to form your own views. Each type is explained briefly below:

Extended family

This was the norm in Scotland before the Second World War. The extended family describes a generational family. In this type of family there can be a blurring of boundaries about who rears or brings up the child. There may also be mutual sharing of financial resources and of economic activity to support the family. A typical example could previously be seen in close-knit areas like fishing or mining communities. In these communities more than one generation (parents, grandparents, aunts, uncles and cousins) all lived within close proximity and all were mutually supportive of each other. This is also sometimes called the horizontally extended family. There is little need for formalised childcare in such families or for elder relative care. Both of these functions are shared responsibilities across the family.

This type of family structure is now commonly associated with Scottish South Asian, Bangladeshi and Pakistani communities and with families from southern European countries.

> **Key term**
>
> **Economic activity** describes work a person or family does to generate an income to support the family. Sometimes called earning a wage.

Nuclear family

This describes a family unit, usually of parents and children living together in the same household. It is a two generational family unit. There may or may not be a close link to other members of the immediate family of grandparents, aunts, uncles

A nuclear family

and cousins, but this will be less strong and probably less mutually supportive than in an extended family. There is not likely to be any financial or economic support given across the wider family membership and it is also likely that child rearing will be the responsibility of the parents. In this type of family structure there may also be the problem of supporting older relatives appropriately.

Lone-parent family

An increasing number of children are part of a lone-parent household. This is partly due to fewer couples marrying and a rise in the number of couples divorcing. It essentially means children are reared by one parent alone. Often this is the mother but sometimes it is the father. There is unlikely to be financial support from other family members and childcare is likely to be an issue for parents who want to go out to work.

Step-families or reconstituted families

Step-families come about when partners who have previously been married divorce and then remarry or cohabit. There are increasing numbers of children and young people being raised by one or other parent who is not their natural parent and with step-siblings with whom there is no blood/kinship link.

Case study 1 *The Cargill family*

The Cargill family have recently moved to Stonehaven from the Scottish Borders. The family consists of Joe Cargill who works in the oil industry, his wife Catriona who is a nurse, and three children, Beth age 9 years, Kirsty age 7 years and Seamus who is just 4 years. Previously Catriona's mum and dad looked after the children for about an hour to cover the time between Joe coming home and her going to work nights. If Catriona's mum couldn't manage, Joe had very close family that lived nearby in the Borders. All previously lived in the small town of Selkirk within a few miles of each other. The Cargill family were pleased to be moving as they thought it would bring good opportunities for the family. However, Catriona was concerned she would be living far from her parents and parents-in-law.

1   What type of family does this describe?

2   In what way might the Cargill family be disadvantaged living so far from their immediate family?

3   What benefits might there be for the family?

Case study 2 *The Ahmed family*

Amjad and Rahima Ahmed live in Dundee with their three children, Tahir (9 years), Uddin (8 years) and Runa (6 years), as well as Amjad's two sisters, his parents and aunt. Rahima works as a classroom assistant at the local primary school and Amjad runs a grocery store. Sometimes Rahima helps out in the store and at other times Amjad's father and aunt help out. The children are all of primary school age and mostly come home with Rahima, but occasionally the boys go to the mosque after school with their father or grandfather. Sometimes, when she is helping out in the shop, Rahima's mother-in-law or aunt-in-law pick up the children and most days they cook family meals. Rahima always tries to get the children ready for bed and tell them their bedtime story. Their home is nearly always filled with relatives and close family friends, and the children are fortunate in having cousins come to stay quite often.

1   What type of family structure does this describe?

2   What are the advantages of this type of structure to the Ahmed family?

Case study 3 *The Allan family*

Jen Allan became a lone parent after divorcing her husband, Jake, who now works abroad. Jake refuses to send any money for the upkeep of their two children, Amy age 4 years and Sean age 7 years.

Jen works at the local branch of the bank. This means she starts at 9 am and doesn't get home until 5.30 pm. She has no relatives living nearby but has a close group of friends who each help the others out when possible. Both her children go to breakfast club and out-of-school care.

1   What family structure does this describe?

2   What are the main issues Jen might need to deal with?

3   What are the advantages to the Allan family from this type of family?

Other family arrangements

'Looked after children'

Unfortunately not all children are able to stay with their birth family. This may be for a range of reasons and when you work with children you will encounter those who may have had disorganised or fractured lives. Some children may need to be provided with care.

The Children (Scotland) Act (1995) introduced a general duty to 'safeguard and promote the welfare of children in need'. This means that in some circumstances children need to be provided with foster care and in other cases children need to be placed in residential childcare homes. These children are referred to as 'looked after children' and are in the care of the local authority whose duty it is to safeguard them and ensure their needs are met. In Scotland, children under 12 years are usually placed with a foster family. Children older than 12 years may also be placed with a foster family, but if none is available those children would be supported in residential childcare units.

Children may become 'looked after' for a variety of reasons, including family breakdown or if they are at risk of harm. The foster family will provide physical, emotional, social and physical care for the child while working with social workers to ensure the child can, wherever possible, go back to his or her family. Often parents are allowed to visit the child while in the foster home, but sometimes for reasons of child protection this cannot happen. Sometimes supervised visits are allowed when the social worker or another key professional is present during a parental visit. Some children are in a range of foster homes during their lives.

Kinship parenting

Kinship parenting is a term used to describe permanent or semi-permanent parenting by a grandparent or other close relative. Some grandparents bring up their grandchildren because the parents are unable to do so. This may be because parents are in prison, have died, or have addictions or mental health problems that prevent them from being safe and effective parents. It is an increasing phenomenon in Scotland. This is quite different from grandparents who may provide informal care for their grandchildren and who may even pick them up from nursery on a day-to-day basis. Grandparents who are providing kinship parenting are effectively being parents again.

Kinship parenting is becoming more common with grandparents and other relatives bringing up children

Consider this

What is your view of how children may be affected by being in a number of foster homes throughout their lives?

Social trends and how they might affect children in Scotland

There is a range of different trends which are highlighted in the specification for Unit DF56 34: contemporary issues for children and families. You will read about some of these in this chapter. It is also recommended that you carry out personal research to find out about some of the trends and demographics that are not mentioned here but which are still important.

Poverty

The Child Poverty Action Group (CPAG) indicates that 25 per cent of children in Scotland are living in poverty, equivalent to approximately 240,000 children. CPAG (2007) describes poverty for families as:

- a lone-parent family with two children living on less than £223 per week

- a couple with two children living on less than £301 a week.

These figures take account of the need to pay for housing, utilities, food, clothing and any additional requirements children may have such as leisure and school trips.

Poverty affects all parts of Scotland, both urban and rural. Even in relatively affluent cities and areas such as Edinburgh or Aberdeenshire there is a high percentage of families on very low income. Some of the effects of poverty on children include poor diet, poor health, poor mental health, living with debt and being caught in a poverty trap and cycle of debt.

Often households that have the least amount of money are not entitled to schemes that could help save money. This can happen with discounts on gas and electricity, with poorer families needing to use special card meters that are more expensive to run. Sometimes families take out additional loans to pay existing debt and find themselves caught in a spiral of debt.

One of the effects of poverty on parents and children is stress. Many children in Scotland today are living in stress-rich households and experience poor mental health as a result. Often children living in the most deprived circumstances are living in substandard housing located in areas where there is a lack of outdoor play opportunities.

Many communities have become actively involved in regeneration schemes to try to

Case study *Living in poverty*

John Millar is employed in the local hospital. He earns a minimum wage working as a hospital cleaner. His wife has a disability that prevents her from working or looking after the children on her own. His pay is supplemented by working families' tax credit which helps to pay for the childcare he needs for his two children, Liam age 2 years and Angus age 8 years, to attend nursery and out-of-school care. John and his wife go shopping every week and try to buy fresh food where possible but they find this drains their income. The children are always well turned out but John finds it hard to buy them all they need. Sometimes their shoes are shabby.

John has been told by the school that Angus will need the new uniform they are introducing and separate trainers for gym. In addition, Angus is quite promising at football and is really keen to be in the school under 9s football team. John doesn't want to discourage his son but he knows that the extra cost of buying football boots would cause him to go into debt.

1   What are the key issues for this family?

2   Are there ways that the school might be able to support them?

3   How might the community be able to support the family?

improve the local environment and to offer support to their local communities. An example of this in action is the use of local cooperatives that source fresh fruit and vegetables at a reduced price for families. Some schools are community schools and provide a community resource for children and families. These include a community wing where parents can learn a new skill and train for work while their children are looked after in the nursery. Other community schools provide specialised health care for families and mother and toddler groups. The Scottish Government document *National Standards in Community Engagement* (Communities Scotland, 2007) outlines ways in which communities can be supported better.

Drug and alcohol misuse

Some children live in households where parents or carers misuse drugs and alcohol or have other addictions. A University of Edinburgh study on behalf of the Joseph Rowntree Foundation (*Parental Drug and Alcohol Misuse: Resilience and Transition among Young People*, Bancroft et al., 2004) highlights the impact of parents who misuse drugs or alcohol on a wide range of children from different socio-economic backgrounds. They describe how children whose parents misused drugs or alcohol felt their parents were sometimes unable to provide consistent practical and emotional care.

- Many young people felt their own childhood was shortened from having to take on adult roles caring for themselves, siblings and for their parents.

- Those with drug misusing parents were more likely to feel socially stigmatised.

- Those with alcohol-using parents were more likely to experience violence and parental absence.

As an early education and childcare practitioner you will be aware that some children in your care encounter this type of disordered life. You need to be able to find ways of supporting such children without stigmatising them further.

Children as carers

Some children care for other siblings or for parents who are ill or who have a disability. National Children's Homes (NCH), a national charity which works with children, has highlighted the needs of children who are carers. Often these children 'lose' their childhood because they are acting as the main carer for a relative. This can be the case even when there is an adult present in the home. Some children care for siblings who have particular disabilities and often take on quite diverse caring roles. NCH consider this can affect the quality of childhood and a child's opportunities for 'normality' (see www.nch.org.uk).

Consider this

What is your view of children as carers? Is there a need to provide them with additional support or is this something you think children would want to do as a matter of course?

Women in work in Scotland

Some social trends can develop because of a particular policy direction. Two key issues in the twenty-first century are the availability of

Further research

Look for papers or articles relating to parental drug or alcohol misuse. You may want to try the following websites:

www.childreninscotland.org.uk
www.jrf.org.uk
www.savethechildren.org.uk
www.children1st.org.uk

Look at some of the statistics relating to the numbers of children affected by parental drug or alcohol misuse, and consider the likelihood of you working with such children day to day. How do you think you, as an early education and childcare practitioner, can best support families in these circumstances?

childcare and employment patterns in women. Later in this chapter you will read about the government policies concerning pre-school provision and how it has been developed to allow more flexibility for women to return to work.

Women in work is not a new phenomenon in Scotland. Some parts of Scotland have traditionally had fairly high levels of female employment. In Dundee the jute industry had a proportionately higher number of women working than men. At the time there were full-day nurseries to support women in work, so women working didn't mean men looking after children instead.

Since the Second World War there has been a drive to get women into the workforce. This trend has included more opportunities for young women to go to colleges and universities to train for professional careers, more part-time working in service industries, and a huge rise in the number of women working in caring services.

Sometimes parents need to juggle their commitments and this can be very hard for families

Fitzgerald and McKay (*Gender, Equality and Work in Scotland*, 2006), in a report for the Equal Opportunities Commission (EOC) and citing the Office for National Statistics (ONS), indicate that in 2006 women made up 47 per cent of the Scottish labour market. However, while 87 per cent of the health and social care labour market is made up of women, only 19 per cent of the top jobs at management level go to women! They also highlighted the pay differentials between men and women, with men still earning proportionately more than women, including in some of the 'top' professions such as law.

One of the issues highlighted by women in the workforce is the need for them to be able to juggle homes, careers and childcare.

Consider this

Why do you think women make up more of the caring services job market than men?

Discuss why you consider fewer women than men have top jobs.

What is your view: should women be juggling children and jobs?

How changing attitudes and perceptions in society affect children and families

Parenting styles

Chapter 2 looked at some of the ways in which childhood is viewed, including children as innocents or as young adults fully responsible for their actions. The way that children are perceived within society can sometimes seem at odds with this. Some parents have expressed concern at letting their children go out to play in case they have an accident – so-called 'cotton wool kids'. Some parents express fear of predatory adults likely to harm their children and some take steps to avoid children being exposed to them. An example of this is where parents prefer children to stay at home with their friends rather than let them play in streets or alone or with friends in parks. Others feel this is overzealous parenting and that children are not being allowed the freedom to choose, to develop resilience and to learn from their own mistakes.

As a result of the anti-social acts of a minority of children, some adults demonise all children as guilty of or contributing to growing anti-social behaviour. This means they often consider children to be guilty of causing harm and vandalising property. Some shops have a blanket ban on more than two children in the shop at a time.

Different types of parenting contribute to different ways of treating children. Chapter 8 outlined these (see pages 250–51).

Fathers as carers

In June 2006 the Equal Opportunities Commission (EOC) in England and Wales published the report *21st Century Dad*. In it they provided some key facts about the contributions fathers now make to child rearing. The report suggests that up to one-third of all male employees have dependent children but that they are less likely to work part-time than women with dependent children might be. They also estimate that there has been a threefold increase since the 1970s in the number of lone-parent fathers. In Scotland there are a number of projects that support lone fathers, including One Parent Families Scotland. Some of their projects include drop-in sessions where fathers are given advice or information or can meet other fathers. They can also take part in organised activities with their children. The 101 Project in Dundee offers a similar range of help and advice, advocacy and support to all lone-parent families that are referred.

Flexible working hours

Flexible working patterns mean that more couples are able to alter their working hours to suit childcare requirements. Thus some parents will choose to start work later to allow them to drop children off at nursery, and some parents will choose to start early and finish early to avoid having to pay high fees for out-of-school care or full day care at nursery. A key advantage of flexible working hours for parents is thus that it enables them to maintain their childcare more affordably.

Case study *An inconsistent parenting style*

You may have overheard an exchange like the one below in the supermarket.

Child: I want those sweets!

Parent: No, you can't have them.

Child: (*starting to get distressed*) I want them!

Parent: No, I'll not tell you again – you can't have them.

Child: (*starting to cry and get into a temper*) Ye-es! (*stamping foot*) I want the sweets!

Parent: No. I really won't tell you again!

(*Child cries and throws a tantrum*)

Parent: All right, just one then no more.

1   What type of parental style is illustrated by this example – autocratic, authoritative or permissive? Explain your answer.

2   Do you think the parent's response is likely to affect the way the child might respond in nursery?

3   Is there a way this situation might have been improved?

A range of industries now have what they describe as 'family friendly working policies'. Flexible working hours can give parents an opportunity to get back into work if they have been long-term unemployed. Some children are in full day care because it's the only way parents who have high levels of personal debt, including mortgage debt, can afford to pay it or can afford luxury items and holidays.

> ### Consider this
>
> Which of the following do you regard as essential to day-to-day living?
>
> Cooker; fridge-freezer; kettle; hair straighteners; cable television; iPod; Xbox; PlayStation Portable (PSP); food; alcohol; car; holidays abroad; holidays at home; football season ticket.
>
> Discuss your decisions in a large group and make up your own list of essential goods if they aren't here. Do you think it is correct that all families should think of these items as essentials?

Despite flexibility in working hours, some parents find key points in the year particularly difficult to cope with. For many the most difficult time is during the summer holidays. Others find the occasional days off school difficult to accommodate and many find it particularly hard to cope when children are ill.

Many private nurseries and out-of-school care clubs do their best to accommodate working parents by offering flexible packages of attendance and different charges according to the time spent. This is less so in local authority nursery schools and classes where children are usually required to attend for a set 2.5 hours a day and where there is less built in flexibility.

Parents admit juggling work and home life is particularly stressful. Many find it particularly difficult if they are required to stay late at work and are late collecting the children. Some nurseries in Scotland impose a 'fine' on parents who are habitually late. A few nurseries now

offer an extended day and overnight service to accommodate working parents or parents who need to travel because of their jobs. Many offer after-school care as part of a package to parents, so school-age children are picked up from school and taken to a nursery centre where they are provided with snacks and play and/or homework activities while they wait for their parents.

> ### Consider this
>
> To what extent do you think it is advantageous for children to be in full day care and out-of-school care?
>
> Do you consider there is a link between the breakdown of the traditional extended family and the increased need for parents to purchase childcare?

Government policy on childcare

Children in Scotland aged 3 and 4 years are entitled to 475 hours of free pre-school education each year. This usually means around 12.5 hours a week depending on the pattern adopted by each local authority. The Scottish Government has indicated that it wants to raise this entitlement to 15 hours per week. Local authorities can purchase places from other providers, including childminders, play groups and private nurseries. It is the work of the childcare partnerships in each authority to support centres that are not local authority centres, and all must be inspected by both the Care Commission and Her Majesty's Inspectorate of Education (HMIE). You will read more about both organisations later in this chapter. Parents can 'top up' the hours by purchasing additional hours from the centre.

Cultural variations

Cultural diversity and immigration

Scotland has always has been a country rich in cultural variation. For generations settlers have migrated into Scotland and Scots have left to settle in other countries. Although it is a large country in terms of land mass, it is a sparsely populated country. Most people in Scotland live in the central belt between the west and the east. Other parts of Scotland are now increasing in population, including towns like Inverness. The 2001 UK census indicates there are around 5.6 million people living in Scotland, with a bulge of people aged between 30 and 60 years. These demographics also indicate there are fewer young people in Scotland, with only around 250,000 people aged from birth to 4 years.

In some parts of Scotland the population is bilingual: for example, in parts of the west, Argyll and the Isles, Inverness, the Highlands and Western Isles, many families speak both English and Gaelic. The 2001 UK census indicated around 58,000 Gaelic speakers in Scotland; you may find you are working in settings where Gaelic is the first language used by children and parents. Other first languages for many parents and children in Scotland include Punjabi, Bengali, Arabic, Chinese Mandarin and Cantonese, Hindi and Urdu. Some settings will have bilingual support assistants to support children for whom English is not their first language.

The Scottish Government's 'One Scotland' campaign (2005) is designed to help people gain a better understanding of different cultures in Scotland and to stamp out sectarianism and racism. It identifies the benefits to Scotland from the diversity of people living in Scotland and, in particular, the benefit to the economy.

Key term

Sectarianism is hatred towards another because of his or her religious beliefs and arising from narrow-minded views.

Since the enlargement of the European Union to include eastern European states, Scotland has seen an influx of around 32,000 workers from Poland, Lithuania and Estonia. This adds to the cultural diversity of the country and to the diversity of children and families using childcare services. Some centres in Inverness and the Highlands now have support assistants to help the growing number of eastern European families in the area.

Consider this

Why is it important to be aware of sectarianism in Scotland? In what way is it harmful to Scottish society?

Asylum seekers

In 1999 the Immigration and Asylum Act provided a legal basis for the dispersal of asylum seekers – that is, their being moved to other parts of the UK. This action was taken to ease pressures arising on local councils from the large numbers of asylum seekers living close to ports of entry to the UK while awaiting a decision on their claim for asylum. The dispersal scheme has resulted in many asylum seekers being relocated across the UK, including Scotland.

Barclay et al. (2003), in their Report *Asylum Seekers in Scotland*, indicate that some asylum seekers found they were subject to racism and abuse in the communities where they lived. Others found that when the community supported them, Scotland was a good country to live in. Many asylum seekers in Scotland who originate from Iran or Iraq are fleeing persecution.

Until a claim for asylum is granted, asylum seekers can't work in the UK. Immigration is a matter reserved by the UK government, so the Scottish Government has limited powers to help asylum seekers. The Scottish Refugee Council, along with other voluntary organisations, provides advice, information and assistance to asylum seekers and campaigns to make sure the UK government meets its humanitarian obligations to them.

Key term

Reserved powers describes the key areas of responsibility that remain with the UK government in London. It describes areas that the Scottish Government has no control over, such as defence and immigration.

Glasgow City Council is the main provider of accommodation for asylum seekers in Scotland and is considered by many to have the best practice on asylum in the UK (*Asylum Seekers in Scotland*). There are many examples of good community projects in Glasgow city that are helping to build bridges between the local population and asylum seekers.

As an early education and childcare practitioner you are likely to work with groups of people who may be persecuted or fleeing persecution. This work can be challenging if there is a language barrier, where you feel culture and customs are different, and where children and parents have been traumatised by the lives they have left behind. Good centres will work with local communities and take advantage of translation and interpreting services as well as psychological services to support the work they are doing. Sometimes, however, children

of asylum seekers may not be entitled to free nursery education or out-of-school care since neither is a statutory obligation. Check this out in your local nursery school or class.

Key term

A **statutory obligation** means the government must provide something by law. In Scotland there is a statutory requirement to provide school for children between 5 and 16 years, but there is no statutory obligation to provide pre-school education or out-of-school care.

Activity

Compare and contrast the following two case studies.

Case study *The Gryzbowskis – an immigrant family in Scotland*

Konrad and Agata Gryzbowski arrived in Inverness from Poland six months ago. They have two children, Ludmilla who is 3 years, and Krzystof who will be 5 years old in two weeks' time. Krzystof is due to start primary school in August and in the meantime Agata wants to get him into a local nursery so he can improve his English and get to know other children.

They approach the local nursery where they are told there is a waiting list for places. However, it is suggested by the practitioner that there may be spaces in a local play group. The practitioner also offers to give the play group a ring to set up a meeting.

They all go to the play group the next day where they meet the manager. Agata is introduced by her to other parents. Both children are offered a morning place and Agata is asked to fill out

admission forms and information. The manager asks Agata if she would like to stay and help some mornings to get to know the centre better and to help Ludmilla settle. She is also told about other local groups to join. She is told how to contact the local authority about Krystoffs school place and the play group manager indicates the authority have some literature published in Polish.

1 What impression do you think the Gryzbowski family might have of Scotland after this encounter?

2 Is there anything else the centres might have offered to do for the family?

3 How likely is it that the children will be supported in settling in to play group?

Case study *The Alams – a refugee family in Scotland*

Atefeh Alam and her three children, Niloufar (3 years), Arash (5 years) and Cirrus (18 months), have recently come from Iran to the UK where they have made a claim for asylum. This is because Atefeh's husband was allegedly beaten and killed for being a political activist. At first

the family were sent to a refugee camp in Kent before being relocated to Glasgow while they await the outcome of their hearing. The children have had no permanent home for the last 12 months and Atefeh is concerned that her children are becoming traumatised by the lack of continuity. When they moved into the high-rise flat in Glasgow some youths taunted them with racist remarks and spray-painted the outside wall of their flat. They still bother them. Atefeh has discovered that most people in the area are friendly, though none seem to want to help her make a complaint against the local youths.

Arash has now started the local primary school and has made friends. Some of the other refugees tell Atefeh about a drop-in centre she can go to. She would like to get Niloufar into nursery but isn't sure how to go about this. She can't pay for a private nursery or a play group place, and doesn't know how to approach the local authority about childcare provision. She still lives in fear because her husband was allegedly taken from their home in Iran by policemen and she is afraid of authority figures.

1 What are the main issues that the Alam family are dealing with?

2 How might a place at nursery help Niloufar and Atefeh?

3 What are your views on this issue?

How policies of inclusion help support children and families in Scotland

In 1999 the then First Minister, Donald Dewar, spoke about the need for Scotland to be an inclusive society where all citizens benefited from prosperity and where everyone had the chance to work and learn. This was because it was recognised that many people in Scotland were poor and lacked real opportunities so that some seemed born to fail. Social exclusion has been described as the effects of combining unemployment, poor skills, low income, poor housing, high crime environments, bad health and family breakdown. The Scottish Government is trying to ensure that this trend is reversed and there is social *inclusion* in Scotland. They don't want to see citizens of the country excluded because of a combination of circumstances. Government surveys have shown that the highest number of areas with poor housing and multiple deprivations are in Glasgow, west central Scotland, Edinburgh and Dundee. It is also true that in some rural areas of Scotland and in smaller towns there can be multiple deprivation.

In 1999, the Scottish Government working in partnership with the Scottish Social Inclusion Network set out a vision for social inclusion in the document *Social Inclusion – Opening the door to a better Scotland*. The document describes a number of key targets for social inclusion in Scotland. These aims are that:

- every child, whatever his or her social or economic background, has the best possible start in life
- there are opportunities to work for all those who are able to do so
- those who are unable to work or are beyond the normal working age have a decent quality of life
- everyone is enabled and encouraged to participate to the maximum of their potential.

The following goals have been worked on:

- to increase participation in the labour market
- to tackle poverty through both national and local action
- to ensure that every child entering primary school is ready to learn and to make best use of their school years
- to tackle specific barriers to participation faced by individuals including ill-health, low self-esteem, homelessness and drug misuse
- to eliminate discrimination and inequality on the grounds of gender, race or disability
- to reduce inequalities in health
- to ensure that decent and affordable housing is available to everyone
- to tackle inequalities between communities by empowering and regenerating deprived communities.

Inclusion of children with additional support needs

Since the Education (Additional Support for Learning) (Scotland) Act (2004), local authorities have had to consider the needs of a wide range of children, including those who are able or gifted, those who are bilingual and need additional support, children with disabilities and children who are travellers, amongst others. For many of these children there is a requirement to identify the need, assess it and make provision for it. For the majority of children that assessment will be based on the child being included in mainstream schools or classes. This is also called inclusion. For a small number of children with specific disabilities, their needs will be better met in a specialist school that has the equipment, level of staff and resources to accommodate their needs. You can read about inclusion of children with additional support needs in Chapter 6.

How local and national policies, strategies and initiatives support healthy lifestyles for children and families in Scotland

Before looking at policies, strategies and initiatives concerned with healthy lifestyles, it is important to understand how some key policies are likely to affect children's lives and the lives of their families. The Scottish Government has identified a vision it has for children in Scotland. That vision is that children should be ambitious for themselves and be confident individuals, effective contributors, successful learners and responsible citizens. You will see that this is the same vision that has been discussed in Curriculum for Excellence in Chapter 4. In order to achieve this vision, the government thinks children need to be safe, nurtured, healthy, achieving, active, respected, responsible and included. This vision for children is included in all documents the government publishes about children, and is at the heart of its policies and strategies. Many of the strategies that affect children in Scotland have evolved since the Children (Scotland) Act (1995) and include *For Scotland's Children: Better Integrated Children's Services* (Scottish Executive, 2001); *It's Everyone's Job to Make Sure I'm Alright* (Scottish Executive, 2002); *Getting It Right for Every Child* (Scottish Executive, 2006); and *Health for All Children: Guidance on Implementation in Scotland* (Scottish Executive, 2004). Each will be explained briefly in this chapter and all can be researched further.

A key theme from each of the strategy documents described above is the need for better integration and coordination of children's services. This is thought to be important because over the last few years there have been a number of tragic incidents in which children have died or suffered appalling abuse or neglect because it was felt professionals working in services to support children were not speaking to each other often enough and were not sharing information effectively. These strategies are designed to help professionals, including early education and childcare practitioners, understand their roles and responsibilities to children and their families better.

Children (Scotland) Act (1995)

This Act was important because it set a new standard for how children in need were to be supported and how agencies working for children were expected to cooperate in a more coherent way. The Act brought in a requirement for a Children's Services Plan (CSP) to be written to show how agencies were working together to meet those needs. The CSP was to be an overall or strategic plan prepared by the local authority to show the way in which they will act to make sure services, such as education, health and social work, cooperate to support children.

In Scotland there are 32 local authorities, each with responsibility for delivering key services to the public such as education and social work. The local health boards have responsibility for health services. So collaboration between agencies meant working across two different structures, each with their own staffing arrangements and funding. This could be problematic. However, since the main aim of the Act was to make services better for children, it was something that had to be done. Since then CSPs have changed and they are now called Community Plans. This may also change so it is important to research what is currently required.

Opposite is the definition of children in need that was made in the 1995 Act.

A child under the age of 18 years is in need because:

- the child is unlikely to achieve or maintain or to have the opportunity of achieving or maintaining a reasonable standard of health or development unless services are provided, or
- the child's health or development is likely significantly to be impaired or further impaired unless such services are provided, or
- the child is disabled, or
- the child is adversely affected by the disability of another family member.

(Children (Scotland) Act (1995): Section 93(4) (a))

The services involved in working with children are universal and targeted services. Universal services are services to which all children are entitled, such as education. Targeted services include social work services which are given to children only when needed. Researchers including Roaf (*Co-ordinating Services for Included Children: Joined Up Action*, 2002) have indicated that it is very difficult to coordinate services that have a different approach and which are managed separately. This has been one of the key difficulties in coordinating children's services since the 1995 Act.

For Scotland's Children (2001)

For Scotland's Children: Better Integrated Children's Services highlighted some of the shortcomings and fragmentation in the way services in Scotland were being provided for children. It raised concerns, using children's and families' own examples, of how frustrating it can be to have to give various professionals the same personal information over and over. The authors challenged local authorities and other agencies to get better at coordinating services and sharing information. The research also listed key action points to try to show those working with children why some of the structures that were in place needed to change to allow integrated working to improve. Structural changes that have since taken place in a number of authorities in Scotland include the merging of education services and children's social work services into new 'Children's Services' departments.

Key term

Fragmentation of services means that services are sometimes in small parts and not joined up, so one department doesn't necessarily know what another one has done.

It's Everyone's Job to Make Sure I'm Alright (2002)

This report by the Scottish Executive outlined the responsibilities that all professionals working with children have to ensure the child's safety and well-being. It highlighted the need for a review of the child protection system in Scotland to make sure it worked well for the children and adults who were involved. Like other reports, it showed the need for all the agencies involved with children and families to work together. Importantly, it reported that parents did not always feel the child protection system was working well. One of the recommendations was that there should be positive initiatives that promoted every child's right to life, health, decency and development.

Getting It Right for Every Child (GIRFEC) (2006)

You read about the Children's Hearings system in Scotland in Chapter 2. *Getting It Right for Every Child* is an important document because

it makes key recommendations about how the hearings system could be improved to ensure that children who need the support of the system get it. The document also sets out aims to make sure all local authorities show how they intend sharing, cooperating and implementing the correct actions for children in need. Some children end up going to Children's Hearings unnecessarily and consequently the system has become very stretched. This document suggests that sometimes children and their families need to receive better services from social work and health services to prevent them going to hearings, and that the help they need has to be coordinated better. The document also addresses children directly when it says:

- when you are having problems you should be able to easily find out what help you can get and how you can get it
- you should be able to say what you feel and know your views are important; you should feel people will do all they can to help you
- you should know that if you keep doing something that puts you at risk now or in later life that action will be taken; for example, if you keep offending or taking drugs
- you should be able to find out easily what help you can get.

Consider this

Have you seen examples of integration at work in your placement? If so, describe them.

Do you think it is helpful for official government reports to address children directly?

Do you think it is important for children and families to receive help before it is necessary to take action at a Children's Hearing?

You will see that the key theme of all these policies is to integrate services for children better so that those receiving the services feel they are less disjointed and so that mistakes are not made. This is also true of the policies designed to support children's health and well-being.

Health for All Children (2004)

One key strategy of the Scottish Government has been to improve the health of Scotland's children. Like other documents, *Health for All Children: Guidance on Implementation in Scotland*, Scottish Executive, 2004 has tried to show the importance of pulling together services for children so that there is a coordinated approach to supporting children and their families' health and well-being. One of the key messages of *Health for All Children* is that it isn't only the health service that can support children's health and well-being: other key professionals, including early education and childcare practitioners, are in a very good position to be able to provide real support to children and their families.

Health for All Children highlights how important it is to remember that although the responsibility for a child's health lies with the parent, there are other services, including nurseries, family centres, schools and community-based support services, that play a key role in making sure children are healthy and maximise their potential.

Health for All Children emphasises the need to move towards a more positive way of looking at children's health, namely through health promotion. This means 'planned and informed interventions that are designed to improve physical or mental health or prevent disease, disability and premature death' (*Health for All Children*, page 3).

Health promotion means that children will continue to be screened and offered routine immunisations. However, the emphasis will be on helping families to make more informed decisions about the health and development of their child, to respond to children who have a particular need better and more effectively, and to recognise that not all parents will need the same level of help. This means targeting help when the parent needs it most. This approach is represented by the diagram below.

Universal Core Programme
All families offered core screening and surveillance programme, immunisation, information, advice on services

FAMILY HEALTH PLAN

Universal core programme – no additional input needed	**Additional support from public health nurse as agreed with family**	**Intensive support required**
Contact or appointments on request	Structured support (e.g. first-time mother, breastfeeding problems, mental health problems)	Structured inter-agency support for individual families or communities (e.g. child on child protection register with inter-agency children protection plan, looked after or disabled child, parental stresses)

Universal core programme from *Health for All Children: Guidance on Implementation in Scotland* (Scottish Executive, 2004)

Childhood immunisations

The purpose of immunisation is to keep children healthy and free from life-threatening illness. Many of the illnesses that children are now immunised against caused disability or death in previous generations. Many are infectious diseases which can easily be spread by contact and which, if there was an epidemic, would have serious consequences for the health of the nation. Because of good immunisation programmes the UK has been free from or has had low numbers of serious childhood ailments for many years. This includes polio, diphtheria and measles. However, some parents have expressed concerns about giving their children the triple MMR (measles, mumps and rubella) vaccine. As a result many more cases of measles have been reported recently. Measles can cause children acute discomfort and can occasionally cause eye and hearing defects and fits.

Immunisations are particularly important in the child's first year of life.

Further research

To find out the schedule for immunisations go to: www.documents.hps.scot.nhs.uk/immunisation/general/immunisation-schedule-2006-08.pdf.

Go to the NHS Health Scotland website (www.healthscotland.com) where you will find leaflets that are given to parents about immunising their children.

Why is it thought important to routinely immunise children for these illnesses? Try to find some research papers that explain the purpose of immunisation more fully.

Consider this

You are working in a private nursery and a parent who has recently arrived to work in Scotland from eastern Europe expresses concern about why her child should need immunisations. Do you consider it your role to explain the reasons for immunisation and reassure this parent? If not, who might you suggest she discusses her concern with?

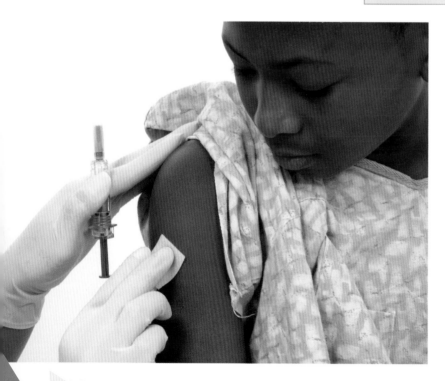

It is important for children to be immunised against potentially life-threatening diseases

Healthy individuals

In December 2005 the Information Statistics Division of NHS Scotland reported that, in Scotland, more than 33 per cent of 12-year-olds were overweight, 19 per cent were obese and 11 per cent were morbidly obese (www.isdscotland.org). Obesity means that a person is extremely overweight. It is usually associated with high levels of body fat that a person carries, and it leads to poor health and long-term illness. When a person becomes morbidly obese it puts their life at serious risk.

Among the issues to be considered in a 'healthy school' is the aspect of children's emotional resilience. This means working with parents and the child's own community to ensure children are given clear messages that they are valued as individuals. Healthy schools also deal with issues of bullying because of the detrimental effect bullying has on children's emotional, mental and physical well-being.

Health Promoting Schools emphasises the need for community collaboration. Central to this is the role of the school as an important feature of the local community and a place that children and families can benefit from using outside of school hours for social and sporting activities and for breakfast clubs and after-school care programmes.

Many out-of-school care clubs are an integral part of local communities in Scotland

One of the main aims of *Health for All Children* is to support a healthy Scotland by putting in place better health education and preventative measures to improve the quality of life and physical and mental health of the population. Different local authorities in Scotland now have their own health policies that are based on the requirements of *Health for All Children*. In north and south Ayrshire there are schemes to support good feeding habits in babies and young children called the 'Best Fed Babies Scheme'. In other parts of Scotland there are healthy living schemes that have been partly funded through the Big Lottery Fund. Nationally there is the Health Promoting Schools initiative that aims to:

- develop and support the physical, social, spiritual, mental and emotional health and well-being of all pupils and staff
- work in partnership with others to identify and meet the health needs of the whole school and the wider community.

Further research

Investigate the publication *Being Well – Doing Well* (Scottish Executive, 2004). It describes some other initiatives such as Tackling Drugs in Scotland and strategies for improving the mental health of the country. Consider how this publication might impact on you as a practitioner and how you might support these initiatives.

Factors that influence children's health

A range of factors affect children's health. Some of these include poverty and deprivation, living in difficult circumstances (including with drug and alcohol misusing parents), living with pollutants including cigarette smoke, poor diet and lack of physical activity, living with chronic or long-term illness and having poor mental health.

Catriona (5 years) lives in a high-rise flat in west central Scotland with her mother and brothers Jamie (7 years) and Jack (10 years). The children don't see their father. It is an area of deprivation where there is a high crime rate and very low employment. Catriona's mum, Sarah, is unable to work because of a chronic illness and the family need to live off the benefits she receives. These include invalidity benefit and child benefit. Sarah has complained to the local council about the damp conditions in her flat and although they say they will do something about it, they haven't done so for at least two years.

Sarah smokes around 40 cigarettes a day and she has noticed Jack is now taking some of her cigarettes. Sarah really cares for her children and tries to do her best on a small budget. She shops locally and usually gets some cheaper foods for the children, including sausage rolls, pies, crisps and burgers, because she thinks this fills them up better. She buys Catriona and Jamie sweets to take to school as they don't have time for breakfast. Jack and Catriona don't get out to play much, especially in the winter. Sarah thinks it's unsafe in the playground where local drug dealers are. Catriona and Jack are both overweight. Both children have been bullied at school because of their weight. They say they prefer to watch DVDs rather than go outside to play.

1 What are the key issues for this family?

2 What initiatives are there to help support families like this?

might already have a respiratory problem such as asthma. Children who live in households where parents smoke are at increased risk of some illnesses including respiratory illnesses.

Key term

Passive smoking is the smoke that is inhaled when a person near to you smokes.

The Scottish Government is trying to encourage children to establish good patterns of eating and exercise from a young age. This is because poor diet and lack of exercise has a long-term effect on children's health. Illnesses that affect adults in Scotland include coronary heart disease, strokes, diabetes and cancers that are linked to smoking. In 2007 the Scottish Government started a trial in an authority in the west of Scotland to provide free school meals for all young children irrespective of their income. This was to see if eating healthier school meals had an impact.

This scheme will continue to the end of the 2007–2008 school year. Ministers will then evaluate the trial for evidence on: changes in attitudes by children and parents to school meals and healthy eating; eating habits; and development of social skills as children eat together. If the evaluation of the trial is positive, all primary one to three pupils in Scotland will be entitled to free school meals.

Consider this

Do you think this type of scheme would be beneficial to all children if it was implemented across Scotland?

One of the key priorities the Scottish Government has is to create a healthier Scotland. To do this they have been investing in schemes, including media and newpaper advertising, to help people understand the implications of an unhealthy lifestyle. On 26 March 2006 Scotland introduced a smoking ban in public places. This was preceded and followed by measures to help people give up smoking. Passive smoking harms children's health, particularly those children who

Nursery schools and classes, primary schools and out-of-school care clubs all need to support a better understanding of good diet and exercise for children. Some schools in Scotland are trying to move towards a Scandinavian system of outdoor play and learning to encourage children to do more everyday activities outside. Other measures being adopted are to encourage healthy eating which includes 'five a day'. This refers to eating five portions of fruit and vegetables a day. So, when planning children's meals you need to make sure fruit and vegetables are included.

Encouraging children to drink more water is also a key consideration in many nursery and primary schools. Research suggests children are able to concentrate better if they are hydrated. Many schools provide children with flasks to drink from or water coolers so they can drink when they want to.

Breakfast clubs are trying to make sure children are given healthy foods to start the day. Some provide foods such as porridge or sugar-free cereals with fruit.

Activity

You are looking after two children aged 3 years and 7 years during the school holidays. Their mother has asked you to provide her with a weekly menu for them and has told you she will make £50 available. You are required to provide a mid-morning snack and a lunch each day Monday to Friday.

What will you provide?

Physical activity and health

You will be asked to support children's physical activity whether you work with very young children, children with additional support needs or children in out-of-school care. Some children will have their own physical activity schedule that has been put together by other professionals such as physiotherapists, and many schools now have access to a healthy schools coordinator. Where children have particular disabilities or need additional support, you need to check with parents and other key professionals about the best programmes to support them, as some children with disabilities need to become more active.

One of the best ways for younger children to get exercise is through outdoor play or vigorous indoor activity or dance. Other ways include walking or cycling to school every day. You should ensure there is plenty of opportunity in the centre for children to get fresh air and exercise. Scotland has pretty poor weather sometimes, but this shouldn't prevent children getting outside. Even in bad weather children can enjoy putting on boots and coats and being outside; the more you move, the warmer you will get.

Sports scientists and other experts suggest children need a minimum of an hour's daily exercise and good diet to prevent them becoming overweight. Useful exercise for children includes weight-bearing exercise to help strengthen bones and cardiovascular exercise to reduce weight gain and improve fitness. Weight-bearing and cardiovascular activities include running, skipping, jumping or cycling. Other activities can help children develop good hand–eye coordination and contribute to their exercise. They might include ball games and throwing and catching games such as bean bags and hoops.

Physical activity is important for children's mental health as well as their physical health. Exercise in childhood will mean children are less inactive and possibly set down good habits for later life. Inactivity and poor diet are contributing factors to weight gain. Physical activity is also beneficial to a child's flexibility, healthy bone structure, muscular strength and endurance.

Walking buses are a healthy way of getting children to school

Some nurseries and out-of-school care clubs feel that health and safety concerns sometimes mean they don't provide the range of outdoor activities they might like. Some settings prevent children from going near water and from climbing trees. It is important to carry out a proper risk assessment before you provide outdoor play, but this shouldn't prevent you from doing a full range of activities. Some centres ensure a health and safety assessment is done and additional staff are present at all times if children are playing near to water or are climbing.

Outdoor play is to be encouraged

Risk assessment

When you are working in an early education and childcare setting, you will be providing a range of activities both indoor and out, including planned visits for children. Many of these will require a risk assessment to be done. Risk assessments mean that you take into consideration a range of factors when planning activities. These factors include any potential harm that could come from the activity and how you will act to make sure this doesn't happen. Risk assessment doesn't mean accidents won't happen, but it means you have done your very best to ensure they don't and have a plan in place for how to minimise risk and how to act in case of emergency.

Activity/equipment: Week beginning 01 October 2007	Hazards present	Date checked	Staff
Climbing frame	Wiped down as it was slippery	01 October	S.W.
Bikes	Removed blue bike to be repaired	01 October	G.P. to discuss
Put out large water tray	Member of staff to supervise to ensure health and safety	02 October	G.P. & S.W.
Outdoor sand tray	Lid left off. Not to be used and sand to be removed because of cat faeces.	03 October	S.W. to discuss at team meeting

Example of a day-to-day risk assessment form used in a local nursery

Another form of risk assessment is risk assessing visits before going on them. A risk assessment form can be used for this and for other activities. When doing this you need to consider what the potential risk is, whether it can be eliminated, and if it can't how you are going to ensure the children's safety. You need to say who has assessed the risk and when this was done. If it is something fairly major that might require action on the part of the nursery, for example providing better security fences for an outdoor play area, you would need to say the timescale you are working to and when you plan to have this completed.

How policies affect children's care, learning and development

Regulation of Care (Scotland) Act (2001)

You have read about some of the policies that support families in Scotland today. Other key policies directly affect children's overall well-being, including the type of care, learning and development they receive. Some of these policies have emerged because of one key piece of legislation: the Regulation of Care (Scotland) Act (2001).

The Regulation of Care (Scotland) Act provided for a system of care regulation in Scotland for a range of people from the very young to the very old. Two main organisations were set up as a result of the Act. They are the Scottish Commission for the Regulation of Care (or Care Commission) and the Scottish Social Services Council (SSSC).

Care Commission

The Care Commission is required to inspect services to make sure those services meet the requirements of the National Care Standards. National Care Standards for Early Education and Childcare up to 16 years are the standards that cover services that children receive, including those provided in nursery schools and classes, in crèches, from childminders, in play groups and in out-of-school care clubs. All care standards are written from the point of view of service users and describe the levels of care every service user is entitled to. In the case of early education and childcare, the service users are children.

Care standards describe the type of environment children can expect, how they will be helped to realise their potential, how they will be given choice and how the service provider (nursery) will make sure they are safe in the setting. They also state the expectation that service users (children) will be treated well and with dignity, will have their privacy respected, and that the centres will make sure there is equality within services.

Care Commission officers (CCOs) make sure services are keeping to the care standards through a system of inspection. Where a service is providing pre-school education, the service will be jointly inspected by the Care Commission and Her Majesty's Inspectorate of Education (HMIE).

Care Commission officers are professionals who have previous experience of working in the sector and who have an additional qualification in inspecting and regulating services: the Regulation of Care Award (ROCA). CCOs help to support children's care, learning and development by making sure the services provided for children offer an appropriate environment for care, play and learning. If CCOs feel this is not happening they can ask centres to put plans in place to make sure improvements are made. At worst they can make a request to the Sheriff to shut down a service. However, CCOs want to work with centres to make them the best they can be, so this would only happen in extreme situations.

Inspections

The Care Commission is bringing in a model of self-assessment for centres. This means that before an inspection the manager and staff of the centre need to sit down and consider how well the service is being run, where their strengths are and where they think they need to make improvements. This is then discussed with the CCO when they come to inspect. By working in partnership it is anticipated that the CCO and the centre can agree on how best to make improvements and pass on examples of good practice.

A system of self-evaluation has been used in Scotland's schools for a number of years. Schools are inspected by HMIE. HMIE use self-evaluation as part of the drive for quality improvement in Scotland's schools and nursery classes. They use the revised *The Child at the Centre: Self-evaluation in the early years* (Scottish Executive, 2000) as the focus for looking at the quality of the learning experience children receive alongside the use of the national Care Standards in nurseries. *The Child at the Centre* highlights the importance of children's successes and achievements and links to key priorities of Curriculum for Excellence. It also highlights the journey towards quality improvements and the importance of effective transitions being made from nursery to school and from home to nursery and school. You can access this document through the website of HMIE (www.hmie.gov.uk).

The Scottish Social Services Council (SSSC)

While the Care Commission inspects care services, the SSSC regulates the people working in those services. This means that practitioners working with children need to meet a required standard, follow the codes of practice and show they are competent by holding a specific qualification. This helps to protect children and to ensure they are supported in their care and learning. The SSSC has key policy objectives which are:

- to strengthen and support the professionalism of the workforce

- to protect those who use services
- to raise standards of practice in care services
- to raise public confidence in the workforce.

The SSSC's main tasks include:

- publishing Codes of Practice for all social service workers and their employers (you can read about Codes of Practice in Chapter 1)
- registering key groups of social service workers, including early education and childcare practitioners
- regulating the workforce and its training and education
- contributing to workforce planning, development of qualifications and promotion of education and training.

The Scottish Social Services Council: Regulation, registration and Codes of Practice, Scottish Social Services Council, 2008)

As an early education and childcare practitioner you will be asked to register with the SSSC as a Day Care of Children Services worker. There are three parts to this register:

- registration as a manager
- registration as a practitioner
- registration as a support worker.

Each part of the register has a specific function, and when you register with the SSSC you are registering against your job *function* not your job title. That is because the same titles can be used in this sector to describe quite different jobs; the register is concerned with *what you do* not what you are called.

The qualifications that are needed to register also relate to a function rather than a job title and can be found on the SSSC's website (www.sssc.uk.com). Below are the job functions the SSSC uses.

Manager

Managers/lead practitioners in day care services for children are defined as workers who hold responsibilities for the overall development, management and quality assurance of service provision, including the supervision of staff and the management of resources.

Practitioner

Practitioners in day care of children services are defined as workers who identify and meet the care, support and learning needs of children and contribute to the development and quality assurance of informal learning activities and/or curriculum. They may also be responsible for the supervision of other workers.

Support workers

Support workers are defined as workers who have delegated responsibility for providing care and support to children.

When you are qualified and look for a job in the early education and childcare sector you will be asked to register with the SSSC. Other workers also need to register to work with children, including nurses and teachers. Teachers are required to register with the General Teaching Council for Scotland and nurses with the Nursing and Midwifery Council. When the Care Commission come out to inspect services, they will ask if you are registered with the SSSC.

Case study *Preparing for an inspection*

Staff at Sunnyside Nursery have been told they are to be inspected by the Care Commission in a month's time. The last inspection report highlighted key areas for improvement, including making sure risk assessments are done before taking children on trips; making sure all staff are aware of the policies on health and safety; and making sure the outdoor environment for children provides better challenge for them.

Since the last inspection a new nursery manager has been appointed. She read the inspection report when she took up the post and has been working with staff since then to make sure they are all aware of policies and understand what they have to do to make sure the nursery is a safe and healthy place. She has developed new risk assessment forms by sitting down with staff and asking their views.

She has also worked with the children and staff, asking their views on purchasing new outdoor play equipment. She has suggested to the staff

that they should bring some of the nursery equipment that is usually indoors – like sand, water and blocks – outdoors.

So far she has had very positive feedback from the children about the new equipment and the relocation of activities. The children are now asking if they can take more of these outside.

The nursery staff are due to meet on Monday to look at self-assessment for the inspection.

1 Do you think the manager will be able to identify key improvements that have been made for the inspection?

2 How effective do you think it is to use the children's views as feedback for an inspection?

3 Why do you think it is more helpful to work with the staff on constructing new risk assessment policies?

How research skills can be used to inform practice and develop strategies

In Scotland's devolved parliament an election is held every four years. Sometimes the government is re-elected; sometimes there is a change of administration. New governments refresh or have new policy proposals. This can be because research indicates a particular need for them.

If you are working with children you need to keep as up to date with initiatives and policies as possible, particularly if they have a direct effect on children's lives and well-being. Sometimes you may need to do some research to find out the main priority of a particular policy or the implications of it for your day-to-day practice.

Chapter 10 describes some of the techniques you need to use for your graded unit, and some of these will be useful when you are looking at policies and initiatives.

Often guidelines will be sent directly to the centre. Good managers will alert you to the fact they have arrived and will take time in staff meetings to explain the purpose and any responsibilities you might have. However, it is good practice to keep as up to date as possible. It's also important to know ways that you can interpret the policies so that you can put them in place for children and families in an understandable way.

Keeping up to date can be hard work

Research skills to inform practice

One of the important skills you will learn on the HNC course is the skill of researching accurately. This is particularly useful as it can help you prepare helpful information for parents and children based on carefully researched facts. When you are undertaking any research it is important to be clear about what you are trying to find out. This is explained in more detail in Chapter 10.

Further research

Any policy the Scottish Government is involved in producing will be put on the government's official website (www.scotland.gov.uk). If the policy is related to children's health it is likely also to be on the 'Healthier Scotland' part of the Scottish Government website. Many government publications are free of charge. You can find this out by looking at the back of the document where you will find out how to order additional copies. It's always helpful if you know the exact title of the document you are looking for, but if you have some key words usually an Internet search engine will provide a list of possibilities for you.

How policies and other information can be presented effectively

Policy provides direction for governments and organisations by suggesting actions that are required. Information in official documents can be quite complex so it is often helpful to go to the Executive Summary where you will find the key points laid out.

Sometimes you will be asked to make new policies known to children and their parents. This requires a great deal of background reading, asking questions and research on your part to be able to do this successfully. You read in Chapter 7 about the importance of clear communication and of body language. If you are presenting complex information to parents and children, all of the skills you read about will be required. In addition, you may need to practise giving the presentation. You might want to use ICT packages such as PowerPoint as a visual aid to your presentation.

No presentation will be clear if you don't understand the content and the context of what you are telling the audience. Preparation and knowledge are essential to providing clear, accessible messages. Good presentation skills are also vital, including the skill of distilling information into key understandable points. Think about some of the lectures you have had on the HNC course – possibly the better ones are those that gave you enough information but not too much, as you can suffer from 'information overload'. This means you may need to cut down on what you are saying without losing your key message.

It is often helpful to practise the skill of public speaking. One of the most difficult audiences is an audience of peers or friends. If you can do a presentation successfully in front of them, it will help when you have to do one professionally. Always remember to speak clearly and concisely and to look at your audience rather than your notes. Remember, practice makes perfect – so practising in front of a mirror can be a good

idea. If your college has video equipment it is helpful to record your presentation then play it back. This will help you pick out any repetitious habits you have and try to correct them. You can practise giving presentations by doing the following activity.

Activity

Prepare a set of no more than six PowerPoint slides or a leaflet for parents explaining how the nursery would like to support children's dental health.

Prepare a set of no more than six PowerPoint slides or a leaflet showing how the out-of-school care club will encourage healthy eating and additional physical activity in the children who attend the setting.

Check your progress

1 What are the key family types and key features of the families highlighted in this chapter?

2 What are some of the advantages to Scotland from migration into the country?

3 How do flexible patterns of working help families to manage childcare better?

4 To what extent does poverty affect children's well-being?

5 How can immunisation support children's health and well-being?

6 In what way is sectarianism harmful to Scotland?

7 What is meant by obesity and how can it have a detrimental affect on children's well-being?

8 How can physical activity make Scotland's children healthier?

9 How does a system of regulation help provide better care and education for children?

10 How can research help you to support a better understanding of policies among children and parents?

References

Bancroft A., Wilson, S., Cunningham-Burley S., Backett-Milburn K. and Masters, H. (2004) *Parental Drug and Alcohol Misuse: Resilience and Transition among Young People*, York: Joseph Rowntree Foundation

Barclay et al. (2003) *Asylum Seekers in Scotland*, Edinburgh: Scottish Executive Social Research

Crown Office (1995), c. 36, *The Children (Scotland) Act* (1995), Edinburgh: HMSO

Crown Office (1999) *Immigration and Asylum Act*, London: HMSO

Crown Office (2001) *The Regulation of Care (Scotland) Act*, Edinburgh: TSO

Crown Office (2005) *Education (Additional Support for Learning) Act (Scotland) 2004*, Edinburgh: TSO

Communities Scotland (2007) *National Standards for Community Engagement*, Edinburgh

Equal Opportunities Commission (2006) *21st Century Dad*, Manchester: Equal Opportunities Commission

Fitzgerald, R. and McKay, A. (2006) *Gender Equality and Work in Scotland: A Review of the Evidence Base and Salient Issues*, Glasgow: Equal Opportunities Commission

Roaf, C. (2002) *Co-ordinating Services for Included Children: Joined Up Action*, Buckingham: Open University Press

Scottish Executive (1999) *Social Inclusion – Opening the door to a better Scotland*, Edinburgh

Scottish Executive (2000) *The Child at the Centre: Self-evaluation in the early years*, Edinburgh

Scottish Executive (2001) *National Care Standards (various)*, Edinburgh

Scottish Executive (2001) *For Scotland's Children: Better Integrated Children's Services*, Edinburgh

Scottish Executive (2002) *It's Everyone's Job to Make Sure I'm Alright*, Edinburgh

Scottish Executive (2004) *Being Well – Doing Well*, Edinburgh: Health Promoting Schools Unit

Scottish Executive (2004) *Health for All Children: Guidance on Implementation in Scotland*, Edinburgh

Scottish Executive (2006) *Getting It Right for Every Child*, Edinburgh

Scottish Executive (2007) *A Curriculum for Excellence: Building the Curriculum 2 – Active Learning in the Early Years*, Edinburgh

Scottish Executive (2007) *National Standards in Community Engagement*, Edinburgh

Useful websites

The Child Poverty Action Group (CPAG): www.cpag.org.uk/scotland

Children First: www.children1st.org.uk

Children in Scotland: www.childreninscotland.org.uk

General Household Survey www.statistics.gov.uk

Joseph Rowntree Foundation: www.jrf.org.uk

National Children's Homes (NCH): www.nch.org.uk

National Health Service in Scotland: www.healthscotland.com

One Parent Families Scotland: www.opfs.org.uk

Save the Children: www.savethechildren.org.uk

Scotland's census: www.scotlandspeople.gov.uk

Scottish Commission for the Regulation of Care (Care Commission): www.carecommission.com

Scottish Government: www.scotland.gov.uk

Scottish Social Services Council: www.sssc.uk.com

Chapter 10
The graded unit: a survival guide

Introduction

The graded unit is a research project and is probably the part of the HNC which causes the most anxiety to students. There is no doubt that this is designed to be a challenging piece of work, but it helps if you can view it as something which is going to be of benefit to you in future. It is my experience that the majority of students who have successfully completed the graded unit have felt that, overall, it was a positive experience. They all reported having learned a lot; with a sizeable number actually admitting to having enjoyed the process.

The graded unit is designed to allow you to demonstrate:

- all you have learned in other units of the course, and how these parts interlink and relate to each other
- a discussion of your practice in a way which proves that you can relate it to relevant theory
- your ability to undertake an investigation which allows you to improve the research skills already acquired earlier in the course, to develop new skills and to critically evaluate your work.

Undertaking the graded unit will enable you to demonstrate your developing skill as a reflective practitioner. You will also be able to enhance your knowledge in a particular area of interest, which will be of real use in your chosen area of work. Reflective practice involves self-evaluation on a regular basis and includes thinking about how and why certain approaches have been taken, examining the effectiveness of what has been done, considering ways of improving, and identifying areas of your own knowledge and skills which need to be updated.

Furthermore, in doing all the work involved in the graded unit, you will be refining and honing your core skills, particularly those of communication (written and oral), ICT, team working and problem solving.

Gaining a good grade in the graded unit may ease your path to further study if you are planning to move on to university. Indeed, some universities are already awarding conditional acceptances to students who achieve a particular grade. This is the one area of the HNC where you can demonstrate your abilities in a formal way and be rewarded by a grade which will indicate to others how successful you have been.

How can you achieve all this? This chapter is your 'survival guide' to the graded unit. It will provide you with guidance and support to help you plan, carry out and evaluate your project successfully.

In this chapter you will learn:

- The structure of the graded unit
- How to select your topic and define an aim
- How to select, devise and use research methods effectively
- How to critically analyse your data
- How to present your work
- How to reflect on your work

The structure of the graded unit

The graded unit consists of three parts:

1. a plan of action
2. an investigative report
3. an evaluation.

You will recognise that this is a familiar context for practitioners, who are involved in the process of planning, doing and reviewing on a daily basis.

Action plan

> **Key term**
>
> The **action plan** consists of the 'What? Why? How? When?' of your project.

In this section you are laying the foundations of your investigation. It is very important to get the planning stage right or you will find yourself in some difficulty at a later stage in the project. Your college tutor should be able to give you some useful guidance at this stage, but do remember that this is supposed to be an independent piece of work with as little input from tutors as possible.

You are entitled to have one formal tutorial to discuss your choice of topic and other issues related to your plan, but apart from that your tutor is not allowed to give you anything other than minimal help with your individual project. It is helpful to keep a note of what was discussed at that tutorial, as it is only too easy to forget important points. Your tutor may suggest that you use the proforma which comes with the unit descriptor for this purpose. Alternatively, your centre may have devised another form for recording the content of your discussion and any advice given.

Translated into practical terms, your planning section should consist of the following:

1. an introduction of your chosen topic with reasons why it has been selected

2. a description of how this fits into current theory, government legislation, local/national guidelines/curriculum

3. ways in which your topic relates to children's rights, needs and interests, and mention should also be made of links to other HNC mandatory units

4. an aim and objectives

5. a description of how you will develop your objectives, giving examples of your proposed methods of research and sources

6. a detailed timescale for each stage of the project.

Stage 1: Getting started

There are guidelines given in the unit descriptor as to how many words should be in each section, but as these are guidelines only your centre may decide to change these slightly.

A word of warning may be useful at this stage: you will be penalised if you go more than 10 per cent over or under the stated word count, so it is worth trying to remain as focused as possible. More guidelines to help you with this will be given later on.

Stage 2: An investigative report

This is where you implement what you have planned so thoroughly in the first stage of the project. Your report should contain the following elements:

1. a discussion of any changes made to the proposed aim/objectives as described in your planning stage

2. an investigation into each of your objectives in order to meet your aim; this may involve carrying out primary and/or secondary research

3. a presentation and critical analysis of collected data

4. a summary which pulls together all the findings of the project, relating them to appropriate units studied within the HNC

5. recommendations as to how the topic could be developed further in relation to the setting identified

6. a conclusion

7. references and acknowledgement of sources.

Stage 3: An evaluative report

Having presented your investigation, you now need to reflect upon the whole process and assess how well you have done in a number of ways. This stage should contain:

1. a brief summary (abstract) of the entire project

2. challenges you faced and how successfully you dealt with them

3. knowledge and skills you gained and how these relate to the HNC units you studied

4. an evaluation of the effectiveness of your research methods

5. an evaluation of how closely you stuck to your original plan and the effectiveness of any changes you made

6. how effectively you used communication and interpersonal skills throughout.

(A more detailed guide to each of the three stages will be given later in the chapter.)

How to select your topic and define an aim

You can find some suggested areas of study in the support notes of the SQA unit descriptor. However, this list is not exhaustive and you may want to consider another topic to investigate. It may be that your tutor has provided a limited selection of topics and you have to choose one of them. Most examples of restricted choice topics do provide students with a wide focus of interest, so it should be relatively easy for you to identify something which will be of interest to you.

Case study *Choosing an area of study*

HNC student Fiona is on a two-day-a-week placement in the baby room of a private nursery. She has been there for several weeks and is thoroughly enjoying it. During a recent class at college, she watched a DVD on heuristic play, and as she watched the babies exploring the items in the treasure basket she could see clearly how much they might be learning about shape, size, texture and sound. She hadn't noticed staff using anything like this with the babies in her placement, and when she was having a chat with her placement supervisor she mentioned the wonderful programme she had seen at college. Her supervisor was very enthusiastic, saying that it was a while since they had used anything like that in the room, and why didn't she put together some appropriate items to make a new treasure basket for the babies.

Fiona was delighted to agree to this, especially as she was beginning to wonder whether this might be an appropriate topic for her graded unit. She could see that she would be able to relate what she had been studying in theoretical perspectives regarding exploratory play to her proposed area of research. She felt that this would demonstrate Piaget's theory of intellectual development, i.e. the child at the sensori-motor stage of learning. In addition, Tina Bruce's view of the importance of heuristic play would be interesting to examine further.

Back in college, Fiona discussed the idea with her tutor. The tutor thought that this was an excellent choice of topic, and asked Fiona to think about some possible aims which would enable her to focus her study more specifically, rather than simply 'An investigation into treasure basket/heuristic play'. The tutor also asked Fiona to consider how the topic might relate to current thinking as regards children's rights, the curriculum and appropriate legislation/guidelines.

After some thought, Fiona came up with the title 'To investigate the benefits of heuristic play using treasure baskets with children between 6 and 9 months'. She was able to see how this aim would link to UNCRC Article 31 (relating to the child's right to play) and to the Birth to Three guidance (*Birth to Three: supporting our youngest children*, Learning and Teaching Scotland, 2005), in particular Section 2: The importance of early experiences.

Alternatively, your tutor may be open to any sensible suggestion you come up with. However, you must arrive at an agreement with your tutor that this is an appropriate area of study before you proceed further.

There are a number of sound reasons to select a topic, even when you are faced with a restricted list. Some of these reasons are described below.

Your own personal interest

This may have developed from your own experiences or from those of your siblings, children or friends. For example, Michelle is very interested in how children's handwriting develops. Her own handwriting is rather untidy and difficult to read, and throughout her childhood she was constantly criticised for 'not trying hard enough to write neatly'. This is an area she would like to explore further.

The results of an observation

Your interest may have been aroused by an observation you made in your work with children. For example, James noticed that the boys in his nursery do a lot of running around and seem to prefer physical play and construction to the more language-based activities. He would like to find out whether this is the case in general or an isolated example.

To improve your knowledge

There may be a topic about which you do not feel as knowledgeable as you think you ought to be and you recognise how important this understanding will be in your future work with children. For example, Paula hears her manager discussing 'free-flow play' with another member of staff, saying how important it is for children. Paula has a reasonable idea what is meant by the term but wants to develop a deeper understanding.

To explore an area of current interest

There may be a topic which is exciting a lot of interest in the media or the subject of recent legislation/new guidelines. For example, Jahi has been surprised by how many references she has seen to outdoor play recently. It seems that this is an area which is attracting a lot of attention from the press and she has read several articles which indicate that children are being prevented by their parents and carers from playing outside. This is due to fears for their safety, fuelled by several recent high profile cases involving the abuse of children. There seems to be a concern that children are being over-protected and that, on many levels including physical and emotional well-being, children's healthy development is being compromised.

You should also consider how your chosen area of study is going to relate to other learning which has taken place in units across the HNC, in particular the mandatory units. You may find the following checklist helpful when you reach the point where you have a possible topic in mind. These are issues which you should also consider before making a final decision.

1. Is this project going to be of practical use in my future work?

2. Am I interested in my proposed topic?

3. Is there plenty of material available for my research (books, magazines, websites, newspapers, journals, etc.)?

4. Can I see links with the HNC units I have been studying, in particular the mandatory units?

5. Is there a link with children's rights, needs or interests?

6. Will it be possible for me to carry out observations (and/or other methods of primary research) in my workplace/placement?

7. If appropriate, can I devise activities/experiences which will aid my research to be implemented in my workplace/placement?

Both of the examples in the spider charts opposite illustrate how you can take an appropriate topic and relate it successfully to each of the mandatory and at least a couple of the optional units. Remember that this is one of the essential requirements of the project.

Let us examine how you might arrive at a specific topic to investigate after having done a spider chart/mind map. This will also help to clarify the links with other HNC units.

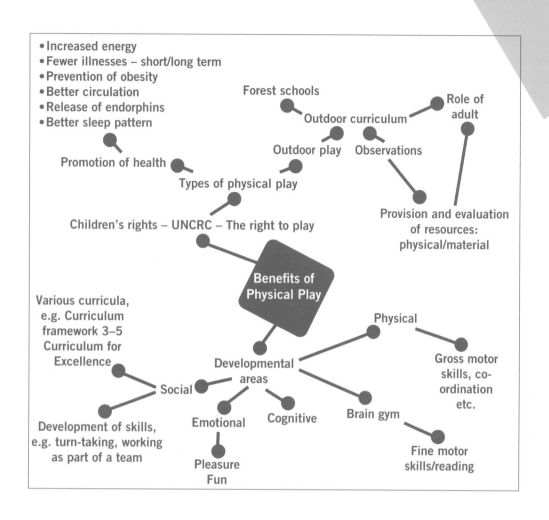

- Increased energy
- Fewer illnesses – short/long term
- Prevention of obesity
- Better circulation
- Release of endorphins
- Better sleep pattern

Promotion of health

Forest schools

Outdoor curriculum

Role of adult

Outdoor play   Observations

Types of physical play

Children's rights – UNCRC – The right to play

Provision and evaluation of resources: physical/material

Benefits of Physical Play

Various curricula, e.g. Curriculum framework 3–5 Curriculum for Excellence

Physical

Developmental areas

Gross motor skills, co-ordination etc.

Social

Development of skills, e.g. turn-taking, working as part of a team

Emotional   Cognitive   Brain gym

Pleasure Fun

Fine motor skills/reading

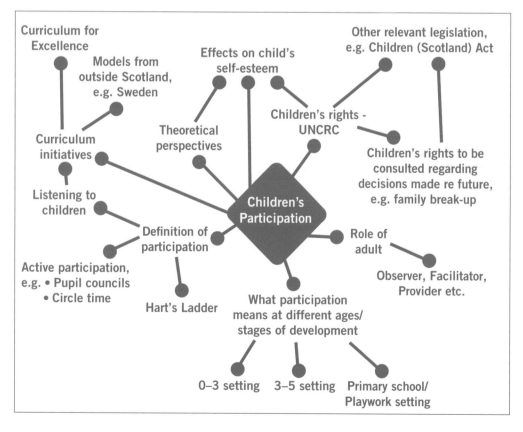

Curriculum for Excellence

Models from outside Scotland, e.g. Sweden

Effects on child's self-esteem

Other relevant legislation, e.g. Children (Scotland) Act

Theoretical perspectives

Children's rights - UNCRC

Curriculum initiatives

Children's rights to be consulted regarding decisions made re future, e.g. family break-up

Listening to children

Children's Participation

Definition of participation

Role of adult

Active participation, e.g. • Pupil councils • Circle time

Observer, Facilitator, Provider etc.

Hart's Ladder

What participation means at different ages/ stages of development

0–3 setting   3–5 setting   Primary school/ Playwork setting

For example, you may have decided that you wanted to look more closely at the benefits of physical play. However, this topic in itself is somewhat large for the scale of project required, so it is important to refine it into something narrower and more manageable. Here are a few suggestions as to what you may decide to choose as an aim:

- to investigate the importance of physical play in promoting children's health
- to examine the importance of outdoor physical play
- to research the possible effects of physical play on social *or* emotional *or* intellectual development
- to consider the role of the adult in the promotion of children's physical play.

Activity

Taking the spider chart on children's participation, try to compile a list of possible aims from this more general topic. You might find this a useful exercise to do with a fellow student, to compare some of your ideas.

Consider the following aims and try to devise an appropriate list of questions which would form your objectives for each. Again, you may find it helpful to work with a fellow student, bouncing ideas off each other.

- To investigate meaningful choices of play opportunity for children in an after-school setting
- To examine recent initiatives regarding children's diet and how they are being implemented in a breakfast club
- To investigate children's learning styles and how they are supported in a P7 classroom
- To study the short-term effects of daily Brain Gym sessions on a group of four children in a P2 class, focusing particularly on handwriting

Having arrived at an appropriate aim which is acceptable to both yourself and your tutor, you need to consider the ways in which you are going to achieve your aim.

Defining objectives

Even though you have narrowed down the focus of study from your original area of interest, you now have to think about forming objectives which will focus your investigation further. You could think about these objectives in terms of being rather like 'bite-sized' pieces of your investigation. They will ease your progress through the project, making it more manageable in that it will be more difficult to stray away from your aim.

A useful way to tackle this would be to examine your aim and think about questions arising from it. It might help to view this from the perspective of someone who knows very little about the subject generally. What are the questions this mythical person might want to ask? These questions will form your objectives. For example, if your aim is 'To examine the ways in which circle time in P1 can support children's self-esteem in becoming "confident individuals" as detailed by 'Curriculum for Excellence'', then the questions arising from this include:

1. What is circle time?
2. Why is self-esteem in children considered to be important?
3. What is Curriculum for Excellence?
4. What are some appropriate activities which could be employed to promote self-esteem for children in P1?

This part of the project is not easy but it is important to define your aim and objectives as clearly and unambiguously as you can. Good, clear objectives will make the next steps of your planning and subsequent investigation much more straightforward.

How to select, devise and use research methods effectively

Once you are satisfied with your objectives, the next step is to consider:

- how am I going to research each objective specifically (i.e. observations, questionnaires, interviews, etc.)
- what reading do I need to do to provide further evidence (websites, textbooks, periodicals, etc.)?

Conducting a piece of research, whether it is a PhD thesis or the graded unit, will involve a variety of ways of gathering information. These can be divided into two categories: primary and secondary research. Your project should have elements of both of these.

> ### Key terms
>
> **Primary research** is concerned with original information which has been gathered by the researcher him/herself. It includes questionnaires, surveys, interviews and observations, photographs and video material.
>
> **Secondary research** is concerned with the gathering of information which has been generated and published by others. This information could be in the form of books, magazines, newspapers, professional journals, research papers, magazines, government papers, curriculum guidelines, national/local policies or resources from the Internet (the list is not exhaustive).

Pros and cons of primary research
Pros

- You can be quite precise about the kind of information you are seeking (e.g. you only ask the questions about which you need an answer). As a result, your data should be relevant to your investigation.

- Your results will be up-to-the-minute and current.

Cons

- There may be practical difficulties associated with actually carrying out this method of research, e.g. people may be unwilling to be interviewed/filmed/answer questions.

- This method of research is only as good as the researcher's questions/interview technique/ selected type of observation.

- Organising and presenting the data can be problematic.

Having said all this, well-planned and organised primary research is an effective and persuasive means of collecting evidence, and is an important part of any valid investigation.

Pros and cons of secondary research
Pros

- You will be able to make use of the work of those who are experts in your area of interest.

- As a result, you will become immensely more knowledgeable about the subject, allowing your opinions and judgements to be better informed.

- There is often a huge amount of available information, easily and inexpensively accessible via public and college libraries together with the Internet.

Cons

- It is very easy to become side-tracked by something which has caught your interest but has no immediate relevance to your study.

- This method can generate huge amounts of material, especially when using the Internet, and the task of organising all this information can feel quite overwhelming. You will need to be very clear about what to use and what to discard.

- It can be very tempting to concentrate most of your secondary research on the Internet. In doing this you could be collecting material which is not necessarily of good quality. You may also miss out on first-class information which can be obtained from other secondary sources. This can make your project rather restricted as regards breadth of sources used, and this would be reflected in a poorer overall mark in your graded unit.

Further research

For more information about research methods generally, read pages 296–305 of *BTEC National Children's Care, Learning and Development* (Squire, 2007).

Information gathered by primary and secondary research is known as either *qualitative* or *quantitative* data. You will probably find that the information you want to gather comes into both of these categories.

Key terms

Qualitative information is concerned with people's experiences, opinions, knowledge/understanding and beliefs, for example, a person's first day at school. It tends to be more in-depth and gained from a relatively small sample, for example, interviews with three people.

Quantitative information is concerned with numbers, for example, how many children are under 5 years old? This data is less in-depth, but gained from a relatively large sample, such as questionnaires completed by 30 people.

By looking at different ways of providing evidence through carrying out primary research, examining others' previous research and reading a variety of source materials, you will be 'triangulating' your research. This will make your findings more convincing (valid).

Activity

Identify whether each of the following questions is concerned with qualitative or quantitative information.

- The highest temperature recorded in Scotland in 2007
- Opinions of the Scottish parliament building
- Public understanding of the effects of global warming
- Debate as to whether there is life after death
- The percentage of the population in Scotland who are vegetarian

Key terms

Triangulation is when more than one research method is used to compare and combine different sources of evidence. This helps to overcome the weakness of using only one research method.

Validity: according to Hucker (*Research Methods in Health, Care and Early Years*, 2001, page 73), 'For data to be considered valid, the method used to collect the data and the focus of the research must be relevant to the conclusion drawn.'

Ensuring your research is valid

If one of your objectives was to investigate the type of play undertaken by 4-year-old boys in the nursery, some valid methods of research to establish this might be:

- observing boys at play in the nursery
- interviewing a selection of boys in the nursery
- giving out relevant questionnaires to nursery staff
- reading appropriate articles in publications such as *Nursery World*
- researching up-to-date findings about the play habits of boys between 3 and 5 years old.

Some examples of methods which would not be valid are:

- sending a questionnaire to parents of boys in the nursery (unless they spend considerable amounts of time there, how do they actually know their sons' play habits? Children do not necessarily display the same behaviours at home and in other contexts)
- observing the girls in the nursery (for obvious reasons!)
- interviewing one boy in the nursery (the play behaviour of one boy cannot be attributed to all other boys of that age and in that context).

Ensuring your findings are reliable

Another factor when considering possible ways of researching may be the reliability of your chosen method.

Key term

Reliability is interpreted by Hucker (*Research Methods in Health, Care and Early Years*, page 72) as follows: 'Reliable data means that if a different researcher carried out the piece of research at a different time, the results would be similar or at least in line with what was previously found.'

If another person carried out an observation under similar conditions to that which you had already done, for example they observed the same boys in the same nursery but on another day, then if the findings were similar the method could be said to have reliability. Of course, you would not be expected to prove this for your project, but you ought to be able to indicate that, at least in theory, your piece of research could be replicated.

Ethical considerations

One extremely important issue to consider when planning how you intend to gather your research data is that of ethics.

Key term

Ethics describes a moral code about behaviour. Ethical behaviour is that which is considered honest and decent.

We all have our own system of ethics which guides and helps us to make decisions about every aspect of our lives. A person's particular code will be determined by the way they have been brought up, their attitudes and beliefs. You will have discussed attitudes and beliefs in Chapters 1 and 4.

Consider this

How do you view the following?

- Gay couples having children
- Smacking children
- Children's television viewing habits
- Eating meat as a moral issue
- Human responsibility towards the planet

It might be interesting to discuss these topics with friends and/or fellow students. Do you all hold the same opinions on these issues? What are some of the factors which may have contributed to individual moral positions?

Ethics have always to be considered in the planning of any research. You have to be very sure that the way in which you go about your research project does not upset or harm others just so that you can gain useful information.

Further research

You will find details of some extremely disturbing research which was done in the fairly recent past on pages 324–5 of *BTEC National Children's Care, Learning and Development*.

Seeking permission

Before starting your research, it is important to gain permission from the appropriate person in a position of authority in your workplace or placement. You can take advice from your supervisor about this. Your supervisor will be able to indicate who needs to grant permission and how this can be gained – whether by letter or by approaching the individual in person.

You might find the following good practice checklist helpful when considering your means of data collection.

1. All information gathered must be treated as confidential – that includes anonymising any information as necessary.

2. All people willing to take part must be assured of confidentiality.

3. People taking part should be made aware of exactly what they are agreeing to do.

4. Participants should also be told how your research findings will be used.

5. Parental permission should be obtained if you plan to involve children directly.

6. Letters should be sent to parents outlining the aim of the project and asking for written permission for their child(ren) to participate, enclosing a tear-off slip to be returned.

7. Young children should be consulted within the limits of their ability to understand, and every effort should be made to explain what you intend to do and what your expectation is of them; this would be done verbally.

8. It should be made very clear to participating children that they do not have to take part, and that they can withdraw their involvement if and whenever they like.

9. Older children might like to be given a simplified information letter detailing the aim of the project, what kind of information you are seeking and what their role would be.

10. You should also seek parents' and children's written permission if asking them to participate in anything which would be outside their normal day-to-day activity within the school/centre, such as questionnaires and interviews.

Case study *Handing out a questionnaire to young children*

Sarah is on placement in a P2/3 class and is basing her graded unit on Golden Time. She has spoken with the head teacher who has given approval for Sarah to write to the parents explaining about her research and asking permission to distribute questionnaires to the children in the class. The questionnaires are designed for very young children to be able to use.

Sarah discusses with the teacher the best time for the children to complete the questionnaire, and they decide to do it the following Monday. Unfortunately the teacher is off sick on the appointed day and the class is taught by a supply teacher. Sarah tells her what has been planned regarding the questionnaire and it is decided that she should just go ahead. Sarah gives out the sheet of questions to the children. She tells them that they must not discuss their answers with anyone else and complete each question as carefully as possible. A few of the children appear to be a little anxious and reluctant to start, but Sarah smiles reassuringly at them and says that they don't have very long to finish as it will soon be lunchtime. The children all complete the questionnaire.

The next morning the head teacher comes into the class and asks to speak to Sarah. She asks if Sarah has any idea why the mother of one of the children in her class would have phoned to complain in the strongest terms about the fact that her daughter had been distraught since coming home from school the previous day. The child had said that they had been given a test that morning by the student, and that she was scared that she hadn't answered the questions properly.

1. Why did the child think that the questionnaire was some sort of test?

2. How should Sarah have approached the distribution of the questionnaire to the children? (You can consider this question in the light of Chapter 2: Children and young people's rights).

3. Suggest what Sarah might do now in order to put matters right:
   - with the child
   - with the parent
   - with the other children in the class
   - with the head teacher.

You may find the sample letter below useful as a proforma for asking permission of parents to involve their children in your research.

The following is a sample of a covering letter which older children could be given in the same scenario.

Dear Parent/Guardian,

I am studying towards a Higher National Certificate in Early Education and Childcare at Queensferry College and am doing a placement in your child's nursery/after-school club/class.

Part of the course requires me to carry out a project about some aspect of early education and childcare. I have decided to base mine on children's reading habits, and as part of the information I need to gather, I would like to include children's questionnaires. The questions will be related to children's favourite type of book and whether they enjoy reading. This will be fully explained to the children, and each child can choose not to take part if they prefer. The questions will be suitable for the children's ages and will be checked over by my supervisor before being distributed.

The children will be asked not to write their names, and all information gathered will be treated as confidential. I would be very happy to discuss any further detail regarding my project with anyone who would like more information. My contact details are below.

Please indicate on the tear-off slip below whether you would be prepared to allow your child to take part in the project (as described above), and return the slip in the addressed envelope provided.

Many thanks for your help.

Dear (use child's name)

As you know, I am a student from Queensferry College on placement with you for the next few weeks. While I am here, I have some work to do for my college which means that I have to find out more about children's reading habits. Perhaps you can help me with this work by answering some questions about the kind of things you like to read and whether you read in your spare time? You would not need to worry about what you write in your answers, as I will be the only person to see them.

This is not something you have to do – it is completely up to you whether you take part or not. The questions are not hard and I will be happy to explain any that you are not sure about. The whole thing will probably take about ten minutes to do.

Have a think about it over the next couple of days and discuss it with your friends and family. You can also have a chat with me if there is anything else you want to know about it.

Thank you for reading this.

Primary research methods

You will now consider some methods of information-gathering in more detail. You will examine what each entails, the pros and cons, some tips and some surrounding issues.

Questionnaires

The questionnaire is one of the most commonly used and potentially effective methods of gathering information by researchers. However, it is important that it is carefully and appropriately structured. Questionnaires can be a positive minefield, where a variety of mistakes will make the finished product at best of limited value and at worst harmful.

It is appropriate to use a questionnaire as a method of primary research for the following reasons:

- it can be custom made to suit your particular needs and that of your project
- you can potentially obtain information from a wide number and variety of people
- apart from the formulation of the questions themselves, it need not be a time-consuming exercise on the part of the researcher, for example, if people are asked to complete them in their own time.

The drawbacks of using questionnaires include the following:

- The number of completed questionnaires returned is often disappointingly low. This may be due to the researcher not having direct contact with the respondent. Also, the questions may be about matters which have no meaning or interest to them.
- It is not the best way of gathering any in-depth information, and there is not the possibility of asking people to expand on answers if they have responded by post.
- People may misinterpret or misunderstand the questions.
- People will not necessarily be truthful when answering. They are more likely to give the answer they think they should or the one they think you would like to hear. For example, if you ask 'How many portions of fruit and vegetables do you eat in a day?', most people know that a healthy diet demands that they eat a minimum of five portions per day and many may be reluctant to admit to not doing so.

It is possible, to gain more in-depth information by administering the questionnaire on a one-to-one basis. In that way you can ask for clarification or expansion of answers. However, this is extremely time-consuming, so you would have to weigh up whether the information gathered is worth the time spent collecting it.

It is also possible to administer the questionnaire to a group of people at the same time. This would be appropriate with groups of children, but the younger the child is the smaller the group should be. The advantage of this is that you would have a larger proportion of completed questionnaires.

In order for a questionnaire to be of real use, a couple of issues should be considered first:

- Is a questionnaire the best way of gaining the information you need?
- Have you done sufficient secondary research to gain a clear understanding of the nature of the evidence to be sought?

If your answer to both of these questions is 'yes', you should then go on to consider how best to structure your questionnaire. Think about:

1. the type of questions you wish to ask
2. who you are going to ask; Hucker (*Research Methods in Health, Care and Early Years*, pages 89–92) provides very useful examples of different types of samples you may wish to consider
3. how your questionnaire will be distributed (by post, by hand, or in some cases by telephone)
4. how many questionnaires you will distribute
5. a covering letter/introduction (sometimes known as a 'preamble') which will include:
   - the nature of your study
   - an assurance of confidentiality
   - clear instructions as to how to complete the questionnaire
   - an estimate of how long it will take to complete
   - the deadline for its return.

Types of questions

Closed questions, are those that require a yes/no (or similarly narrow) response. They are useful if you are only looking for a simple answer, such as whether or not something has happened. It would be the type of question you might pose when seeking quantitative data. However, this type of question has little value if you want to elicit more detailed information. Example of closed questions include:

- Do you eat fish?

- What time did you get up this morning?

- Did you watch *X Factor* last night?

The main advantage of closed questions is that it is easy to organise and present the data, perhaps in the form of a table or graph (there will be more detail on data presentation later in the chapter). The downside is that the information will lack depth and detail.

Open questions will encourage more than a minimum response, for example:

- How would you describe your first day at college?

- Supposing you won £5,000, how would you spend the money?

- How do you like to pass the time while on holiday?

Open questions are useful in that they can provide detailed, interesting information often based on people's views and experiences. However, as these are likely to differ from person to person, you may find it difficult to find a concise way of presenting the data.

Scale questions are where a statement is put forward with which the reader has to agree or disagree. This is not as straightforward as it may appear, as often people's opinions are not definite. An example of this type of question would be:

- To what extent do you agree with the following statement? Please circle your preferred answer.

The age when children start school should be delayed until 6 years.

Strongly agree – Agree – Neither agree nor disagree – Disagree – Disagree strongly

Ranking questions are those seeking information about people's opinions and views. The reader is asked to number a list of options by their importance. An example of this type of question might be:

- In order of preference, from most to least, number your favourite type of film (1 being your favourite):
  - Thriller
  - Horror
  - Romantic
  - Science fiction
  - Costume drama

Choosing from a list of options is another type of ranking question. For example:

- If you were invited out for a meal, which of the following types of restaurant would you choose? Please circle your response.
  - Indian
  - Italian
  - Chinese
  - French
  - Mexican
  - Other (please state which)

Some common pitfalls of questionnaires

Examples of common pitfalls when asking questions are described below.

- *Questions which are too wide in their scope* are easy to misinterpret. This will result in responses that provide too much information which is then difficult to analyse and present. For example, the question 'What do you think of the prime minister?' could be interpreted in many ways depending on the perception of the person being questioned. For instance, it could be understood as inviting comment on the prime minister as a person, a politician and leader of his party, an international statesperson or even his/her appearance! Therefore, it is extremely important to carefully word the question to prevent ambiguity and to ensure responses will provide the right amount of information.

- *Asking questions which are not specifically relevant to your aim* will mean that you are left with a lot of superfluous material that you do not know what to do with! (What would this indicate about the *validity* of your questionnaire?)

- *Questions which assume something* about the person you are questioning will be flawed if your assumptions are incorrect. The activity below shows some examples of this.

Activity

Spot the assumption:

1. Last time you travelled by plane, which airport did you leave from?
2. Did you send your dad a Father's Day card?
3. Do you prefer beef or venison?
4. What method of transport do you use to go to and from work?
5. What did you get for Christmas?

- *Asking questions which are intrusive or inappropriate* is likely to cause offence and must be avoided. It would be safe to say that rarely, if ever, are these type of questions designed deliberately to upset; all the more reason to examine the wording and the subject matter carefully.

> Even with the best intentions, researchers can touch upon subjects which may be painful or difficult for their subjects. (*Doing Your Early Years Research Project: A Step-by-Step Guide*, G. Roberts-Holmes, 2005, page 56)

It is good practice, and should be mandatory, for you to run questions intended for a questionnaire past your work/placement supervisor and your college tutor.

Consider this

Why might the following questions cause offence/upset?

1. Why are you a single parent?
2. Research tells us that parents should read to their children as often as possible. Do you read bedtime stories to your children?
3. Do your children eat the recommended five portions of fruit and vegetables a day?
4. How much time does your child spend watching television on an average day?

- *Asking leading questions* is one of the recognised disadvantages of questionnaires and will result in participants giving you the answer they think you are looking for. Therefore, you have to be very careful not to encourage them to think that you are looking for a particular response. For example, the question 'Would you agree that watching television is bad for children's social development?' leaves the respondent in no doubt as to what the questioner's position is on this issue. Perhaps a better way of expressing this question would be 'How do you think that children's social development may be affected through watching television?'

- *Asking questions which include too much jargon* will discourage participants from answering them. People want to answer questions where the language is accessible.

Key term

Jargon is a specialised kind of language used among particular groups (e.g. professions such as doctors or lawyers, sportsmen/women, actors, etc.) which is easily understood by its members. Jargon poses no problem when used only within these groups, but can sound almost like another language to others, e.g. the terms 'adjuvant therapy' and 'bilge rat' are jargon that are likely only to be understood by those working in medical and naval engineering professions respectively. Inappropriate use of jargon can make people feel alienated and excluded.

Consider this

Can you think of any professional words/ phrases which you use in early education and childcare which might be incomprehensible to those not in this line of work? How might you phrase them differently?

If your questionnaire is too long or too complicated, the participant may choose not to respond

Checklist for effective questionnaires

1. Have you written a covering letter which includes the following:

    - details of your research and how the respondent's information will be useful (and used)
    - clear instructions on how to complete the questionnaire
    - an estimate of how long the questionnaire should take to complete
    - an assurance of confidentiality
    - an assurance that any participant has the right to change their mind at any point
    - details of the date by which the completed questionnaire should be returned
    - an addressed envelope for its return (stamped if it has to be posted)
    - your contact details in case somebody wishes to contact you regarding any aspect of the questionnaire or the information you require
    - your thanks for the respondent's time and effort?

2. Have you made your questionnaire as short as possible? Most of the people you are targeting are extremely busy, so will take one look at an over-long list of questions and consign it to the nearest drawer to be completed 'later'. Very often 'later' never comes! It is a good idea to keep your questionnaire as brief as possible.

3. Have you kept your questions as simple and straightforward as possible?

4. Is the language you have used reader friendly and jargon free?

5. Have you placed the easiest questions at the beginning, increasing in difficulty towards the end?

6. Have you used a variety of types of question to keep the reader's interest?

7. Have you kept the questions which require a longer answer for the latter part of your questionnaire, and provided adequate space for longer responses? It can put people off if they are faced with longer questions at the beginning.

8. Have you made sure that the layout and print are clear and easy to follow?

9. Have you run your questionnaire past your college tutor and workplace/placement supervisor to see whether they approve it?

Activity

In the text box below and on the next page is an example of a questionnaire which has several design faults. Can you spot them?

Clearly, this exaggerated example contains many more mistakes than you are likely to make if you have followed the guidelines carefully. However, one or more of these may occur in your questionnaire if your preparation is not meticulous.

Dear Parent

I am an HNC student on placement in your child's school, and would like to ask you to complete a questionnaire about your children's eating habits. This would be very helpful for my research, and I would appreciate your participation.

Please return the completed questionnaire to me at the school as soon as possible.

Question 1   How many children do you have and what are their ages?

Question 2   Do any of the family have specialised dietary requirements? If so, what are they and how many follow this regime?

Question 3   Do your primary school age children take school lunches? (If yes, proceed to Question 5, if no, please go to Question 4)

Question 4   Do your children take packed lunches to school / come home for lunch? (Please circle which one applies)

Question 5 (Complete this if your child takes packed lunches)

Please circle which of the following your child(ren) is likely to have in their lunchbox on a daily basis:

- Sandwich
- Cake
- Biscuit
- Crisps
- Chocolate

- Sweets
- Fruit
- Fizzy drinks
- Fruit juice
- Water

Question 6 If you have not included fruit, please say why, bearing in mind that we are advised by HEBS (Health Education Board for Scotland) to eat at least five pieces of fruit or vegetables daily.

Question 7 (Please complete this question if your primary-school aged children usually come home from school for lunch)

What do you provide for lunch for your children?

- A cooked meal containing vegetables
- Home-made soup
- A ready meal (junk food)
- Sandwiches
- Crisps
- Yogurt
- Cake

- Biscuits
- Chocolate/sweets
- Fizzy drinks
- Water
- Fruit juice
- Milk

Question 8 Does your child take a snack to school for playtime? Yes/No

Question 9 What is it likely to be?

Question 10 Does your child have a choice as to what they eat, or are they expected to eat whatever is provided?

Question 11 Would you say that, as a family, you eat at least five fruit and/or vegetables per day?

Question 12 If not, please indicate why.

- Don't like fruit
- Don't like vegetables
- Can't afford to buy them
- Other reason

Question 13 Are you aware of the constituents of a good balanced diet, vis-à-vis vitamins and minerals, monounsaturated and polyunsaturated fats, proteins, simple and complex carbohydrates?

Question 14 (a) Would you say that any of your children are overweight?

(b) If yes, do you relate this to their diet?

(c) What other factors do you think may have caused their tendency towards obesity? (Please circle those you think may be contributory factors)

- Lack of exercise
- Too much TV and/or computer games
- Heredity

Interviews

The advantages of interviews include:

- it is possible to gain a lot of qualitative information and in more depth than from other forms of research

- any misunderstandings regarding questions can be explained at the time, reducing the likelihood of inappropriate answers

- because interviews are dependent on the interaction between two people, if you are able to develop a good rapport with your interviewee, you may get far more information than if a questionnaire had been used

- you can ask for more details or for the answer to be explained more clearly.

The disadvantages of conducting interviews include:

- interviews tend to be extremely time-consuming, which is an important issue to consider when you are involved in small-scale research over a relatively short period

- you need to have very good social interaction skills so that you can communicate effectively; it is important to be able to put your respondent at ease and to spot any signs which may indicate that they are finding the interview difficult or stressful

- it is relatively easy to influence answers without intending to, for example your body language, facial expressions, tone of voice and gestures can give clues as to your own attitudes and opinions, and this may affect the objectivity of your results

- it can be difficult to analyse and record your results, as you may have gathered large amounts of varied information; consequently, you may find it difficult to draw conclusions based on this method alone.

Consider the following points before going any further with planning to use interviews.

- Will the information gained through interviewing be useful to you in meeting the aim of your project?

- Can you use it to triangulate other findings?

- Do you have sufficient time available to make this a realistic method of researching?

- Do you have appropriate interviewees in mind? If so, are they likely to consent?

- Is the time during which you could carry out interviews likely to be convenient to your prospective interviewees, given that they are likely to be busy people?

Having asked yourself these questions, and as a result being relatively certain that this is a valid method of research for your project, you should then consider what type of interview you will carry out.

Structured (formal) interviews

This type of interview involves constructing an interview schedule. This is a list of the questions you intend to ask, written in the order in which you will ask them, and is similar to a questionnaire. It is important to use only the questions as they are written, in the same order with no additional questions.

The advantages of structured interviews include:

- because you are asking exactly the same questions to each interviewee, the results should be easier to analyse and present

- it makes the results more reliable

- it is likely to be less time-consuming.

The disadvantages of structured interviews include:

- you may be missing out on very useful and interesting information

- if your questions are not as well thought out as they should have been, there is no opportunity for you to address this during the interview.

Unstructured (informal) interviews

This method of interviewing consists of the interviewer having only a list of points or issues to be discussed. It allows the interviewee more scope for answering and enables the interviewer to 'probe' for more details. This may be required when the respondent does not give a very full answer and you feel that more detail would be preferable. Probing questions ask for deeper, more thoughtful answers. Here are some examples of how you might phrase such questions.

- What do you think might happen if…?

- Why do you think that this happened/didn't happen?

- Have you considered other ways to…?

- How do you feel about…?

- How did you come to this conclusion?

- If you had the choice…?

- What did you have in mind when you…?

- What were you expecting to happen?

- Can you say a little more about…?

- Could you give me an example of the kind of thing you are talking about?

However, remember to use these questions with sensitivity. You should not probe so deeply that you make your respondent feel uncomfortable, or stray into territory which is neither relevant nor appropriate.

The advantages of unstructured interviews are:

- it is possible that you will gather extremely interesting and useful information

- if you do not get satisfactory responses, you can make use of probing questions.

The disadvantages of unstructured interviews are:

- it may be very difficult to analyse and present your findings

- your results may be less reliable

- this can be an incredibly time-consuming method of interviewing

- potential respondents may not be so keen to participate if they are not assured that everyone will be asked the same questions.

Semi-structured interviews

This type of interview is a combination of the other two, in that there is a mixture of structured questions together with a more informal list of topics for discussion. It also allows an opportunity for 'follow-up' discussion.

How should I record the interview?

You need to consider whether you will try to write down answers as people give them, perhaps using a kind of shorthand (either your own or the real thing). This is probably not the best way of doing it, as it will be difficult for you to give the interviewee your full attention at the same time. There is also the danger of missing part of the response and perhaps having to interrupt the flow by having to ask the interviewee to repeat something.

A better alternative is to use a digital recorder or tape machine to record the interview, bearing in mind that you would first need the interviewee's permission. The beauty of this is that you can relax and concentrate on the interview itself. However, it could have the result of making the interviewee feel a little self-conscious, which can affect the quality of response. The other important issue is that you will then have to transcribe the interview, which is extremely time-consuming.

What do I need to do next?

- Approach the person or people who you have decided to interview, asking them formally if they would be prepared to take part.

- As with questionnaires, you should give them details about the nature of your research, tell them how their information will be used and assure them of confidentiality.

- Give the interviewee a rough idea of how long the interview might take.

- Ask whether they would agree to the interview being taped.

- Ask whether they would like to see a copy of the questions beforehand.

- Assure the participant that they can ask you anything related to the project and see your completed work.

- Try to arrange a mutually convenient time and place where the interview can be held.

Having obtained your participant's permission, you need to decide on the format for your interview.

Constructing your interview

If your interview is to be even partly structured, you need to compose the questions with care. Many of the rules applying to questionnaires apply here also, for example:

- questions should be clear and unambiguous

- language should be jargon free and comprehensible, without being patronising

- leading questions should not be used nor those which make assumptions about prior knowledge and experiences

- care should be taken to avoid intrusive questions or deeply contentious issues.

Conducting the interview – a good practice checklist

1. Make sure that you are sufficiently prepared in terms of your background reading and research into the subject.

2. Indicate how long the interview will take and then aim to stick to this timescale.

3. Ensure that the venue you have chosen is suitable, for example that there are no distractions such as noise or excessive heat or cold.

4. Beforehand, make sure that you have all you require, for example notebook, pens, pencils and tape recorder with all necessary accessories.

5. Arrive in good time.

6. Remember to thank the interviewee for agreeing to participate.

7. Give a brief summary of what you intend to do, explaining how this will contribute towards your project (the preamble).

8. Try to put the interviewee at ease by starting with simple, unchallenging questions.

9. Keep an eye on the time, as you do not want to take up any more of the interviewee's precious time than you have negotiated.

10. If using an unstructured/semi-structured approach, be prepared to 'probe' if you need more information than is being offered.

11. Remain sensitive at all times to any possible distress or discomfort your questions may be causing.

12. If there are visible signs of stress, such as difficulty in answering, a quavering voice or obvious physical agitation, you need to move on quickly.

13. Adopt a non-judgemental approach and listen to answers respectfully, whether you agree with what is being said or not.

14. Be an active listener. If you find it difficult to concentrate on what the other person is saying, try to mentally repeat their words, which will help you to focus. If you use techniques such as smiling, nodding and leaning forward slightly towards the person, they will feel that you are paying attention.

15. Do not interrupt the interviewee.

Case study *Conducting an interview*

Robbie, an HNC student working in an after-school club, had decided to carry out a number of interviews with appropriate people whom he hoped could provide some insight into his graded unit topic. As he wanted to find out more about the ways in which the children in the club could be motivated towards choosing more outdoor play, he approached one of the lecturers in health and recreation at his local FE college to ask whether he would be prepared to take part in an interview. The lecturer (Paul) agreed to do so enthusiastically. They agreed that the interview would take place the following Thursday, at 4.30 pm, at the college.

For several days beforehand, Robbie thought about the kind of questions he might ask, telling himself that he really ought to be writing them down. However, Robbie was pretty busy and he was also trying to arrange his flatmate's surprise 21st birthday party, which was due to take place the night after his interview with Paul. He didn't really feel the need to do too much background reading, as he felt quite confident that this would not be necessary for the interview.

On Wednesday, just before finishing work, Robbie told his manager about the fact that he would need to leave work early the following day to reach the college by 4.30 pm. The manager was furious, as this was the first she had heard of it, and told him that his lack of appropriate organisation was unacceptable.

Robbie spent the evening with some friends at his local pub quiz night. After the quiz had finished and he had enjoyed a few pints, he decided that he had better go home and do some reading to prepare for tomorrow's interview. However, by this time he was feeling a little sleepy, and decided that a good night's sleep would be more beneficial.

On Thursday afternoon Robbie played football with some of the children. Suddenly, he realised that it was 4.10 pm, and there was no way that he could get to the college by bus and still arrive in time. He phoned his mum who gave him an earful but agreed to drive him to the college where they arrived at 4.35 pm. Rushing into reception, he couldn't remember the room number that Paul had given him, so several minutes more were wasted while the receptionist tracked Paul down.

Naturally, Paul wasn't too pleased at being kept waiting, but he agreed to go ahead anyway. Robbie had remembered to check with Paul beforehand about whether he would object to being taped, but when he turned to take the tape recorder from his rucksack the horrible realisation hit him that he had left it at work. By this time, he was feeling extremely stressed, especially as he had to ask Paul for a pen and some notepaper.

Paul gave Robbie some very useful information and ideas for strategies he could develop in the club. During the interview, Paul mentioned some recent initiatives related to outdoor play, which he thought would be of help. Robbie was so busy writing down the previous thing Paul had said, that he didn't fully catch the name of the initiative (which he had never heard of) and he was too embarrassed to ask him for clarification.

The interview had to be concluded by Paul, who had become very late for a meeting. Robbie quickly thanked Paul for his help, apologising profusely for having held him up.

- List the mistakes made by Robbie in the run-up to his interview

- What could Robbie have done to be better organised?

Take care to use positive body language while conducting an interview

Observations

All those working in the early education and childcare sector are familiar with observations. This applies to both doing them and the

Observational evidence will be invaluable in your research study

reasons why they are such a popular form of assessing a number of issues related to children's needs and interests, developmental progress, curriculum and resources (human, material and physical). The 'whys and wherefores' of observation have been addressed in Chapters 1 and 4. Observational evidence is invaluable in the research study because:

- observing is a skill you already have, albeit one which is developing with practice

- it should not be difficult for you to observe children, as you have regular access to them and this is already an expectation of you

- it will probably require less preparation than interviews and questionnaires (although of course you should still consult with your supervisor/line manager before carrying out an observation and make sure that you have all the resources you need)

- it may be possible, and very beneficial to you, to use observations already carried out as a starting point for your project – in that way you will be reducing your workload, which is always something to be desired!

Other forms of primary research

Using a video/camcorder

The advantages of this primary research method include:

- it can capture wonderful detail of children's behaviour which would be impossible to record in any other way

- it can be played over and over again, when other details which may have been missed can be noted

- filming an activity allows you to examine the context more easily.

The disadvantages of this research method include:

- written parental permission is necessary; in cases where this is not forthcoming, it can restrict your opportunities as particular children may have to be excluded

- successful use is dependent on the technology running smoothly – this does not always happen

- children's behaviour may be less natural with the presence of video, although this is likely to be short-lived as they become used to it

- transcribing and analysing the material is extremely time-consuming.

Audio recording (e.g. with a digital or tape recorder)

Most of the issues regarding audio recording have been discussed with regard to recording interviews. However, there are additional factors to consider when recording children:

- written parental permission must be gained (as previously discussed)

- as this method only records verbal exchanges and other auditory material, it is difficult to obtain the 'whole picture' as regards any activity involving the children

- if the quality of the recording is poor or there is a lot of background noise, it may be very difficult to follow what is going on and important points may be missed.

However, this method can be extremely useful depending on what kind of information you are looking for.

Photographs

On their own, photographs have limited value and you should avoid using them just to make your project look more attractive. Any photograph you include should provide some evidence to support or explain your findings (such as an observation), and you should provide an appropriate commentary when discussing and analysing your results. It is important to remember that a photograph is merely a record of what is happening at that instant, and does not indicate events leading up to it or what happened afterwards. However, photographs can provide very convincing supplementary evidence, so it is worth considering whether their use will be a positive addition to your project.

Again, you will need written parental consent and the consent of the centre before taking photographs.

Other important points to consider when undertaking primary research are those related to questions such as:

- cultural/religious differences

- race

- gender

- family circumstances

- disability, additional support needs and the inclusion agenda

- age/stage of development.

It is important to include appropriate reference to any of the above issues which relate directly to your project at the planning stage, in the analysis of data and in your evaluation.

Secondary research

Using books

There are a bewildering number of books currently available in the area of children's health and well-being, education, rights, development, protection and play. You need to develop the ability to make the best use of your time in finding appropriate books for your topic. You should probably start with books from your course booklist, as these will provide you with at least some of your essential reading. Your college library will have others, as will some of the larger public libraries. You may also find that you can access the reference books from another college or university.

Here are a few tips to help you access the relevant information you need.

- Look at the summary of the book's contents on the back cover.

- Read the list of chapter titles.

- Scan through the index for any key words, phrases or people's names which indicate that it is worth looking further.

- Choose what appears to be a useful chapter and read the first and last paragraphs. This may help you decide how relevant the chapter is going to be.

Effective reading for information requires you to be able to:

- *skim*, i.e. rapidly look through a page/pages, trying to get a sense of what it is all about, without actually reading it word for word

- *scan*, i.e. quickly look over a page/pages with a few key words in mind, which will enable you to find particular information more quickly

- *take notes*: always write all necessary information you will need to reference a book correctly as you use it (see more detail about referencing below); it is extremely frustrating, not to mention time-consuming, to have gained some very useful information from a book, taken notes and perhaps a quote, only to find that you can't source it, so make a note of any page number where there is something of particular interest you may wish to return to later

- *analyse the usefulness of what you have read*, e.g. is the material relevant, not just to your topic, but to your specific aim and/or objectives? Try to be as focused as possible; you may come across a lot of information which is very interesting, but not of particular relevance – try to put it aside as it has the potential to divert you from your intended path and waste precious time.

Issues when gathering secondary evidence

Let us now examine some of the issues which emerge during the gathering of evidence which has been written by others.

- *Author bias:* every author has their own opinion on the topic they write about which can affect the way material is displayed. This does not mean that you should not use a particular author's work, but you should be wary of how any bias will affect the validity of your findings. Do not rely solely on the writings of one author, read around to get views from a variety of authors.

- *How current is the material?* Be aware of when a particular piece was written. Within the early education and childcare field, there have been many changes over the last few years. These may be the result of new knowledge gained, for example about genetics or brain function, or the consequence of new curricula, guidelines or legislation. Of course not all issues about which you may be writing would be made invalid by using older secondary material, for example if you were referring to early years pioneers such as Montessori, Froebel or Steiner.

However, using older material which no longer applies might make a particular aspect of your work obsolete and therefore of extremely limited value.

Plagiarism

Over the last few years, plagiarism has become much more of an issue, mainly due to the Internet and the ease with which students can access and use others' work without acknowledging it. In academic circles, plagiarism has always been strictly judged; in some cases leading to people failing exams or even being asked to leave a course. There is no easy way to say it: plagiarism is dishonest as it involves the theft of another person's intellectual property – that is, their expressed thoughts and ideas.

The importance of referencing secondary sources

It can be difficult to write about a topic where you are expected to use the writing of others to support your argument or viewpoint without using their words or ideas. That is why it is important in a piece of work like your HNC project to include material written by others in a particular way.

Referencing your work is relatively simple if you follow the guidelines. There are various systems of referencing used in academic circles. One of the most straightforward and commonly used is the Harvard system. The Internet has numerous guides to using the Harvard system, but you may find the following summary helpful.

1 If you are alluding to another's ideas, or are paraphrasing (rewording) something they have written, you would present it like this:

> Munn and Drever (2004) state that one of the weaknesses of questionnaires is that the information gathered tends to be descriptive rather than explanatory.

(You would then go on to reference this fully in your bibliography – see overleaf for more details on how to do this.)

2 You may wish to use exactly the words used by the author to illustrate a point, or provide additional supporting evidence (remember 'triangulation' as discussed earlier in the chapter). You would do so as follows:

> The information collected tends to 'describe' rather than 'explain' why things are the way they are. (Munn and Drever, 2004, page 5)

When using the author's own words, they should be placed within speech marks, as above, and referenced fully in your bibliography.

Note: It is important to say at this point that while direct quotes can enrich a piece of work if used appropriately, they should be used sparingly and judiciously. Use a quote only when you really feel that it adds weight to your argument or if there is a particularly first-class expression which has been used by an author, the impact of which would be lost if it was paraphrased. In addition, quotes should be no longer than a sentence or two at most.

3 If the work is written by more than two authors, the first time it is cited you should use all the authors' names, date of publication and page numbers. If you use the same source later in your work, you should use the name of the first author and 'et al.'

(meaning 'and the others'). For example, as first mention:

> 'The value of play has been open to some debate.' (Dryden, Forbes, Mukherjee and Pound, 2005, page 121)

And the second mention would be:

> 'Young children's ability to plan and work cooperatively is most effectively learned through play.' (Dryden et al., 2005, page 115)

4 If you are citing an author's work which has been mentioned in another text, you should use the following way of referencing this:

> According to Stephen and Cope (2003; cited in Dryden et al., 2005, p. 133)…

5 If you are referring to a chapter from an edited book, you should use the chapter author's name in the body of your work (e.g. Mukherji, 2005) and reference the book fully in the bibliography. Include the chapter title and full details of the book from which it is taken.

6 Whether you are quoting from a newspaper, journal, magazine article or from the Internet, the rule is the same as regards the reference within the body of your writing. Use the author's name and date, referencing them fully in the bibliography as illustrated in the table below.

There is often debate about how the texts you have read and used in your work should be displayed at the end of your work. To simplify matters for the purposes of this project, it is suggested that you list all written materials under the heading 'Bibliography' or 'References', setting them out as shown in the table below.

Books should be listed first, in alphabetical order of the surname of the author (or first author if there are two or more), and where there are several titles by one author these should be listed in order of the date of publication. Other secondary resources used, such as research papers, Acts, magazines and websites, should be listed thereafter.

In the references section at the end of this chapter you will find a list of helpful titles, including journal, newspaper and Internet articles, together with suggested magazines for your research. These are valuable sources to get you started.

Timescale for your project

It is difficult to project yourself into the future and estimate how long it is going to take to complete each part of your investigation. It is a good idea to take your final submission date and work backwards from there. Your college tutor may give you hand-in dates for the action plan and the investigation, or these dates may be negotiated with people individually. However these dates are decided, you need to be able to give a realistic estimate of when each constituent part of the project will be finished.

One very good strategy is to fill out a timetable for each week of the foreseeable future. This is a 24-hour timetable and can help enormously with your time management. You start by plotting the hours which you know will be taken up with classes and/or work. You then enter any events which you know will be happening on a particular day. Make sure that you also put in leisure time, as it is important that you manage to keep a sensible work/life balance. What remains after all this is the time you will have available to do your project. Of course some of your primary research may be carried out during your working hours (or at placement), but you

Surname and initials of author	Date of publication	Title (and edition if more than one)	Pages	Place published	Publisher
Hucker, K.	2001	*Research Methods in Health, Care and Early Years*	XXX	Oxford	Heinemann
Roberts-Holmes, G.	2005	*Doing Your Early Years Research Project*	XXX	London	Paul Chapman Publishing

need to consider time for reading, looking for appropriate materials, note-taking, collating and analysing your findings, etc.

The length of time each element of your project is going to take will depend on a number of factors, namely:

- how organised you are
- family and other commitments in your life
- the level of cooperation you receive from people from whom you want to gather information
- the amount of available resources and your skill in accessing them
- how quickly you read, note-take, etc.
- your IT skills
- your ability to use appropriate graphic representation (if this is how you decide to organise your primary data).

The chart below gives an example of a detailed timescale stating completion dates for each of the significant elements of the project. This is just one way in which you could do the timescale. You may find it easier, for example, to divide your investigation into dates by which you would complete each objective.

You do not need to worry unduly about meeting each of your target dates exactly, although of course you will have to meet the dates set by your tutor. You cannot foresee what may interfere with your ability to meet these targets, but you must be prepared to account for any changes to your initial estimates when writing your evaluation.

Good practice tip: Keeping a diary

It is an excellent idea to jot down events occurring at each stage of your project. This does not need to be a detailed account, but it will help you to remember things to refer to when it comes to writing up your evaluation.

	Element of project	Date for completion by
Action plan	Select topic; initial reading; meet with tutor; identify aim and objectives	
	Identify how topic fits into children's needs, interests and rights	
	Select sources for secondary research – reading	
	Selection of appropriate primary research with details of how this will meet objectives	
	Submit completed action plan	
Investigation	Questionnaire composed, distributed and returned; interviews carried out; observations done; reading	
	Analysis of data; writing up of results and analysis	
	Write up secondary research	
	Conclusion and further recommendations	
	Check references; add bibliography, appendix and Contents page	
	Final editing of investigation	
	Submit investigation	
Evaluation	Complete abstract	
	Complete evaluation	
	Final editing and contingency time	
	Submit completed project	

How to critically analyse your data

It is important to take a systematic approach to your investigation. Constantly remind yourself of your aim and your objectives, asking the question as to whether the material you are collecting is relevant or just interesting!

One way of organising yourself may be to take each objective and carry out all the research, primary and secondary, before moving on to investigate the next one. In that way you can be more focused and less likely to stray from the point.

How you do this depends very much on whether the material you have collected is qualitative or quantitative. As mentioned previously, qualitative data can be more difficult to analyse than quantitative data, which can often be analysed by generating graphs or charts.

A critical analysis involves not just a description of your findings but an assessment of their usefulness in terms of supporting or refuting your other findings or those of other people.

Your findings should not simply be listed in the analysis section. The skill of critical analysis is being able to explain your findings and present informed conclusions and decisions.

It is important to organise all the data collected through your primary research and relate it to each of your objectives/research questions. Then think about how each of these goes towards answering the question posed. There may be a lot of material which has been gathered incidentally, but only that which is significant to your objective should be discussed. An example is given below.

Objective: To investigate boys' play in the pre-school room of a nursery

Data collected:

- time sample observations detailing how three boys use play areas
- frequency samples of particular areas detailing the instances of use by boys

It is important to take a systematic approach to your investigation

- interviews with nursery teacher and one practitioner
- interviews with three boys chosen randomly
- articles from *Nursery World*: 'Superhero Play'; 'Admit it, boys will be boys'
- notes taken from *Boys and Girls: Superheroes in the Doll Corner* (Paley, 1986)*
- notes from *Developing Learning in Early Childhood* (Bruce, 2001)*
- notes from *Understanding Children's Play* (Lindon, 2001).*

(* fully referenced in bibliography)

How to organise and analyse your material

- It may be appropriate to start with a discussion of some of the material you have read relating to your objective.
- Write up and present the results of your primary research in an appropriate format (some tips to support you in the presentation of these details can be found on pages 331–4). In the case of the example above, you might wish to present the results of your time sample on a grid which demonstrates your findings at a glance.

- You then need to comment on this result, highlighting significant features of it, for example you could say that it was noteworthy that two out of the three boys were not observed in the book corner all day, and the third was observed there only on one occasion. In addition, what was also very significant was that all three of the boys were observed playing outside or at the large brick corner for at least 50 per cent of the recorded time.

- You might then go on to talk about the findings from your frequency sample, where you have tallied the number of times a particular area of the nursery was used by the boys. Perhaps because of your findings in the time sample, you may opt to look at the book corner and the brick area – this would give you a wider picture of whether your findings were generalised in a wider sample of boys in the nursery.

- Let us say that the brick corner was visited six times more frequently than the book corner by boys – does this support the findings from your time sample? Does the information gathered in your interviews add further weight to this?

- Now discuss how your findings relate to what you have read regarding the play habits of boys.

Analysing quantitative data

The example below is adapted from the work of a previous HNC student. This is based on the results of quantitative data gathered from a questionnaire completed by teachers on learning styles (27 questionnaires were returned out of 63 distributed).

You can see that as well as having collated and presented the results of the questionnaire, the student has commented on the results, indicating possible reasons for some of them. The limitations of this method of research are highlighted clearly. Comparisons are then made to other secondary research completed.

Analysing qualitative data

This type of analysis is far less straightforward than that of quantitative data, and therefore more time-consuming. The other issue to consider is that as the researcher you have to make the decision about which elements of the data are significant and relevant. It can be tempting to include material that is interesting but irrelevant. Don't let yourself stray from your objectives and ultimately your aim. Remember that your word limit is not particularly generous, so you cannot afford to include pieces of writing that are not going to make a positive contribution to your project. Therefore, when organising the data collected through narrative observations, unstructured/semi-structured interviews and the open-ended questions in questionnaires, focus on the relevant responses. It can be helpful to go through your data with coloured highlighter pens, using a different colour for each distinctive category of response.

Results of quantitative data questionnaire

The data shows that 100 per cent of the teachers are aware of some learning style models. Five teachers did not complete the space to name the style they know about. This could indicate that while they were aware of different models, they had no specific knowledge or that they could not remember the name. VAK was named by 63 per cent as the style they knew about. One named multiple intelligences and one mentioned experiential learning (unclear whether this refers to Kolb model or Piaget's theory).

This data cannot be viewed as representative of the views of the teaching profession as a whole, as the sample is too small. However, it does give some insight into the views of primary teachers, and supports what is stated in Peacock's report to the Education Committee (2005) where he said: 'The aspiration for there to be greater scope and space for pupil-centred learning which takes account of multiple learning styles amongst pupils was a recurrent theme during the enquiry.'

For example, if the original question was related to beliefs about the age at which children should begin formal education, you could loosely categorise the responses using colour coding as follows:

> All those who believe that children start formal education too soon

> Those who think that formal education should begin earlier

> Those who think that the age of starting school is about right, but that children should still be learning through play

Having done this, it then becomes easier to present your results and comment on them in relation to your objective and aims, as the example below shows.

Analysis of qualitative data collected

Of all the people responding to the questionnaire (16 out of 25, i.e. 64 per cent) 13 out of 16, i.e. 81.3 per cent expressed the view that formal education begins too early for children in this country. Two people stated that children should not start school until they are 7 years old. Four more mentioned in one form or another that children from other European countries start school later 'and it would appear that their children do well'. Interestingly, no one thought that formal education should begin earlier. This is of particular significance when you consider that all the respondents are teachers.

If you have carried out a completely unstructured interview, your results will be far more difficult to analyse. However, try to extract what is relevant and comment on that. (At this stage of the project, you do not need to comment on issues such as reliability and validity of your research methods; you will do this in the evaluation section.)

As well as critically analysing your primary research data, you should also consider your secondary material. For example, who has written this and what are their credentials? Consider issues like author bias and unsupported claims.

One example of this may be an article you have found in a magazine or newspaper where claims have been made about a particular issue without any evidence to substantiate them. While not saying that you should disregard material such as this entirely, you should treat it with caution. When discussing the content in your investigation report, you should allude to the fact that although this material is very interesting and may back up other evidence collected by you, it is not necessarily wholly dependable.

Changing/adapting your aim and objectives

You may find that once you have started to read and research in more detail, after having initially formulated your aim and objectives, you may wish to adjust the focus of your research somewhat. Any change made should be relatively minor, and you should consult with your college tutor about the proposed alteration.

One reason for deciding to make a change may relate to an aspect of the topic which you had not considered in depth before. Having read more widely, you might now feel that this is something which is more beneficial and relevant. For example, on the subject of boys' play, you may not have considered looking at recent research into brain development specifically. However, if a lot of the material you had been reading alluded to this, your understanding of the topic would be greatly enhanced by including an objective that required you to study this further. This objective may replace one which you have decided is of less importance to your project.

If you do decide to make a change, you must justify it in the introduction to your investigation.

Considering the implications of your research findings

When you have completed the development of your aim and objectives, having presented and critically analysed your findings, you should then go on to make suggestions as to what the next steps might be to develop the project within your chosen setting. This could be one of the following:

- details of further research which could be undertaken as a result of questions arising during your research, which you were unable to investigate due to the remit and constraints of the project

- strategies which could be implemented in the workplace/placement as a result of your research findings

- a combination of both.

Below is an example of next steps based upon findings within a particular project.

Summary and conclusion to the investigation

This part of your investigation is where you pull together all the information gathered for your objectives and relate it back to your aim. You will discuss how your various forms of research served to support (or refute) each other, and to what extent you have achieved your aim. You should also include a brief discussion of how your project links in with the different HNC units, and how you have taken account of issues concerning children's interests, needs and rights.

Fundraising could increase opportunities for outdoor play by raising money for waterproof boots and clothing

How to present your work

Appearance

- While there is nothing in the SQA unit descriptor which states that your work should be wordprocessed, there is little doubt that

---

Consideration of potential further development of issues arising from the research

Based on secondary research and observations, I have implemented outdoor play for a certain portion of every day, no matter what the weather conditions. In the analysis of the findings, based on further observation, video recordings, photographs, reading, interviews and surveys of the children, I feel that this is an area which could be developed further.

- Some of the parents were objecting to the children having to go home in wet coats. This had led to some parents stating that they did not want their children to go outside if it was wet. One suggestion is therefore *fundraising* so that rain-proof outdoor clothing and wellies can be bought for the children to use so that their own clothes are kept dry until it is time to go home.

- The organisation of a *coffee morning* would provide parents with the opportunity to be shown evidence of some of the results of the children's outdoor play, in terms of art and craft work produced and photographs with captions relating to learning within each of the curricular areas.

- Someone with expert first-hand *knowledge of Forest Schools* (or similar) could give a talk to parents and staff. Following this, the parents could be asked to complete a questionnaire about whether they now had a more positive view towards outdoor play in all weather conditions.

- *In-service training and further reading* for staff would be invaluable. Perhaps it would result in them all approaching the idea of being outside in all weathers as something of benefit to everyone, rather than just 'the latest fad' as you heard it described.

this adds a great deal to the readability of any piece of work.

- It will also improve the presentation if your project is bound, or at least placed in a folder that holds the pages firmly and securely, and is not likely to spill everywhere as soon as someone starts turning the pages.

- Consider the font you will use – the Dyslexia Association recommends Arial or Comic Sans as being the clearest and easiest to read. Font size 12 should be used for the bulk of the script.

- You should have a *Contents* page at the beginning of your project, which gives details of the page numbers where the different parts of your project can be found.

- Each page should be numbered.

- Your name, college/centre, SQA candidate number and SQA unit number should be clearly written on the front cover.

- Also on the front cover (or on the first page), you should write the title/aim of your project.

- A *numbered appendix* (see page 333) should be placed at the end of your project, with each item titled and numbered in the contents page (e.g. Appendix 1 – copy of letter to parents).

- An abstract of the project (see page 334) should be placed immediately after the Contents page.

- Make sure that you have made no spelling or major grammar mistakes. Use the spelling and grammar check on the computer. It is also a good idea to ask someone to proofread your work: if it does not make sense to them, then it is unlikely to make much more sense to the person marking it.

- Remember to include paragraphs and subtitles and to use underlining, italics, etc. to break up the density of script. These will improve the readability of your work.

- Avoid over-long sentences. This is a very common mistake, and can make written pieces much more confusing and difficult to understand. If you come across a sentence that looks too long, rework it into two separate sentences.

Presentation of quantitative (numerical) data

One of the most efficient ways of presenting numerical data is pictorially, by means of:

- a variety of graphs (line, bar)
- histograms/pictograms
- pie charts
- tables.

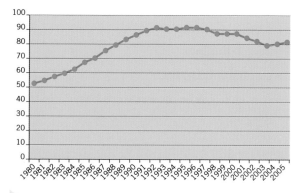

Example of a line graph

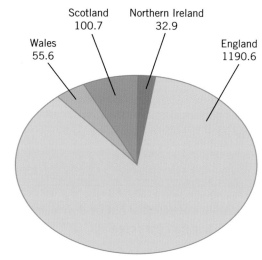

A pie chart

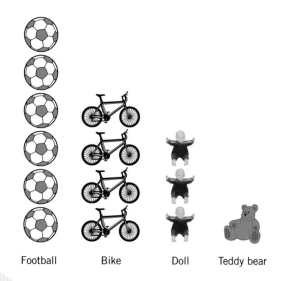

| Football | Bike | Doll | Teddy bear |

Example of a pictogram

Commonly used pictorial representation

Type of graph/chart	When it may be appropriate to use	Particular features
Bar chart	For presenting data in several categories, e.g. number of different day care settings in Scotland	Easy to both produce and understand the data
Line graph	Useful for presenting considerable amounts of information which covers a long period of time, e.g. numbers of children in local authority nurseries between 1997 and 2007 in Scotland	1. Good for comparing data, i.e. another line can be inserted on the same graph which compares data (in the example given – perhaps from another country) 2. More use when handling large amounts of data
Pie chart	Used for representing numerical information as a percentage of the whole, e.g. types of pets owned by children within a class	1. Each number is worked out as a fraction, e.g. five children out of 20 own a dog, i.e. ¼ = 25%. This then has to be calculated and presented as a fraction of a circle 2. Only works when there are a limited number of categories
Pictogram	Used to present information pictorially – uses pictures or symbols	Can be very effective visually – if used properly it is clear and easy to understand

Pictorial representations of data present your results in a clear and concise form, which should be relatively easy to interpret. The table above briefly describes some of the more commonly used types. If you are able to use a spreadsheet into which you enter your data, there are computer programs which will transform it into tables and graphs.

Chapter 2 in *Research Methods in Health, Care and Early Years* gives an excellent overview of all the ways in which you can present your data pictorially. Your college tutor may feel that you might benefit from a group teaching session on this aspect of the project. It is certainly an opportunity for you to improve your core skills, or learn a completely new skill. (This is something to bear in mind when you come to do your evaluation.)

The appendix

> **Key term**
>
> An **appendix** (plural appendices) is a collection of material which is presented at the end of a book or piece of work. It includes any sources of information helpful to understanding the book's/research project's main content.

There are differing opinions about the appropriate contents of an appendix. Here are some suggestions of what you could consider including in your appendix:

- a copy of any letters sent out, for example asking permission or giving information

- a copy of a questionnaire or interview schedule, with *one* completed copy of each

- a copy of anything which is essential to illustrate the discussion in the main body of your investigation, such as a list, table or assessment schedule which you make specific reference to

- a copy of each different type of observation carried out (for example, one time sample, one participant observation, etc.)

- one or two examples of children's drawings and/or writing, if relevant and referred to in your text.

Each category of appendix should be numbered. For example, any letters would be Appendix 1. If there are more letters, you should number them 1a, 1b, etc. Details of what is included in the appendix should be entered into your list of contents at the front of your project, as the following example shows.

What not to include in an appendix

You should not include the following in your appendix:

- all raw data (i.e. completed questionnaires, interview schedules, etc.)

- copies of magazine or newspaper articles

- photocopied pages of textbooks

- downloads from the Internet

- numerous examples of children's work

- posters, leaflets, booklets, etc.

Word count

Keeping within the required word limit is something students often find difficult, so here are a few tips to help.

- Check that everything you are writing about is relevant to your objective.

- Cut down on any unnecessary language used; for example, you may be expressing something in a long sentence which could be expressed equally well in a short one.

- Look for any instances of repetition or dwelling too long on a particular topic, discussion or argument.

- Do you need all the quotes and examples you have included? Perhaps you can cut them down slightly.

Still too many words? You should then go through your work prioritising its contents in order of importance and relevance to your project. This is where you may have to be ruthless!

How to reflect on your work

The final part of your project – the evaluation – gives you the opportunity to reflect on every aspect of your work, from the planning stages through to the conclusion. All you need for this section is the ability to look back over what you have done and critically evaluate it in terms of the criteria stated below. (This is where your diary will come in handy.)

However, before we consider the evaluation in more detail, this is the point at which you should produce an *abstract* of your project. This is important in order to introduce the reader to your topic. The abstract should be placed on the first page of your project, immediately after the contents page.

Key term

An **abstract** is a brief summary of your research which should include your aim/objectives, research questions, methods of research, main findings, recommendations and conclusion. It should be no longer than 200 words.

The evaluation

This section will be divided into different headings, each of which should be considered. Under each heading you will find a number of questions to ask yourself. If you work through each of these, reflecting carefully and honestly on your answers, you will write a good evaluation.

1 Identification of challenges

- How well did you meet timescales – those set by yourself and those set by others?

- Were you able to carry out your planned tasks/activities/research? If you were unable to do any of these, why was that the case? What did you do about it?

- How would you rate your team-working skills? Give examples to illustrate your answer.

- Did you face any personal difficulties which interfered with the progress of your project? (Keep any explanation of these brief.) What did you learn from this?

- Which aspects of the project were particularly successfully carried out, in your opinion? Why do you think that was so?

- How easy was it for you to stay within the word count? What did you do in order to ensure that you did not go too far over/under?

2 Evaluation of how learning undertaken in the HNC was used to carry out the project

- Was any new learning/skill acquired? (This should include the content of appropriate HNC units.)

- Have you considered each of the mandatory units separately, detailing how you have integrated learning acquired in each of these into your project, together with any appropriate optional units?

- Are there any areas of your knowledge and/or skills which have improved over the course of the project? (Consider: IT skills, time management, reading for information, using the Internet, personal organisation, etc.)

3 Reflection on the effectiveness of the research methods used

- Were your primary research methods effective? If so, why? If not, why not?

- Were your secondary research methods effective? Did you use a wide enough variety of sources? Too wide? Was there too much dependence on Internet sources?

- Did you collect sufficient and relevant data? Did you collect too much data?

4 Discussion as to how closely the original plan was followed

- How closely did you follow your original planning in terms of:

    (a) your aim

    (b) your objectives

    (c) your proposed primary research

    (d) your proposed secondary research, including sources used?

5 Effectiveness of communication/ interpersonal skills used throughout the course of the project

- How well did you communicate *verbally* with:

    (a) your college tutor

    (b) your placement/workplace supervisor

    (c) children

    (d) other members of placement/workplace staff

    (e) other appropriate adults, e.g. parents, interviewees?

    (This may include explaining, discussing, negotiating and clarifying. It involves listening as well as speaking.)

- How good was your *written* communication in terms of:

    (a) letters

    (b) information sheets

    (c) emails, etc.?

    Having put the finishing touches to your last sentence, it is important that you then check your project thoroughly before handing it in. The checklist in the Check your progress box on the next page will help you with this.

1. Do your action plan, investigative report and evaluation have all the necessary elements? Look back to the beginning of this chapter where you will find them listed.

2. Have you laid out your project as advised? (This concerns the Contents page, front cover, numbered pages, appendices, etc.)

3. Have you checked that all pictorial representations of data have been clearly labelled? (This also applies to any photographs used.)

4. Does your appendix contain appropriate materials only?

5. Have you kept within the limits of the word count for each section?

6. Are you certain that you have not plagiarised anyone else's work?

7. Have you referenced your sources correctly within your text?

8. Have you constructed your bibliography using Harvard referencing?

9. Have you read over the entire project using a spell/grammar check and edited it where appropriate?

10. Have you asked at least one other person to proofread the finished project before you finally submit it?

Congratulations on completing your HNC graded unit!

References

Books

Boak, A., Bulman, K., Butcher, J., Daly, M., Griffin, S., Hill, K., Horne, S., Hucker, K., Snaith, M., Squire, G., and Tassoni, P. (ed. Squire, G.) (2007) *Children's Care, Learning and Development*, Oxford: Heinemann

Hucker, K. (2001) *Research Methods in Health, Care and Early Years*, Oxford: Heinemann

Learning and Teaching Scotland (2005) *Birth to Three: supporting our youngest children,* Dundee

Lewis, I. and Munn, P. (2004) *So You Want to Do Research! A Guide for Beginners*, Glasgow: Scottish Council for Research in Education SCRE

Munn, P. and Drever, E. (2004) *Using Questionnaires in Small-Scale Research*, Glasgow: SCRE

Roberts-Holmes, G. (2005) *Doing Your Early Years Research Project: A Step-by-Step Guide*, London: Paul Chapman Publishing

Simpson, M. and Tucson, J. (2003) *Using Observations in Small-Scale Research*, Glasgow:

Squire, G. (ed.) (2007) *BTEC National Children's Care, Learning and Development*, Oxford: Heinemann

Publications

Journal articles

Jarvis, P. (2007) 'Dangerous activities within an invisible playground', *International Journal of Early Years Education* 15, October 2007, pages 245–59

Newspaper articles

Macleod, F. (2007) 'Scots schools accused of letting down children from poor families', *The Scotsman*, 11 December 2007

Internet articles

Trevarthen, C. (2004) *Learning about Ourselves from Children: Why a Growing Human Brain Needs Interesting Companions* (available at: www.perception-in-action.ed.ac.uk/PDF_s/Colwyn2004.pdf)

Useful magazines, periodicals, newspapers and other publications

You will probably find that your college library stocks these, and may keep back copies of some.

Your early education and childcare department may also subscribe to some of the following:

Nursery World
Child Education
Early Education
Children in Scotland
Early Years Educator
Times Educational Supplement (Scotland)

In addition, some of the better quality newspapers may have an education section published on a weekly basis. For example, every Wednesday *The Scotsman* has a section called 'Education Scotsman' which often has interesting and thought-provoking articles.

Useful websites

Your college may have a licence for a website called 'Childlink' (www.childlink.co.uk) which has back copies of child-related articles which have appeared in a variety of newspapers, periodicals, etc. This is a superb resource, and if you have an Athens account you can access it from home.

Children in Scotland: www.childreninscotland.org.uk – here you can find details of current research being undertaken among other interesting articles

The British Association for Early Childhood Education: www.early-education.org.uk – a national voluntary organisation which provides help, support and information for early education and childcare practitioners

University of Exeter website on the Harvard system of referencing: www.education.ex.ac.uk/dll/studyskills/harvard_referencing.htm

National Literacy Trust: www.literacytrust.org.uk – an independent charity dedicated to the provision of support to families and professionals involved in literacy development

Learning and Teaching Scotland: www.ltscotland.org.uk – an invaluable website with reports of good practice, current research, curricular matters. This is especially useful for keeping up to date with developments in the new Curriculum for Excellence. Follow the links to a monthly newsletter called 'Early Years Matters'

Nursery World: www.nurseryworld.co.uk – a very useful website where you can register free of charge and search through the magazine's archives for articles relevant to your topic

The Scottish Government website: www.scotland.gov.uk – following the links on this website can provide information on a variety of issues, including health, early education and out-of-school care

SureStart: www.surestart.gov.uk – Sure Start is a government-funded organisation which brings together early education, health and families in an effort to give children the best possible start in life

Under5s Early Years Website: www.underfives.co.uk – this website offers the opportunity to download resources for early education and childcare free of charge

Index